Zucca barucca (slices of grilled pumpkin) was originally a festive dish for Venetian Jews. It was then adopted by the rest of the city's inhabitants and is sold by street vendors, especially during Carnival.

The Venetians collected rainwater in deep cisterns dug in the campi of the city. This water was drawn from wells set into each cistern.

Shown here are the wells at San Martino (below) and the Doge's Palace (inset).

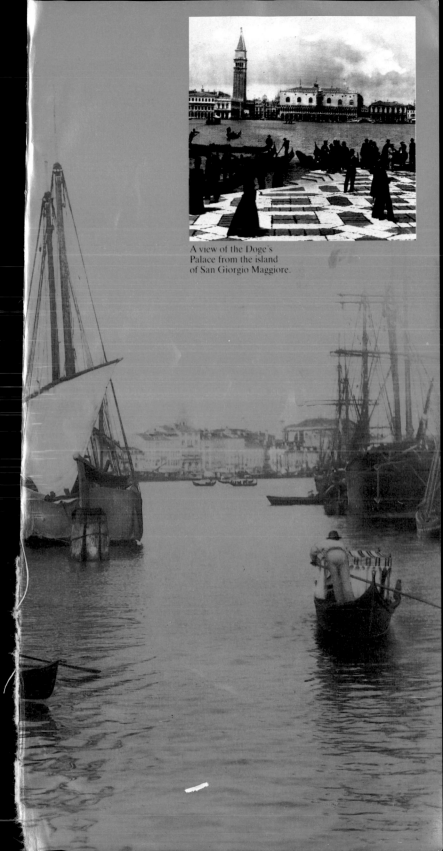

A view of the Doge's
Palace from the island
of San Giorgio Maggiore.

NUMEROUS LOCAL SPECIALISTS AND ACADEMICS HAVE CONTRIBUTED
TO THIS GUIDE. SPECIAL THANKS TO SANDRA STOCCHETTO
AND SABINA VIANELLO (SOGGETTO VENEZIA).

CONTRIBUTORS
Alberto Giulio Bernstein, Giuseppe Cherubini (cooperativa Limosa, Venice),
Eleonora Cicotti (Laboratorio di Ecologia Sperimentale e Acquacoltura, Rome),
Margherita Fusco (cooperativa Limosa, Venice), Roberta Manzi (cooperativa
Limosa, Venice), Roberto Rosselli, Maria Colombo, Jean-Louis Fournel,
Paola Ancillotto, Roberto Fontanari, Tullio Ortolani, Ugo Pizzarello,
Giovanni Roman, Roberto Valese, Giovanni and Mario Valese,
Maroun El Daccache, Dominique Fernandes, Luciana Miotto, Silvia Moretti,
Loredana Pellarini, Patrick Jusseaux, Maria Grazia Gagliardi,
Donatella Perruccio Chiari, Caterina Bonomi, Jean-Carlos Carmigniani,
Bruna Caruso, Barbara Di Maio, Roberto Ellero, Andrea Fabiano,
Chiara Galli Rosso, Pascaline Vatin Barbini, Jean-Claude Zancarini,
Piero Zanotto.

WE WOULD ALSO LIKE TO THANK:
Stefano Barbieri, Jacopo Barovier, Alberto Bianchi, Maria Raffaella Caprioglio,
Francesco Capuzzo, Giorgio Ciriotto, Consorzio Venezia Nuova, Gisèle D'Antony,
Gianni De Checchi, Margherita De Cunzo, Stefania De Marchi,
Maddalena Di Sopra, Ornella Fontanari, Francesca Galli Aliverti,
Donatella Gibbin, Irina Ivancich Biaggini, Costanza Jori, Maria Teresa Menotto,
Isabelle Pinna, Caterina Rossato, Marina Tassinari,
Muriel Toso and Ian Littlewood.

TRANSLATED BY ANTHONY ROBERTS
EDITED AND TYPESET BY BOOK CREATION SERVICES, LONDON
PRINTED IN ITALY BY EDITORIALE LIBRARIA

VENICE

KNOPF GUIDES

CONTENTS
KEY ASPECTS OF LIFE IN VENICE

CONTENTS
A JOURNEY THROUGH VENICE

▲ Venice

MARCO POLO AIRPORT

MESTRE

VENICE

Porto di Marghera

GIUDECCA

ALBERONI

Porto di Malamocco

LITORALE DI PELLESTRINA

PELLESTRINA

Porto di Chioggia

CHIOGGIA

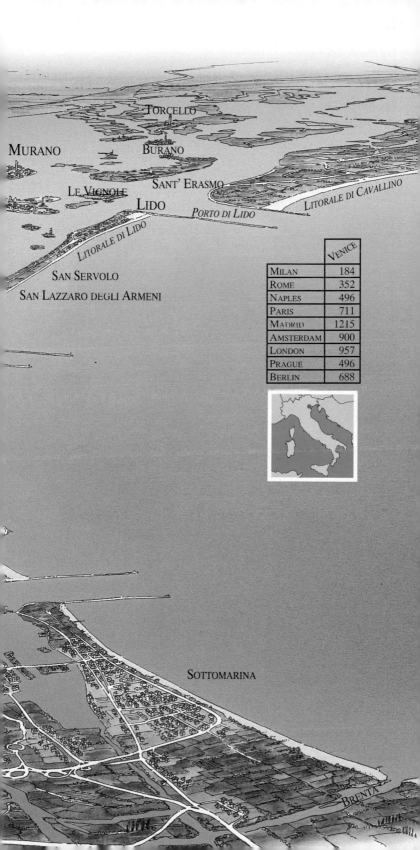

MURANO

TORCELLO

BURANO

SANT' ERASMO

LE VIGNOLE

LIDO

PORTO DI LIDO

LITORALE DI CAVALLINO

LITORALE DI LIDO

SAN SERVOLO

SAN LAZZARO DEGLI ARMENI

	VENICE
MILAN	184
ROME	352
NAPLES	496
PARIS	711
MADRID	1215
AMSTERDAM	900
LONDON	957
PRAGUE	496
BERLIN	688

SOTTOMARINA

BRENTA

HOW TO USE THIS GUIDE

The symbols at the top of
each page refer to
the different parts
of the guide.

■ NATURAL ENVIRONMENT

● UNDERSTANDING VENICE

▲ ITINERARIES

◆ PRACTICAL INFORMATION

The itinerary map
shows the main points
of interest along the
way and is intended
to help you find
your bearings.

The mini-map
locates the particula
itinerary within
the wider area
covered by
the guide.

*The gateway to
Venice: after all, is
neither the Piazzal,
nor the Grand Canal
below us, churned
by propellers,
turbulent as a
great river.*
Fernand Braudel,
France

Santa Lucia Station.

Immediately outside the railway station lies Cannaregio, the first of the six *sestieri* of Venice. Situated at the north-west end of the city, this is the second largest *sestiere* after Castello, covering an area of 150 hectares. Nearly a third of the population of Venice is concentrated here, amounting to more than twenty thousand people. There are two theories about the origin of the name Cannaregio: according to one, it comes from the *regio* (the Royal Canal), meaning the one broad waterway which once provided convenient access to the city from the mainland by prolonging the lagoon canal of San Secundo (which runs parallel to the railway bridge). The other hypothesis is that the word derives from the reeds and canes which used to abound in this area. In any case, a system of straight, parallel canals with long fondamenta abutting houses which intersected this crossroads zone of workmen's homes and linked the calli...

THE GATEWAY TO VENICE ★

PONTE DELLA LIBERTÀ. Built by the Austrians 50 years after the Treaty of Campo Formio in 1797 ● *34*, to link Venice with Milan. The bridge ended the thousand-year separation from the mainland and shook the city's economy to its roots as Venice, already in the throes of the industrial revolution, saw its dependence on the mainland grow...
SANTA LUCIA STATION. The present station still bears the name of the Renaissance church demolished in 1861 to make way for it...
dome of the Church of San Simeone Piccolo...

★ The star symbol
signifies that a particular
site has been singled out
by the publishers for its
special beauty,
atmosphere or cultural
interest.

● ▲ ■ ◆
The symbols alongside a
title or within the text
itself provide cross-
references to a theme
or place dealt with
elsewhere in the guide.

At the beginning of each
itinerary, the suggested
means of transport to be
used and the time it will
take to cover the area are
indicated:

🚤 By boat
🚶 On foot
🚲 By bicycle
🕐 Duration

THE GATEWAY TO VENICE ★

PONTE DELLA LIBERTÀ. Built by the Austrians 50 years after
the Treaty of Campo Formio in 1797 ● *34*, to link Venice with
Milan. The bridge ended the thousand-year separation from the
mainland and shook the city's economy to its roots as
Venice, already in the throes of the industrial revolution, saw

🚶 Half a day

BRIDGES TO VENICE

NATURAL HISTORY

THE VENETIAN LAGOON

The Venetian Lagoon extends over 135,903 acres, 123,548 of which are water and 12,355 dry land.

About six thousand years ago, after the last Ice Age, rising water levels created the Venetian Lagoon. Located at the junction of the sea and the river currents of what was once the Po delta, this is a highly complex environment which is probably unique in the world, and includes a wide variety of highly active biological ecosystems. For five centuries now, humans have been working in order to balance their needs with the requirements of nature. The Lagoon is also surrounded by some thirty-one miles of remarkably well preserved coastline.

Sand carried down by the rivers and shaped by marine currents eventually formed bands along the coastline, which in due course locked the Lagoon in on itself. Work began in the 14th century to divert the principal rivers emptying into the zone and to block four rivermouths, in order to prevent the clogging of the estuaries. Today the Lagoon is linked to the open sea by just three *bocche di porto* (Lido, Malamocco and Chioggia).

As an area of extraordinary natural wealth, the Lagoon has been much affected by human intervention. Industrial zones and natural preserves now have to survive alongside each other.

The recently enlarged industrial complex of Porto Marghera is one of the biggest in the Mediterranean, and scarcely a stone's throw from Venice.

The islands, pools and fish farming *valli* ■ *20* (39,535 acres), *barene*, *velme* ■ *19* and canals (96,368 acres) are home to many animal and plant species.

Mestre

Porto Marghera

Canale V. Emanuele III

Canale della Giudecca

La Giudecca

F

Canale di Malamocco Marghera

BACINO DI MALAMOCCO

BACINO DI CHIOGGIA

Sile

Iesolo

PALUDE
MAGGIORE

Torcello

Mazzorbo

Burano

ACINO
I LIDO

Murano

Canale di
San Felice

Treporti

Canale di Murano

Canale di Treporti

San Erasmo

NICE

Le Vignole

Porto di Lido

Lido

San Michele

ZONA
DI
TIACQUE

Malamocco

Porto di
Malamocco

Navigable entry canal

San Pietro
in Volta

Pellestrina

Porto di Chioggia

Chioggia

Sottomarina

Brenta

Some 27 major
rivers and canals hold
more than half of the total
volume of water found in
the Lagoon.

Where it is not left to the wild,
the Lagoon can be cultivated
and used for fisheries, salt pans
and other commercial purposes.

Freshwater recovery canal
(for irrigation)

Fish farming area

Barena

Fortified islet

Canal

Deep water

Coastal islet

Beach

Dyke protecting
reclaimed land
from high tides

Fortified islet

Murazzi

Breakwater

MURAZZI These embankments
have protected the shoreline from
erosion on the Lagoon's seaward
side ever since the 13th century.

The 10 or so
fortified islets in the
Lagoon were
originally built as
part of a defensive
network to protect
the city against
foreign attack.

Breakwaters
extending seawards
on either side of the
Lagoon's entry
channels protect
them from the
encroaching sand.

■ BARENE AND RUSHES

LITTLE EGRET This small member of the heron family is a common sight in parts of the Lagoon where it searches for food.

Sea and river currents meet and mingle in the former delta of the River Po, and the resulting brackish water covers the Venetian Lagoon to an average depth of about twenty inches. Clay and sand deposits carried in by both currents have gradually created raised banks called *barene* (salt-flats). These broad, wet expanses are the home to large numbers of water-loving plants and contain food for many species of bird. Near the river estuaries, where the water is less salty, thick rushes grow, providing shelter for much of the Lagoon's bird population.

MARSH HARRIER A tireless hunter of rodents in and around the rushes and *barene*.

BEARDED TIT It can often be seen and heard singing among the rushes.

BITTERN A species of heron that hunts mainly after dark

Velme

The *barene* are colonized by "pioneer" plants – species that are capable of thriving in this brackish environment. They filter and then retain in their plump foliage the fresh water that they need to grow. In late summer, the blossoming of wild aster and sea lavender covers the Lagoon with patches of pink and blue color.

Ghebi

GLASSWORT   **ASTER**   **SEA LAVENDE**   **OBIONE**

RUSH BEDS The brackish water at the mouth of the river estuaries is the ideal place for beds of rushes to grow and spread.

VELME Muddy and usually submerged parts of the Lagoon which appear at low tide, revealing carpets of algae.

BARENE Islets covered in thick vegetation that are only submerged when the tides are at their highest.

RUSH

REED BUNTING

REED WARBLER

SEDGE WARBLER

REDSHANK

The birds of the rush beds generally have drab plumage, but make up for this with a range of complex cries and song patterns.

Rush beds

Barene

SPOTTED REDSHANK (1) AND GREENSHANK (2)
Regular visitors to the *velme* during the winter months, where they feed on *policheti* (mudworms).

REDSHANK (1), BLACK-TAILED GODWIT (2) AND CURLEW (3)

SANDPIPER
A diminutive wading bird that uses its long beak to find food beneath the mud of the *velme*.

WATER RAIL
The harsh calls of this extremely shy bird is often the only thing that betrays its presence.

19

FISH FARMING

SPOONBILL
This distinctive bird is a common sight in the marshes and around the rush beds and banks of the Lagoon.

The *valli da pesca* cover 21,764 acres of the Lagoon, about a sixth of its total area.

Vallicultura is a tradition in the Lagoon, and is one of the most ancient forms of fish farming. The *valle*, which is entirely man-made, is a banked-up area which is linked to the open Lagoon by a series of channels. Fish locks located at these outlets allow the fish to enter on a seasonal basis. The catches then take place in the spring, when the young fish return to the gulf, and during the winter, when the adults move into the open water to reproduce or in search of warmer currents.

Female

MALLARD

Shooting occasionally takes precedence over fishing among the *valli*. Both activities are strictly regulated, allowing species to come into season at different times of year.

COMMON TERN

MUTE SWAN AND CYGNET

Immature

Wildfowl are plentiful in the *valli*, where they can find large quantities of food.

There are about twenty-four *valli* in the Lagoon, most of which are privately owned. They range in size from 250–750 acres.

1. Parts of the Lagoon in which fish move about freely.
2. Winter ponds and growing ponds.
3. and 4. Fish locks.
5. Sluices, which allow operators to control the water level in the *valle*.

Winter ponds enable the younger fish to survive during the colder months.

The *lavoriero,* or fish lock, is positioned at the neck of the channel linking the *valle* with the Lagoon. It usually consists of two successive dams, which are moveable. The first lock filters out vegetable flotsam, admitting fish only. The second works as a kind of antechamber, from which the fish are graded and directed into different ponds depending on their size.

Baicolere are ponds reserved for young sea bass.

The water in the *valli* requires constant monitoring, with periodical dredging, lock maintenance and regulating of the environment.

FLOUNDER

The average *valle* produces 50 percent eel, 30 percent mullet, 10 percent sea bream, 5 percent sea bass, and 5 percent flounder and other species indigenous to the Lagoon.

21

■ THE FISH OF THE LAGOON

The sails and rigging of the *bragozzo* used by fishermen on the Lagoon have now been replaced by diesel motors.

The fish sold in the markets of Venice come mostly from the Adriatic Sea. Only a few species remain within the confines of the Lagoon during the summer months, notably eels and mullet. The latter move in shoals along the coastline and come into the Lagoon to feed on the animal and vegetable matter that is their major source of nourishment. The astonishing variety of fishing techniques and fishing vessels generated by Venice is the result of many centuries of experience in managing the Lagoon and its resources.

LARGE-HEADED MULLET This most prized member of the mullet family can grow to 24 inches in length

BRAGOZZO The fishing boat of the Lagoon's interior, equipped for harvesting scallops.

GOLDEN MULLET These fish swim into the Lagoon in the winter after reproducing at sea in the fall. They taste less good if caught near a port.

MUSSETTO The young sea mullet, bass and sea bream netted by these vessels are later released into the *valli*.

SQUILL An abundant Lagoon crustacean.

SARDINE AND ANCHOVY Frequently on the menus of Venetian restaurants, these coastal fish are usually netted in the northern Adriatic.

SOLE The fishermen of the Lagoon search for sole at night, attracting them with lamps and then netting or spearing them.

CUTTLEFISH The only member of the squid family found in the Lagoon – and then only if it does not rain, because if the salt content of the water is reduced they head for the open sea. The delicious Venetian dish *spaghetti al nero* is prepared with the ink of the cuttlefish.

SHRIMPS

MAGGION

On nights when the sirocco blows, the surface of the Lagoon glows with a phosphorescent light. At such times, the fish create luminous wakes in the water, making it easy for fishermen with square dipping nets to spot them.

Each species of fish found in the Lagoon is caught in a different manner. One method uses a stationary net, pegged upright with poles, which guides the fish into a central circular pocket net, where they are captured.

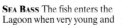

HOOP NET Spread at the bottom, the wings of the hoop net guide mullet, sea bass and eels into a pocket at its end.

SEA BASS The fish enters the Lagoon when very young and eventually grows to a length of between 12 and 30 inches.

VIERI These wicker baskets hung along the sides of boats allow the Lagoon fishermen to keep crabs, eels and other fish alive after they are captured (*vieri da barca*). The largest (*vieri da bisatti*) can hold up to 330 pounds of fish.

SEA BREAM Present in the Lagoon from March to November, and caught using either rod and line or nets.

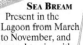

EEL In the fall, shoals of baby eels move into the Lagoon in the form of translucent elvers. They remain there for between 6 and 12 years before going back to the sea to reproduce.

RED MULLET A sea fish, caught in the Lagoon during the fall.

RED GURNET Lives in open sea, but often caught near ports.

OYSTERS Either dredged from the bottom of the Lagoon, or pulled from the sand by men with rakes.

GREEN CRAB In winter, these crabs reproduce near the open sea, but re-enter the Lagoon with their young from February.

MUSSEL ROPES

MUSSELS Attached to ropes suspended in the water, mussels are heavily cultivated in the Lagoon.

■ Bollards and Beacons

This bollard shrine shows how much the water was an integral part of Venetian life.

The Lagoon of Venice and its maze of waterways would be totally impassable if the navigation channels were not marked out by beacons and bollards, known as *bricole*. These groups of pilings, which are found everywhere in the Lagoon, vary widely in color, shape and number, and follow a precise code of reference. They are much appreciated by the seabird population of this broad and otherwise unrelieved expanse of water. Similarly their submerged parts are home to thriving colonies of animal and vegetable life, with many mollusks and seaweed species sheltering around them.

BRICOLA Made of massive baulks for stability, the *bricole* mark the limits of navigable channels.

DAMA These announce the entrance of a canal, or a junction between two waterways.

PALINA Single pilings which are mostly used as mooring posts in Venice.

COLORED PALINE The colors signify that the palina belongs to a specific family.

Gengiva

Pilings up to 20 feet long were driven into the Lagoon just behind the *gengiva*, or bank.

BARNACLE

RED SEAWEE

ACTINIA The colonies of this star-patterned anemone are cloaked in a shiny gelatinous layer.

ATHERINE FISH This fish lives in sandy coastal areas, but reproduces in brackish water.

GOBY A very common Lagoon fish, the goby spends the winter months in the mud at the bottom of the canal, where it lays its eggs.

The numbers on the *bricole* are duplicated on charts to aid navigation.

The *bricole* tend to rot quickly, and so have to be replaced every 20 years.

HERRING GULL
Perched on the *bricole*, the gulls patiently await the return of the fishing boats.

The channel passes beside the *bricola*, which bears a white mark.

BLACK-HEADED GULL
During its mating season, this species' head turns a dark brown color.

GREAT CORMORANT A powerful hooked beak and swimming speed give the cormorant an advantage in fishing.

The *bricole* are made out of one or more trunks of oak, olive or chestnut, chosen for their weight and solidity. Their top ends are tapered so that they can be assembled in bunches, then tarred to prevent infiltration by rainwater.

LIMPETS

GREEN SEAWEED
More abundant on the canal bottoms than nearer the surface.

MUSSEL A single mussel may filter as much as 13 gallons of water a day to feed.

ASCIDIAN

SEA ANEMONE

GREEN CRAB

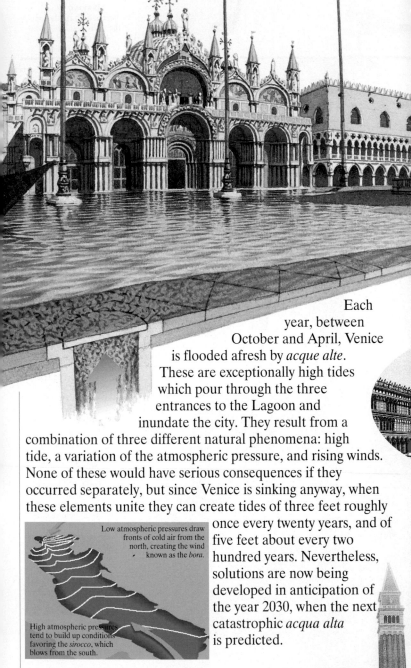

Each year, between October and April, Venice is flooded afresh by *acque alte*. These are exceptionally high tides which pour through the three entrances to the Lagoon and inundate the city. They result from a combination of three different natural phenomena: high tide, a variation of the atmospheric pressure, and rising winds. None of these would have serious consequences if they occurred separately, but since Venice is sinking anyway, when these elements unite they can create tides of three feet roughly once every twenty years, and of five feet about every two hundred years. Nevertheless, solutions are now being developed in anticipation of the year 2030, when the next catastrophic *acqua alta* is predicted.

Low atmospheric pressures draw fronts of cold air from the north, creating the wind known as the *bora*.

High atmospheric pressures tend to build up conditions favoring the *sirocco*, which blows from the south.

Because it is a virtually closed sea, the Adriatic is as susceptible to tidal variations (the consequence of the moon's gravitational pull on the oceans) as to the variations of atmospheric pressure which generate high winds. The *sirocco*, a wind blowing out of Syria, pushes the Adriatic towards the Gulf of Venice. The *bora*, a wind from the Hungarian steppes, impedes the tide from flowing back out of the Lagoon. Between them, these two winds are responsible for raising waves more than 8 feet high, and when all these elements combine, an *acqua alta* is unleashed.

Rainwater run-off from St Mark's Square is channeled along a system of drains that flows directly into the Grand Canal. When the water rises in the Lagoon, this process is reversed.

Because the drains are all linked together, the water from the Grand Canal can pour up into the square.

Year by year, the frequency and dimensions of the *acque alte* have steadily increased. During the 1920's, high tides of about 3 feet (24 inches in St Mark's Square) occurred an average of once a year; today the phenomenon is often repeated up to 10 times annually. Among the 15 exceptional *acque alte* recorded since 1867, the worst was in November 1966; in that year St Mark's Square, the lowest point in Venice, found itself under more than 4 feet of water.

Since 1966, research has been carried out with a view to finding ways to protect Venice from flooding. The regulation of

rising and falling tides at the three entrances to the Lagoon will be achieved by a system of mechanically operated sea-locks. The Consorzio Venezia Nuova, which is in charge of the project, has already tested an experimental module known as MOSE.

When one enters the St Mark's Basilica from the Piazza, one has to go down several steps. This is due to a compacting of the subsoil, a characteristic which is now a common feature in all the oldest quarters of the city – which are also the richest areas from an architectural point of view. It therefore follows that the subsidence of the soil and the effect of continual *acque alte* are a very serious menace to the palaces of Venice.

Here the floodgates are shown in the closed position, preventing the water from entering the Lagoon. When open and regulating the currents back and forth, the floodgates will be completely submerged.

By about the year 2000, the plan is that 40 floodgates like the one above will be protecting the Lido channel, 20 the one at Malamocco, and 20 others the one at Chioggia.

THE FLORA AND FAUNA OF VENICE

The seaweed on the *bricole* attracts small insects, which are much appreciated by Venetian sparrows.

The labyrinth of Venice's canals, which brings the sea into the very heart of the city, is its most original feature. Green crabs, shrimps, mollusks and several species of fish survive in this brackish environment, adjusting to the rise and fall of the tides. On the surface, between the paving stones of the calli and the stones in the walls, the observant walker can find many different plants that have adapted to this unusual milieu; likewise, the bird population, which thrives in the city's old quarters and hidden gardens.

So large is the city's population of stray cats that an international adoption center for Venetian cats has been set up.

BLACKBIRD (MALE)

SWIFT
They nest under the eaves of houses.

SWALLOW
Mostly to be found on the smaller islands of the Lagoon.

CRYSTHE MARINE
Normally found on sea cliffs, this little plant also grows in the chinks of masonry along the sides of the canals.

FERAL PIGEON
Present in huge flocks not just in St Mark's Square but all over the city.

GREAT TIT

HOUSE SPARROW In contrast to the sparrows of Northern Europe, the race found south of the Alps has a brown head.

The layers of algae and micro-organisms which can be seen along the sides of the canals subject to tidal fluctuations (those in the intertidal zone) testify to one of the richest theaters of biological activity in the Mediterranean.

BROWN RAT
or Sewer Rat.

High water.

Low water.

Alternate layers of sand and clay, topped with a mixture of the two (1000m).

Layer of closely packed clay, or *caranto*.

Superficial layer, mostly detritus.

28

HISTORY

6th – 10th Centuries   The Founding of Venice

306–37
Reign of Constantine.

THE ORIGINS. In the 1st century BC, the name *Venetia* designated an administrative region within the Roman Empire, including the present Veneto, Friuli and Trentino areas. In 568 the Lombards encroached from the north and between the 6th and 7th centuries the population of the Veneto (by now a province of Byzantium) was pushed back to the coast and the islands. Conventional wisdom has it that Venice was founded by these forced migrants, but some now think it was already a flourishing Roman port well before then. No one knows for sure.

330
Transfer of the capital of the Roman Empire to Constantinople.

401
Start of the barbarian invasions.

493–553
The Ostrogoth kings rule in Northern Italy.

554
Justinian, the Byzantine Emperor, restores imperial authority on the peninsula with Ravenna as capital.

TOWARDS POLITICAL AUTONOMY. In the 7th century, the Christian patriarch resided at Grado and the Byzantine administration at Heracleia; the latter subsequently moved to Malamocco. Those inhabiting the Lagoon began to elect their own governors, though the links with Byzantium were still close and the Byzantine fleet defended them when the Franks invaded in 810. A pact was made with the Franks and the Lagoon was confirmed as part of the Byzantine Empire.

THE BIRTH OF A STATE. At the same time, the elected governor – or Doge, from the Latin *dux*, or leader – left Malamocco for Rivoaltus in the heart of the Lagoon. In 827 the archipelago came under the religious authority of Aquileia, and found itself again threatened with Frankish domination. Two merchants stole the relics of St Mark the Evangelist and brought them to the Lagoon in 828. Invigorated by this psychological coup, the Realtine Islands achieved religious independence from Grado and established political autonomy. St Mark's emblem, the lion, became the symbol of the new state, and the first stable forms of government were put in place. By the 10th century, the city of Venice had emerged.

The Realtine Islands.

11th – 14th Centuries   A Mediterranean Power

727–8
Revolt against Byzantium in Italy.

751
The Lombards occupy Ravenna.

800
Charlemagne is crowned Emperor in Rome.

936
Otho I is crowned Emperor. Italy is assimilated with Germany.

POLITICAL AND ECONOMIC GROWTH. Venice was soon dealing with its former Byzantine masters on equal terms. In return for her financial and military support in the struggle against Islam and the Normans, Venice received commercial advantages in the Byzantine-controlled Orient. Her influence soon spread along the Dalmatian coast, and her war galleys dominated the Adriatic. Like other maritime republics, such as Genoa and Pisa, Venice took advantage of the crusades by supplying ships, food and money to the Christian forces, and opening commercial exchanges around the Mediterranean. By the 12th century, the city's rulers were powerful enough to act as mediators between Pope Alexander III and Emperor Frederick I Barbarossa, who signed

In 828, two merchants from Torcello stole the body of St Mark the Evangelist in Alexandria and brought it home. St Mark became the patron saint of Venice.

a peace treaty in Venice in 1177. In 1204 the Doge Enrico Dandolo took advantage of Constantinople's growing weakness to demand the soldiers of the Fourth Crusade pay for their Venetian transportation by laying siege to the capital of the Eastern Empire. Constantinople fell and another empire was installed, of which the Venetians took the lion's share. But Genoa, envious of the success of its rival, formed an alliance with the deposed Byzantine emperors and reconquered the Eastern Empire in 1261. The Venetians lost a portion of their territory and most of their commercial privileges. After a truce lasting from 1270–90, the struggle with Genoa resumed until 1299, when a fresh peace was concluded. Despite the defeat of the Venetians at the Battle of Curzola in 1298, neither of the adversaries gained a decisive advantage.

THE DEVELOPMENT OF INSTITUTIONS. Meanwhile, economic expansion had modified the social structure of the city. A wave of newly rich families were eager to take their place in government alongside older patrician clans. The quasi-monarchical authority of the Doge was also becoming irksome at a time when free cities were prospering elsewhere in Italy. Councils of "Sages" were set up between 1130 and 1148 to curb the Doge's powers, and in 1172 a committee was formed to monitor his election. But Venice's incessant warfare with Genoa and Constantinople made domestic unity a strong priority, and this probably explains the famous measure of 1297 to "close" the Grand Council, after which only members of families inscribed in the Golden Book (containing the record of births and marriages of the Venetian nobility) could be admitted ● 231. In this way Venice endowed herself with a tightly knit political class, with powerful bodies like the Council of Ten (established in 1310) to complement it.

A DIFFICULT 14TH CENTURY. Venice lost half her population to the Black Death of 1348. A serious economic crisis followed, and Ludwig I of Hungary seized the opportunity to annexe Dalmatia from Venice. At the same time the rulers of Padua and Ferrara, and especially the powerful Viscontis of Milan, began to threaten Venetian interests. The ancestral struggle with Genoa, which had allied itself with Florence, Padua and Hungary, intensified from 1378 onwards.

A THREAT TO SURVIVAL. In 1379, the Genoese fleet penetrated the Lagoon and seized Chioggia, but the Venetian forces made a desperate counterattack which enabled them to conclude a peace at Turin in 1381 and save the situation. The treaty strongly favored Venice's enemies; but Genoa, exhausted by the conflict and wracked by domestic strife, never again posed a serious threat to the Venetians.

EARLY 11TH CENTURY
First Norman invaders appear in Southern Italy and are defeated by the Venetians.

1054
Schism in the East.

c.1080
The principal cities of Northern and Central Italy win their independence: the comuni.

1075
The Turks conquer Jerusalem.

1096–9
The First Crusade.

1154–83
Wars between Barbarossa and the comuni. Treaty of Constantinople in which the freedoms of the comuni are confirmed.

1309–77
The papacy is transferred to Avignon.

15TH CENTURY THE HEIGHT OF VENETIAN POWER

Corfu, a Venetian possession.

1385–1437
Hapsburg expansion into Northern Italy.

1414–18
End of the Great Schism.

1434
The Medicis assume control in Florence.

1453
Constantinople falls to the Ottomans and becomes Istanbul.

1488
Bartolomeo Diaz reaches the Cape of Good Hope.

1492
Christopher Colombus discovers America.

1494
Charles VIII sets out to conquer the kingdom of Naples: the start of the Italian Wars.

The Venetian conquests.

1494–8
Piero de Medici leaves Florence. The establishment of Savonarola's republican government.

THE DEFENCE OF THE LEVANT. Venice steadily extended her Mediterranean Empire. Taking advantage of the Genoese decline, she once again took control of the Adriatic, which for many centuries thereafter became known as the Gulf of Venice. Corfu fell in 1386, the Albanian coast submitted a few years later and Dalmatia was finally reconquered between 1409 and 1420. But now another threat was looming in the shape of the Ottoman Empire. The Turkish fleet had been defeated in 1407, but went on to victory in a battle of 1429. The Turkish army captured Constantinople in 1453, advanced into the Balkans, and seized Negroponte (Euboea) from Venice in 1470.

Nevertheless the Republic not only maintained but also strengthened its positions in the eastern Mediterranean, extending its domination to Cyprus in 1489, although fresh defeats by the Turks were in store between 1499 and 1503. In the late 15th century expansionism and the safeguarding of one's own interests could be justified as the defence of Christianity.

THE CONQUEST OF THE MAINLAND. At the close of the 14th century, Venice formed an alliance with Florence to counter the expansionist politics of the Viscontis in Northern Italy. It was important to keep her powerful Milanese neighbors in their place if Venice was to control the trade routes into Northern Europe and protect the assets of the wealthy Venetian families which had invested in mainland property. But to do so meant she was obliged to abandon her isolation. Although Treviso and the surrounding countryside had been overrun in 1339, Venice's first real effort to extend her authority deep into mainland Italy did not begin until 1404. Within twenty years she had annexed Padua, Vicenza, Verona, Belluna, Feltre and all of Friuli. The Venetian government now divided its activities into two spheres: the *stato da mar* (the colonial sea-state) and the *stato da terra* (the land-state). Venice's advance along the Po valley resumed in 1425–6, and before long the Republic's boundaries had reached the banks of the river Adda, a state of affairs officially sanctioned in 1454 by the Treaty of Lodi. War with Ferrara (1481–4) led to yet another attempt at expansion, which failed in the face of combined resistance from Florence, Milan and Naples. By now, the Italian powers were profoundly suspicious of Venetian ambitions to upset the balance of power and dominate the peninsula: the threat from Milan was forgotten.

Recruitment of sailors for the
Venetian fleet.

THE ITALIAN WARS.

THE ITALIAN WARS. Taking advantage of the confusion
created by the French invasion of Italy in 1494, Venice
attempted to seize control of the ports of Apulia and to
annex Pisa, which had risen in revolt against Florence.
After this the Republic sought to overrun papal
Romagna, and this was the last straw. At Cambrai in
1508 the monarchs of Europe and the Italian city-states
formed an alliance against Venice under the aegis of
Pope Julius II. The army of the Republic was routed at
Agnadello on May 14, 1509; part of Venice's mainland
empire was occupied by French and Imperial forces, and
the rest rose in revolt. For a few weeks, the fall of the
Venetian state appeared inevitable.

16TH – 17TH CENTURIES   A FORCED NEUTRALITY

THE TURNING OF THE TIDE. Thanks to the support of
Pope Julius II, who switched alliances as
soon as the Papacy was assured of
retaining Romagna, Venice was able to
take advantage of the rivalries between her
Imperial, French and Spanish enemies. By
playing off Francis I of France and the
Emperor Charles V against each other,
within ten years she contrived to regain
and consolidate all her lost possessions,
relinquishing only Cremona and the
Venetian claim to the ports of Apulia.

Pope Julius II.

VENETIAN NEUTRALITY. After this
episode, Venice opted for armed
neutrality. Over the next two centuries she
remained a force to be reckoned with but
never again took sides in the quarrels of
the great European monarchies.

THE GOLDEN AGE. After Florence and Rome, the Venice
of Titian, Tintoretto and Veronese became the third great
center of the Italian Renaissance, while the stability of her
institutions became a byword in Europe.

RETREAT FROM THE MEDITERRANEAN. The state of
Venice's maritime empire was less promising. From the
beginning of the 16th century, the islands of the Aegean had
been falling into the hands of the Turks. The fruit of a
Venetian alliance with Spain and Rome, the victory of
Lepanto on October 7, 1571, had no lasting effect and Cyprus
was effectively lost. Corsairs on the Bosnian and Dalmatian
coasts harried Venetian shipping on the Adriatic, and the

city's resources
were steadily
depleted by the
wars. The
government
ran deep into
debt and had
to impose
heavy taxes on
the economy.

1517
Martin Luther
proclaims his reforms.

1519
Charles V is crowned
Holy Roman Emperor.

1525
Francis I is defeated at
Pavia.

1527
Sack of Rome by the
imperial troops.

1530
Venice refuses to
acknowledge the
dominion of Charles V.

1545
The Council of Trent.
Start of the Counter
Reformation.

1556
Abdication of Charles
V. Italy ceded to Spain.

1559
Treaty of Cateau-
Cambrésis: France
renounces all claim to
Italy.

Daniele Manin, leader
of the Venetian
uprising in 1848.

1618–48
*The Thirty Years' War
between the great
European powers.*

Right, a Venetian
plague doctor.

1702–12
*War of the Spanish
Succession between
France and a coalition
of European powers.*

THE START OF A DECLINE. An economic
crisis beginning in 1620 followed by the great
plague of 1630 heralded the start of an
irreversible decline. Europe's commercial
focus shifted to the North Sea, the volume of
shipping in Venice dropped, and the city's
luxury industries began to suffer from French
competition. In the 17th century Venice's
attempts to influence European politics met
with failure, though for a while she held her
own against Ottoman encroachment in the
East. Her loss of Crete (1645–69) was balanced by the
reconquest of Morea and Athens at the end of the century;
but both fell back into Turkish hands between 1714 and 1718.

18TH CENTURY THE DEATH OF THE REPUBLIC

1706–7
*French setbacks in
Italy. Austria conquers
Milan and the
kingdom of Naples.*

1776
*Independence of the
United States.*

1789
*The French
Revolution.*

CRISIS OF CONFIDENCE. The ruinous conflict with the
Turks had, on several occasions, obliged the Venetian ruling
class to open its ranks to newly enriched families, in exchange
for lump payments to the state. However the number of
candidates for this honor fell sharply during the course of the
18th century – a sign that confidence was eroding. In fact, the
social and political fabric of Venice was in crisis, and the
tentative reforms of the second half of the century came too
late. Almost inevitably, the Republic was swept away in the
turmoil of the Napoleonic Wars.

VENICE, BONAPARTE'S PLAYTHING. Venice's decision in
1793 to adopt a policy of "unarmed neutrality" was such an
admission of weakness that in 1796

Napoleon Bonaparte marched into the
Veneto, ostensibly to fight the Austrians.
In April 1797 he "ceded" part of Venice's
territory to the Hapsburgs and then, on
May 1, 1797, he declared war on Venice
herself. Before long French forces were
picketed before the Doge's Palace and
Bonaparte was offering peace on his own
conditions – with the proviso that the
Venetians "reform" their government,

1802
*Napoleon Bonaparte
becomes president of
the Italian Republic.*

which they hurriedly did on May 12. At the subsequent Treaty
of Campo Formio, the French abandoned Venice to Austria,
whose armies entered the city on January 18, 1798.

19TH CENTURY FROM AUSTRIA TO ITALY

1804–5
*Napoleon is crowned
Emperor and King of
Italy.*

FOREIGN DOMINATION. Venice was reconquered by
French troops in January 1806; the French were driven out
again by the Austrians in April 1814. The creation of a free
port provided only
temporary relief from
the city's inexorable
decline between 1830
and 1848. An
insurrection led by
Daniele Manin and
Nicolò Tommaseo on
May 22, 1848,
temporarily expelled

Garibaldi
in Venice.

the Austrians, who responded in 1849 by laying siege to the city. On August 24, the provisional government fell, and the Austrians, returning for the third time, punished Venice by stripping her of administrative authority over the Veneto. Over the next two decades, Austria governed the city with increasing severity.

VENICE REVERTS TO ITALY.

Venice was finally absorbed by the new Italian monarchy in 1866, when the king received Venice and the Veneto after the Austrian defeat at Sadowa, in return for his support of Prussia.

VENICE IN THE 20TH CENTURY

Venice's splendid isolation was broken by the construction of a railway bridge (in 1846) and a road bridge (in 1932) linking the city with the mainland Between the end of the 19th century and the start of the First World War, several attempts were made to stimulate the Venetian economy by developing the port, the industrial zone at Mestre and the seaside resort of the Lido, in addition to the creation of cultural events such as the Biennale. Between the wars, Venice's trading economy, centered around the port of Marghera, remained buoyant. But following the Second World War the attempt to turn Venice into a modern center, like its neighbors in Northern Italy, ended in failure. There were numerous problems; the city's economy was forced to rely on ancillary activities, and the price of living space became prohibitively high. The population also dwindled and aged; the steady flow of migrants to Mestre and Marghera turned into a flood. At the same time the ecological balance of the Lagoon was damaged and the phenomenon of the *acqua alta* attained disturbing dimensions. The city's architectural heritage began to deteriorate rapidly under the combined assaults of pollution and heavy canal traffic. Finally, the plight of Venice began to attract world attention, and in 1973 a special law was passed by the Italian government which allowed the provision of billions of lire in subsidies. Nonetheless the fundamental question still remains the same: should we allow this city, home to 79,000 inhabitants, to become no more than a huge museum? Should we let Venice die, or should we make the necessary radical changes in one of the few great capitals of the past to have survived the 20th century miraculously intact?

1814–15
Fall of Napoleon and restoration of the old regimes in Italy.

1831
Several Italian cities rebel and Austrian forces intervene.

1846–7
Economic crisis and famine in Europe.

1848
Revolution spreads throughout Europe. The first Italian War of Independence ends with an Austrian victory.

1859
The second Italian War of Independence ends with victory for the Piedmontese.

1861
Proclamation of the Kingdom of Italy

1870
Rome becomes the capital of Italy.

1896–1911
Conquest of Abyssinia and Libya by the Italians.

1915
Italy enters the Second World War on the side of the Allies.

1922
The march on Rome and the establishment of a Fascist regime in Italy.

1933
Hitler seizes power in Germany.

1945
Uprising in Northern Italy against the Germans and the Fascists.

1946
Proclamation of the First Italian Republic.

● THE BATTLE OF LEPANTO

In 1570 the Turks attacked Cyprus, a Venetian possession. Christian forces, galvanized by the spirit of the Counter Reformation, responded by forming the Holy League (Venice, Spain and the Papacy) to repel the invader. On October 7, 1571, the Christian fleet engaged the Ottomans off the port of Lepanto on the south-west Hellenic coast. In one of the greatest battles fought in the Mediterranean, the Christian forces crushed an enemy undefeated since 1538.

PHILIP II
On May 19, 1571, the King of Spain, Philip II, joined the Holy League to "bring ruin and destruction upon the Turk", committing his country to fight alongside Venice, Genoa and the Papacy. Philip's brother, Don Juan of Austria, who was a natural son of Charles V, was named commander-in-chief of the allied fleet.

THE DEFEAT OF THE TURKS
The Turkish admiral Ali Pasha underestimated the Christian strength and, against the advice of his squadron commanders, ordered his fleet to leave Lepanto. In the ensuing battle thirty thousand Turks were killed or captured, nine thousand died on the Christian side, and many were wounded, including the Spaniard Miguel de Cervantes, author of *Don Quixote*.

Figures of Moors (in fact, these represent Turkish prisoners in chains) adorning the Morosini galley: after the Battle of Lepanto, it became customary for prisoners to row the galleys of Venice.

LA MERAVIGLIOSA ET C[...]N VITORIA DATA DA DIO A CHRISTIANI CONTRA TVRCHI ALLI SCOGLI CVRZOLARI L'ANO 1571 A 7 OTO

THE OPPOSING FLEETS

Against the Turks' 230 galleys and 60 galliots, the Christians had only 214 warships, more than half of which came from the Arsenal at Venice. The Christian firepower, however, was vastly superior. To avoid encirclement, the Christian right flank had to spread itself thinly; fortunately the brunt of the action was borne by Don Juan's squadron in the center.

The round ships ▲ *178*, remained in the rearguard while six Venetian galeasses ▲ *180* led the van; these were the only cannon-equipped heavy vessels to be present at the Battle of Lepanto.

THE OTTOMAN SULTAN SELIM II (1524–74)

Selim's attempt to annexe Cyprus in 1570 provoked a Christian retaliation.

PIUS V, INSTIGATOR OF THE LEAGUE

Determined to roll back both the Turkish and Protestant threat to the Roman Church, Pope Pius V moved heaven and earth to form his Holy League. Every soldier who fought under Don Juan's banner of Christ was absolved of all sin by the Pope's special dispensation.

The name of "Bucintoro" is probably derived from *bucio*, which was a type of boat used in medieval times: hence *bucio in t'oro* (gilded *bucio*). This Doge's galley was a spectacular symbol of the Serene Republic. It was launched for state visits and other official ceremonies, such as the Doge's marriage with the sea, which took place on Ascension Day. This feast apparently commemorated a 10th-century expedition that was led by the Doge Orseolo II, and which delivered Dalmatia and Istria from the grasp of Slavic pirates and transformed the Adriatic into a Venetian gulf.

THE "OSELLE"

When the last Bucintoro was built at the Arsenal in 1729, the Republic struck an *osella*, or medal. One side of it showed the Doge on his knees before St Mark, the city's patron saint, and the other a picture of the Bucintoro.

THE DOGE'S CORTÈGE

As soon as the ceremony was over, the cortège was reorganized for the procession back from the Lido. Directly astern of the Bucintoro were the most elaborate vessels, belonging to prominent individuals; then came everyone else. Those who had been present at the ceremony joined in the festivities that followed as open-air banquets and parties were held on the islands along the route of the procession.

IMPORTANT VISITORS

The Bucintoro was customarily placed at the disposal of state visitors to Venice. On July 15, 1574, Henry of Valois formally entered Venice aboard the Bucintoro, which carried him up the Grand Canal to the lodgings that had been prepared for him by the Seignory at the Ca' Foscari ▲ *331*.

In 1311, the Senate decreed the construction of a triumphal vessel which would be capable of carrying up to 200 men. The only evidence of how these different Bucintori looked is to be found in engravings, paintings and models; no other trace of them remains. The last Bucintoro was gutted by Napoleon's soldiers in 1798, before being finally scrapped in 1824. Opposite, the prow of a scale model, with the traditional effigy of Justice.

«IT IS A KIND OF GALLEY, COVERED AND GILDED. [...] THE INSIDE OF IT IS A SINGLE, BROAD CABIN, FLOORED WITH WOOD, WITH DIVANS ALL AROUND AND A THRONE AT ONE END FOR THE DOGE.» CHARLES DE BROSSES

THE CEREMONY OF THE DOGE'S "MARRIAGE"

Dressed in gold and ermine and wearing his *corno* hat, the Doge was carried by the Bucintoro to the port of San Nicolò di Lido, where he was awaited by the patriarch of San Pietro. He was then "married" to the sea. Throwing a ring into the water, he uttered the words: "We marry you, oh sea, in token of our true and perpetual possession", and invoked God's protection for all who worked on the water.

THE NUPTIAL RING

Legend says the ring was given to the Doge by a fisherman, who himself received it from St Mark. The chronicles record it was the gift of Pope Alexander III to acknowledge the Republic's control of the Adriatic.

SCALE MODEL OF THE LAST BUCINTORO

This model is preserved at the Naval Museum.

It was built by a worker at the Arsenal on the request of a vice-admiral of the Venetian navy, the Marquis Amilcare Paolucci delle Roncole.

FRAN.^{CO} MOROS: CAP.^N GN.^{ALE} CON POCHE GAL.^E E QVATRO NAVI DA LA FVGA A 17 NAVI TVRCHES:
DA GVERRA, NE FA ROMPERE, E NAVFRAGARE DVE, E NE PRENDE VNA CARICA DI MILIZIE.
TERMINA COSÌ LA CARICA DI CAP. GN.^{ALE} LA PRIMA VOLTA, E SE NE RITORNA A VENEZIA DOPO ESSERV
STATO LONTANO CON L'ARMA IN MANO LO SPAZIO DI 23 ANNI CONTINVI, SENZA MAI RIVE I AE
PATRIA NE PVR PER MO F N I L E SVBITO ANZI VIENE SPEDITO PROVED GN.^{ALE} STRAORDIN IN FR^{LI} PER V VA
TEMVTA IRRVCION   ROHI IN QVELLA PROVINCIA MAGGIO 1661

FRAN.^{CO} MOROS: STATO VICE CAP.^N DELLE NAVI, POI CAP.^N IN GOLFO E E ELETTO DOPO CAP.^N DELLE GAL.^E
NELLE ACQVE DI PARISI, E DI NIXIA, OVE SI INCONTRANO LE DVE, ARMATE, BENCHE LA TVRCA SVPERIOR
DEL DOPPIO, DISFA LA GALERA DEL CAP.^N BASSA, CHE RESTA SOTTOMESSA ROMPE ED ACQVISTA VN GA
MAGNA ABBORDA PER VLTIMO CON LA SVA GALEA ZZA LA NAVE CAPITANA DI COSTANTINOPOLI GVERNI
DI PIV DI 70 CANNONI E DOPPO VN SANGVINOSO CONTRASTO LA SOTTOMETTE, FATTO GRAN NVMERO
DI SCHIAVI, E PRESO VIVO IL, CAPO SVPREMO DELL'ARMATA GROSSA NEMICA DETTO NICOLO D
NADALINO, FVRLANO RINEGATO FAMOSO, CHE, SI CHIAMAVA MVSTAFA BASSA QVAL MVORE NELLE CARCER
DELLA DOMINANTE.   LVGLIO   1651

FRAN.^{CO} MOROS: CAP.^N GN.^{ALE} INSEGVISCE L'ARMATA TVRCA, CHE FVGGE SEBENE PIV
NVMEROSA ASSAI DELLA VENETA, ARRIVA DVE DELLE PIV GROSSE GALERE, E LE
PRENDE.   APRILE 1659.

Francesco Morosini (1619–94) was one of the last great admirals of the Venetian Republic. His many naval expeditions were recorded in a series of paintings of the late 17th century, which are now displayed in the Correr Museum (the Morosini Rooms, first floor). His glorious victories and his reconquest of the Peloponnese earned him the title of Doge in 1688.

FRANC. MOROS. K. PROC. E CAP. GNALE ACQVISTA NAVARIN VECCHIO CHE VNA VOLTA DICEVASI IL ZONCHO FORTEZZA NELA MOREA. E VI PRENDE MONI. DI OGNI GENERE E CANONI DI GRAN NVMERO GIVGNO 1686

FRANC. MOROS. SOPRACOMITO NEL PRIMO COMBATTIM. MARITIMO NELLA GVERRA DI CANDIA VA PRIMO DI TVTTI AD ASSALTARE LA PIV GRANDE DELLE NAVI TVRCHE NELL. ACQVE DI MILO, PER CORRISPONDERE ALL' IMPEGNO PRESO NEL MOTO DA LVI FATTO SCRIVERE SOTTO L'INSEGNA DELLA SVA GALERA, QVALE DICEVA IN CERTAMINE PRIMA. VNA GRANDE BORASCA SEPARA LA BATTAGLIA, CHE CONTINVÒ MOLTO, E SANGVINOSA. OTTOBRE 1648.

FRANCESCO MOROSINI CAP. GNALE ESPVGNA CISME FORTEZZA POSTA IN TERRA FERMA DI RINCONTRO A SCIO, FACENDO CON STRATAGEMA VSCIRE IL PRESIDIO TVRCO DALLA PIAZZA QVALE PERCIÒ NON POTENDO PIV DIFENDERSI, CEDE.. VI ACQVISTA MONIZIONI, BOTTINO CONSIDERABILE, CANNONI DI PIV GENERE IN COPIA. GIVGNO 1689.

● THE VENETIAN DIALECT

GOLDSMITHS' EMBLEM
The goldsmiths (*oresi* in Venetian) gave their name to a street in the Rialto where their shops were concentrated ▲ 283.

PANTALOON
The Venetians owed their nickname of *pantaloni* to a local saint, St Pantaloon. This name is also applied to one of the masked figures in the Commedia dell'Arte, who wears short trousers, hence the French name for trousers, *pantalon*.

In the Middle Ages, Italy was divided into a multitude of states, giving rise to an enormous diversity of dialects. With Latin as a common denominator, the various regions developed different modes of speech according to the commercial contacts and foreign influences to which they were exposed. Thus the Venetian dialect, which was used in official documents and for the composition of literary works, quickly gained the status of an official language spoken in the Republic's various colonies. Furthermore Venice was among the first Italian centers to evolve family names (from the 11th century). This system, with characteristic phonetic structures, was unique in Italy and was universally respected until the fall of the Republic.

PROPER NAMES

There are many odd features about Venetian names. Some derive from local distortions of Italian names, which were then adopted by the Italian language. Hence Alvise (for Luigi or Ludovico), Tomà (for Tommaso) and Anzolo (for Angelo). In other cases, a proper name has served to describe a type of person and has subsequently been transformed into a common name. Hence Zanni, the Venetian form of Gianni/Giovanni; In the Commedia dell'Arte this name applied to the characters of Harlequin and Brighella ▲ 291.

PLACE NAMES

Apart from a few *vie* driven through the city in the 19th century and given ubiquitous titles like Via Garibaldi, the streets of Venice mostly have extremely old and curious names. Some, which hark back to bygone professions and crafts, occur frequently: for example, the Calli del Pestrin (milksellers), del Pistor (bakers), del Frutarol (fruit and vegetable merchants). Others refer to the original geographical divisions between various specialized economic activities. Thus the Fondamenta degli Ormesini of Cannaregio probably owes its name to the presence of workshops specializing in fabrics from Hormuz in the Persian Gulf, or perhaps even from the furs with which the hats of nobles were edged. In the St Mark's–Rialto zone we find the Frezzerie (arrowsmiths) the Mercerie (clothsellers) and the Spadaria (swordsmiths). Venetian street names also preserve the memory of religious communities, as in the various Calli dei Preti (priests) and delle Muneghe (nuns); and the vanished influence of great patrician families who lived in the vicinity, such as Calle Contarini. Venice's traditionally large foreign contingent is also reflected in place names such as Calle dei Ragusei (after emigrants from Raguso, today's Dubrovnik), Calle delle Turchette ("little Turkish women"), Riva degli Schiavoni (Dalmatians), Calli degli Armeni (Armenians) and dei Tedeschi (Germans).

CRAFTS AND TRADITIONS

In the first half of the 18th century the graceful and luxurious Rococo style became increasingly popular in Venice, as a reaction against the more formal splendor that dominated the Baroque period. The Republic had begun its slow decline, but the great Venetian families were still embellishing their palaces, particularly the interiors. Rooms became more intimate, and lacquer and fine gilding were the norm for furniture, with swelling, undulating lines, softer hues and a growing preference for flowers and pastel backgrounds over the Baroque chinoiseries.

CONSOLES
The console table was a practical place on which to put things down (gloves, books) temporarily, hence it became known as a *servidor* (servant) in Venice.

LACQUERED FURNITURE ▲ *333*
Prior to the lacquering process, furniture was dressed and polished, then decorated and gilded. Finally it was given 15–20 coats of varnish. Furniture like this served to brighten many a Venetian interior.

ARMCHAIR
The delicate tones of satin and lacquer and the inward-curving lines of this armchair reflect the refined taste of Venetian society.

A lacquered **COMMODE** decorated with flowers and garlands against ivory. Commodes like this, with light backgrounds, were much in demand.

In response to the changing domestic and social norms, furniture became increasingly functional and comfortable.

PIER GLASS-DESK
One of the rare larger pieces of furniture produced by the Rococo style; multifunctional, it might serve as a commode, desk or looking-glass.

SMALL COMMODES could be adapted to the less spacious rooms of the 18th century. In response to a growing demand for lacquered furniture, *lacca povera* ("poor" lacquer) was developed. This was basically a painted décor reproduced on a thin sheet of paper, then stuck to the wood and covered with several coats of varnish.

MIRRORS
The great mirrors of 18th-century Venetian salons often had rich gilt-wood frames decorated with carved ribbons and fluting. Their effect was to scale down the elegant outlines of furniture and boiseries, by creating optical illusions (the impression of greater space) and by reflecting ad infinitum the light shed by multitudes of wall-brackets.

CHINOISERIES
These began as simple Baroque imitations of oriental décors, sometimes in relief, against red or black backgrounds. Later, Venetian craftsmen enriched the genre by introducing scenes of Venetian life.

In the 18th century, Venetians followed French fashions. Abandoning the rigid outlines of the two preceding centuries, clothes became graceful, sensual and highly colored. Silk was all the rage, often picked out with gold and silver thread and adorned with pearls and precious stones. Dyes took their names from contemporary habits (as in "coffee", Spanish tobacco), or poetry (as in "Angel's feather", a bright Tiepolo red). Pastel tones so dear to the Rococo style were popular, and white predominated in every aspect of human finery. Powder was used to emphasize the pallor of the skin, and jewelry was mainly of diamonds or pearls.

THE "VELADA"
Venetian men wore the *velada*, a kind of coat that had much in common with women's clothing, with its tight waist and flared skirts.

WIGS
Men wore wigs from beginning to end of the 18th century, while women adopted the fashion only after 1750.

SHOES
In the 18th century, Venetian women abandoned the high heels of the 16th century in favour of rather flatter shoes.

MEN'S CLOTHING
The *velada* allowed the shirt and the richly decorated waistcoat to show through. Skin-tight breeches ran down to the knee, and were worn with white silk stockings. Shoes had silver or gold buckles, sometimes set with pearls.

> «THE WOMEN OF VENICE ARE BEAUTIFUL BUT, MORE TO THE POINT, THEY ARE FLIRTATIOUS.»
>
> ANGE GOUDAR

HAIRSTYLES

In the first half of the 18th century, women wore their hair pulled back with no ornament except perhaps a flower on the left side of the head. Towards the end of the century the fashion returned for more voluminous coiffures, with towering wigs and ribboned bonnets. Depending on the type of bow, ribbon or other decoration, wigs took different names: "à la Turque", "Figaro", "chaste Susan" or "sentimental". In this last example, tiny portraits of dear ones would be pinned to the hair.

BEAUTY SPOTS

Hair, face and throat were powdered, and beauty spots would be added wherever required. An elaborate code revolved around the beauty spot: for example, placed near the eye, it signified the word "irresistible".

THE TRICORN HAT

A black, three-cornered hat completed a man's coiffure.

WOMEN'S CLOTHING

The 18th-century fashion extolled femininity above all else. The décolleté was low and deep, edged with lace. The corset was stiffened with steel or wooden rods. It cinched the waist down to the hips, and the silhouette ballooned. Skirts bulged outwards like contemporary chests of drawers, so much so that chairs had to be widened to receive them ● 44. Voluminous hoop-petticoats were worn on a framework of iron hoops, attached to the waist by bands of fabric and padded at the hip. Women's clothes always had French names, even when invented in Venice.

OFFICIAL CEREMONIES

Religious, civil, political and military ceremonies took place in Venice throughout the twelve months of the year. Public buildings were festooned with flags for these occasions; streamers and fabrics from the East were hung across house fronts and palace loggias; porticos and triumphal arches were raised on the city's campi. Citizens participated wholeheartedly in grandiose ceremonials attended by the Doge, and in the various parades and processions through the city. All in all, such events might best be understood as direct celebrations of the spiritual and political life of Venice.

THE DOGE'S CHAPLAIN
The chaplain of St Mark's, bearing his candle, was present in all of the Republic's processions.

RECEPTIONS
Red letter days in the life of the Republic were marked by lavish receptions in honor of ambassadors and European sovereigns visiting the city. A series of memorable parties was given when Henri de Valois came to Venice in July 1574.

PROCESSION TO SAN ZACCARIA
On the first Monday after Easter, the Doge and Seignory proceeded to San Zaccaria to pay homage to the sisters of the convent, who gave up their garden to permit the square to be widened ▲ 172.

THE FEAST OF CORPUS CHRISTI
This ceremony, which took place at the start of June, was renowned for the richness of its costumes and its kaleidoscope of flowers, candles and colors. The religious and civil authorities of the Republic, as well as the members of the scuole, paraded with great pomp around St Mark's Square (seen here at the close of the 15th century) ▲ 296.

THE FESTIVAL OF LA SALUTE

In gratitude to the Virgin for her intervention against the plague of 1630, the Venetians go in procession to the Basilica of La Salute on November 21. On the third Sunday of July, another procession commemorates the end of the epidemic of 1575 at the Church of the Redentore.

For this occasion a pontoon bridge is constructed across the Grand Canal from Santa Maria del Giglio to the Basilica of La Salute.

PROCESSION OF CORPUS CHRISTI

This procession was held more or less under cover, since the cortège (which left the basilica by one door and re-entered it by another) walked under a gallery specially erected for the occasion. A white flag was hung beneath the arcade, which was held up by columns covered in red damask and draped with branches of laurel.

MARITIME PROWESS

The "captain-general of the sea" was chosen by the Grand Council. This nomination to the highest post in the Venetian navy was sealed by the presentation of the commander-in-chief's baton in St Mark's Basilica, after which the captain-general walked in procession to the Piazzetta, with a guard of honor firing a salute over his head. This ceremony, in which the Doge and the Seignory took part, was also an occasion for Venice to celebrate her maritime power.

As part of the Venetian government's deliberate policy to promote "social stability", street entertainments and games were regularly organized in the city, especially at Carnival time. Shows and sports that were thought to build up the citizens' patriotism and fighting spirit were sponsored by the state; but as far as the Venetian populace was concerned, any excuse for a good time was entirely welcome.

THE SKATERS
Very occasionally the Lagoon would freeze over and the canals of Venice would become impassable by boat. At such times, children and young people went about the city on rudimentary ice-skates, probably imitating the ones that the Venetian merchants had seen being used in Northern Europe.

Every February 2, numerous games were organized on Campo Santa Maria Formosa.

CRUEL SPORTS
Two particularly nasty sports were organized at Candlemas. One (on the left in the engraving below) entailed battering a plump white cat to death with one's head while the cat was free to use its claws to defend itself. The cat-killer's skull had to be shaven, whence a Venetian expression (still in use) that roughly translates as "to kill a cat with your shaven head". In another Candlemas event (below right) the competitors leaped from a bridge after a live goose, which was dangled from a balcony by a rope; the winner who managed to grab the wretched creature carried it in triumph through the streets. For bull-baiting, the bull (or ox) was tethered by a rope lashed to its horns, while dogs worried its most vulnerable parts (mostly the ears).

> «I WAS ON THE PIAZZETTA AND I SAW THE FLIGHT OF THE ANGEL,
> AND ALSO THE DANCE OF THE MOORS;
> BUT WITHOUT YOU, MY DEAR, I WAS ALONE.»
>
> I.V. FOSCARINI

THE FEAST OF MARDI GRAS ON THE PIAZZETTA
In the background of this painting by Bella are human pyramids and the *svole dell'angelo* (flight of the angel). This latter trick was performed by an acrobat, who slid down a rope from the top of St Mark's campanile to the Doge's Palace, carrying a bunch of flowers for the Doge.

WHEELBARROW RACES
This 18th-century sport was a speciality of Venice's street-sweepers. The first team to cross the finishing line and grab the flag won a cash prize.

STILTS
During Carnival, Venice was haunted by masked men on stilts, who raced around the streets, bestrode the canals, ate their meals on high, and leaned artlessly against the upper balconies of palaces. Probably because of an association of ideas between stilts and crutches, it was popularly believed that to walk on stilts was to attract the evil eye.

51

Carnival began on Boxing Day, December 26, and reached its climax the day before Ash Wednesday. While it lasted, the law was more or less held in abeyance: the wearing of masks and disguises abolished social divisions for the duration, whereas for the rest of the year the strict orders of precedence observed for official ceremonies did the opposite. During Carnival, the campi, St Mark's Square and the main thoroughfares were thronged with people dancing, singing, carousing and playing games.

The use of masks was so widespread that the maskmakers had their own official artisan status as early as the 15th century.

In its parody of Venice's civil and religious rituals, Carnival also featured the enemies of the Republic. Seen here is a richly dressed Moor.

CARNIVAL AT THE CAFÉ FLORIAN
The mask began as a means for nobles to mingl
incognito with ordinary citizens in the casini ▲ 2
and theaters. Today, people meet more prosaical
in the cafés around St Mark's Square.

Carnival opened with a series of balls on Venice's largest campi; these were followed by spontaneous parties which continued for several weeks until Shrove Tuesday, when the bells of San Francesco della Vigna tolled at midnight to mark the beginning of Lent.

"TABARRO" AND "BAUTO"
The *bauto* was composed of a black silk hood and a lace cape; the costume was completed by a voluminous cloak (*tabarro*) and a three-cornered hat. Wearing *bauto*, *tabarro* and a white mask covering most of the face, one could go anywhere completely incognito.

During Carnival, St Mark's Square was invaded by street vendors selling *frittele* (fritters) and other sweetmeats.

CARNIVAL TODAY
Since 1980, the masks have reappeared in Venice, and 18th-century garments and traditional costumes again mingle with other grotesque disguises. The old custom of giving balls and theatrical performances has been revived, along with an array of ancient Venetian games. On the final day, the effigy of Carnival is burned on St Mark's Square, in accordance with tradition.

THE COMMEDIA DELL'ARTE
Some disguises (in this case, Harlequin) are borrowed from the Commedia dell'Arte, which was played on all the city's campi ▲ *291*.

The regattas of Venice began as military exercises for crossbowmen on the Lido and developed into popular events for all Venetians, for whom the sea and everything to do with it was a way of life. The oarsmen of the galleys assigned to transport soldiers to and from St Mark's whiled away the time with races; the government, seeing a convenient way of training the people for war, introduced the first official regatta in about 1300, on the Feast of the Marias ▲ *167*. Regattas proliferated and the tradition still continues today, with events held from March to September, in Venice itself and across the Lagoon.

THE HISTORIC REGATTA
In 1825, after the loss of Venice's precious Bucintoro, it was decided that an annual regatta should be held to preserve the traditions of the Republic.

THE BANNERS
A platform was erected for the judges in front of Ca' Foscari, the traditional finishing line for races. These judges presented the first boats in each category with banners of several different colors (red for the winner).

A DARING COMPETITOR
In 1574, the winner of one of the races, a woman, had to leap from boat to boat to collect her red banner from the judges.

PARADE IN RENAISSANCE COSTUME
Venice's main historic regatta takes place on the first Sunday in September. Large vessels filled with people in costume parade down the Grand Canal, accompanied by a fleet of smaller boats. After this there are four races involving the different types of boats in use on the Lagoon. Opposite, the *bissona Veneziana*, an eight-oared boat featuring the lion of St Mark on its bows.

Right, a *sandalo*, or flat-bottomed boat, taking part in the Vogalonga. The two oarsmen row standing up, Venetian style.

THE WOMEN'S RACE
The first women's race took place in 1493, in honor of Béatrice d'Este, the wife of Lodovico il Moro, Duke of Milan. Fifty girls entered this race, which is still run each year.

THE VOGALONGA, OR LONG-DISTANCE RACE
This tremendous event has been organized every year since 1975. On Ascension Day, when by tradition the Doge was "married" to the sea, hundreds of boats of all kinds race from St Mark's Basin to Burano and back again, a distance of about 18 miles. The final stretch is through the Cannaregio and Grand Canals, where a huge and enthusiastic crowd awaits the competitors. The Vogalonga is a test of endurance and skill with the oar; entrants train for months in advance around the city's canals.

Once the nobles of Venice had got into the habit of traveling about the city in their own personal gondolas and employing a private gondolier, the latter inevitably became something of a confidante, since he accompanied his master to even the most private rendezvous. Nowadays, the gondoliers still form a "caste" of their own, and the profession is passed down from father to son. Today, the gondola mostly survives as a tourist attraction, and the gondoliers of the city number about four hundred all told.

Gondolas were originally so gaudily decorated that the Republic decreed in 1633 that they should all be painted black.

GONDOLIERS RESTING
A *stazio* is both a mooring place for gondolas and an embarkation point. One of the biggest is near the columns of the Piazzetta, at the feet of which the gondoliers gossip and wait for passengers.

RACING IN THE LAGOON
Gondoliers were able to demonstrate their skill and speed during duck hunts.

A BIZARRE CONSTRUCTION

The gondola is designed so that one of its sides is nine inches broader than the other ● 68. Thus the gondola heels and yaws naturally to starboard, but the gondolier, standing in its stern with one leg forward, can right its course with his oar ● 70.

THE GONDOLAS OF THE SUN KING

The Republic of Venice often presented gondolas as gifts to foreign sovereigns and ambassadors. Thus in 1687 Louis XIV of France had no fewer than 15 gondoliers in his service, who were lodged in his "Petit-Venise" on the canal at Versailles.

TRAGHETTI

The traghetti, which are collective gondolas propelled by two oarsmen, provide a ferry service to and fro across the Grand Canal at seven different points.

VENEZIA

Black clothes and a red or blue ribboned straw hat make up the uniform of the modern gondolier; formerly he was dressed in much brighter colors.

"FELZE"

This small, cabin-like structure, with a roof like a half-barrel, was usually installed on the gondolas during the winter months. It provided a measure of privacy and warmth for passengers.

1. The glassblower starts by collecting a certain quantity of molten glass on the red hot end of a hollow tube.

2. He lays the tube across a bench, turning it in a wooden mold until the ball of molten glass is round and compact.

5. Using steel pincers, he chokes the collar of the glass ball near the end of the tube.

6. The glass is then reheated and reblown.

9. The glassblower then widens the hollow of the glass and begins the shaping process.

11. A second tube is fixed to the inside of the glass, and the first one is detached. The upper part of the glass is now finished.

STAGES IN THE MANUFACTURE

13. Meanwhile, the glassblower prepares the foot and the stem.

14. A little molten glass is applied to the stem to make it adhere to the upper part of the glass.

3. He blows down the tube to pierce the ball, then blows again to form a rough shape.

4. The glassblower continues to rotate his tube to counter the downward-pulling effect of gravity and to stop the glass stretching out.

7. The spherical form is given to the base of the glass and drawn out to a point with the pincers.

8. The point is removed to allow the pincers to be introduced.

OF A WINE GLASS

10. The lip of the glass is widened.

12. The glass is heated once again.

15. The glass is pivoted in the pincers to make sure its alignment is true.

16. The glass is reheated, then finally placed in a special oven to cool.

Venetian lace is made with the needle, although the product is also made with a bobbin at Chioggia and Pellestrina. The Venetian technique of *punto in aria* ▲ *371* first appeared in the mid-16th century; the embroidery technique used until that time still required a canvas backing, which gave a perforated effect. The anonymous invention of *punto in aria* dispensed with this constraint, since a single strand of thread fixed to a piece of parchment served as its support.

The lacemaker arranges the openwork and varies her stitches according to strict conventions imposed by the designer.

The basic stitch is the simple (or triple gauze) stitch, which produces effects as light as tulle.

The lacemaker then executes the relief, or alternatively embroiders a thread of greater or lesser thickness.

MOUNTING THE LACE
Several layers of fabric, and then the paper bearing the design to be copied, are spread on a cushion. After passing the stitches through both the paper and the fabric, the design is fixed by running the thread around its contours.

GREEN PAPER is commonly used, as it is less tiring on the eyes.

THE LACEMAKER'S ACCESSORIES
Needles and thread.

THE ROUND CUSHION is mounted on a wooden frame.

The lacemaker attaches her first row of bars to the design.

THE CHAIR
Lacemakers sit on chairs with foot rests, usually facing daylight by the window.

POSTURE
Seemingly made of stone, with only her fingers in constant motion, the lacemaker in her traditional white apron sits for hours at a time, her head bent over her work.

"SAN MARCO" ARS (LAGUNA)
LABORATORIO DI SCIALLI
VENEZIA di Ponte dei Barateri, Calle di Mezzo 673
Tel. 3617   Tel. 3617

SHAWL FACTORY   SCHALTUCHERSTRICK F
Handwork   Handarbeit
ATELIER DE BRODERIES A LA MAIN
Châles

17TH-CENTURY LACE
In the 17th century, Venetian *gros point* lace, thick and modeled against a background of bare stitches, was all the rage. Towards the end of the century, smaller, more delicate patterns came into fashion.

Hanks of thread.

Burano's lacemakers have revived the Venetian lace technique. They also work lace in *Alençon point*, thus perpetuating the finest traditions of their craft, both local and foreign.

When finished, the stitches holding the design are removed, and the lace is separated from it.

● MARBLED PAPER

The technique of marbling paper originated in Japan around the year 1000, and spread to Persia and Turkey, where craftsmen had the idea of using gum instead of water as a base for the dipping liquid. Known through the Arab world in the Middle Ages, marbling finally reached Europe in the 15th century and, in the 18th century, developed in France, where its former use for holy texts was extended to ordinary bookbindings and boxes. Outside France, marbling largely disappeared with the Industrial Revolution, only to be reborn in Venice during the 1970s.

The technique offers unlimited decorative possibilities, for each sheet of marbled paper is entirely unique.

3. (Center) Once all the colors have been placed on the liquid surface, they are drawn out in lines with a pointed instrument. After this an upright comb is pulled across them.

4. The comb must be manipulated very slowly, otherwise all the colors risk being displaced.

1. Using a brush, droplets of the first color are flicked on to the surface of a colorless, liquid gum. These dilate little by little until they cover the entire surface of the tray.

2. Ox-gall is added to the colors. The second color must contain more gall than the first, so as to push it aside, float and spread. The third contains more than the second, and so on.

The colors are diluted with water, or oil when the support is a fabric of some kind. Today, turpentine is also used.

The most important tool of the trade is a marbling tray, in which liquid gum and colors are laid. Other tools (brushes, combs, mortar and pestle for pounding the colors to powder) vary according to the technique used.

Alberto Valese working in his shop. It was on his initiative that ancient marbling techniques were revived in Venice in 1970. He has continued to enrich the craft with innovations.

5. The sheet of paper is delicately placed on top of the mixture, taking care that no air is trapped beneath.

6. The sheet is then lifted with extreme care, after which it is hung from a cord or spread out on a table.

The art of metal casting reached its zenith during the Renaissance period, when the taste for bronzes became widespread. Today, the tradition is still maintained by a few old foundries in Venice, which produce objects in copper and bronze. These objects are in many cases beautifully finished sculptures, with forms inspired by the maritime traditions of Venice. Examples are the dolphins that are used to decorate gondolas, and which have long snake-like tails wrapped around tridents.

1. The fusion of the metal takes place at 900°C and lasts between 60 and 90 minutes. The furnace (above) can contain up to 330 lb of metal.

Some palace doors still retain their original bronze handles. These are often extremely refined busts, such as the ones above.

Among the familiar brass objects are these sea-horses, which traditionally decorate the sides of gondolas.

2. The resulting metal is poured into an ingot mold for re-use.

1. PREPARING THE MOLD
The mold containing the model is filled with a fine refractory sand. Once the model has been removed, the form to be reproduced will remain printed on it.

2. POURING THE METAL
The mold is closed, and then the liquid metal is poured in through a tiny hole.

DOOR KNOCKERS
Many of the knockers on Venetian doors are in the form of a lion's head, with a large ring in its jaws. Variations on this theme range from the simple to the highly intricate. Other designs include Moors, grotesque heads, and clowns.

The model below is called a *trevisan*, after a gondolier of that name.

3. REMOVING THE CAST
The inside of the mold has been carefully powdered prior to pouring, to ensure the cast can be easily removed afterwards.

4. FINISHING
After its removal from the mold, the bronze or brass object is finished by hand with a chisel. Finally it is carefully polished.

MOSAICS

The small shards for mosaics are obtained by breaking large plates of colored glass into pieces with a hammer.

Mosaic was a technique of the Greco-Latin era, which was commonly used throughout the Byzantine Empire, and reached a very high level of accomplishment in both Venice and Ravenna. Although no description of it dating from the Venetian-Byzantine period has survived, scholars have been able to work out how it was done from the mosaics of St Mark. The technique of mosaic apparently remained unaltered from antiquity to the Renaissance.

Mosaic craftsmen probably worked from small-scale pictures, taking their cues from the ancient models of Byzantium or from miniatures (as in the Genesis Dome above the narthex of St Mark's). Mosaic work was team work, in which the various tasks were precisely distributed.

Gold and silver are applied in leaf form to colorless or bottle green cubes, then covered with a thin layer of transparent glass.

Sticking like a skin to a building's interior, mural mosaic work is designed to cover broad surfaces and to be viewed from a distance as an ensemble. This characteristic, like the near invulnerability of mosaic images to the effects of passing time, lends it great symbolic value.

1. First, the surface is covered with either one or two layers of cement, which is scored to make the next layer stick properly.

2. After tracing out the broad lines of the image, a thin layer of mortar is then spread over a part of the surface small enough to be completed in a single day.

3. On the prepared surface, part of the décor is painted, down to the last detail, in the colors to be used.

4. The shards of glass are applied. They are pressed two thirds their thickness into the mortar, and care is taken to vary the angles of their setting so they will refract light in different ways. The shards must also be placed irregularly, with spaces of varying width between them.

● THE CONSTRUCTION OF A GONDOLA

1. Positioning of the stem and stern of the boat, with three main frame elements of oak. These are the first of the 280 pieces of wood which together make up the gondola.

2. Installation of the *cerchi* (sheathing) on the upper flanks of the gondola. These oak planks are profiled by wetting and gradual warping over a fire of dried rushes.

3. Gradually the other 33 frame elements are added, along with the sides and decking at prow and stern.

4. Finally, thwarts are put in place to strengthen the structure; the shape of the *forcola* and the curve of the hull are adjusted to suit the weight and height of the gondolier.

THE "FERRO"
The *ferro*, or decorative prow of the gondola, is supposed to represent the Doge's hat (or *corno*) ▲ *231* and the six sestieri of Venice. The seventh (on the other side) is supposed to symbolize the Giudecca. In fact, the *ferro* acquired its present form after a long period of evolution. As late as the 17th century, Venetian painters were recording *ferros* on gondolas in the shape of finely wrought crosiers.

THE LAST GONDOLAS
The *squeri*, derived from *squadra* (square), are now rare in Venice. None of them makes more than three or four gondolas a year.

THE GONDOLA, A MASTERPIECE OF BOAT BUILDING, HAS A HULL THIRTY-SIX FEET LONG AND LESS THAN FIVE FEET WIDE, WITH ONLY HALF ITS BOWS IN CONTACT WITH THE WATER; HENCE ITS FLOATING SURFACE IS REDUCED TO A MINIMUM.

PROFILE

PLAN

The gondola is protected by no less than seven coats of black paint.

Gondola seen from the stern.

THE "FORCOLA"

The rowlock (*forcola*) is carved from a single piece of walnut or cherry wood.

Stages of construction.

The twisted *forcola* is a crucial element of the gondola; its *morso* (notch) is cut so as to cradle the gondolier's oar. The part is cut out with a saw, shaped with a plane and adze, and thoroughly oiled.

THE "SQUERO"

The *squeri*, or gondola yards, are always by the water, with a wooden shed where the boat builders can work in winter and store their tools. The owner usually lives on the floor above, or else in an adjoining building. In front of the buildings a piece of open ground slopes down to the edge of the canal; here the gondolas are worked on during the summer, and construction materials are deposited. Below is the 17th-century Squero di San Trovaso ▲ 324, the oldest in Venice.

THE OAR

The gondolier's oar is made from a single piece of beech, fined down with a drawknife to make a ribbed surface on the blade end, and a round, smooth surface where it works in the rowlock.

Venetian rowing is different from conventional rowing because the oarsman stands upright facing the bows and plies his oar from fore to aft.

Rowing forward.

Gondola stationary, rowing forward.

The gondolier stands upright in the stern of the boat, facing forward.

Pushing the oar backward. To veer left, the gondolier puts extra effort into this stroke.

Movement to stop the gondola.

Rowing forward in narrow canals.

Bringing the oar forward. This corrects the advance of the boat; if the gondolier puts more power into the action, he alters his course to the right.

Rowing backwards.

Rowing by pushing the oar forward.

BEFORE THE DEVELOPMENT OF MOTORIZED VESSELS, THE VENETIAN TRANSPORT SYSTEM DEPENDED ON MEN ROWING BOATS. SINCE 1975, ROWING HAS BECOME A FASHIONABLE PASTIME AND A GROWING NUMBER OF RACES ARE HELD.

"DESDOTONA"
Eighteen oars, usually leads parades.

"VOGARIZZO"
A variation on the rowlock for *peate*, or delivery boats.

"CAORLINA"
Rowed by six oarsmen, this boat is a popular feature of the historic regatta.

RACING **"GONDOLINI"**
The star attraction of the historic regatta ● *54*, specifically designed for racing.

"FORCOLA DA REGATA"
Racing rowlock. The notch is always the same.

RACING **"MASCARETA"**
Usually rowed by women. The light, painted hull is characteristic of the Lagoon skiff.

"FORCOLA A DUE MORSI"
Double rowlock, for fishing boats.

"SANDALO VOGATO ALLA VALESANA"
Here the rower stands inside the boat and rows with crossed oars.

FUNERAL GONDOLA

71

TAXI
Very practical if you are in a hurry, but always the most expensive mode of transport in Venice.

MOTOSCAFO
Smaller than the traditional vaporetti, the motoscafi serve the two main departure points from the Piazzale Roma. LINE 5 goes right round Venice via the Grand Canal, the Arsenal, Murano and the Canareggio Canal, with frequent halts. The DIRECT LINE also passes along the Giudecca Canal but does not stop there, since its purpose is to provide a fast link between the Piazzale Roma, the railway station and St Mark's.

PUBLIC SERVICES
In Venice, the police, the firemen and the ambulance service all operate by boat. In an emergency, they are not obliged to respect the speed limits on the Grand Canal.

GARBAGE COLLECTORS
Garbage is a major practical problem in Venice. Since everything both arrives in the city and leaves it by boat, the Venetians are obliged to leave their garbage alongside the canals for collection.

VAPORETTO
LINE 1 (*accelerata*) is paradoxically the slowest vaporetto in Venice, affording passengers ample leisure to admire the palaces along the Grand Canal. On LINE 34 (*turistica*) there are fewer stops. During the day, the *accelerata* passes every 10 minutes; in the evenings, it does so every 30 minutes.

TAXI

POLICE

MOTOSCAF DIRECT LINE

AMBULANCE

FIRE BOAT

GARBAGE COLLECTORS

VAPORETTO

«I LAY DOWN TO REST, LISTENING TO THE BLACK BOATS
STEALING UP AND DOWN BELOW THE WINDOW ON
THE RIPPLING WATER, TILL I FELL ASLEEP.»

CHARLES DICKENS

PUPARIN

TOPO

SANPIEROTA

CAORLIN

S'CIOPÒ

"PUPARIN"
Assymetrical like the gondola, this approximately 30-foot-long vessel owes its name to the lean, raking shape of its stem, and also to the fact that the man rowing it stands on a sort of small platform at the back.

"TOPO"
These sailing boats were developed at Chioggia, where the biggest of them were used for fishing. The *topo* is not entirely decked over; its middle part is left as an open hold so that the fish can be thrown into it. In Burano, they use motorized *topi* whose size has been modified to enable them to transport all types of cargo.

"SANPIEROTA"
The *sanpierota* was originally a fishing vessel but, because of its exceptional stability, it is now widely used for excursions around the Lagoon.

"CAORLINA"
The *caorlina* (from *caorle*) is nearly symmetrical in shape and is among the better looking boats to be found on the Lagoon. It was originally designed to pass through the mainland canals, but today it is mostly used for racing.

"S'CIOPÒN"
The full name of this small boat is *sandalo da s'ciopo*, hence the abbreviation *s'cipiòn*. Because it lies low in the water, it was used for shooting (*s'cipiòn* means a duck boat in Venetian). It is still used for negotiating the shallower waters around the Lagoon.

73

This very ancient recipe was born of a need to preserve fish for as long as possible; Venetian sailors could take these marinated sardines with them on voyages, as a preventive against scurvy.

2. Brown pinenuts and raisins together in a pan.

1. Fry onions gently in 1 cup of oil until brown and soft.

5. Place a layer of fish on the bottom of a terrine and cover with a layer of the onion mixture.

4. Roll the fish in a plate of flour, then fry. Add vinegar and cook until liquid is reduced.

> «LOOKING OUT, I BEHELD THE GRAND CANAL SO ENTIRELY
> COVERED WITH FRUITS AND VEGETABLES, ON RAFTS AND IN
> BARGES, THAT I COULD SCARCELY DISTINGUISH A WAVE.»
>
> WILLIAM BECKFORD

INGREDIENTS (for four people)
1½ lb of fresh sardines, 2 lb of sweet white onions, 1 cup of virgin olive oil, 1 glass of white wine vinegar, a little flour, a pinch of salt, 2 oz of Smyrna raisins and 1 oz of pinenuts (optional).

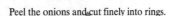

Peel the onions and cut finely into rings.

Remove scales from fish, then remove heads and intestines. Wash and drain on paper towels, add salt.

3. Add pinenuts and raisins to onions.

6. Continue adding alternate layers until the terrine is full. Top with onion mixture.

7. Leave in a cool place for at least two days, then serve with grilled polenta.

● Typical Venetian Products

BURANO BEADS
Formerly made and painted by hand, one by one.

MINIATURE GLASS OBJECTS
Discarded shards of glass are used for making costume jewelry, small glass figures, bottles, trinkets, and the like. This is an important outlet for Venetian glass production.

CHANDELIERS
Venetian chandeliers are lightweight, and usually in the form of a pagoda hung with polychrome glass and beads.

THE SYMBOL OF VENICE
Miniature gondolas made of plastic, wood or glass are sold to tourists by the thousands.

MASKS
The Venetian mask has regained its popularity since the revival of the Carnival.

LACE
That seen on the Venetian streets is mostly a pale imitation of Burano work.

MARBLED PAPER
There are still craftsmen in Venice who marble paper by hand, sheet by sheet.

SWEETMEATS
Try *baicoli* accompanied by zabaglione and sweet wine; also *bussolai* from Burano, which are ring-shaped biscuits, salted or dusted with sugar.

LOCAL NEWSPAPERS
Street kiosks stock two local dailies, the *Gazzettino* (with the higher circulation) and *La Nuova Venezia*. There is a monthly, *Marco Polo*, and *L'Ospite di Venezia*, a review found in hotels.

76

ARCHITECTURE

Venice's network of waterways.

The urban fabric of Venice clearly distinguishes two separate communication networks – that of the waterways (canali, rii) and that of the pedestrian thoroughfares (calli, piazza, campi, fondamenta, salizzade, rive and rughe). The choice of network is governed by the nature of the site and its formation, for Venice is essentially a cluster of small islands joined together by bridges and separated by canals and basins.

OPEN SPACES AND PEDESTRIAN THOROUGHFARES

On the islands, a dense maze of footpaths emerged, mostly regularly spaced and running at right angles to the canals, like the teeth of a comb. Across this network and parallel to the canals ran the calli, broken at intervals by larger open spaces. These were the campi, the smaller campielli, and the piazza, as in Piazza San Marco (St Mark's Square). In time, the pedestrian thoroughfares and bridges became a maze of interlinking alleys, and the cluster of islands became a real city, regulated by a hierarchy of open spaces – public campi, semi-private courtyards and private gardens.

THE CAMPO

The Venetian campo varies in form. Campo Santi Giovanni e Paolo ▲ 157 (right), for example, is L-shaped. Sometimes it has canals running along its edges. Earlier campi were paved with bricks in herringbone patterns and bordered with bands of Istrian stone, but in the 18th century they acquired hard stone flags of flint (*masegni*) which bore up better under constant use.

STATUES

Statues placed in campi, like that of Colleone ▲ 147, 157, are the exception in Venice, where the glorification of the state mostly took precedence over praise of individual achievement.

THE HOUSES

While patrician palaces and the mansions of the wealthy bourgeoisie (notaries, lawyers and civil servants) gave a hierarchical flavor to the campi, more modest dwellings tended to fill in the narrow spaces behind them.

CANALS AND QUAYS

Indispensable for loading and unloading goods headed in and out of the campo's *fondachi* (warehouses), the side of the campo opening on the canal also provided the best access to the church, and to other major buildings around it.

Pedestrian
network.

THE WELLS
There might be
between one and four
cisterns of drinking
water on any given
campo.

CHURCH AND MONASTERY
Each campo has its own church;
most of these churches have façades
fronting a canal. The monastery beside
the church was usually the center around
which the district originally grew up; and this
is one reason why the spacious cloisters of the
Dominican monastery of Santi Giovanni e Paolo
insula, so
much so that the projecting church dictates the
shape of the campo.

THE SCUOLA
Sometimes secondary
oratories stood near the
main churches, but more
often there were scuole.

If they were scuole grandi
(here, the Scuola San
Marco ▲ *159*) these
might be as large as the
church itself.

79

8TH–9TH CENTURY

10TH CENTURY

11TH CENTURY

13TH CENTURY

14TH CENTURY

15TH CENTURY

18TH CENTURY

FOUNDATIONS OF THE WATER CISTERN

DRAINS ARE LAID, AND THE CISTERN IS FILLED WITH SAND

THE WELL IS INSTALLED

CROSS-SECTION

A. Clay
C. Sand
D. Istrian stone

E. Brick conduit
F. Clay lining
G. Box drain
H. Well

> «A REALIST, IN VENICE, WOULD BECOME A ROMANTIC,
> BY MERE FAITHFULNESS TO WHAT
> HE SAW BEFORE HIM.»
>
> ARTHUR SYMONS

FOUNDATIONS AND TEMPORARY WOODEN SURROUND

FIRST ELEMENTS OF VAULTING IN ISTRIAN STONE,
BRICK VAULTING, AND KEYSTONE

FINISHED BRIDGE, WITH BALUSTRADE AND STEPS

THE WELLS

The wells, which performed the essential task of providing Venice with fresh water, were usually privately owned, and they were to be found throughout the city in every campo and thoroughfare. The carved well-lip was the only visible feature of what was a complex underground system; beneath the surface, the Venetian well consists of a surrounding 16-foot-deep cistern, with an impermeable clay lining. At the center of this cistern is a shaft with walls of bricks specially made with fissures in their downsides. The cistern is filled with sand, and the rainwater, running through gratings in the pavement of the campo, flows into connected box-drains running around the edge of the cistern. It then filters through the sand until it reaches the central well-shaft.

THE BRIDGES

Venice's earlier wooden bridges were soon replaced by stone and brick constructions. The building of these permanent bridges involved a partial emptying of the canal, sinking foundations on either bank, raising a wooden arch on which to mount stones and brick, and constructing steps and parapets on top of these. With only a few exceptions, the bridges of Venice have single, semicircular arches.

In 1033, seventy parishes were established around Venice's churches. These later coalesced into *contrade*, the smallest administrative units of the state framework. By the 18th century there were more than two hundred churches in Venice, ample proof if any were needed of Venetian piety. With their decoration, they served as showcases for the majesty of the state (San Marco ▲ *234*), for the wealth and influence of religious orders (Gesuiti ▲ *152*) or for the glorification of important patrician families (Santa Maria del Giglio ▲ *264*).

THE VENETIAN-BYZANTINE STYLE
The basilica of SANTA MARIA E SAN DONATO ▲ *368* (12th century), famous for its extraordinary octagonal apse, is built on the basilical plan with three naves, as is clear from its restrained three-part exterior in red brick. The vertical thrust of the main body of the building is accentuated by the small double aperture just below the roofline, and by the elegant Lombard blind arches.

Detail of the right pinnacle of the Gothic church of La Madonna dell'Orto ▲ *146*.

Detail from the door of the Baroque Church of the Gesuiti ▲ *152*.

THE GOTHIC STYLE
Like Santi Giovanni e Paolo ▲ *157*, SANTA MARIA GLORIOSA DEI FRARI ▲ *292* was built by a minor religious order. Its traditional three-part façade in brick is studded with the Gothic vocabulary of rosewindow, pinnacles, cornices and elaborate portal. The wavelike line of the coping is similar to that of San Giovanni in Bragora ▲ *176*.

THE RENAISSANCE STYLE

SANTA MARIA DEI MIRACOLI ▲ 151 (1490) was one of the first churches in Venice to adopt the classicism of the Renaissance, which predominated in Venice after Palladio's arrival in 1527. Note the novelty and originality of the broad, curving tympanum and the lush polychrome marble façade.

Detail from the door of the Gesuiti ▲ 152.

THE PALLADIAN STYLE

SAN GIORGIO MAGGIORE ▲ 340, one of Palladio's last masterworks, was built in the years after 1565 to plans completed in 1559. Taking his inspiration from the buildings of the ancient world, Palladio skilfully divided the church's façade into two planes and pediments. In this way he achieved the fusion of the classical temple form (on the outside) and the Roman, Latin-cross form (on the inside).

NEO-CLASSICISM

Tommaso Temanza's Church of the MADDALENA (c.1760) is an example of renewed classical severity, in reaction to the current fashion for Baroque. In this adaptation of the classical temple, the architect worked to a centered plan, with a circle on the outside and a hexagon on the inside.

THE BAROQUE STYLE

With the church of the DERELITTI, Longhena abandoned the classical vertical arrangement for a Baroque style influenced by Mannerism.

The campanile is basically a tower-belfry set apart from the main body of the church. Traditionally the tower is square, with an upper, open chamber containing bells. This, in turn, is topped by a conical or pyramidal spire, or an onion-shaped dome. Sometimes a smaller, arcaded campanile will be joined to a church. Those Venetian campaniles which have not been destroyed altogether are today the object of constant restoration work, because their foundations so frequently subside.

CATHEDRAL OF SANTA MARIA ASSUNTA
(Torcello). This 11th-century campanile is a robust tower cadenced by tall Lombard blind arches. The generous openings of the belfry at its top and its simple, low roof are typical of Venetian-Byzantine architecture.

SANTA FOSCA
▲ *145*
The present campanile was built shortly after the collapse of the first bell tower in 1410, and the tower was unaffected by the reconstruction of the church, which was carried out in the late 17th and early 18th centuries. Gothic elements here, such as the double-arched belfry and the four corner pinnacles, are blended with Romanesque holdovers like the Lombard blind arches, reinforcing the body of the tower, and the Byzantine flavor of its dome.

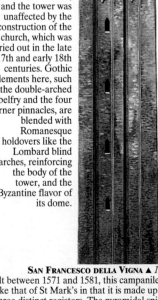

SAN FRANCESCO DELLA VIGNA ▲ *161*
Built between 1571 and 1581, this campanile is like that of St Mark's in that it is made up of three distinct registers. The pyramidal spire, resting on its square base, accentuates the soaring nature of the construction, which is otherwise traditional with classical Renaissance elements.

SAN PIETRO DI CASTELLO ▲ *157, 182*
This campanile, with its original arrangement of two superimposed stone arches, crowned the polygonal base of a dome that is no longer there. It is the only surviving example of its kind in Venice, because the ground was too unstable for weighty construction of this type.

ARCHED BELFRIES
of the sacristy of SANTO STEFANO (above) and of the Church of SANTI GIOVANNI E PAOLO ▲ *157* (left).

BELFRY OF THE ORATORY OF SANT'ANGELO

SANTI APOSTOLI ▲ *150, 198*
The upper parts of this campanile, which was begun in the 15th century, were not completed until between 1720 and 1730. They are separated from the rest of the building by a projecting cornice. The high classical stem, topped by an octagonal tambour and picturesque onion-dome, lends the campanile grace and harmony.

SAN GIACOMO DI RIALTO ▲ *283* is dominated by its bells and by a huge 24-hour clock, which once rang out the hours for the Rialto's merchants.

From the 13th century onwards, the scuole became the headquarters of the charitable and mutual assistance guilds of Venice. They are most readily identified by their façades, which suggest strictly organized interiors behind them.

As a rule, the ground floor of a scuola would be used for religious functions; the chapter room above it was for large assemblies, and it was usually connected to the *sala dell'albergo*, the scuola's treasure house and the meeting place of its dignitaries. Because they were symbols of civic status, prosperity and the power of the guilds, special attention was paid to the decoration of the scuole's exteriors.

SCUOLA DI SAN MARCO ▲ *159*
The elegant façade of this scuola is one of the most refined in Venice. The humanist approach of Pietro Lombardo and the marble perspectives which he designed for the ground floor are in marked contrast to Codussi's elaborate coping.

SCUOLA VECCHIA DELLA MISERICORDIA (1450)
Discretion and harmony are the keynotes of this particular façade. The pinnacles, windows and coping all reflect the flamboyance, charm and refinement of Gothic style.

Scuola di San Rocco (1517–49) ▲ *294* The imposing
height of this building carries echoes of the triumphalism
that was found in ancient Rome. Columns, pilasters and
cornices emphasize the composite Codussi-style windows
on the lower level and the long pedimented series of double
bay windows on the first floor.

**Scuola di San
Teodoro** ▲ *275*
The balanced
composition of this
façade, completed by
Sardi and Longhena
in 1649, perfectly
reflects the interior,
with its two capacious
chambers one above
the other.

Scuola dei Carmini ▲ *329* Between 1668 and 1670
Longhena designed the perfect formal symmetry of
this façade around the axis of its central bay. The
high coping of the upper floor, the grotesque masks
on the window arches, and other projecting elements
all reflect the taste of 17th-century architects.

**Scuola dei Battiloro
e Tiraoro (1711)** ▲ *351*
The capricious spirit of Rococo
predominates in this vividly
colored façade.

Scuola della Carità
This scuola now looks like
a Neo-classical, triumphal
arch, after Massari failed
to complete his
1765 project.

The layout of the Venetian palazzo conforms to certain functional and climatic imperatives. The rooms distributed on either side of a central space (the *portego*) admit the ventilation so essential during periods of humidity or summer heat. The façade, which was usually in three sections, answered both the commercial and residential purposes of the building. The shop areas were on the ground floor, porch or portico areas, offices and archives were between floors, and residential *piani nobili* and *salone* on the upper floor. Servants' quarters were in the attics. Thus the palace served as both a home and a kind of warehouse, or *casa-fontego* ● *104*.

PALAZZO FALIER ▲ *150, 208*
This palace, in the Cannaregio sestiere, belonged in the mid-13th century to the family of the traitor Doge Manin Falier, who is thought to have lived here for several years. A portico on the ground floor reconciled the public and private functions of the building: its façade has many arches on both floors, with windows in the Venetian-Byzantine style and zoomorphically carved Gothic cornerstones.

CA' D'ORO ▲ *148, 196* (Cannaregio). Built between 1424 and 1434 for the procurator Marino Contarini on the foundations of an earlier palace, this masterpiece was originally covered in gold leaf. Here Flamboyant Gothic vies with the refined, soaring play of pillars and arches. The Milanese Matteo Raverti and the Venetians Bartolomeo and Giovanni Bon planned the Ca' d'Oro as a blend of the traditional palazzo, closed in and compact, with the freshness and grace of a façade wide open to the exterior. Much of the decorative repertoire of the Doge's Palace is copied from the Ca' d'Oro.

FONDACO DEI TURCHI ▲ *193, 347–48.* (Santa Croce) The Ca' Palmieri-Pesaro, which was built in c.1227, became the Turks' warehouse in 1621..From the start it was one of the biggest palaces on the Grand Canal.

Despite Berchet's misguided restoration in 1869, the Fondaco dei Turchi has remained an important example of Venetian-Byzantine civil architecture, with its two lateral towers framing the Romanesque arcades of a portico (on the ground floor) and a loggia (on the floor above).

PALAZZO BERNARDO ▲ *204* (San Paulo) As the epitome of Flamboyant Gothic (c.1442), the Palazzo Bernardo has a symmetrical "triptych" design, with three levels of bay windows and colored marbles maximizing the effect of elevation. The lateral watergates mean two families living in the building can have their own entrances.

● PALAZZOS

PALAZZO VENDRAMIN-CALERGI ▲ *144, 194* (San Marcuola) Designed by Mauro Coducci, this palazzo introduced Tuscan Renaissance sophistication to the Gothic Venice of 1502–4. The usual three-part design is respected, but the twin bay windows, the three classical orders, one on top of the other, the heavily emphasized cornice and the all-stone façade are essentially new.

PALAZZO MALIPIERO-TREVISAN (Castello). Built between 1520 and 1530 by Sante Lombardo, nephew of the more famous Pietro, this palace shows a liveliness of form which is typical of the North Italian Renaissance. The semi-circular arches which crown the windows and doors, the side niches and carefully wrought balconies, all create subtle variations at each level of a classical white façade, the refinement of which is heightened by antique *tondi* in porphyry and green materials. Centered on the building is a small stone bridge, on either side of which are watergates. This bridge links the palace to Campo Santa Maria Formosa ▲ *166*.

PALAZZO TREVISAN ▲ *368* (Murano) Daniele Barbaro was the architect of this 16th-century Palladian building. Here the façade makes use of the play of light and shade to stress its stronger elements – the rich central area, the projecting balcony held up by fluted corbels, the tall niches and masks on the two lower levels, and the extravagent outline of the topmost cornice. The severity and regularity of these contrasts was originally attenuated by the colors of Prospero Bresciano's frescoes.

CA' PESARO ▲ *351* This superb Grand Canal palazzo was begun by Longhena in 1652 and completed in 1710.

A triumphalist façade and powerful effects of chiaroscuro make Ca' Pesaro the archetype of a certain aspect of patrician taste, and a masterpiece of Venetian Baroque. Its bossage of diamonds, monstrous heads, *putti* and genies add decorative weight to the more sober elegance of its purely architectural elements.

PALAZZO BELLONI-BATTAGIÀ
▲ *194* Built by Longhena (1645–9), this palazzo in the Santa Croce sestiere is one of the loveliest of its period. The façade is relatively small, but cunningly balanced. The design of it respects the traditional framework by relying on the vertical interplay of Corinthian pilasters on the *piano nobile*. The family coat of arms and Venetian admirals' obelisks, which were commissioned by the owner, blend easily here with the architect's chosen vehicle of expression.

Venetian dwellings are often clustered around an inner courtyard, which is closed off from the outside world and is usually square in shape. From the 13th century, this courtyard commonly depended on a main house, but after the turn of the 16th century it expanded lengthwise to open on to a canal or calle.

GOTHIC HOUSE, RIO MALPAGA (LATE 14TH CENTURY) Located on a narrow islet near San Barnaba ▲ *334*, this building belongs to a group of 60-foot-wide medieval units, by which all the adjoining building sites were strictly regulated. A long courtyard opens onto a major thoroughfare, and the distribution of space follows the Venetian pattern of warehouse on the ground floor, residence above, and loggia under the eaves.

THE VENETIAN-BYZANTINE HOUSE
A number of 13th-century houses around the Campo San Lio have retained their distinctive Venetian-Byzantine character. They are tall, with narrow façades, small windows and ground floors reserved for commercial use.

PALAZZETTO CONSTANTINI (14TH–15TH CENTURY)
Built on the Rio terrà ai Saloni, this little building used to adjoin the Rio terrà dei Catecumeni, which is now filled in. It still has its original wooden Renaissance portico.

HOUSE ON CAMPO SAN TERNITA (LATE 16TH CENTURY) A traditional 3-section structure combines with the style of the Renaissance.

BLOCKS OF FLATS BUILT AS LODGINGS FOR RENTAL ON THE CALLE DEL PARADISO (13TH CENTURY) ▲ 171 Commissioned by the Foscari and Mocenigo families, whose coats of arms appear on the Gothic gables, these buildings have first-floor overhangs, which create more space inside without encroaching on the street.

GHETTO NUOVO ▲ *140*
(Cannaregio). Since it was impossible to extend the Jewish quarter beyond the canals surrounding it, space had to be created vertically, by adding new floors to existing buildings and creating communal areas to be shared by several blocks. Hence the unusual tallness of the Ghetto structures, which also show how densely Venice was populated in the 16th and 17th centuries.

FONDAMENTE DELLE PROCURATIE E DEI CERERI
This complex was built at the end of the 16th century in Venice's poorest quarter. Most of the lodgings in it were apportioned to indigents free of charge by the Procurators of St Mark, the government officers who administered charitable bequests. The symmetrical arrangement of the façade betrays the equally strict layout of the interior.

CALLE DEL TRAGHETTO
(San Marco). This asymmetrical 17th-century palazzetto has its main entrance and first floor bay windows grouped to one side, so that the main reception room on the upper floor (the *portego*) has other rooms on only one side of it. The whole building stands on a relatively high base of Istrian stone, while the Greek symmetry of the top floor restores a sense of vertical balance.

The two substantial wings of the building stand directly on the canal that skirts its island site. Each contains its quota of cheap lodgings overlooking the courtyard, and more expensive ones overlooking the fondamenta, the difference being visible in the façade. A connecting arch lends unity to the ensemble and makes the courtyard a semi-public area.

Chimneys were always an important element of Venetian architecture. The most common is the "inverted bell" type, which has a conical flue top (left). This was eventually supplanted by the cubic flue top, more or less elaborately decorated. In both cases, a frieze of small corbels normally separates the upper and lower sections of the shaft. Some time later, a much more ornate "obelisk" type of chimney came into vogue ● 96.

CAMPO OGNISSANTI
A stone mask is set into the wall of one of the houses overlooking this Dorsoduro campo (16th–17th century).

RIO TERRÀ DEGLI OGNISSANTI
Nothing in the appearance of this substantial building gives any clue to the layout of its interior, except perhaps the two tall chimneys constructed against the façade. These chimneys, which are typical of standard Venetian houses, actually serve two separate lodgings on every floor.

OBELISK CHIMNEY Renaissance period, on a house on the Salizzada San Antonin.

CUBE CHIMNEY on a house on Campo San Trovaso. The cap has an elaborate, curving outline (seen below).

INVERTED BELL alongside Rio di Sant'Anna. Variations on this conical silhouette are found all over Venice.

VENICE IS NOT BUILT ON PILINGS BUT ON THE UNSTABLE ISLETS OF THE LAGOON. THE CITY'S ARCHITECTS HAD TO FIND SPECIALLY ADAPTED WAYS TO GIVE THEIR BUILDINGS LIGHTNESS AND FLEXIBILITY.

THE FOUNDATIONS were set on a series of pilings which were rammed into the ground to the depth of the *caranto*, a layer of solid clay and sand some way beneath the surface. Where the *caranto* was too far down, wooden barriers were erected around the site, which was then drained and reinforced with baulks of oak and larch. After this, a *zattaron* would be laid. This was a kind of pontoon made of two layers of larch planks which were cemented with a mixture of stone and brick. This was a practice that prevailed in Venice from the 16th century onwards. On the *zattaron* rested the foundations of Istrian stone, and eventually the upper parts of the building.

THE FAÇADES were usually made of brick, often left bare but sometimes rendered in either pale grey (*rovigno*) or brick red (*pastellone*).

THE FLOORS were constructed in the normal way using oak beams and boards, which were then covered with a layer of mortar and spread with shards of stone and marble. This final layer would be firmly packed down to create a smooth, shiny but still relatively elastic surface.

THE ROOF was usually made of Roman tiles, which were rested on a layer of flat, hollow bricks. These tiles were then set on rafters. Around the roof ran the *gorne*, which were stone gutters connected to the drainpipes which led directly to the well.

CLOCKS AND CLOCKTOWERS

For the Venetians, monumental clocks were vital references which kept them informed of the hour, the movements of the planets, the terrestrial months and the signs of the Zodiac. In the 16th century, the San Marco Clocktower became one of the symbols of the Republic's power; all the major Venice-dominated cities of the mainland were similarly equipped. The mechanisms were regulated seasonally according to a solar hour that varied from forty minutes in summer to eighty minutes in winter. The time was calculated visually, according to the light.

The clocktower (1496–9), which incorporates the gateway between St Mark's Square and the Merceria, has the most beautiful clockface in Venice. The hours, months and phases of the sun and moon are all recorded on it. Studded with stars against a blue background, with the signs of the Zodiac and the planets in relief, the very concept of this tower lends additional force to the majestic beauty of St Mark's. With its face turned to the sea, the clockface is a symbol that is both awe-inspiring and beneficial by turns. For centuries it provided vital information to merchants and ships' crews about to sail from St Mark's Basin bound for the Orient. It was also for centuries a silent witness to grisly public tortures and executions.

Beneath the main clockface is a niche containing statues of the Virgin and Child, on either side of which are small doors. One of these shows the hour in Roman numerals, the other the minutes by multiples of five in Arabic numerals. On Ascension Day, which used to be one of the principal festivals celebrated in Venice, wooden automata representing the Three Kings are trundled out of the doors and pass one by one in front of the Virgin.

The two bronze giants which ring the hours on the top of the clocktower are represented clothed in the skins of wild animals, like the demi-gods of antiquity.

In the Doge's Palace ▲ 224 a single mechanism set into the wall regulates the clockfaces in the Senate and College Chambers. Its workings were devised by Raffaele Penzin in about 1530, and remade after the fire of 1574. The original contraption of wheels and weights was eventually replaced by a regular clock mechanism in 1755. There is a second clockface in the Senate Chamber, decorated with the symbols and signs of the Zodiac, whose usefulness is limited to recording lunar months and the phases of the moon.

The great clock of the Church of San Giacometto di Rialto kept time for the crowds of merchants in the heart of Venice's commercial quarter▲ 85, 283.

ROMANESQUE AND VENETIAN-BYZANTINE

Capital, Ca' da Mosto, 13th century

Arcades, Cloister of Sant'Apollonia, 12th–13th century

Capital, Ca' Loredan, 12th–13th century

Re-used arcades, House on the Riva del Carbon, 12th century

Arcades, Church of Santa Maria e San Donato, c.1140

Re-used frieze, Palazzo Contarini, 17th century

Arcades, Ca' Loredan, 12th–13th century

Capital, St Mark's Square, 12th century

Tympanum, St Mark's Basilica, 9th–13th century

Arcades, Ca' Locanda al Selvadego, 13th century

Arcades, Ca' Loredan-Ca' Farsetti, 13th century

Grille, Ca' Loredan, 12th–13th century

Re-used frieze, Polo house, 13th century

Loggia, Ca' da Mosto, 13th century

Arched bay window, Casa Zane, 13th century

Crenellations, Doge's Palace, 14th century

Ca' d'Oro, 1424–34

Palazzo Foscari, c.1430

Double windows, House of Calle del Pistor, early 14th century

Bay window, Palazzo Sagredo, end 14th century

Single window, Palazzo Soranzo, Ponte de l'Anzolo, mid-14th century

Loggia, Palazzo Soranzo, San Polo, 15th century

Loggia, Palazzo Giovannelli, early 15th century

Crenellations, Palazzo Cavalli, late 14th century

GOTHIC

Doorway, Palazzo Contarini, 15th century

Bay windows and pinnacles, Doge's Palace

Loggia, Doge's Palace, 14th century

Grille, Palazzo Soranzo, San Polo, 15th century

Loggia, Palazzo Sagredo

Loggia, Palazzo Ariani, c.1349

Rose window, Palazzo Soranzo Van Axel, c.1470

Loggia, Ca' d'Oro, 1420–34

Loggia, Palazzo Agnusdio, 14th century

Vegetable frieze, Palazzo Pesaro degli Orfei, now the Museo Fortuny, 15th century

Capital, Palazzo Giovannelli, Santa Fosca, early 15th century

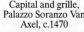
Capital and grille, Palazzo Soranzo Van Axel, c.1470

Bay window, Palazzo Foscari, c.1430

Step on the staircase, Palazzo Contarini, Porta di Ferro, late 15th century

Crenellations, Fondaco dei Tedeschi, 1508   Procuratie Vecchie, 1500–32

RENAISSANCE AND MANNERISM

Double bay window with balcony and bay window, Palazzo Zorzi, 15th century

Niche, Ponte dei Becchieri, late 15th century

Staircase, Palazzo Contarini del Bovola, 1499

Grille, Palazzo Cappello, Ponte della Canonica, early 16th century

Single bay window, Palazzo Zen, 1523

Bay window and grill, Scuoletta San Rocco, 15th century

Pediment, Scuola di San Marco, 1490–1533

Niche, Church of San Giorgio dei Greci, 1539–61

Double bay window with tympanum, Palazzo Vendramin-Calergi, 1504–9

Window, Palazetto, Via Garibaldi, c.1581

Window with balcony, Palazzo Corner, 1553–6

Grille, Palazzo Trevisan, Murano, 16th century

Bay windows with pediments, Palazzo Balbi, 1582–90

Bay window, Palazzo Foscarini, c.1600

Bay window, Palazzo Priuli-Ruzzini, late 16th century

Calle Vendramin, 16th century   Ramo della Pagia, 17th century   Rio della Celestia, 17th century

Arched window with balcony, Procuratie Nuove, 1582–1619

Central bay window, Palazzo Pisani, Santo Stefano, 1614–15

Window, pediment, balcony, Procuratie Nuove, 1582–1619

Window, bay window and balcony, Palazzo Canal, 17th century

Bay windows and balcony, Palazzo Barbaro, 1694

Arched window, balcony, Ca' Pesaro, 1652–82

Door and window, Scuola dei Battiloro e Tiraoro, 1711

Central bay window, Palazzo Zenobio, late 17th century

Doorway, Convent of the Terese, early 17th century

Doorway, Church of Santa Margherita, 18th century

Bay window with balcony, Palazzo Frizier, 18th century

Bullseye window, Palazzo Labia, late 17th century

103

This idealized representation by Viollet-le-Duc of a Venetian Gothic Palace illustrates the dual function (commercial and residential) of the great patrician house. The French architect has taken certain liberties with the layout of the interior, but in general he has portrayed the salient features correctly ● *88*. The elements of the façade are all carefully detailed. Note particularly the porticos, windows, balconies, loggias, arches, cornices and moldings ● *100* to *103*.

The warehouse area is on the ground floor, with offices and archives at mezzanine level.

The attic area is mostly occupied by kitchens.

One side effect of the sumptuary laws, and the physical constraint of building on pilings, was that three stories was about as high as the Venetians dared go. Here, the main façade presents a stone front to the city, while at the back, a garden, or *cortile*, with a well reminds us that these palazzos were designed to create a hermetic, intimate world of their own.

The ornate *portego* was the largest room on the *piano nobile*, running from one side of the building to the other. Lavish banquets and receptions would be held in this area.

Venice as Seen by Painters

Auguste Renoir (1841–1919) arrived in Venice in late 1881. After visiting Florence, which rather bored him, he was in turn captivated by Venice; nevertheless the paintings that he did here were all of conventional subjects (probably because he badly needed to sell them and raise some money). His *Grand Canal*, which was shown at the 7th Impressionist Exhibition in 1882, received a cold reception, being criticized for its over-careful brushwork which was deemed an unfortunate departure from the naturalness and freshness of his earlier Impressionist work. From the 1870's onward, Renoir belonged firmly to the Impressionist group, which was then revolutionizing painting in general and landscape art in particular. Like Monet, he had

concentrated on light tones, eliminating browns and blacks from his palette. Better than anyone else, he knew how to capture fleeting light effects through the suppleness of his technique. In *Grand Canal*, however, he was accused of freezing this suppleness into a mechanical procedure.

« WHEN I WENT TO VENICE, I DISCOVERED THAT MY
DREAM HAD BECOME – INCREDIBLY, BUT QUITE
SIMPLY – MY ADDRESS.»

MARCEL PROUST

Félix Ziem (1821–1911) was successful from 1849. His ability to blend changing skies and glittering water was much admired, as in *Venice: The Doge's Palace* (1). But his art did not develop much after this, and his repertoire remained limited.

JMW Turner (1775–1851) only visited Venice three times, but succeeded wonderfully in evoking the city's atmosphere in paint. With his mastery of watercolor, he caught the subtler effects of Venetian light, which he developed later in oils in his London studio, retaining the watercolor technique. Turner took care to give his canvases of Venice a preliminary coat of white paint. This was a break with the tradition of starting a picture with a backing of red or another dark color. While other painters exploited contrasts of light and shade to construct their forms, Turner concentrated on delicate tonalities of pink, blue and yellow, as in *Leaving for the Ball* (2). Eventually he was painting white on white, a highly innovative practice for the 19th century.

1
2

> «WE MUST LOOK AT NATURE PURELY AS A MOSAIC OF DIFFERENT COLORS, TO BE IMITATED ONE BY ONE IN COMPLETE SIMPLICITY.»
>
> PAUL SIGNAC

Paul Signac (1863–1935) was influenced early on by the Impressionists; later, after meeting Seurat, he adopted the style of pointillism. This consisted of covering the surface of the canvas with regular dots of color, which created an intense, uniform effect of light, along with a meticulous serenity and calm unknown to art hitherto. A keen sailor who revelled in seascapes, Signac discovered Venice at the end of 1903 and went there again in

1904. He was deeply receptive to the color and oriental flavor of the city, and was fascinated by the mosaics of St Mark's which, he believed, confirmed many of his theories about painting. Signac's experience of Venice yielded canvases such as *The Green Veil* (1).

Henri Edmond Delacroix, known as Henri Cross (1856–1910) was another leading pointillist, but hesitated to go too far in "fracturing" his brushwork – as this watercolor of a *Canal in Venice* shows (2, 3 detail).

1

2   3

111

Like many other symbolist painters of his generation, Lucien Lévy (alias Lévy-Dhurmer, 1865–1953) was partial to misty atmospheric effects. For him they offered the "only pathway by which the eye might penetrate the world's mysteries".

VENICE
AS SEEN BY
WRITERS

THE SERENE REPUBLIC

From the 13th century onwards the Venetian Republic
was engaged in expanding its control over most of
Northern Italy. At the same time it was imposing its
authority as a great Mediterranean power, whose
empire was acknowledged up to the very rim of the
Orient. The stability of Venetian institutions, which
remained practically unaltered between 1297 and
1797, was in the eyes of many an ideal of
government, and in pre-Revolutionary Europe was
something of a political myth.

THE CITY OF THE VENETI

*Petrarch (1304–74) first visited Venice in
1354 as the ambassador of Giovanni
Visconti, Duke of Milan, and he moved
permanently to a palace on the Riva degli
Schiavoni in 1362. This palace was given to him by the Republic, in the hope
that he would leave his precious library to Venice.*

❝The august capital of the Veneti is today the only home of liberty, peace
and justice, the only refuge of the good, the only port of destination for
those who desire to live well and whose vessels have been tossed and
battered by the storms of tyranny and war. Venice is a city rich in gold, but
richer still in beauty, mighty in its possessions, but mightier by its virtue,
founded on solid marble, but with the yet more solid moral foundation of civil
concord, girt about with salt waters, but in the true salt of the spirit how much
better encompassed than all others.❞

PETRARCH, *LETTERS*, 1364

THE DECLINE OF THE REPUBLIC

*In 1816, two years after the beginning of Austria's second occupation of
Venice and the Veneto, Lord Byron (1788–1824) arrived in the city, newly
separated from his wife. Byron moved into the Hotel Gran Bretagna on the
Grand Canal, where he lived for the next five years; his profligacy was the talk
of the town. In the Fourth Canto of* Childe Harold's Pilgrimage, *Byron turns
from his fictional Harold character to describe the "dying glories" of Venice.*

I stood in Venice, on the Bridge of Sighs;
A palace and a prison on each hand:
I saw from out the wave her structures rise
As from the stroke of the enchanter's wand:
A thousand years their cloudy wings expand
Around me, and a dying Glory smiles
O'er the far times, when many a subject land
Look'd to the winged Lion's marble piles,
Where Venice sate in state, throned on her hundred isles!

. . . In Venice Tasso's echoes are no more,
And silent rows the songless gondolier;
Her palaces are crumbling to the shore,
And music meets not always now the ear:
Those days are gone – but Beauty still is here:
States fall, arts fade – but Nature doth not die,
Nor yet forget how Venice once was dear,
The pleasant place of all festivity,
The revel of the earth, the masque of Italy.

LORD BYRON, *CHILDE HAROLD*, 1817

A LAMENT

William Wordsworth (1770–1850) took Venice very seriously and reverently; there is little of light-hearted contemporary Venice in his lines as, say, in Byron's Beppo, a Venetian Story, *or Shelley's* Julian and Maddalo. *His private life was troubled after the death of his brother in 1805, and many poems of this period have an elegiac quality. Much of Wordsworth's later work was inspired by his travels in Europe.*

Once did She hold the gorgeous east in fee;
And was the safeguard of the west; the worth
Of Venice did not fall below her birth,
Venice, the eldest child of Liberty.
She was a maiden City, bright and free;
No guile seduced, no force could violate;
And, when she took unto herself a Mate,
She must espouse the everlasting Sea.
And what if she had seen those glories fade,
Those titles vanish, and that strength decay;
Yet shall some tribute of regret be paid
When her long life hath reached its final day:
Men are we, and must grieve when even the Shade
Of that which once was great is passed away.

WILLIAM WORDSWORTH, *ON THE EXTINCTION OF THE VENETIAN REPUBLIC*, 1807

A CITY ON THE WATER

VENICE THROUGH THE EYES OF AN ARTIST

In September 1786, Johann Wolfgang von Goethe (1749–1832), the German poet, novelist and dramatist, left Weimar to travel to Italy. Before moving on to Florence and Naples, he stopped in Venice, keeping a journal which was later to become the basis for his book Italiensche Reise *("Italian Journey").*

❝ My old gift of seeing the world with the eyes of that artist, whose pictures have most recently made an impression on me, has occasioned me some peculiar reflections. It is evident that the eye forms itself by the objects, which, from youth up, it is accustomed to look upon, and so the Venetian artist must see all things in a clearer and brighter light than other men. We, whose eye when out of doors, falls on a dingy soil, which, when not muddy, is dusty, – and which, always colourless, gives a sombre hue to the reflected rays – or at home spend our lives in close, narrow rooms, can never attain to such a cheerful view of nature.

As I floated down the lagoons in the full sunshine, and observed how the figures of the gondoliers in their motley costume, as they rowed, lightly moving above the sides of the gondola, stood out from the bright green surface and against the blue sky, I caught the best and freshest type possible of the Venetian school. The

sunshine brought out the local colours with dazzling brilliancy, and the shades even were so luminous, that, comparatively, they in their turn might serve as lights. And the same may be said of the reflection from the sea-green water. All was painted 'chiaro nell' chiaro', so that foamy waves and lightning flashes were necessary to give it a grand finish. ❞

JOHANN WOLFGANG
VON GOETHE,
ITALIENSCHE REISE,
1816

THE SONG OF THE GONDOLIERS

After a quarrel with his first wife, Minna, Richard Wagner (1813–83) fled to Venice with a friend, poet Carl Ritter. He stayed in the Palazzo Giustinian, on the Grand Canal, from August 29, 1858 to March 24, 1859, where he composed the second act of Tristan and Isolde *in solitude. Years later, Wagner returned to Venice, where he died in the Palazzo Vendramin-Calergi. His works of prose were translated into English and published in the 1890's in eight volumes.*

❝One night, suffering from insomnia, I went out on my balcony at about three o'clock and there heard for the first time the celebrated and ancient song of the gondoliers. It seemed that the first harsh, plaintive cry that echoed through the night's quiet came from the Rialto, about a quarter of an hour's walk away from me. A similar chant answered it from even farther off. This strange, melancholy dialogue continued at intervals, sometimes long intervals, and I was so moved that I could not fix in my memory the few notes, probably very simple ones, that modulated it. Another evening I was able to understand by direct experience the full poetry of this popular air. I was returning late in a gondola, through dark canals; suddenly the moon rose, flooding with light the indescribable palaces and my gondolier, who stood slowly plying his gigantic oar in the stern of the boat. At that moment he uttered a cry like a wild creature, a kind of deep groan that rose in crescendo to a prolonged 'Oh!' and ended with the simple exclamation 'Venezia!' Something else followed, but already the cry had stirred in me so violent a commotion that I forgot the rest. The sensations I experienced at that moment did not leave me throughout my sojourn in Venice; they remained in my mind until I had completed the second act of *Tristan* and may even have suggested the plaintive, trailing clarinet at the beginning of Act Three.❞

RICHARD WAGNER, *MEIN LEBEN*, 1911

FLOATING IN A GONDOLA

George Eliot (1819–80) was a frequent visitor to Italy throughout her life and its influence can be seen in her work. Her novel Romola *is set in Florence and her poem* The Spanish Gypsy *was inspired by the works of Tintoretto. Seven months before her death, she married her financial adviser, John Walter Cross, whom she had met in Rome. Her letters and journals were edited by Cross and published posthumously in 1885.*

❝Of all the dreamy delights, that of floating in a gondola among the canals and out of the Lagoon is surely the greatest. We were out one night when the sun was setting, and the wide waters were flushed with the reddened light. I should have liked it to last for hours . . . Another charm of evening was to walk up and down the Piazza of San Marco as the stars were brightening and look at the grand dim buildings, and the flocks of pigeons flitting about them; or to walk on to the Bridge of La Paglia and look along the dark canal that runs under the Bridge of Sighs – its blackness lit up by a gaslight here and there, and the plash of the oar of blackest gondola slowly advancing.❞

GEORGE ELIOT, *LETTERS AND JOURNALS, 3 VOLS*, 1885

THE VIEW FROM TORCELLO

John Ruskin (1819–1900) had a lifelong interest in landscape painting and between 1834 and 1860 he prepared a five-volume series on Modern Painters. *He spent seven months in Italy researching this series, and wrote passionately of the buildings and the natural beauty of Venice.*

❝ On this mound is built a rude brick campanile, of the commonest Lombardic type, which if we ascend towards evening (and there are none to hinder us, the door of its ruinous staircase swings idly on its hinges), we may command from it one of the most notable scenes in this wide world of ours. Far as the eye can reach, a waste of wild sea moor, of a lurid ashen grey; not like our northern moors with their jet-black pools and purple heath, but lifeless, the colour sackcloth, with the corrupted sea-water soaking through the roots of its acrid weeds, and gleaming hither and thither through its snaky channels. No gathering of fantastic mists, nor coursing of clouds across it; but melancholy clearness of space in the warm sunset, oppressive, reaching to the horizon of its level gloom. ❞

JOHN RUSKIN, *THE STONES OF VENICE*, 1851–3

PROUST IN VENICE

An avid reader of Ruskin, two of whose books he translated into French, Marcel Proust (1871–1922) visited Venice for the first time in 1900.

❝ My gondola followed the course of the small canals; like the mysterious hand of a Genie leading me through the maze of this oriental city, they seemed, as I advanced, to be carving a road for me through the heart of a crowded quarter which they clove asunder, barely dividing with a slender fissure, arbitrarily carved, the tall houses with their tiny Moorish windows; and, as though the magic guide had been holding a candle in his hand and were lighting the way for me, they kept casting ahead of them a ray of sunlight for which they cleared a path.
One felt that between the mean dwellings which the canal had just parted and which otherwise would have formed a compact whole, no open space had been reserved. With the result that the belfry of the church, or the garden-trellis rose sheer above the rio as in a flooded city. But with churches as with gardens, thanks to the same transposition as in the Grand Canal, the sea formed so effective a way of communication, a substitute for street or alley, that on either side of the canaletto the churches rose from the water in this ancient plebeian quarter, degraded into humble, much-frequented mission chapels, bearing upon their surface the stamp of their necessity, of their use by crowds of simple folk, that the gardens crossed by the line of the canal allowed their astonished leaves or fruit to trail in the water and that on the doorstep of the house whose roughly-hewn stone was still wrinkled as though it had only just been sawn, little boys surprised by the gondola and keeping their balance allowed their legs to dangle vertically, like sailors seated upon a swing-bridge the two halves of which have been swung apart, allowing the sea to pass between them.
Now and again there appeared a handsomer building

that happened to be there, like a surprise in a box which we have just opened, a little ivory temple with its Corinthian columns and its allegorical statue on the pediment, somewhat out of place among the ordinary buildings in the midst of which it had survived, and the peristyle with which the canal provided it resembled a landing-stage for market gardeners. **"**

MARCEL PROUST, A LA RECHERCHE DU TEMPS PERDU, 1925

DEATH IN VENICE

Death in Venice by Thomas Mann (1875–1955) tells the story of a disillusioned writer, Gustav Aschenbach, who comes to Venice for an extended rest. His meeting with a beautiful young Polish boy awakens in him a mystical joy. Aschenbach is torn between his desire to complete his life's work and his mute and violent passion: meanwhile Venice, the omnipresent backdrop to the story, is in the grip of a cholera epidemic.

" Tadzio and his sisters at length took a gondola. Aschenbach hid behind a portico or fountain while they embarked, and directly they pushed off did the same. In a furtive whisper he told the boatman he would tip him well to follow at a little distance the other gondola, just rounding a corner, and fairly sickened at the man's quick, sly grasp and ready acceptance of the go-between's role.

Leaning back among soft, black cushions he swayed gently in the wake of the other black-snouted bark, to which the strength of his passion chained him. Sometimes it passed from his view, and then he was assailed by an anguish of unrest. But his guide appeared to have long practice in affairs like these; always, by dint of short cuts or deft manoeuvres, he contrived to overtake the coveted sight. The air was heavy and foul, the sun burnt down through a slate coloured haze. Water slapped gurgling against wood and stone. The gondolier's cry, half warning, half salute, was answered with singular accord from far within the silence of the labyrinth. They passed little gardens, high up the crumbling wall, hung with clustering white and purple flowers that sent down an odour of almonds. Moorish lattices showed shadowy in the gloom. The marble steps of a church descended into the canal, and on them a beggar squatted, displaying his misery to view, showing the whites of his eyes, holding out his hat for alms. Farther on a dealer in antiquities cringed before his lair, inviting the passer by to enter and be duped. Yes, this was Venice, this the fair frailty that fawned and that betrayed, half fairy tale, half snare; the city in whose stagnating air the art of painting once put forth so lusty a growth, and where musicians were moved to accords so weirdly lulling and lascivious. Our adventurer felt his senses wooed by this voluptuousness of sight and sound, tasted his secret knowledge that the city sickened and hid its sickness for love of gain, and bent an ever more unbridled leer on the gondola that glided on before him. **"**

THOMAS MANN, DEATH IN VENICE, 1912

VENICE BY NIGHT

Frederick Rolfe, "Baron Corvo", ambivalent English novelist and Catholic convert, spent many years of his life in Venice and died there in 1913.

" It was unfortunate that his pockets were empty. With threepence, he might have spent the greater part of a cold wet night in a dry warm caffè.

He walked briskly, over the Academy bridge, as far as the Public Gardens eastward. About 23 o'clock, the rain became drizzle. He turned westward, going by Santazustina and Sanzanipolo and millions of little back alleys to the long solitary quay of Santamaria Odorifera, and on through the Ghetto to the three-arched bridge of Cannarezo. There, he turned, crossing the iron-bridge by the station; went round by Santachiara and Santandrea and Sanraffael to the Marittima end of the Zattere. He had walked, so far, as though on definite business; but now he slackened to a leisured dawdle. There was only a night to get through without exciting notice. In the morning, he could arrange better for the future.

The whole quay of the Zattere extended itself before him. He set himself to pace it from end to end. The drizzle ceased, and a warm haze bloomed on the darkness. He kept moving, to dry his drenched clothes.

Midnight sounded, and the stroke of one. The last ferries left the pontoons by the church of the Gesuati . . . On the distant bank of the wide canal of Zuecca, the lengthy line of lights along Spinalonga fluttered like little pale daffodils in a night-mist coloured like the bloom on the fruit of the vine. Great quiet reigned. He prayed, to comfort the minutes as they fled by . . . Dawn, misty, pink and glittering grey like salmon-flesh and scales, came. Very tired and stiff and sodden, he put the night behind him; and crossed Canalazzo, walking by Sanvidal and Sammaurizio and the Piazza to the club. **99**

BARON CORVO, *THE DESIRE AND PURSUIT OF THE WHOLE*, 1934

IMPRESSIONS OF VENICE

CARNIVAL

John Evelyn (1620–1706) is probably best remembered for his Diary, *in which he recounts the details of his travels abroad, providing an invaluable record of the period.*

66 1646. In January Signor *Molino* was chosen *Dodge*, but the extreame snow that fell, & the cold hindred my going to see the solemnity, so as I stirrd not from *Padoa* til *Shrovetide*, when all the world repaire to *Venice* to see the folly & madnesse of the *Carnevall*; The Women, Men & persons of all Conditions disguising themselves in antique dresses, & extravagant Musique & a thousand gambols, & traversing the streetes from house to house, all places being then accessible, & free to enter: There is abroad nothing but flinging of Eggs fill'd with sweete Waters, & sometimes not over sweete; they also have a barbarous costome of hunting bulls about the Streetes & Piazzas, which is very dangerous, the passages being generally so narrow in that Citty: Likewise do the youth of the severall Wards & parrishes contend in other Masteries or pastimes, so as tis altogether impossible to recount the universal madnesse of this place during this time of licence: Now are the greate banks set up for those who will play at Basset, the Comedians have also liberty & the *Operas* to Exercise: Witty pasquils are likewise thrown about, & the Mountebanks have their stages in every Corner. **99**

JOHN EVELYN, *DIARY,* 1818

VENICE IN SPRING

Georges Sand (1804–76) left her husband in 1831 and embarked on a life as a writer. Venice is at the center of several of her works, such as the prose poem entitled Lettres d'un Voyageur.

66 You can't imagine what Venice is like at present, my friend. When you saw those ancient pillars of Greek marble whose colour and shape reminded you of bleached bones, she hadn't yet discarded the mourning drapes she puts on in winter. Now the spring has blown an emerald dust over all that. The base of the *palazzi*, where oysters used to cling to stagnant moss, are covered in mosses of tender green, and the gondolas glide between two carpets of velvety, beautiful verdure, while the sound of the waves languidly dies away in the foam of their wake. All the balconies are covered with vases of flowers, and the flowers of Venice, planted in a warm soil and blossoming in a humid atmosphere, have a freshness, rich texture and languid air which makes them resemble the women of this clime, whose beauty is as dazzling and as shortlived. Brambles twine around each pillar and hang their garlands of tiny pink and white rosettes from the black wrought-iron balconies. **99**

GEORGES SAND, *LETTRES D'UN VOYAGEUR*, 1837

SAINT MARK'S SQUARE

Guy de Maupassant (1850–93) thought Venice would be a place of surpassing grandeur; he was surprised to arrive there and find the city "resembled a bibelot" threatened by time.

66 I had dreamed of a great city filled with immense palaces, such is the renown of this antique queen of the seas. Amazingly, everything is tiny, tiny, tiny! Venice is no more than a bibelot, an old, charming, bibelot d'art, poor, ruined, but proud with a great sense of her former glory. Everything here is ruinous, on the point of crumbling into the water that floats this poor, worn city on its surface. The facades of the palaces are ravaged by time, stained by humidity, eaten up by the leprosy which destroys stone and marble. Some lean slightly to the side; they are ready to fall, tired of standing so long on their pilings.

Suddenly the horizon widens, the Lagoon widens: over there on the right are mist-shrouded islands, and to the left a fine Moorish monument appears, a marvel of oriental grace and imposing elegance, which is the Doge's Palace.

I shall not speak of the Venice that everyone else has described. Piazza San Marco resembles Place du Palais Royal in Paris; the façade of the church looks like the pasteboard front of a café-concert; but the inside of it is everything one imagined and is moreover absolutely beautiful. The penetrating harmony of the lines and the colour tones, the glinting soft light of the old gold mosaics in the midst of austere marbles, the marvellous proportions of the vaults and the distances, something of divine discovery in the whole basilica, and in the very sunbeams which become calm and religious around its pillars, in the sensations it casts like beams upon the spirit through the eye: all these things make St Mark's the most completely admirable thing on earth. **99**

GUY DE MAUPASSANT, *CYRABIAS*, 1851

THE SPECTACLE OF VENICE

Edward Gibbon (1737–94) author of History of the Decline and Fall of the Roman Empire, *was not impressed by Venetian architecture.*

66 The spectacle of Venice afforded some hours of astonishment and some days of disgust. Old and in general ill-built houses, ruined pictures, and stinking ditches dignified with the pompous denomination of canals; a fine bridge spoilt by two rows of houses on it, and a large square decorated with the worst architecture I ever yet saw. 99

EDWARD GIBBON, *MISCELLANEOUS WORKS*, 1796

THE EFFECTS OF VENICE

Born in Orel, in central Russia, Ivan Turgenev (1818–83) was the first major Russian writer to find success in the rest of Europe. He lived mostly in Western European countries, and his writing examines the social, political and philosophical issues of the times.

66 No one who has not seen Venice in April knows the full, the indescribable charm of that magical city. The gentleness and softness of spring are to Venice what the bright sun of summer is to majestic Genoa, what the gold and purple of autumn are to that grand old man among cities, Rome . . . 'Venice is dying, Venice is deserted' – so her inhabitants will tell you, but it may be that in the past she lacked such charm as this, the charm of a city fading in the very culmination and flowering of its beauty. No one who has not seen her, knows her: neither Canaletto nor Guardi (not to speak of more recent painters) was able to record the silvery delicacy of her air, her vistas, so near and yet so fugitive, her marvellous harmony of graceful lines and melting colours. To the visitor, soured and broken by life, Venice has nothing to offer; to him she will be bitter as the recollection of early unrealized dreams are bitter. But for him who still has strength and confidence within him, she will be sweet; let him bring his happiness to her and expose it to her enchanted skies, and, however radiant his happiness may be, she will enrich it with her own unfading light. 99

TURGENEV, *ON THE EVE*, 1859

COLLECTING MEMORIES

Besides novels, short stories, plays and essays, Henry James (1843–1916) wrote several books of "sketches" based on his extensive travels through Europe. His views about the effects of Venice on visitors seem the opposite to those of Turgenev.

66 I know not whether it is because San Giorgio is so grandly conspicuous, but with a great deal of worn, faded-looking brickwork; but for many persons the whole place has a kind of suffusion of rosiness. Asked what may be the leading colour in the Venetian concert, we should inveterately say Pink, and yet without remembering after all that this elegant hue occurs very often. It is a faint, shimmering, airy, watery pink; the bright sea-light seems to flush with it and the pale whiteish-green of lagoon and canal to drink it in. There is indeed a great deal of very evident brickwork, which is never fresh or loud in colour, but always burnt out, as it were, always exquisitely mild.

Certain little mental pictures rise before the collector of memories at the simple mention, written or spoken, of the places he has loved. When I hear, when I see, the magical name I have written above these pages, it is not of the great Square that I think, with its strange basilica and its high arcades, nor of the wide mouth of the Grand Canal, with the stately steps and the well-poised dome of the Salute; it is not of the low lagoon, nor the sweet Piazzetta, nor the dark chambers of St Mark's. I simply see a narrow canal in the heart of the city – a patch of green water and a surface of pink wall. The gondola moves slowly; it gives a great smooth swerve, passes under a bridge, and the gondolier's cry, carried over the quiet water, makes a kind of splash in the stillness. A girl crosses the little bridge, which has an arch like a camel's back, with an old shawl on her head, which makes her characteristic and charming; you see her against the sky as you float beneath. The pink of the old wall seems to fill the whole place; it sinks even into the opaque water. Behind the wall is a garden, out of which the long arm of a white June rose – the roses of Venice are splendid – has flung itself by way of spontaneous ornament. On the other side of this small water-way is a great shabby façade of Gothic windows and balconies – balconies on which dirty clothes are hung and under which a cavernous-looking doorway opens from a low flight of slimy water-steps. It is very hot and still, the canal has a queer smell, and the whole place is enchanting.

It is a fact that almost every one interesting, appealing, melancholy, memorable, odd, seems at one time or another, after many days and much life, to have gravitated to Venice by a happy instinct, settling in it and treating it, cherishing it, as a sort of repository of consolations; all of which to-day, for the conscious mind, is mixed with its air and constitutes its unwritten history. The deposed, the defeated, the disenchanted, the wounded, or even only the bored, have seemed to find there something that no other place could give. **99**

HENRY JAMES, *ITALIAN HOURS*, 1909

LINGERING IMPRESSIONS

Hugh Honour's Companion Guide to Venice *was first published in 1965, and has since become one of the standard reference works on the city. He lives in Tuscany.*

66 When the moment for departure comes, the impressions which are strongest in the memory are more likely to be of the city and the lagoon than of its artistic treasures. No cicerone can indicate, no guide-book can predict, what these will be. It may be no more than a glimpse through an escutcheoned gateway to a cortile hung with washing, or the elation on emerging from a long dark calle on to a smiling fondamenta. A wedding party in a train of gondolas, a greengrocer and a porter abusing each other in the sibilant dialect of Goldoni's pantaloons, a gondolier polishing the brasswork on his boat, an old woman crouched in devotion in some quiet cool church where a Bellini Madonna stares down in compassion, the flicker of candles before a shrine illuminating the carved marble flowers of a Tullio Lombardo, or perhaps some sight as simple as a cat sunning itself on an old well-head, or a pair of pigeons silhouetted against the sky on one of those arches which thrust the palaces apart across some narrow calle. Though they may be sinking, the buildings of Venice will see out our time; but such scenes as these, which form an essential part of the memory of every lover of Venice, neither will nor can be quite the same again. **99**

HUGH HONOUR, *THE COMPANION GUIDE TO VENICE*, 1965

COURTESANS AND DESPERATE VILLAINS

Thomas Coryate (c.1577–1617) was well known in his day as an eccentric character. In 1608 he travelled through France, Italy, Switzerland, Germany and Holland, most of the journey being undertaken on foot. An amusing account of his travels, entitled Coryate's Crudities, *was published in 1611.*

66 As for the number of these Venetian Cortezans it is very great. For it is thought there are of them in the whole City and other adjacent places, as Murano, Malomocco, &c. at the least twenty thousand, whereof many are esteemed so loose, that they are said to open their quivers to every arrow. A most ungodly thing without doubt that there should be a tolleration of such licentious wantons in so glorious, so potent, so renowned a city . . . For so infinite are the allurements of these amorous Calypsoes, that the fame of them hath drawn many to Venice from some of the remotest parts of Christendome, to contemplate their beauties, and enjoy their pleasing dalliances. And indeede such is the variety of the delicious objects they minister to their lovers, that they want nothing tending to delight. For when you come into one of their Palaces (as indeed some few of the principallest of them live in very magnificent and portly buildings fit for the entertainement of a great Prince) you seeme to enter into the Paradise of Venus. 99

66 There are certaine desperate and resolute villaines in Venice, called Braves, who at some unlawfull times do commit great villainy. They wander abroad very late in the night to and fro for their prey, like hungry Lyons, being armed with a privy coate of maile, a gauntlet upon their right hand, and a little sharpe dagger called a stiletto. They lurke commonly by the water side, and if at their time of night, which is betwixt eleven of the clocke and two, they happen to meete any man that is worth the rifling, they will presently stabbe him, take away all about him that is of any worth, and when they have thoroughly pulled his plumes, they will throw him into one of the channels: but they buy this booty very deare if they are after apprehended. For they are presently executed. 99

THOMAS CORYATE,
CORYATE'S CRUDITIES, 1611

MORALITY

Lord Byron maintained a regular correspondence with his good friend and publisher, John Murray, throughout the five years that he spent in Italy. By all accounts, he had rather a riotous time in Venice in 1817.

66 The general state of morals is much the same as in the Doges' time; a woman is virtuous (according to the code) who limits herself to her husband and one lover; those who have two, three or more are a little wild; but it is only those who are indiscriminately diffuse and form a low connection such as the Princess of Wales with her courier who are considered as overstepping the modesty of marriage. In Venice the nobility have a trick of marrying with dancers or singers; and truth to say the women of their own order are by no means handsome; but the general race, the woman of the second and other order, the wives of Advocates, merchants and proprietors and untitled gentry are mostly bel'sangne and it is with these that the more aleatory connections are usually formed: there are also instances of stupendous constancy. I know a woman of fifty who never had but one lover, who dying early she became devout renouncing all but her husband: she piques herself as may be presumed upon this miraculous fidelity, talking of it occasionally with a species of misplaced morality which is rather amusing. 99

LORD BYRON,
LETTER TO JOHN MURRAY, JANUARY 2, 1817

THE EASTERN INFLUENCE

Son of a Lord Mayor of London, William Beckford (1759–1844) was a wealthy traveler and collector of paintings and curios. He is remembered chiefly for an oriental tale entitled Vathek, *but he also wrote two travel books, including* Dreams, Waking Thoughts and Incidents. *This was originally suppressed by the author in 1783 and republished in a revised edition in 1834.*

❝I like this odd town of Venice, and find every day some new amusement in rambling about its innumerable canals and alleys. Sometimes I pry about the great church of St Mark, and examine the variety of marbles and mazes of delicate sculpture with which it is covered. The cupola, glittering with gold, mosaic, and paintings of half the wonders in the Apocalypse, never fails to transport me to the period of the Eastern empire. I think myself in Constantinople, and expect Michael Paleologus with all his train. One circumstance alone prevents me observing half the treasures of the place, and holds down my fancy just springing into the air: I mean the vile stench which exhales from every recess and corner of the edifice and which all the incense of the altars cannot subdue. When no longer able to endure this noxious atmosphere, I run up the campanile in the Piazza, and seating myself amongst the pillars of the gallery, breathe the fresh gales which blow from the Adriatic; survey at leisure all Venice beneath me, and its azure sea, white sails, and long tracks of islands shining in the sun. Having thus laid in a provision of wholesome breezes, I brave the vapours of the canals, and venture into the most curious and murky quarters of the city, in search of Turks and Infidels, that I may ask as many questions as I please about Cairo and Damascus.❞

WILLIAM BECKFORD, *DREAMS, WAKING THOUGHTS AND INCIDENTS*, 1783

THE SMELL OF VENICE

Three years after her husband Henry Thrale's death, Hester Thrale (1741–1821) married an Italian musician named Gabriel Piozzi, amid much opposition from family and friends (including Dr Johnson). She published several books of poems and anecdotes.

❝But it is almost time to talk of the Rialto, said to be the finest single arch in Europe, and I suppose it is so – very beautiful, too, when looked on from the water, but so dirtily kept and deformed with mean shops, that, passing over it, disgust gets the better of every other sensation. The truth is, our dear Venetians are nothing less than cleanly. St Mark's Place is all covered over in a morning with chicken-coops, which stink one to death, as nobody, I believe, thinks of changing their baskets; and all about the ducal palace is made so very offensive by the resort of human creatures for every purpose most unworthy of so charming a place, that all enjoyment of its beauties is rendered difficult to a person of any delicacy, and poisoned so provokingly, that I do never cease to wonder that so little police and proper regulation are established in a city so particularly lovely to render her sweet and wholesome.❞

HESTER PIOZZI,
OBSERVATIONS AND REFLECTIONS, 1789

remarkable. The light of a
Venetian dawn in early
summer – you must be about at
four o'clock in the morning to
see the market coming to life – is so
limpid and so still that it makes every separate
vegetable and fruit and fish luminous with a life of its
own, with unnaturally heightened colours and clear stencilled
outlines. Here the cabbages are cobalt blue, the beetroots deep rose, the
lettuces clear pure green, sharp as glass. Bunches of gaudy gold marrow-flowers
show off the elegance of pink and white marbled bean pods, primrose potatoes,
green plums, green peas. The colours of the peaches, cherries, and apricots, packed
in boxes lined with sugar-bag blue paper matching the blue canvas trousers worn by
the men unloading the gondolas, are reflected in the rose-red mullet and the
orange *vongole* and *cannestrelle* which have been prised out of their shells and
heaped into baskets. In other markets, on other shores, the unfamiliar fishes may
be vivid, mysterious, repellent, fascinating, and bright with splendid colour; only in
Venice do they look good enough to eat. In Venice even ordinary sole and ugly
great skate are striped with delicate lilac lights, the sardines shine like newly-
minted silver coins, pink Venetian *scampi* are fat and fresh, infinitely enticing in the
early dawn.

The gentle swaying of the laden gondolas, the movements of the market men as
they unload, swinging the boxes and baskets ashore, the robust life and rattling
noise contrasted with the fragile taffeta colours and the opal sky of Venice – the
whole scene is out of some marvellous unheard-of ballet. **99**

ELIZABETH DAVID,
ITALIAN FOOD, 1954

THE CATS

*Jan Morris is the author of a prodigious number of travel books, and has
writtten about many of the world's great cities. Among these works is her
classic guide to Venice, which was published in 1960.*

66 For myself, I love the cats of Venice, peering from their pedestals,
sunning themselves on the feet of statues, crouching on dark staircases to escape
the rain, or gingerly emerging into the daylight from their fetid subterranean lairs.
Shylock defined them as 'necessary and harmless', and Francesco Morosini, one of
the great fighting Doges, thought so highly of them that he took one with him on
his victorious campaigns in the Peloponnese.

There are few more soothing places of refuge than a Venetian garden on a blazing
summer morning when the trees are thick with green, the air is heavy with
honeysuckle, and the tremulous water-reflections of the canals are thrown
mysteriously upon the walls. The rear façade of the palace before you, with its
confusion of windows, is alive with gentle activity. On the top floor an elderly
housekeeper lowers her basket on a string, in preparation for the morning mail.
From a lower window there issues the harsh melody of a housemaid's song as she
scrubs the bathroom floor. In the door of the ground-floor flat a girl sits sewing, in
a black dress and a demure white apron, with a shine of polished pans from the
kitchen lighting her hair like a halo. From the canal outside comes a pleasant buzz
of boats, and sometimes the throaty warning cry of a bargee. On a neighbouring
roof-garden an artist stands before his easel, with brush in one hand, coffee-cup in
the other.

And dotted all about you in the grass, in attitudes statuesque and contented, with
their tails tucked around them and the eyes narrowed in the sunshine, one licking
his haunches, one biting a blade of grass, one intermittently growling, one twitching
his whiskers – all around you sit the cats of the garden, black, grey or obscurely
tabby, like bland but scrawny guardians. **99**

JAN MORRIS,
VENICE, 1960

TOURISM

Pietro Aretino (1492–1556) wrote several comedies and satires. Here he writes to his landlord in Venice.

❝ It seems to me, Honoured Sir, that I would commit the sin of ingratitude if I did not repay with praise some part of the debt which I owe to the heavenly situation of your house . . . Certainly its builder chose the finest position on the Canal. And since that Canal is the patriarch of all others and since Venice is a female pope among cities, I can truthfully say that I enjoy both the fairest highway and the most joyous view in the world. Whenever I look out of my windows at that time when the merchants foregather I see a thousand persons in as many gondolas . . . To my left I behold the much frequented Bridge and the warehouses of the German traders. There are grapes in the barges below, game of all kinds in the shops and vegetables laid out on the pavements. There is no need for me to long for meadows watered by streams when I can marvel at dawn over waters covered with an endless variety of merchandise, each article in its due season. What sport it is to watch those who bring in great quantities of fruit and vegetables handing them out to others who carry them to their appointed places! All is tumult and bustle, except where about a score of sailing-boats laden with melons are moored together, making a sort of island to which crowds hurry off to count, sniff and weigh, so as to test the quality of the goods. Of the ladies, gleaming in gold and silk and jewels, though they are mere housewives, I will not speak, lest I grow tedious with the description of such pomp and circumstance. But what makes me roar with laughter are the whistles, catcalls and jeers directed by the boatmen at those whose rowers are not equipped with scarlet hose.

And who would not laugh till he cried at the sight of a boatload of Germans who had just reeled out of a tavern being capsized into the chilly waters of the Canal? ❞

PIETRO ARETINO, *LETTER*, 1529

A COSMOPOLITAN CITY

Following his father's death in 1640, John Evelyn spent a lot of time traveling in Europe until 1652, when he married and decided to settle in England.

❝ Nor was I less surprised with the strange variety of the several nations seen every day in the streets and piazzas; Jews, Turks, Armenians, Persians, Moors, Greeks, Schiavonians some with their targets and buckles, and all in their native fashions, negotiating in this famous Emporium which is always crowded with strangers . . . It was evening, and the canal where the Noblesse go to take the air, as in our Hyde Park, was full of ladies and gentlemen. There are many dangerous stops, by reason of the multitudes of gondolas ready to sink one another; and indeed they affect to lean them on one side, that one who is not accustomed to it, would be afraid of oversetting. Here they were singing, playing harpsichords, and other music, and serenading their mistresses; in another place racing and other pastimes on the water, it being now exceeding hot. ❞

JOHN EVELYN, *DIARY*, 1818

ECHOES

Mary McCarthy, American novelist and critic, spent a winter in Venice in the early 1960s. In her classic Venice Observed, *she applied an ironic objectivity to her subject and its people, pointing out that in addition to building the loveliest city on earth, the Venetians invented income tax, statistical science, the floating of government stock, state censorship, anonymous denunciations (the Bocca del Leone), the gambling casino – and the ghetto.*

❝ When the Venetians stroll out in the evening, they do not avoid the Piazza San Marco, where the tourists are, as the Romans do with Doney's on the Via Veneto. The Venetians go to look at the tourists, and the tourists look back at them. It is all for the ear and eye, this city, but primarily for the eye. Built on water, it is an endless succession of reflections and echoes, a mirroring. Contrary to popular belief, there are no back canals where a tourist will not meet himself, with a camera, in the person of the other tourist crossing the little bridge. And no word can be spoken in this city that is not an echo of something said before. 'Mais c'est aussi cher que Paris!' exclaims a Frenchman in a restaurant, unaware that he repeats Montaigne. The complaint against foreigners, voiced by a foreigner, chimes querulously through the ages, in unison with the medieval monk who found St Mark's Square filled with 'Turks, Libyans, Parthians, and other monsters of the sea'. Today it is the Germans we complain of, and no doubt they complain of the Americans, in the same words. Nothing can be said here (including this statement) that has not been said before. One often hears the Piazza described as an open-air drawing-room; the observation goes back to Napoleon, who called it 'the best drawing-room in Europe'. A friend likens the ornamental coping of St Mark's to sea foam, but Ruskin thought of this first '. . . at last, as if in ecstasy, the crests of the arches break into a marbly foam, and toss themselves far into the blue sky in flashes and wreaths of sculptured spray . . .' Another friend observes that the gondolas are like hearses: I was struck by the novelty of the fancy until I found it, two days later, in Shelley: 'that funereal bark'. Now I find it everywhere. A young man, boarding the vaporetto, sighs that 'Venice is so urban', a remark which at least sounds original and doubtless did when Proust spoke of the 'always urban impression' made by Venice in the midst of the sea. And the worst of it is that nearly all these clichés are true. It is true, for example, that St Mark's at night looks like a painted stage flat; this is a fact which everybody notices and which everybody thinks he has discovered for himself. I blush to remember the sound of my own voice, clear in its own conceit, enunciating this proposition in the Piazza, nine years ago. ❞

MARY MCCARTHY, *VENICE OBSERVED*, 1961

A Journey
through Venice

SERVIZIO
GONDOLE

▲ Gondolier at the landing stage.

Taxi launches. ▼

CAVALLI

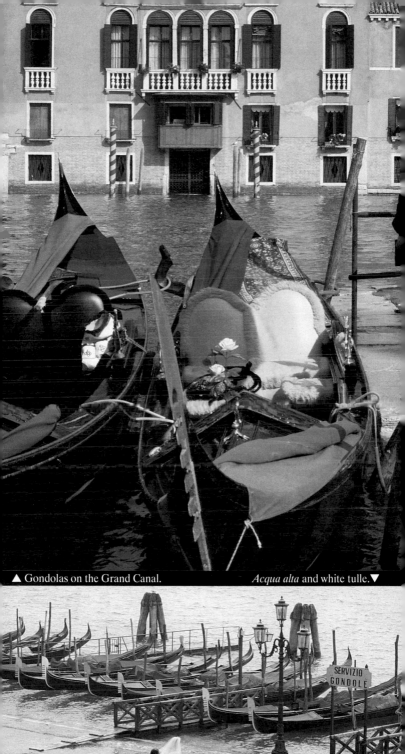

▲ Gondolas on the Grand Canal.

Acqua alta and white tulle.▼

▲ Ponte degli Scalzi on the Grand Canal.

▲ St Mark's Square in the snow.

Café Quadri on St Mark's Square. ▼

▲ Riva degli Schiavoni.

Taxi on the Grand Canal.

Fishing boats. ▼

▲ General view of Torcello.

Torcello. ▼

▼ Fishing nets in the Lagoon.

CANNAREGIO

CHURCH OF SANTA MARIA DEGLI SCALZI
CHURCH OF SAN GIOBBE
PALAZZO LABIA
GHETTO
CHURCH OF SANTA M... DEI SERVI

SANTA LUCIA STATION
CHURCH OF SAN SIMEONE PICCOLO
CHURCH OF SAN GEREMIA
CHURCH OF SAN MARCUOLA
PALAZZO VENDRAMIN-CALERGI
CHURCH OF SANTA MARI... DELLA MADDALENA

> **"The gateway to Venice, after all, is neither the station nor the Piazzale, but the Grand Canal before us, churned by propellers, turbulent as a great river."**
>
> Fernand Braudel, *Venise*

Immediately outside the railway station lies Cannaregio, the first of the six sestieri of Venice. Situated at the northwest end of the city, this is the second largest sestiere after Castello ▲ 155, covering an area of 150 hectares. Nearly a third of the population of Venice is concentrated here, amounting to more than twenty thousand people. There are two theories about the origins of the name Cannaregio; according to one, it comes from *Canal regio* (the Royal Canal), meaning the broad waterway which once provided convenient access to the city from the mainland, by prolonging the lagoon canal of San Secondo (which runs parallel to the railway bridge). The other hypothesis is that the word derives from the reeds and canes which used to abound in this area. In any case, a system of straight, parallel canals, with long fondamenta abutting southwards and linked by calli, criss-cross this zone of workmen's houses interspersed with magnificent palaces. To the south, behind the palaces of the Grand Canal, a wide street known as the Strada Nuova was built at the end of the last century. Now pedestrianized, this street runs from the station to the Campo Santi Apostoli, crossing the sestiere from one side to the other and adopting a number of different names as it goes. Few people lived in this sestiere until the 11th century, and it seems to have taken form only gradually, as the process of draining and consolidating the site progressed. From the 15th

Santa Lucia Station.

century onwards, Cannaregio was a definable quarter, though it was still peripheral to Venice proper. Before the railway bridge and the station were built, manufacturing was the principal industry in the district, despite attempts to create a new area of growth with the Fondamente Nuove. A similar project in the 16th century, the draining of the Sacca della Misericordia, was also never realized.

PALAZZO MASTELLI
CHURCH OF THE MADONNA DELL'ORTO
PALAZZO CONTARINI DAL ZAFFO
SCUOLA NUOVA DELLA MISERICORDIA
CHURCH OF SANTA MARIA DELLA MISERICORDIA
CHURCH OF SANTA SOFIA
CHURCH OF SANTI APOSTOLI
CHURCH OF THE JESUITS
CHURCH OF SAN CANCIANO
CEMETERY OF SAN MICHELE
MURANO

CA D'ORO
CHURCH OF SAN FELICE
CHURCH OF SAN MARZIALE
CHURCH OF SANTA FOSCA
RIALTO BRIDGE
FONDACO DEI TEDESCHI
TEATRO MALIBRAN
CHURCH OF SANTA MARIA DEI MIRACOLI
CHURCH OF SANTI GIOVANNI E PAOLO

THE GATEWAY TO VENICE

PONTE DELLA LIBERTÀ. Built by the Austrians 50 years after
the Treaty of Campo Formio in 1797 ● *34, 243*, to link Venice
with Milan. The railway bridge ended the thousand-year
separation from the mainland and shook the city's economy
as Venice, already in the throes of the industrial revolution,
saw its dependence on the mainland grow ever larger.
SANTA LUCIA STATION. The present station dates from 1955,
but still bears the name of the Renaissance church
demolished in 1861 to make way for it. Opposite is the green
dome of the Church of San Simeone Piccolo.

Half a day

BRIDGES TO VENICE
The Austrians
conceived a project
for a bridge between
Mestre and Venice as
early as 1814, but it
was not until 1846
that construction of
the Ponte della
Libertà was finally
begun. The span of
this new viaduct was
almost 11,500 feet,
and it included 222
stone arches. On
April 25, 1933, the
Ponte delle Littorale
was opened. Built in
less than two years by
the engineer
Umberto Fantucci,
this bridge was
intended for use by
motor cars.

137

THE CHURCH OF THE SCALZI. Almost adjoining the station is a church commissioned from Longhena by the Discalced (barefoot) Carmelite order. This Baroque building was constructed between 1660 and 1680. The Carmelites brought an image of the Virgin from the island of Lazzaretto Vecchio ▲ *384*; at that time the image was known as that of Santa Maria di Nazaretta, and the new church was then named after it. The façade, by Giuseppe Sardi, dates from 1680, and one of the vaults was decorated with a fresco by Tiepolo, the *Trasporto della Casa del Loveto* (1743–5). This vault was destroyed by an Austrian bomb on the night of October 27, 1915. Only two fragments remain, and these are preserved with Tiepolo's original sketch at the Accademia. The church's other fresco by Tiepolo, the *Gloria di Santa Teresa,* on the lower right-hand side of the church, was not damaged by the bomb. The second chapel on the left-hand side contains the tomb of Lodovico Manin, the last doge of Venice. (Take the Lista di Spagna, which was formerly the site of the Spanish Embassy, to Campo San Geremia, one of the few piazzas that has four separate wells.)

Ponte delle Guglie.

A WAY INTO VENICE
Before the construction of the bridge, the Cannaregio canal provided the main means of access to Venice: all traffic from the mainland had to pass by way of San Giuliano and Lizza di Fusina (today's Marghera). Fusina, at the mouth of the Brenta, was the scene of constant comings and goings, with vessels carrying provisions to the city. Until the 19th century, the waterway was kept open, even when sea-traffic to St Mark's Basin was jeopardized by the spread of the marshes and *barene* (mudflats) ■ *18,* in the 16th century. At that time, boats had to have empty barrels lashed to their sides, to reduce their draft and enable them to unload directly on the wharves.

FROM SAN GEREMIA TO SAN GIOBBE

THE CHURCH OF SAN GEREMIA. The present church was built in the mid-18th century by Carlo Corbellini, who took as his model the Greek Cross floorplan of the Church of La Salute ▲ *318*. Apart from several Baroque altars, the main point of interest is Palma the Younger's *Madonna Assisting at the Coronation of Venice*. The left-hand extension of the church was modified to house the relics of the Sicilian martyr St Lucia after the destruction of the church named after her. Beside the adjoining Fondamenta Labia is one of Venice's oldest campaniles, which dates from the 12th–13th century. **PALAZZO LABIA.** Beside the campo, right next to the church, is the Palazzo Labia, one of the most imposing buildings of its type in Venice. Now occupied by the RAI (Italian national television), it was built at the beginning of the 18th century by the Labia, a family of rich Catalan merchants who were admitted to the Venetian Patriarchate in 1646 in exchange for a large donation to support Venice's war in Crete ● *34*. They

«In these sullen streets there is the silence of towns that are dead, [...] the rusty brick backdrops that Tintoretto looked out on from his window in the Campo dei Mori.»

Goncourt Brothers

commissioned Giambattista Tiepolo to decorate the main room on the first floor. Taking the life of Cleopatra as his theme, the artist attempted to portray the pomp of contemporary Venetian aristocracy, and by so doing he contrived indirectly to exalt his own clients as members of that aristocracy. (From here, take the Salizzada San Geremia and then, just before the Ponte delle Guglic, turn along the Fondamenta Savorgnan.)

Ponte delle Guglie. This stone bridge, which spans the Cannaregio canal, replaced a wooden one in 1580. It takes its name from the obelisks that stand at either end, and occupies a key position between the Grand Canal and the Lagoon. Only three waterways in Venice possess the status of canal – the Giudecca, the Cannaregio and the Grand Canal – the rest being known as rii. The majority of Venice's food supplies used to arrive along the Cannaregio canal. On the other side of the bridge, on the Rio terrà San Leonardo, there is an attractive flower, vegetable and fish market.

The Church of San Giobbe. This church was begun in 1450 by Antonio Gambello, among others, and its construction was continued little by little as donations were raised to pay for it – notably a bequest from the Doge Cristoforo Moro. When Pietro Lombardo took over the project in 1470, he decided to alter much of its original style in order to accommodate some pure Renaissance elements in the portal, the decoration of the dome of the choir, and also in the **Martini Chapel,** whose vault is covered with shiny terracotta that came from the workshop of the Florentine sculptor Luca della Robbia. (Cross over the **Ponte dei Tre Archi,** a 17th-century structure which is unique in Venice, since arches like these would have hindered the barge traffic.) On the Fondamenta di Cannaregio stands Giuseppe Sardi's **Palazzo Surian-Bellotto,** in which the French Ambassador, de Montaigu, stayed during the 18th century, accompanied by his secretary, Jean-Jacques Rousseau.

The golden plates
At a banquet which he held for his fellow patricians, Gian Francesco Labia had the dinner served on golden plates. When they had finished eating, he apparently hurled the plates into the canal, with the remark *"Le abia, o non le abia, saro sempre Labia"* (Whether I have these or not, I shall always be a Labia). Malicious gossip has suggested, however, that he may have subsequently retrieved his treasures from the water.

THE GHETTO

THE JEWS IN VENICE DURING THE 14TH AND 15TH CENTURIES.
The first signs of a Jewish presence in Venice date from the
early 14th century, when Jewish merchants first came to buy
and sell in the port and *fondachi*, without receiving the right
to settle permanently in the city. During the second half of the
century, the Jews began to establish themselves more or less

illegally, until the
Chioggia War of 1381
● *31* yielded a first
condotta. This
officially authorized
them to live in Venice
and to practise usury
and *strazziaria* (the
sale of secondhand
clothes and objects).
The *condotta*, which
defined the financial
conditions and status
under which they were
allowed to stay in the
city, was no more than

Inside the Schola
Spagnola.

a renewable, temporary contract, however, and, on August 27,
1394, a decree was passed which stipulated that the Jews were
to be expelled from Venice at the end of the current *condotta*
– on February 20, 1397. From that time onwards, they were
permitted to stay for no more than 15 consecutive days, and
they also had to wear an emblem which would identify their
religion. The pretext for this decision came from certain
irregularities that had been uncovered in the management of
the Jewish *banchi,* but what really prompted it was the fear
that Jewish bankers and merchants would start to penetrate
into other sectors of Venetian commerce. Nevertheless, the
measure was deflected and the Jewish presence continued
undiminished through much of the following century until
1496, when a more restrictive order
was put into force which again
allowed Jews to stay in Venice for
only two weeks in every year.

**THE ORIGINS OF THE
WORD "GHETTO"**
In the 14th and 15th
centuries, foundries
were set up in
Cannaregio. Their
cinders were piled
nearby, on a spot
where new foundries
were to be built. The
Venetian word for "to
smelt" was *gettare*,
hence the name *geto
veccio* (old foundry)
for the first site, and
geto nuovo for the
second. With the
arrival of the Jews,
the meaning and
pronunciation
changed as the *ghetto*
became the place
assigned to them.

Circumcision
(late 18th century).

**THE ESTABLISHING OF THE FIRST
GHETTO.** The war waged against
Venice by the allies of the League of
Cambrai, and the appalling Venetian
defeat at Agnadello in the spring of 1509 ● *33*, altered this
situation again. Fearing the advance of the Imperial army,
mainland Jews took refuge in Venice, where some of them
gave much-needed funds to the Republic, despite the severe
losses they had already suffered. Under these circumstances,
Venice as usual opted for political realism: she tolerated the
Jews, and at the same time proceeded to organize their
segregation from the rest of the population. On March 29,
1516, a substantial majority in the Senate approved Zaccaria
Dolfin's proposal that the Jews in Venice should move en bloc
to the Ghetto Nuovo, a sort of urban islet that was linked to
the rest of the city by two points of access which might be
closed at night. This decision meant the Jews could remain as
pawnbrokers and textile merchants, while still ensuring they

«ALL THE FORGOTTEN DISEASES OF THE LEPROSERIES OF THE
ORIENT SEEMED TO GNAW THESE BLISTERED WALLS.»

THÉOPHILE GAUTIER

were kept apart from the rest of the city. It ran contrary to the
tide of public opinion (fuelled by the sermons of the
Franciscans, who proclaimed that God would punish the city
if the Jews were admitted), while still taking shrewd account
of it, for the chosen site made it possible not only to protect
the Jews from violence and looting, but also to impose an
effective curfew upon them and to keep them apart from
the rest of the Venetian population. As half-fortress and half-
gathering point, the Ghetto soon became the symbol of
Venice's ambiguous attitude; one which was prepared to
accept the Jews and to make the most of their skills, but at the
same time was still determined to demonstrate their
inferiority to Christians.

La Giudecca ▲ 336,
contrary to what one
sometimes reads
about it, was never a
place where the Jews
were concentrated in
Venice. Moreover,
the name probably
does not derive from
giuderi (Jews) at all,
but from *zudega*, a
Venetian corruption
of *giudicati*, meaning
"condemned men".

VENETIAN AMBIVALENCE. The Republic's
policy was most clearly demonstrated
when, in 1524, a group of patricians
proposed that a pawnshop should be
established in the city. This operation, by
lending money at a low rate of interest,
would have rendered the Jews
superfluous. But an alarmed Council of
Ten persuaded the patricians to drop
their project "on pain of death";
moreover, a decree was then passed
which forbade the Council to reconsider
the matter except with the unanimous
consent of all its members. Most wanted
the Jews to carry out the task of lending
money, because they could be easily
controlled and heavily taxed. The
condotte were regularly renewed. In
December 1571, during the crusade
against the Turks ● 36, in which Venice
played so prominent a part, a decision

was once more taken to expel the Jews; but this again was
never applied and, in 1573, a fresh *condotta* authorized them
to stay in Venice and to lend money at a maximum interest
rate of five per cent. After this there was no further talk of
driving the Jews from the city.

DAILY LIFE IN THE GHETTO. By consigning the Jews to the
Ghetto Nuovo, the Senate made what Brian Pullan has called
"the Venetians' contribution to the
language of persecution". From the
16th century onwards, the word *ghetto*
signified the segregation of the Jews in
Venice and gradually became a generic
term used all over Europe. After 1541,
the Jewish quarter was enlarged to
include the Ghetto Vecchio. In 1633,
the Ghetto Nuovissimo was also added
but, in spite of these extensions, the
population density remained very
high, and this explains the
relative tallness (for
Venice) of the buildings in
the Jewish quarter, which
frequently grew to heights
of six, or even nine stories.
The Jews were forbidden to

In the 9th century,
two noble families
which had been
involved in an
insurrection were
banished to the
Giudecca, where they
lived under house
arrest. The only clear
link with the Jewish
community dates
from 1515, when a
Venetian patrician,
Giorgio Emo,
proposed that the
Jews be consigned to
the Giudecca. But the
Jewish community,
represented by the
banker Ascher
Meschullam, pointed
out that the presence
of a military barracks
on the island might
lead to trouble with
their community, and
the senators
recognized the force
of this argument.

The *aron* of Schola Spagnola, with the Ten Commandments.

THE CLOSURE OF THE GHETTO
The decree of 1516 stated that the Jews were "required to go without delay and to abide all together in the block of houses at the Ghetto, by San Girolamo . . . and in order to prevent them from moving about the streets at night . . . we decree that on the Ghetto Vecchio side, where there is a small bridge, and likewise at the other end of said bridge, two gates shall be raised, which shall be opened at dawn and closed again at midnight by four Christian sentries employed for the purpose and appointed by the Jews themselves at a wage that our college shall deem to be suitable." The entrance to the Ghetto on the Rio San Girolamo was also closed off, and the Jews were forbidden to leave the area during certain religious festivals.

leave their quarter during the night, or during Christian religious festivals; they also had to wear an identifying emblem, initially a yellow skullcap, then a turban or a hat, first yellow then red. Although they were placed under the control of a special magistrature, they were able to run their own affairs within the Ghetto. Butchers and bakers could ply their trades in the proscribed area according to the prescriptions of the Jewish faith. Community life was close-knit, and benevolent associations were as numerous as the synagogues, which were known as schole, like their Christian counterparts, the scuole ▲ 295. The synagogues were usually on the upper floors of buildings with discreet façades: nothing on the outside gave any indication of the rich premises contained within. But the whole of Venice shared the same passion for music and theater, and the Campo del Ghetto Nuovo, although it housed no fewer than sixty tailors' shops and three moneylenders' offices and was full of busy crowds during the day, nevertheless contrived to double up as a venue for theatrical performances, which were often attended by Christians. Indeed, many of the Christians were happy to break the curfew during the feast of Purim, when there were masks and street dancing in the Ghetto, just as at Carnival time in the rest of Venice.

FROM THE FALL OF THE REPUBLIC TO MODERN TIMES. The gates of the Ghetto were finally demolished on June 10, 1797, during the French occupation, "so that there shall no longer be any apparent division between the citizens of this town". But, with the arrival of the Austrians, to whom Napoleon Bonaparte was soon to surrender the city, the Jews once again found that they were confined to the Ghetto in a kind of unofficial segregation. It was not until the Unification of Italy that Victor Emmanuel II was able to grant the Jews an equal status in law as the rest of his subjects. The history of the Jews of Venice was subsequently no different from that of all the other citizens, until the Fascist regime promulgated its racial laws and began to deport the Venetian Jews to concentration camps – a fact of which we are today reminded by a carved plaque on the wall of the Schola Spagnola.

THE SYNAGOGUES AND MUSEUM. In 1719 there were a total of nine schole; today there are just five remaining. Their names reflect something of the diversity which was to be found within the Jewish community in Venice.

In this scene from Luchino Visconti's 1954 masterpiece, *Senso*, Contessa Livia (Alida Valli) hurries through the labyrinthine Ghetto Nuovo (below) on a way to a tryst with her handsome young Austrian lover.

There was the SCHOLA GRANDE TEDESCA, which appeared on the Campo del Ghetto Nuovo in 1528; the SCHOLA CANTON (1532), which followed the Ashkenazi rite and was so named either after a family or because it stood in the corner of the piazza; and the SCHOLA ITALIANA (1575). The foundation dates of both the SCHOLA LEVANTINA (Eastern Mediterranean) and of the SCHOLA SPAGNOLA, or PONENTINA (Western Mediterranean) are rather less certain. Both were

Sephardic and they stood on the Campiello del Ghetto Nuovo. The main halls of each of these synagogues are extremely impressive. The synagogue in the Ponentina was rebuilt during the course of the 17th century by Longhena, but its rival can still boast a fine portal and, on the inside, some 17th-century carved wood columns. Religious ceremonies are still conducted today in one or other of these two schole, depending on the season. The Schola Grande Tedesca contains a museum of Hebrew art on its ground floor which displays both religious and secular items that were collected from the 17th to 19th centuries. (After the Ponte del Ghetto Nuovo, continue along the Fondamenta degli Ormesini, and then turn right at the second bridge into the Rio terrà Farsetti.)

in the 18th century, whose tombstones were gradually sinking into the sand and vegetation. In 1386, the Jews had obtained permission to bury the dead in this plot of ground by the Lagoon at San Nicolò di Lido. The brotherhood of the Misericordia was responsible for carrying out the burials, and every nation was allotted its own corner of the graveyard.

▲ CANNAREGIO

The gate of SANTA MARIA DEI SERVI.

THE SCUOLA DEI LUCCHESI (Luccans) Many natives of Lucca were forced into exile when Castruccio Castracani took control of their city in 1317. According to the chronicles, thirty Luccan families and at least three hundred artisans arrived in Venice at this time, where they perfected (and perhaps introduced) the art of silk weaving. From the 14th century, these artisans had their own guild, which assembled at the Scuola del Volto Santo. This building burned down in the 1789 fire (see the painting on the right by Francesco Guardi). But the symbol of the Scuola dei Lucchesi, the *volto santo*, is still visible on some of the *patera* decorating the well and the entrance of the Corte del Volto Santo (which looks onto the Rio terrà della Maddalena).

FROM SAN MARCUOLA TO SAN MARZIALE

THE CHURCH OF SAN MARCUOLA. This church's name is an odd contraction of Ermagora and Fortunato, the two saints to whom it was dedicated. Founded in about 1000, and rebuilt in the 12th century on a basilical plan, the building was rebuilt twice more during the 18th century.

The second of these restructurings was supervized by Antonio Gaspari, and then by Giorgio Massari; between them, these two architects made a large portal in the side of the church flanking the Grand Canal, as part of a plan to make this the church's main façade (never completed). So, when you enter the south portal, you discover to your surprise that the high altar is not in front of you but to your right. The single-nave interior is relatively modest in its décor. The altars are by Gianmaria Morlaiter, who sculpted the high altar of La Salute ▲ *318*. Note also Tintoretto's *La Cena* (1547). In 1789 the San Marcuola quarter was seriously damaged by fire, and among the many buildings destroyed was the SCUOLA DEI LUCCHESI. (Take the Rio terrà Dietro la Chiesa and continue as far as the Via Larga Vendramin.)

PALAZZO VENDRAMIN-CALERGI. This is undoubtedly one of the noblest examples of Renaissance architecture in Venice. Francesco Sansovino, official chronicler of the Republic and son of the great architect, called it the finest structure on the Grand Canal. It was probably designed by Mauro Coducci; d'Annunzio has described its "ethereal aspect . . . like a sculpted cloud suspended on the water". The palace was completed at the start of the 16th century. Its owners, the Loredan family, were famous for their pride and, as if to refute this reputation, they had the Templars' motto of humility carved on the base of the façade. After passing through a succession of distinguished owners, the palace became the property of the Calergi, a great feudal family of Cretan origin, and was then passed on to their cousins the Vendramin. The composer Richard Wagner lived and died here in 1883; in 1946 the house was bought by the city of Venice and turned into a winter casino. (At the end of the Calle Larga Vendramin, turn right into the Rio terrà della Maddalena, the first street in Venice to be constructed over a filled-in canal, in 1398.)

THE CHURCH OF SANTA MARIA MADDALENA ● 83. With its smooth, shadowless surfaces, this round Neo-classical building covered in white marble is architecturally unique in

Venice. Built by Tommaso Temanza in the second half of the 18th century, it replaced a demolished 13th-century church. On the outside, it forms a perfect circle; on the inside the plan is hexagonal, with four radial chapels. (After the Ponte Sant'Antonio, take the Salizzada Santa Fosca.)

CAMPO SANTA FOSCA ● 84. A statue of the monk Paolo Sarpi stands at the center of this campo, with the CHURCH OF SANTA FOSCA to one side. Santa Fosca was founded in the 10th century, then rebuilt in 1297 using Byzantine canons to determine its floorplan and orientation. It was demolished in 1679 to make way for a church which had a single nave (as opposed to the previous three naves). Consecrated in 1733, it was completed by Domenico Rossi in 1741, but had to be restored again after a fire near the end of the century. To the left of the façade is a fine 15th-century brick campanile.

THE CHURCH OF SANTA MARIA DEI SERVI. Nothing remains of the group of buildings that was formed by the original 14th-century church and monastery here, except a few interesting elements such as the Gothic portal of the convent. Paolo Sarpi lived in the monastery and Veronese painted his *Supper at Simon Peter's House* (1570–6) for the refectory. This painting was later presented to Louis XIV by the Venetian Republic and is now at Versailles.

THE CHURCH OF SAN MARZIALE. According to legend, a boat ran aground here in 1286, at a point close to the church. It contained an image of the Virgin, placed there by a shepherd from Rimini; the image was removed on the orders of the Doge and displayed inside the church. The building we see today dates from the 17th century. Inside are Tintoretto's *St Martial* and, in the sacristy, Titian's *Tobias and the Angel Gabriel* (1530). (After the bridge, turn left down the Fondamenta della Misericordia and take the Calle Larga).

THE DEATH OF WAGNER
This celebrated death in Venice inspired the Cuban writer Alejo Carpentier: "Passing by the Palazzo Vendramin-Calergi, Montezuma and Filomeno noticed some black figures carrying a coldly glinting metal coffin down to a gondola. 'It's a German, who died yesterday of apoplexy,' said the boatman, pausing for a moment. 'Now they are taking his remains back to his country. They say he wrote peculiar operas . . .' " (*Baroque concert*)

THE ATTACK ON PAOLO SARPI
The monk Paolo Sarpi (1552–1623) was a resolute opponent of Church interference in politics. He defended Venice at the risk of his own life when Rome laid an interdict on the city in 1606. On October 5, 1607, he was wounded by five unknown assailants; afterwards, he accused the Pope, claiming that he recognized the *stylus* (the style, but also the blade) of the Roman Curia.

CAMPO DEI MORI

Beyond the Ponte dei More lies an intriguing "Venice within Venice". **CAMPO DEI MORI.** The name of this campo probably alludes to the presence in the vicinity of the *fondaco,* and houses used by Arab merchants. Three 18th-century statues in front of the houses on the campo, and a fourth on the *fondaco*, are supposed to represent the three

SIOR ANTONIO RIOBA Adorned in the last century with an iron nose, this statue, bearing a burden on its back, stands at the foot of the Ponte dei More. The Venetians invented a character for it, Sior Antonio Rioba, and used him as their mouthpiece when they wanted to criticize the government.

Moorish brothers, Rioba, Sandi and Afani. They were merchants who left Morea (the Peloponnese) to escape civil war. They arrived in Venice in 1112, where they acquired the name of Mastelli, purportedly because "they possessed thousands of buckets (*mastelli*) filled with gold sequins". The

figure in a turban and oriental costume leading a camel, who inhabits the bas-relief on the façade of PALAZZO MASTELLI (on the Campo della Madonna dell'Orto), is a reference to the family's involvement in the spice trade. On the fondamenta, at the foot of the bridge, stands number 3399, Tintoretto's house, where he died in 1594.

MADONNA DELL'ORTO

THE CHURCH OF LA MADONNA DELL'ORTO. This church was dedicated to St Christopher (there is a statue of him by Bartolomeo Bon above the portal); it was rededicated to the Virgin after the discovery of a miraculous statue in a neighboring garden. The building was begun in the late 14th century and completed a hundred years later. It was restored by the British Save Venice Commission after the 1966 floods ■ *26*. Along its red brick façade are a frieze and garlands, ridge ornaments and niches containing statues of the twelve Apostles (from the workshops of the dalle Masegne). The elegant portal belongs to the transition period between Gothic and Renaissance. More than any other church in Venice, this is the shrine of Tintoretto, who is buried in the chapel to the right of the choir. While still a young man, he painted a *Last Judgment* and *Adoration of the Golden Calf* on the choir walls, *The Martyrdom of St Christopher* and the *Vision of the Holy Cross to St Peter* in the apse, and the *Presentation of Mary in the Temple* (above the entrance to the San Mauro chapel on the right of the nave). Also in the church are a masterpiece by Cima da Conegliano from his early days in Venice, *St John the Baptist among the Saints*, and a *Virgin and Child* by Giovanni Bellini in the Valier Chapel.

The Casino degli Spiriti.

SCUOLA DEI MERCANTI. An elegant CLOISTER of the former convent adjoins the church on one side, and on the other stands what was, after 1570, the headquarters of the SCUOLA DEI MERCANTI. As the owners of many houses in the Rialto, the commercial heart of the city, these merchants could, with the profits they made there, indulge in works of charity and assistance to widows and orphans. The interior was decorated with paintings by Tintoretto and Veronese, which were lost during the Napoleonic occupation of Venice. (Leave the campo, which has retained its original herring-bone brick paving, and turn right down the Fondamenta della Madonna dell'Orto.)

CORTE DEL CAVALLO. This courtyard owes its name to the workshop of Andrea del Verrochio and Alessandro Leopardi, in which was cast Bartolomeo Colleoni's famous bronze warhorse, which now stands at the center of the Campo Santi Giovanni e Paolo ▲ 157, 159. (Retrace your steps and continue along the fondamenta.)

PALAZZO CONTARINI DAL ZAFFO. A patrician mansion dating from the late 16th century, the Palazzo Contarini dal Zaffo was famous for the literary debates which took place in its gardens and in the CASINO DEGLI SPIRITI – a small building at the end of the park which overlooks the Sacca della Misericordia and the wide expanse of water beyond. Titian and Aretino, among others, took part in these intellectual joustings. The palazzo is now occupied by a charitable institution.

"This is the derelict palazzo in which Tintoretto lived for 20 years, and later died. He was author of that *Crucifixion*, which contains so many figures bursting with life that one is at a loss to understand how they sprung from a single brain. "
Maurice Barrès,
La Mort de Venise

THE COLLEONE ▲ *159* Andrea del Verrocchio was working on his equestrian statue of Colleone when he heard that another sculptor was to get the commission for the rider, and his work would be confined to the horse. He left Venice in a rage, but not before he had smashed the legs and head of his newly completed warhorse. Threatened with the death penalty, he replied that this would be a great pity . . . "since alive I can still make a more beautiful head for my horse". The authorities were charmed by his humor and aplomb, and doubled his fee.

THE MISERICORDIA

SACCA DELLA MISERICORDIA. This is the "missing piece" of Venice, the cove that was never filled in. (After the bridge, which makes an angle with the fondamenta, continue straight on and turn left along Fondamenta dell'Abbazia.) The route leads past one of the last SQUERI ● 69, ▲ 324 in Venice. These boatyards, which combine work-shops and houses for the gondola builders, are always on the banks sloping down to the water. The buildings themselves are not unlike mountain chalets, a reminder that the first Venetian shipwrights were carpenters from the villages of Northern Italy. (Turn left.)

SCUOLA VECCHIA DELLA MISERICORDIA ● 86. An elegant 14th–15th-century brick construction which was enlarged several times before being remodelled in the Gothic style in about 1451. Also on the CAMPO DELL'ABBAZIA, one of the quietest and most picturesque squares in Venice with its herringbone paving, is the former CHURCH OF SANTA MARIA, called *"di val verde"* ▲ 295 after the island on which it was founded in the 10th century. Note the allegorical statues (by Clemente Moli) on the façade, and the portrait of the patrician Gaspare Moro, who paid for the church to be rebuilt (1651–9).

SCUOLA NUOVA. This was commissioned from Sansovino in 1534 by the brotherhood of La Misericordia, who sold their original building to the silk weavers' guild. It was 50 years before the interior was completed, and the exterior was never finished. (When you reach the PONTE CHIODO – the only bridge in Venice with no parapet – turn down the Fondamenta di San Felice and continue to the Strada Nuova.)

THE STRADA NUOVA

STRADA NUOVA. The Austrians planned to push this major arterial road through to the north of the city, but the project was not realized until 1871–2. Originally named Via Vittorio Emmanuele, it quickly became known as the "Strada Nuova". Running along the Grand Canal, it links the station with the Rialto Bridge. Today it is lined with shops and is very busy, especially at Christmas time and during the Carnival, when it is filled with multi-colored stalls.

THE CHURCH OF SAN FELICE. This 11th–12th-century church was demolished when it threatened to fall down and was rebuilt in 1531. It has a painting by Tintoretto, *St Demetrius and a Votary*. (Turn right and go on to the Ponte Pasqualigo.)

PALAZZO GIOVANELLI. This palace presents an early 15th-century Gothic façade on the Rio di Noale side. It was once famous for its art collection, assembled by the Giovanelli family, which included Giorgione's *Tempest* ▲ 307. It is now the office of a firm of auctioneers. (Turn back and take the Calle della Ca' d'Oro, to the right.)

THE CA' D'ORO: "A DIVINE PLAY OF AIR AND STONE". This mansion is, along with the Doge's Palace, the loveliest expression of the oriental, flowered Gothic style in Venice. Marius Contarini bought the site in 1412. He wanted his palace to be more splendid than all the others, so he involved himself closely in the works,

Before the Campo della Misericordia, pause to admire the GOTHIC GATEWAY to the Corte Nuova. In its three-part lunette, the Madonna opens the folds of her cloak, receiving under her protection the genuflecting brotherhood of the Scuola Vecchia della Misericordia.

The intensely dramatic *St Sebastian* by Andrea Mantegna (1431–1506), on the first floor of the Ca' d'Oro.

> «YOU CANNOT IMAGINE WHAT AN UNHAPPY DAY I SPENT [...] BEFORE THE CA' D'ORO, VAINLY ATTEMPTING TO DRAW IT WHILE THE WORKMEN WERE HAMMERING IT DOWN BEFORE MY FACE.»
>
> JOHN RUSKIN

which were carried out first by Lombard artisans directed by Matteo Raverti, and then by Venetians under Giovanni and Bartolomeo Bon. Before long the building began to be called the "Golden House" (Ca' d'Oro). This gives some idea of the effect of its asymmetrical façade, on which a profusion of gilt was blended with polychrome marble and other adornments; and indeed it must have been staggering to have impressed a city as vivid and luxurious as 15th-century Venice. But decline quickly set in; the Ca' d'Oro changed hands many times and deteriorated over the centuries. It was almost a ruin when the Russian Prince Troubetskoy bought it in 1847, and set in motion a programme of ill-advised restoration. Finally, Baron Giorgio Franchetti, who acquired the building at the end of the century, reconverted the Ca' d'Oro to its original state; the façade recovered its brightness, and the courtyard its staircase and well. In 1916, Franchetti donated his collections, along with the palace, to the state. A museum was opened in 1927, which today contains Carpaccio's *Annunciation* and *Il Transito della Vergine*, Titian's *Venus* and Mantegna's *St Sebastian*. The Franchetti gallery also possesses rare examples of Gothic and Renaissance furniture, 15th- and 16th-century Flemish tapestries, and an interesting collection of medallions, some of which date back to the 15th century. The Ca' d'Oro has been frequently restored this century and is again swathed in scaffolding because its marbles have proved vulnerable to pollution and the vibrations of the vaporetti.

CAMPO SANTA SOFIA. The Church of SANTA SOFIA is only distinguishable by its square campanile, being otherwise invisible among the houses on the Strada Nuova. Near the traghetto, linking the campo to the Pescheria ▲ 285 on the other bank, is the PALAZZO SAGREDO, with its staircase and frescoes by Pietro Longhi (*La Caduta dei Giganti*, 1734).

A FAMOUS OWNER
In 1847, the Russian Prince Alexander Troubetskoy bought the Ca' d'Oro for the great ballerina Maria Taglioni, who collected palaces on the Grand Canal, and commissioned Meduna to restore it. The architect set about disfiguring the building before the horrified gaze of the art critic, John Ruskin, who was then staying in Venice. The "glorious" inside staircase was dismantled; the well, designed by Bartolomeo Bon, was sold; and the marbles of the façade were thrown away, along with the floor tiles.

SANTI APOSTOLI

THE CHURCH OF SANTI APOSTOLI. The original church is thought to have been founded during the 9th century. Partly rebuilt in 1575 and restored several times since then, the present building owes its appearance to restoration work carried out during the mid-18th century. Only the CORNER

CHAPEL of the 16th-century building remains today. Attributed to Mauro Coducci, it contains the tomb of Caterina, Queen of Cyprus ▲ 352. The most notable pictures here are Veronese's *Manna from Heaven* and Tiepolo's *Communion of St Lucia*. The campanile ● 85 is one of the tallest in Venice, and has a tiny shop at its base. Aretino lived nearby, on Rio di San Giovanni Crisostomo, before he moved to the Rialto.

PALAZZO FALIER ● 88. This Venetian-Byzantine palace, which dates from the 13th century, was the home of the Doge Marin Falier, who was beheaded in 1355 after being found guilty of plotting against the Republic ▲ 232.

THE CHURCH OF SAN GIOVANNI CRISOSTOMO. Founded in the 11th century, San Giovanni Crisostomo was then rebuilt in the Renaissance style by Mauro Coducci (late 15th century). The façade bears some resemblance to that of San Zaccaria ▲ 171 and San Michele ▲ 153, both of which were also designed by the same architect. Inside is one of Giovanni Bellini's final works, *St Jerome, St Christopher and St Louis of Toulouse* (1513). At the high altar is Sebastiano del Piombo's celebrated *St John Chrysostom and Saints* (1509–11).

CORTE SECONDA DEL MILION ★. Marco Polo ▲ 281 lived in this small courtyard until the time of his death in January 1324; his house was subsequently burned down in 1596. The courtyard's name recalls the sobriquet that was given to the great explorer by his fellow Venetians, and also the story of his travels, which Marco Polo himself dictated to Rusticello of Pisa during his imprisonment by the Genoese in 1298. Rusticello transcribed the text into Old French, and this subsequently became the basis for the *Livre des Merveilles* (known as *Il Milione* in Italian). On the walls of the houses around here are some fine Venetian-Byzantine friezes and *patera*.

TEATRO MALIBRAN. This theater is thought to occupy part of the site on which Marco Polo's house stood, an unproven theory which is nevertheless commemorated by two plaques: one old one, in Latin, is at 5864 Calle della Chiesa, and a rather more recent one has been erected opposite the Ponte del Teatro. Built by the Grimani family in 1677, the theater was inaugurated as Teatro San Giovanni Crisostomo during the following year. At that time it was the largest and most lavish of all the Venetian lyric theaters. After the Fenice ▲ 262 opened in 1792,

The Church of San Giovanni Crisostomo, flanked by a campanile which was built between 1532 and 1590.

« THE CA' D'ORO IS LIKE THE SMILE OF A WOMAN.
[...] ITS FACE BREATHES HAPPINESS AND SERENITY;
AND THE GRAND CANAL REFLECTS IT.»

ANDRÉ SUARÈS

the Malibran's repertoire was mainly confined to drama –
until Gallo, who purchased it in 1819, brought the programme
back to include operatic works. It was during this time that
the theater was renamed after its benefactor, the Spanish
soprano Malibran. Since then it has been closed down and
reopened on several occasions: today it once again awaits
some further restructuring work. (Return to Campo San
Giovanni Cristostomo, then proceed down Salizzada San
Canciano and turn right into Calle Boldù.)

LA MALIBRAN
Maria Malibran
(1808–36) arrived in
Venice in 1835. She
took lodgings at the
Grand Hotel, near
Palazzo Contarini-
Fasan, where the
legendary
Desdemona is said to
have spent her
childhood. With an
eye to Desdemona's
story, Malibran
elected to sing in
Rossini's *Otello* at the
Fenice. During her
stay in Venice she
heard that a small
local theater was
going bankrupt, and
offered to sing there
for nothing; however
there was still not
enough money, so
Maria threw in
the fee she
received
from the
Fenice. In
gratitude,
the theater
changed
its name to
Malibran.

PALAZZO BEMBO-BOLDÙ. There
is a remarkable statue of
Saturn, or Father Time, set in
the façade of this Gothic
building. The figure is shown as
an old man holding a solar disc.
**THE CHURCH OF SANTA MARIA
DEI MIRACOLI ● *83* ♥.** This

"precious jewel of the
Renaissance" was built between
1481 and 1489 by Pietro
Lombardo as a shrine in which
to house Nicolò di Pietro's
miracle-working *Virgin and
Child*. Like a casket decorated
with marquetry, the entire
building is covered both inside and out with polychrome
marbles. The façade is encrusted with medallions,
porphyry panels and green marble. The interior, with
its tones of light pink, silver-grey and white, is
haloed in a soft light. The beautifully finished
coro pensile (raised choir) was linked to the
adjoining monastery until 1865 and is built
over a kind of crypt. The curious bas-
reliefs, which feature mermaids, Tritons,
small animals, flowers and other figures,
run along the length of the pilasters and
also around the base of the church. The
coffered ceiling is decorated with fifty
panels depicting prophets and
patriarchs.
PALAZZO SORANZO-BAROZZI. The door
to this magnificent Gothic palace on the
Fondamenta delle Erbe is of particular
interest since all of its features are
original, including the spy-hole and
knocker.
THE CHURCH OF SAN CANCIANO. Inside
this ancient and frequently rebuilt
sanctuary, the WIDMANN CHAPEL (which
was built by Longhena and then
subsequently decorated in sumptuous
Baroque style by Clemente Moli) is
particularly worth a visit. The painters
Jacopo da Ponte (who was otherwise
known as Bassano), Leonardo Corona
and Titian all lived within the
surrounding parish. (Cross over the
charming little Campiello del Cason, and
then take the Rio terrà Santi Apostoli.)

The frozen Lagoon from the Fondamente Nuove (right).

THE JESUITS

On the façades of some of the houses in the Campo dei Gesuiti are inscriptions and insignia associated with the old guilds of *sartori* (tailors), *tessitori* (weavers) and *botteri* (coopers).

Young patricians used to play ball games on the Campo dei Gesuiti, but their habit upset the Jesuits, and in 1711 they were asked to find another location. Thenceforth the games were held at San Giacomo dell'Orio ▲ *349*, in the sestiere of Santa Croce. Rather different from early football ▲ *169*, the game involved teams of three men each. The batsman, who wore a studded armband, had to strike the ball while it was in flight, after it had been thrown by another player.

❝On the walls and church squares, green and white marbles are set in one another to form blossoms and floral designs.**❞**
Hippolyte Taine,
Voyage en Italie

ORATORIO DEI CROCIFERI. The order of the *Crociferi*, or Bearers of the Cross, were closely associated with the crusades, during which they wore a grey cross on their tunics. From the mid-12th century, they built a convent, church and hospice on this site. The buildings were burnt down in 1514 and were then rebuilt on a much larger scale. The hospice (which gave shelter to pilgrims and cripples) and the oratory were altered at the end of the 16th century on the intervention of the Doge Pasquale Cicogna. Palma the Younger was commissioned to paint a cycle of canvases which illustrated some of the high points in the history of the order. The artist responded with some of his finest work. Denounced for the laxness of its morals, the order was consequently suppressed in 1656 by Pope Alexander VII. A year later, the Jesuits (who had been driven out of Venice in 1606 as a result of the Republic's rift with Pope Paul V) returned to the city and purchased the Convent of the *Crociferi*.

THE CHURCH OF SANTA MARIA ASSUNTA, OR DEI GESUITI. In 1715, the Jesuits commissioned Domenico Rossi to build them a completely new sanctuary, but without changing the height of the building because a huge monument built by Sansovino for the Da Lezze family occupied the reverse of the façade. Rossi's church was completed in 1729; it took the form of a Latin cross and was decorated in lavish Baroque style. The church reflected favorably not only on the Jesuits, but also on the Manin family, which contributed large sums to the works, and thereby gained the right to burial in the choir, close to the high altar. After the suppression of the Jesuits in 1773, the convent served first as a public school and later, in 1807, as a barracks. With the rehabilitation of the order by Pius VII in 1814, Santa Maria Assunta once again

The cemetery gate
of San Michele.

reverted to the Jesuits, who proceeded to build themselves
another convent on the Fondamente Nuove. It is still
occupied today by members of the order, and is the seat of
the American Jesuit University. Inside Santa Maria Assunta
are several masterpieces, notably Tintoretto's *Assumption of
the Virgin*, and Titian's altarpiece *The Martyrdom of St
Lawrence* in the transept, as well as canvases by Palma the
Younger in the sacristy. Beneath a baldachin, on four
wreathed columns in green and white marble, stands a
colossal Baroque altar, whose tabernacle is encrusted with
lapis lazuli. (Carry on towards the Fondamente Nuove and
turn right. Take the first right-hand street, Calle della Pietà, as
far as the Ramo del Tiziano on the left.)

TITIAN'S HOUSE. A plaque at number 5182–3 marks the site of
the house where Titian lived, and in which he died in 1576.
The Fondamente Nuove were not constructed until 1589, and
thus during the artist's lifetime his house and garden would
have looked directly on to the Lagoon. Returning to the
Fondamente Nuove, you can board the ferry to Burano ▲
370, Torcello ▲ 374,
Murano ▲ 364, or
San Michele.

THE ISLAND OF
THE DEAD

**THE CEMETERY OF
SAN MICHELE.**
Before entering
Venice proper,
travellers and fishermen from Murano, Burano, Torcello or
the other islands in the lagoon used to stop off at the two
small islands just off the Fondamente Nuove – San Cristoforo
della Pace and San Michele (which at one time was called
"Cavana de Muran", or the Murano shelter). San Cristoforo
was chosen as a site for a public cemetery in 1807 by the
Napoleonic authorities. The architect Antonio Selva was
commissioned to carry out this project, which was
subsequently interrupted for a while

due to a lack of funds. In 1836 the canal between the two islets was filled in, but the building works were not finally completed until 1870. A plaque at the cemetery gate recalls that this island also served as a prison. Arrested in 1820 by the Austrian occupants of Venice, the Italian patriot Silvio Pellico, author of *My Prisons*, was held captive here after a year in the "Leads" ▲ 252. He was to spend the final period of his long imprisonment at the Spielberg near Brno, a Hapsburg state jail.

THE CHURCH AND MONASTERY OF SAN MICHELE. These two buildings, which stand at the cemetery entrance, were constructed between 1469 and 1535. The Renaissance church, in white Istrian stone, was the first of its kind designed by Mauro Coducci. In front of the main portal is the tombstone of Fra Paolo Sarpi, whose ashes were transported to the Church of Santa Maria dei Servi ▲ 145 in 1828. The cartographer Fra Mauro was a distinguished 15th-century inmate of the monastery. He was the author of a celebrated planisphere (which is now held at the Libreria Marciana ▲ 254). The small 15th-century Gothic CLOISTER is well worth seeing.

CAPPELLA EMILIANA. Built by Guglielmo dei Grigi, known as Guglielmo Bergamasco, this "round, white chapel, sculpted with shells and adorned with pink and green marble cabochons", as Michèle Manceaux describes it, is crowned by an unusual dome entirely covered with white stones.

DEATH IN VENICE. San Michele, hidden behind its pink walls and shaded by cypress trees, is one of the few cemeteries on earth to which the dead are brought by boat. In the old days, they would have been borne gently across the water from the city in funeral gondolas, which were richly decorated with gold-winged angels. These vessels were subsequently replaced by modern motorboats, which were fitted out as floating hearses. Today the island can accommodate no further graves, and Venice now has to send her dead to the mainland for burial.

THE TOMBS OF THE FAMOUS AT SAN MICHELE. In a section of the cemetery set apart for foreigners (Greek Square, XIV), among the tombs of Russian princesses and Greek queens, lie the mortal remains of the composer Igor Stravinsky (1882–1971) and Serge Diaghilev of the Russian Ballet (1872–1929). The grave of the American poet Ezra Pound (1885–1972) is located in square XV.

DIAGHILEV
In 1929, Diaghilev came to Venice. Convinced his end was near, he called his friend Misia Sert to join him. On August 18, he fell into a coma and died the following day. His body was put on a funeral gondola and carried across the Lagoon for burial.

CASTELLO

ARC DEL PARADISO
CHURCH OF SANTA MARIA FORMOSA
SCUOLA DI SAN MARCO
CHURCH OF SANTI GIOVANNI E PAOLO
PALAZZO PRIULI
CHURCH OF SANTA MARIA DEI DERELITTI
CHURCH OF SAN GIORGIO DEI GRECI
SCUOLA DI SAN GIORGIO DEGLI SCHIAVONI
CHURCH OF SAN F DELLA VIGN

RIALTO BRIDGE
HOTEL DANIELI
PALAZZO QUERINI-STAMPALIA
CHURCH OF SAN ZACCARIA
CHURCH OF LA PIETÀ
PALAZZO GRITTI-BADOER
CHURCH OF SAN IN BRAGORA

THE DOGE'S DREAM
Tradition has it that Giacomo Tiepolo, the 41st Doge of Venice (1229–49), had the following dream one night: a swamp area of the Lagoon, which later became Campo Santi Giovanni e Paolo, was covered with magnificent flowers. White doves with the sign of the cross on their heads flew overhead. Then he heard a voice saying: "I have chosen this place for my ministry." Having informed the senate of this divine message, the Doge obtained leave for the Dominicans to build a monastery on the spot. The order had been established in Venice for a decade, but they were living in difficult conditions, in tents under the portico of the Church of San Martino. The monastery church was dedicated, perhaps on the request of the Doge himself, to the martyred brothers John and Paul, who were put to death in Rome during the 4th century.

The maps show Venice as shaped like a fish, and Castello is its tail. It is the largest and most varied of the six sestieri and also, most importantly, the home of the Arsenal, which stands behind its high towers like a forbidden city within a city. The establishment of this naval dockyard on the Isole Gemini (twin islands) at the start of the 13th century was crucial to the area's development. All kinds of related activities grew up around what was to become the largest naval complex in Europe, along with the modest homes of dockworkers and sailors; later, foreign communities sprang up and even a few palazzos. The northern part of the sestiere was controlled by the Mendicant orders (Dominicans and Franciscans), whose charitable institutions (*ospedali*) proliferated. Their presence became an overwhelming feature of the area. The Arsenal lay halfway between the political and mercantile centers of San Marco and the Rialto to the west, and the religious center of the island of San Pietro to the east. Already, during the time of Aretino, a fortress (*castello*) had been built on San Pietro, from which the name of the sestiere probably derives. There was another island in the vicinity, known for centuries as l'Olivolo on account of its olive shape,

Veduta di SS. Giovanni, e Paolo.

156

THE ARSENAL   PUBLIC GARDENS   BIENNALE GARDENS   CHURCH OF SAN PIETRO DI CASTELLO   SANT'ELENA

which
had its own
Church of San
Pietro; in 775 this church
became the seat of the Venetian
episcopate and remained so for a
thousand years. While San Pietro is one of the
islands longest inhabited by man in the Lagoon of
Venice, its neighbor Sant'Elena (which now constitutes the
most south-eastern point of the sestiere) was not built upon
until very late. Napoleonic town planning was responsible for
creating a whole series of public gardens here, which today
provide the location for the Venice Biennale, and he also

🗎 One day

opened up the Via Eugenia,
now known as the Via
Garibaldi. In the great museum-
city that Venice has become
since the passing of her glory, in
this city where nothing can be
changed or taken away, Castello
is one of the few districts to
have been substantially modified in the 20th century – hence
the new quarters of Sant'Elena, Celestia and the south-
eastern tip of San Pietro.

SANTI GIOVANNI E PAOLO ● 78

THE CAMPO SAN ZANIPOLO, a Venetian dialect
contraction of the Christian names of Giovanni
and Paolo, was proudly referred to by Venetians
until the 19th century as the *Campo delle
Maravege* (campo of marvels). Some say this was because of
certain remarkable happenings that occurred there, while
others think the name derives from the campo's splendid
monuments. At the center of the square, which was paved in
1592 by Dominican friars, stands the great equestrian statue
of the *condottiere* Colleoni.

CAMPO
DI SS. GIOVANNI
E PAOLO

"This deserted
square between San
Zanipolo, the cloister
of the Scuola and, in
the background, the
Rio dei Medicanti,
spanned by a little
bridge that looks
like
two
hands
joined
at the
fingertips – this
square looks like a
theater set after the
play is over."
Louis Aragon,
*Les Voyageurs
de l'impériale*

157

CONSTRUCTION OF THE CHURCH OF SANTI GIOVANNI E PAOLO.
The Dominicans began building this church at the end of the 13th century, after draining the swamp given to them by the Republic in 1234. A donation from the Grand Council in 1390 allowed them to enlarge it, and it was consecrated in 1430.
GOTHIC GRANDEUR. This church, and the Frari ▲ *292*, between them represent the most ambitious expression of Gothic

MARSHES AND LAGOON
The strip of land which extends from the bridge across the Rio dei Mendicanti to the Fondamente Nuove ▲ *153* was reclaimed by determined hard work.

architecture in Venice. The five apses at the rear of the building, like the façade with its soaring central structure, are remarkable examples of the architectural style of the 14th century. The red brick main entrance, built in 1458 to plans drawn up by Antonio Gambello, is representative of the transitional period between Gothic and Renaissance. The entrance is flanked by columns from a church on Torcello which has now been demolished.
A VENETIAN PANTHEON. Like the Frari, SANTI GIOVANNI E PAOLO is something of a memorial to the glories of Venice's past. No fewer than twenty-five Doges, whose tombs were in many cases sculpted by great masters such as Lombardo or Giovanni Buora, lie buried in this sanctuary. It was here, from the 15th century, that the funeral rites of the first magistrates were invariably celebrated. The church also contains the tombs of such legendary figures as Vettor Pisani, Ludovico Diedo and Sebastiano Venier, the victor of Lepanto ● *36*.

«I STOOD IN FRONT OF THE CHURCH OF SAINTS JOHN AND PAUL, CONTEMPLATING THE SMALL HEAD AND SQUARE JAW OF BARTOLOMEO COLLEONI, THE DREADED CONDOTTIERE.»

HENRY JAMES

There is even an urn containing the skin of Marcantonio Bragadin who, after the fall of Famagusta in 1571, the last Venetian citadel in Cyprus ● *33, 36*, was flayed alive by his Turkish captors.

THE TREASURES OF SANTI GIOVANNI E PAOLO. Among the most notable works of art in the church are a *Polyptych of St Vincent Ferrier* by Giovanni Bellini, *The Almsgiving of St Anthony* by Lorenzo Lotto, *St Dominic in Glory* by Piazzetta and, in the CAPPELLA DELLA ROSARIO, several paintings by Veronese. There is also an altarpiece by Longhena (1638) and a large narrative stained glass window fashioned by the master glassblowers of Murano.

THE CONDOTTIERE Bartolomeo Colleoni was one of the most noteworthy figures in Italian political and social life during the 15th century. A *condottiere* from Bergamo, Colleoni reached the summit of his career when he was appointed to be permanent captain-general of the Venetian army. As a reward for his loyal service, the Republic gave him the fiefdom of Malpaga, on the Milanese border. But they failed to fulfill exactly all the conditions of Colleoni's will, by which he bequeathed his possessions to the Republic. One of these conditions was that a statue should be erected in his memory in Piazza San Marco soon after his death (1475). Since it was forbidden by law to build any monument in the great square, the Senate solved this dilemma by placing the statue in front of the Scuola Grande di San Marco. The figure was sculpted by the Tuscan artist Andrea del Verrocchio ▲ *147*, and then cast in bronze after his death by Alessandro Leopardi, who also added a pedestal and signed his name on the horse's girth. The statue of Colleoni was finally unveiled on March 21, 1496.

THE SCUOLA DI SAN MARCO ★ ● *86*

This charitable institution, founded in 1260, had many prominent Venetians among its members. First established in the Santa Croce quarter, it was transferred to the Campo Santi Giovanni e Paolo in 1437. In 1485 a fire destroyed the original wooden structure, which had a fine spiral staircase designed by Gentile Bellini. The reconstruction was assigned in 1489 to Pietro Lombardo, who was then working on the Doge's Palace ▲ *224*, and to Giovanni Buora. The two architects decided to retain the original plan of the building and place a smaller gallery for restricted meetings above the main hall, with its double row of columns. Mauro Coducci, who was later called in to mediate in a quarrel between the Grand Guardian of the brotherhood and the architects, himself ended up as the *proto* (commissioned architect) for the scuola. His contribution to the façade, which has a broad projecting portal, may be seen in its upper parts. In terms of its art treasures, the Scuola di San Marco was for many years the richest guild in Venice. It held the *Miracles of St Mark* by Tintoretto (now divided between the Accadamia ▲ *301* and the Brera Museum in Milan), and canvases by Palma the Elder and Paris Bordone. In 1815 the Austrians demolished Coducci's monumental outside staircase, along with some of his other additions, and converted the building into a hospital, which it remains to this day. (Walk along the façade of the scuola.)

I MENDICANTI

THE CHURCH OF THE MENDICANTI. Now closed, this church was once dedicated to the patron saint of lepers who, until the 16th century, were treated in the same way as indigents in Venice. It was attached to the charity hospital, the two wings of which enclose it. The architect was Scamozzi (1552–1616), and the façade was executed by Giuseppe Sardi (1673). While adopting his predecessor's design, this Baroque architect still respected the church's original classical form. (Return to the campo.)

I DERELITTI

> "The light from the bright sky reflected through to the courtyard. . . . In this small space, half-room, half-garden, the air was tepid, smelling of grapes. The silence was so complete that one heard the flutter of a bird hopping from perch to perch."
>
> Hugo von Hofmannsthal, *Andreas*

BARBARIA DELLE TOLE. The street owes its name to the great timber warehouses (*tole* in Venetian) that once stood here. The term *barbaria* (Barbary) is more debatable; it may allude to the formerly somewhat lawless character of the place, to the tough lumberjacks from the mountains who handled the timber, or to its exportation to North Africa (Barbary), from where the Venetian word *barbe* (wooden planks) comes.

THE CHURCH OF SANTA MARIA DEI DERELITTI ● 83. This is also known as the Church of the Ospedaletto, because it is an integral part of this nearby charitable institution. The façade (1670–2) and high altar were designed by Longhena. His forcefully projecting architectural elements lend emphasis to the whole, which is made more interesting by the grotesque masks, lion heads and caryatids in the façade's upper register (sculpted by Josse Le Court). Inside is *The Sacrifice of Isaac*, an early masterpiece by Giambattista Tiepolo.

THE OSPEDALETTO. The Republic created this institution in 1527 as a shelter for cripples, old people and indigent young women. In 1661 Sardi accepted the task of enlarging and restructuring the building, but he soon became embroiled in legal difficulties with his clients and was replaced by Longhena. Like many other institutions of its type, the Ospedaletto gradually changed its function with the passing of time. As in the Mendicanti ▲ 159, the Incurabili ▲ 322 and the Pietà ▲ 174, which housed poor or illegitimate girls, orphans and abandoned children, the education of the young inmates was heavily biased in favor of music. In the 18th century, these four *ospedali* became conservatories in all but name, with music taught by Venice's greatest masters; by the same token, the churches attached to the *ospedali* became concert halls, where talented pupils regularly performed.

TOWARDS SAN FRANCESCO DELLA VIGNA

I DERELITTI
The church beside the hospice contains artworks from the 17th and 18th centuries, which combine to make it a mini-museum. Note especially *The Sacrifice of Isaac* and *Two Apostles*, which are early works by Giambattista Tiepolo. The entrance is by way of a rest home which includes the Ospedaletto.

THE FORMER CHURCH OF SANTA GIUSTINA. Today, the only vestige of what used to be a substantial religious complex of church and monastery is a mutilated 17th-century façade. The Church of Santa Giustina may date from as far back as the 9th century, although it first appears in Venetian chronicles during the 12th century. During the 15th and 17th centuries the building was extensively altered; then a bequest by Giovanni Soranzo, procurator of San Marco, made possible the construction of its celebrated façade. Work began in 1640

The Corte Nuova, photographed at the turn of the century.

under the direction of Baldassare Longhena. Four columns were raised in order to support a high coping, whose curvilinear pediment was then crammed with various statues of the benefactor and his children; they were removed in 1844, when the church was turned into a military school. On October 7 every year, the Doge attended Mass at Santa Giustina to give thanks for the victory of Lepanto ● *36*. (Walk from here along the Fondamenta Santa Giustina and the Calle San Francesco.)

SAN FRANCESCO DELLA VIGNA
In this zone of the Castello sestiere, the Venetian nobles used to practise archery and horsemanship.

THE CHURCH OF SAN FRANCESCO DELLA VIGNA. The name *della vigna* would seem to evoke the vineyards with which this site used to be covered. In 1253 the vineyards were given to the Franciscans by Marco Ziani, son of the Doge Pietro Ziani. They immediately set about building a monastery and church on the site, at a time when this northern part of the sestiere was largely undeveloped. The Franciscan church was rebuilt in 1534 by Jacopo Sansovino. It took the form of a Latin cross, flanked by five chapels on either side of its nave. For the façade (1562–72) the friars chose Andrea Palladio, the architect of the Church of the Redentore ▲ *338* and of San Giorgio Maggiore ▲ *340*. He applied his own balanced, rational brand of classicism, creating architectural harmony through a subtle play of triangles and rectangles. Inside is Veronese's altarpiece *Sacra Conversazione* (1562). Between the church and lagoon, the monastery with its three cloisters offers one of Venice's better examples of 14th-century Gothic.

The covered walkway that runs between the Palazzo Gritti and the Church of San Francesco della Vigna.

PALAZZO GRITTI. This Renaissance building at the corner of the campo once belonged to the Doge Andrea Gritti. It was nicknamed "La Nunziatura", because the government bought it for use as a residence for papal nuncios under Pope Pius IV. Ceded to the Franciscans in the 19th century, it was linked to the convent by footbridge. (Take the Salizzada San Francesco, then the Salizzada delle Gatte, to reach CAMPIELLO UGO FOSCOLO, where a plaque indicates the house of the poet Foscolo, who spent his adolescence in Venice between 1792 and 1797. Turn right, after the Ramo Ponte, take Salizzada Santa Giustina and Calle Zorzi to the Corte Nuova. Note, in passing, the tiny chapel under the *sottoportego*. From here, take the Fondamenta San Giorgio degli Schiavoni.)

THE SCHIAVONIA
Dalmatia (which roughly corresponds to today's Croatia) was the first foreign region to be conquered by the Republic, and the first jewel in Venice's crown. It was much prized by succeeding generations.

SAINT GEORGE AND THE DRAGON
The lance emphasizes one of the diagonals which divide the painting shown below into four triangular masses – the monster and the city, the bone-strewn foreground, the knight on horseback and the young girl, and the sky. Here, color acquires value in the overall construction, because each of these four zones has its own color scheme.

SAN GIORGIO DEGLI SCHIAVONI ★

SCUOLA SAN GIORGIO DEGLI SCHIAVONI. People from Dalmatia (Schiavoni) began to establish themselves in Venice at the start of the 15th century. Most were sailors or artisans, who quickly formed themselves into a scuola, the regulations (*mariegole*) of which were approved by the Council of Ten on May 19, 1485. The new scuola started out at the hospice of the Knights of Malta, who later allotted its members an altar of their own in the hospice church. The Dalmatian community grew rapidly in importance and eventually resolved to build its own headquarters. Between 1480 and 1501 the scuola raised a modest structure with a brick façade fronting the Fondamenta San Antonin. To decorate it, the Dalmatians commissioned ten paintings from Carpaccio, which they placed in a gallery on the upper floor. In 1551, the scuola was pulled down and rebuilt by Giovanni de Zan, but he decided to retain the original plan of two galleries and a sacristy. The paintings were moved to the ground floor, to the panelled gallery where they may be seen today. This scuola is one of the very few in Venice which has preserved its artistic heritage intact: moreover, it reveals a side to Venice that is unexpectedly tranquil and intimate.
CARPACCIO'S PAINTINGS ▲ *306.* Carpaccio's décor, created between 1502 and 1507, includes nine canvases that illustrate episodes from the lives of the three Dalmatian patron saints,

> «IN THIS LITTLE CHAPEL [...] SATURATED WITH THE ODOR OF
> INCENSE, [...] CARPACCIO'S PAINTINGS ARE MORE MOVING
> THAN THEY WOULD EVER BE IN A MUSEUM.»
>
> JEAN-LOUIS VAUDOYER

St George, St Tryphon and St Jerome. He took his theme
from the *Golden Legend* of Jacobus de Voragine, Archbishop
of Genoa, an excellent version of which (translated from

Latin by Nicolao
Manerbi) was printed in
Venice in 1475. The
order in which the
canvases are exhibited
bears no relation to the
chronological order in
which they were painted.
Thus the two paintings
dedicated to St George (painted in 1507) are placed at the
beginning of the cycle.

SAINT GEORGE. The *Golden Legend* relates that George, a
tribune and native of Cappadocia, happened to pass through
"Silcha, a provincial town in Libya". Here he saved
the life of the king's daughter, who was about to
be devoured by a dragon then terrorizing the
neighborhood. After slaying this monster,
the intrepid youth converted the entire
local population to Christianity.
Carpaccio's rendering of this tale is one
of his most celebrated masterpieces: *St
George and the Dragon*. In all the history
of painting there is perhaps no
handsomer St George than this young,
blond knight, mounted on a black charger,
whose silhouette against a clear background
evokes a design from heraldry. The next
painting shows the triumph of the knight
finishing off the dragon in the town square.

OTHER WORKS. The two paintings that follow were the last
that Carpaccio did for the Dalmatians. They represent *The
Baptism of the King* and *The Miracle of St Tryphon*. This saint,
a patron of the town of Cattaro on the east coast of the
Adriatic, was born in Bithynia (in Asia Minor) and died a
martyr. He is shown liberating the daughter of the Emperor
Gordian from the clutches of the Devil. Next to this painting
are the first two pictures commissioned from Carpaccio by the
Scuola. These are the only ones that do not relate to patron
saints of the Dalmatians: they are *The Vocation of Saint
Matthew* and *Christ at Prayer on the Mount of Olives*.

THE SAINT JEROME TRILOGY. These three paintings, which
date from 1502, are dedicated to St Jerome, father of the
Vulgate Latin translation of the Bible and a reformer of the

**THE VISION OF SAINT
JEROME**
Pure wealth of detail
makes this work
unique in the history
of Venetian art.

The
meticulousness and
realism of the
Flemish school are
both to some extent
echoed here, but they
are expressed within
an architectural
concept of space
which appears to
have been a heritage
of Tuscan art. Finally,
there is exquisite
color, which is always
a fundamental
component of
Carpaccio's poetical
insight.

**THE DEATH OF SAINT
JEROME**
Here, the background
is dominated by
browns, while in
the foreground
monks in white and
blue vestments form
a circle around the
body of the saint,
suggested by a light
stroke of the brush.

163

Christian liturgy. The first painting represents *The Miracle of the Lion*, with the saint seen pulling a thorn from a lion's paw. Although this event is supposed to have occurred in the East, the background depicts the Scuola and the Church of the Knights of Malta (the building on the right with the wooden porch). Next to it are *The Death of St Jerome* and a painting known as *The Vision of St Jerome*, which in fact is a representation of St Augustine hearing his own death announced by the voice of Jerome. In a concession to contemporary taste, the saint is portrayed with the features of Cardinal Bessarion, first patron of the Scuola ▲ *254*. (Take the Fondamenta dei Furlani and turn right onto the Salizzada dei Greci.)

SAN GIORGIO DEI GRECI ★

Standing out starkly in this quiet backwater, the buildings of the community form a tightly knit architectural ensemble and an enclave of silence and calm.

THE GREEK COMMUNITY. Already present in Venice from the early 11th century, Greeks began to arrive in substantial numbers during the 14th and 15th centuries under the pressure of Ottoman expansion. After the fall of Constantinople in 1453, a large proportion of Greek refugees were taken in by the Venetians; before long they formed the city's largest ethnic community after the Jews. About four thousand resident Greeks were counted by a census in the second half of the 15th century. Most of these were merchants, book publishers, artists, scribes and literary scholars. To begin with they were authorized to celebrate orthodox rites in several churches (among them San Stae ▲ *350*), but from 1470 onwards, a decree of the Council of Ten restricted them to a single chapel in the church of San Biagio. In 1526, the Greek community was given autonomous status vis-à-vis the patriarchate of Venice and authorized to celebrate its own orthodox cult. Permission was also given to the Greeks to acquire a large site beside the Rio di San Lorenzo. This they cleared, demolishing several buildings in the process, and then went on to build a church, a college, a scuola, a cemetery and a number of private houses. Most of this new complex was designed by Longhena. In 1678, the site was closed off on the Rio dei Greci side with a barrier which was designed by Longhena in such a way that it did not obstruct the view from the buildings.

The campanile, built between 1587 and 1592, leans to one side because of subsidence beneath its foundation.

THE CHURCH OF SAN GIORGIO DEI GRECI. The original architect of this church was Sante Lombardo, who was succeeded by Giannantonio Chiona in 1539. The simple, elegant lines of the façade resemble the work of Sansovino, the architect of the Libraria Marciana on St Mark's Square ▲ *254*. Distinctive elements on the inside are the women's stalls (above the entrance) and the iconostasis. Most of the icons here

The Madonna with the symbols of the Passion, an icon by Emmanuel Lombardos dating from the early 17th century.

were painted by Michele Damaskinos, a 16th-century Cretan artist and a fellow citizen and contemporary of Domenikos Theotokopoulos, better known as El Greco. The atmosphere in this church is perhaps more intimate than in other Venetian sanctuaries, and the Orthodox rites are still celebrated here, despite the fact that the Greek community in Venice has dwindled to barely a hundred souls.

SCUOLA DI SAN NICOLÒ DEI GRECI. Founded in 1498 to defend the rights of the Greek community, this scuola was first located at San Stae; after the acquisition of the Rio di San Lorenzo site, it moved to buildings of its own designed by Baldassare Longhena. Today, the scuola is an icon museum, containing one of the most important collections of its kind in Europe. It also possesses a number of other religious objects, many of which are marvels of Byzantine art, along with the works of celebrated Greek artists who lived in Venice (notably the 15th–17th century painters Michele Damaskinos, Giorgio Klotzas, Emmanuel Zane and the Cypriot Giovanni da Cipro).

THE HELLENIC INSTITUTE. This scholarly foundation occupies the Palazza Flanghini, a short distance farther on, which was formerly the Collegio Greco and was designed by Longhena. The Institute specializes in Byzantine and post-Byzantine studies, and has extraordinarily rich archives, as one would expect given the rôle played by Venice in the Mediterranean basin. They contain, among other things, some rare documents on Crete, the Ionian Islands, Cyprus and the Peloponnese, which for centuries were colonies of Venice in the Levant.

Inside the Church of San Giorgio dei Greci: the dome, the iconostasis and a detail of an icon.

This water-colored lithograph (opposite) by Joseph Nash shows the iconostasis as a partition dividing the nave of San Giorgio dei Greci from the choir, a feature which was obligatory in Greek Orthodox churches.

165

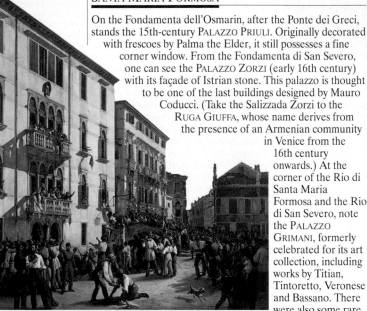

SANTA MARIA FORMOSA

On the Fondamenta dell'Osmarin, after the Ponte dei Greci, stands the 15th-century PALAZZO PRIULI. Originally decorated with frescoes by Palma the Elder, it still possesses a fine corner window. From the Fondamenta di San Severo, one can see the PALAZZO ZORZI (early 16th century) with its façade of Istrian stone. This palazzo is thought to be one of the last buildings designed by Mauro Coducci. (Take the Salizzada Zorzi to the RUGA GIUFFA, whose name derives from the presence of an Armenian community in Venice from the 16th century onwards.) At the corner of the Rio di Santa Maria Formosa and the Rio di San Severo, note the PALAZZO GRIMANI, formerly celebrated for its art collection, including works by Titian, Tintoretto, Veronese and Bassano. There were also some rare coins and Greek and Roman statues, but these were donated to the city of Venice in 1586 and two centuries later became the first treasures of the Museum of Archeology ▲ 255.

CAMPO SANTA MARIA FORMOSA. This campo, which cuts through the dense urban fabric of the Castello sestiere, is one of the largest open squares in Venice. Around it stand a variety of palaces. Immediately to the left of the Ruga Giuffa is the PALAZZO MALIPIERO-TREVISAN, which was mostly rebuilt at the start of the 16th century by the Trevisan family and boasts an all-white façade studded with medallions of porphyry and green marble. PALAZZO VITTURI, a 13th-century Venetian-Byzantine building, has a quadriform window with the point of each arch crowned by a *patera*, like the dot on an "i". Farther on, PALAZZO DONA has a 15th-century lunette in which an angel and *putti* brandish the arms of the Dona family. The corner of the campo is occupied by PALAZZO RUZZINI, with its elegant openwork balcony designed by Bartolomeo Manopola, one of the architects of the Doge's Palace. The Ruzzina, a rich family from Constantinople, built this mansion here after a fire destroyed their residence at San Giovanni Crisostomo.

THE SACK OF PALAZZO QUERINI-STAMPALIA During Manin's provisional government ● 34, ▲ 275, the palace was the lodging of Jacopo Monico, patriarch of Venice, who lived on its upper floor. There was a rumor that the patriarch and a group of patricians favored the capitulation of the city. On August 3, 1849, a group of rioters penetrated the patriarch's apartments in his absence and wrecked the lower floor, which was the home of Count Giovanni, the last of the Querinis.

THE CHURCH OF SANTA MARIA FORMOSA. Santa Maria Formosa is supposed to have been one of the eight sanctuaries founded in the 7th century by St Magnus, Bishop of Oderzo in Friuli. Using the foundations of the 11th-century building, the architect Mauro Coducci reconstructed the church in 1492 with three naves, giving it

A canal adjoining the campo Santa Maria Formosa.

the form of a Latin cross. In 1542, the wealthy Cappello family built on a main façade as a memorial to Vincenzo Cappello, admiral of the Venetian fleet and conqueror of the Turks. In 1604, a second façade overlooking the campo was added: here again, three busts of the admiral attest to the contemporary fashion for transforming church fronts into monuments to individuals. The interior, characterized by an odd chromatic play of grey and white, contains paintings by Bartolomeo Vivarini (*Triptych*, 1473), Palma the Younger, Palma the Elder and Giambattista Tiepolo. The dome was rebuilt twice, after an earthquake in 1668, and after an Austrian bombardment in 1916. Numerous scuole and corporations had altars and chapels in the church, notably the SCUOLA DEI BOMBARDIERI (mortar manufacturers) and SCUOLA DEI CASSELLERI (artisans who made lavish nuptial chests for young brides). The CAMPANILE, which is decorated on all sides with geometrical motifs in relief, was designed by the priest Francesco Zucconi (1611–88). Its entrance is crowned with a grimacing face ● *84* which looks like the mask of an actor. This type of decoration became common in 17th-century Venice due to the success of a new theatrical genre, the melodrama. (Go round the church to the Campiello Querini-Stampalia.)

THE QUERINI-STAMPALIA FOUNDATION. Several members of the Querini family were banished from Venice for their part in the plot hatched against the Seignory in 1310 by Bajamonte Tiepolo ▲ *214*. They took refuge on Stampalia, a Greek island which they owned, and their branch of the patrician family became known thereafter as Querini-Stampalia. In 1868 the last bearer of the name, Count Giovanni, bequeathed his palace, complete with furniture, works of art and historical documents, to the city of Venice. His wish was that a library should be opened in his apartments, and that his collections should be properly preserved: in addition to the house, this man of science left a substantial sum of money to pay for his foundation. In accordance with the count's will, the Palazzo Querini-Stampalia now contains an immense library and museum. In rooms which were occupied during the mid-19th century by the patriarch of Venice, there is a collection of furniture, bibelots and sculptures. The picture gallery contains more than seven hundred works of the Venetian school, notably paintings by Pietro Longhi and a collection of canvases by Gabriele Bella illustrating the daily life of Venice during the 18th century. In the 1960's this Renaissance palace on the curve of the canal was restored and restructured by the architect Carlo Scarpa ▲ *346*, who added a little bridge spanning the canal and laid out new gardens. (Return to the campo.)

FEAST OF THE MARIAS
On January 30 every year, as a token of thanks to the *casselleri* for freeing some young girls who were kidnapped by pirates from Istria and Trieste in the 10th century, the Doge went to Santa Maria Formosa, where he was given two gilded straw hats (an example is at the Correr Museum). On the same occasion, the six sestieri endowed twelve poor but pretty girls, known as the "Marias"; they were dressed in rich clothes and paraded down the Grand Canal to San Pietro di Castello ▲ *182*.

The gardens of the Palazzo Querini-Stampalia, restored by Carlo Scarpa.

BELLA was born in Venice in 1730. In his modest but prolific work, he chronicled the customs and daily life of the Serene Republic at the time when Venice was at the height of her power. Bella's paintings are invariably enlivened by crowds of people and illustrate political institutions, official receptions, lay and religious feasts and public sports .

CEREMONIES OF VENICE
Following his election, the Doge mounted the *pozzetto*, which was carried shoulder high across Saint Mark's Square by the workers of the Arsenal (right). As he went among the crowd, he scattered coins that were newly minted with his effigy.

RECEPTIONS

In 1782, the heir to
the throne of Russia
and his wife visited
Venice incognito, as
the "Comte and
Comtesse du Nord".
They attended a
concert given in their
honor by the young
orphans of the four
ospedali (left).

GAMES

In order to keep
themselves fit and
active, Venetian
nobles often played
various types of
ballgames. Spectators
stood around the
pitch, cheering on the
players representing
their particular
faction.

RELIGIOUS FEASTS

The Good Friday procession (above), attended
by patricians, members of the Scuole Grandi
▲ 295 and various prelates. The Church of San
Geminiano, destroyed in 1808 to make way for
Napoleon's new building, is in the background.

"After dinner, I went out by myself, into the heart of the enchanted city where I found myself wandering in strange regions like a character in the Arabian Nights. . . . I had plunged into a network of little alleys, *calli,* dissecting in all directions by their ramifications the quarter of Venice isolated between a canal and the lagoon, as if it had crystallized along these innumerable, slender, capillary lines. All of a sudden, at the end of one of those little streets, it seemed as though a bubble had occurred in the crystallized matter. A vast and splendid *campo* of which I could certainly never, in this network of little streets, have guessed the importance, or even found room for it, spread out before me flanked with charming palaces silvery in the moonlight. It was one of those architectural wholes towards which, in any other town, the streets converge, lead you and point the way. Here it seemed to be deliberately concealed in a labyrinth of alleys, like those palaces in oriental tales to which mysterious agents convey by night a person who, taken home again before daybreak, can never again find his way back to the magic dwelling which he ends by supposing that he visited only in a dream.**"**

Marcel Proust,
Albertine Disparue

> «NOTHING IS SIMPLER THAN TO LOSE ONESELF IN VENICE; AND NOTHING IS MORE FUN THAN TO BE IN THIS LABYRINTH WITHOUT A MINOTAUR, AS A THESEUS WITHOUT AN ARIADNE'S THREAD! »
> JEAN-LOUIS VAUDOYER

CALLE DEL PARADISO ● 93. This calle, lined with overhanging buildings, owes its name to the lanterns with which it was decorated on Good Friday. It is entered through a 15th-century Gothic archway, on which is sculpted (between the arms of Foscari and Mocenigo) a Madonna protecting a bride and groom beneath her mantle. They are members of the families to whom the corner houses belonged. (In the Salizzada di San Lio, turn left. At number 5484 in the CORTE PERINA stands the house of the painter Canaletto.)

THE CHURCH OF SAN LIO. The original Church of St Catherine (11th century) was rebuilt in 1054 and dedicated to Pope Leo IX (*Lio*, in the Venetian dialect), who joined Venice in defending the cause of the Patriarch of Grado against the pretentions of Aquileia. The Renaissance GUSSONI CHAPEL, built by Pietro and Tullio Lombardo, contains *Saint James on the Road*, a late work by Titian, and *St Leo Exalting the Cross* and *Angels and Virtues* by Giandomenico Tiepolo.

THE CHURCH OF SANTA MARIA DELLA CONSOLAZIONE. The original name of this church was "della Fava", prior to the construction of the present building, which was begun in 1704 by Gaspari and completed by Massari in 1750. It contains an early work by Giambattista Tiepolo, *St Anne, the Virgin Child and St Joachim*, along with *The Madonna and St Philip Neri* by Piazzetta. This artist, who died in abject poverty, was buried in the tomb of his friend Giambattista Albrizzi. (Return to the Campiello Querini and from there take the Fondamenta del Rimedio.)

THE CHURCH OF SAN GIOVANNI NUOVO. This former church is now the Guidi Museum, dedicated to the Roman painter Virgilio Guidi, who worked in Venice for many years. Baldassare Longhena lived and died in this parish. (Continue to Campo Santi Filippo e Giacomo, then follow Rughetta Sant'Apollonia as far as the bridge; from here you can see the Renaissance PALAZZO TREVISAN CAPPELLO, bought by Bianca Cappello ▲ *286*. Turn left before the bridge.)

PONTE DEL DIAVOLO

THE CLOISTER OF SANT'APOLLONIA. First dedicated to St Philip and St James, this church reverted to St Apollonia, patron of the linen weavers whose scuola was nearby. Today it is the Diocesan Museum of Religious Art, with collections made up of articles from Venice's deconsecrated churches. (Return to Campo Santi Fillippo e Giacomo and take the Salizzada San Provolo, which culminates in a florid Gothic portal with a Virgin and Child depicted in its marble lunette.)

THE CHURCH OF SAN ZACCARIA

San Zaccaria stands on a campo whose two entrances used to be closed at night, because the whole square was considered to be the private property of the nuns in the adjoining convent.

LA FAVA
The curious name of the Ponte della Fava was applied by extension to the church adjoining it. There are three theories about the origins of the word "fava": one, that it was the name of a local family; two, that a pastryshop here made special little cakes called *fave dolci* for All Souls' Day; and three, that a merchant of the quarter used to hide his contraband salt under a pile of broad beans (*fave*).

THE CLOISTER OF SANT'APOLLONIA
This cloister (12th–13th century), a unique example of Romanesque architecture in Venice, has remained intact; with its square floorplan, broad arches, colonnades of Istrian stone and brick paving, it has the air of a small campo in the center of which stands a well.

THE DOGE'S VISIT TO SAN ZACCARIA
Each year, the Doge went to San Zaccaria on the first Monday after Easter to pay homage to the nuns of the convent who gave up their vegetable garden to permit the enlargement of Saint Mark's Square ▲ 220. Preceding him was an individual holding the ducal *corno* ▲ 231. If tradition is to be believed, this hat was presented to one of the doges by Agnesina Morosini, who was Mother-Superior of the convent in the mid-9th century.

CALLE DELLE RASSE
In 1172, the Doge Vitale Michiel II was stabbed to death on the Riva degli Schiavoni, opposite the Calle delle Rasse, by an assassin who hid in the door of a house here. No subsequent doge was ever to pass down this dangerous alley again. Instead the Ponte della Canonica was built, so that state dignitaries could travel safely to the annual ceremony at San Zaccaria.

ARCHITECTURAL DEVELOPMENT. The Church of San Zaccaria was founded at the beginning of the 9th century, under the Doge Giustiniano Partecipazio. Towards the mid-10th century, the Byzantine basilica was radically altered and adapted in the Romanesque style. The crypt, which today is beneath the CHAPEL OF SAN TARASIO, dates from this era. The building as a whole was renovated between 1170 and 1174, at which time a campanile was added in alignment with the façade, to the right of the church. At the turn of the 14th century major new works were begun, at which time the building lost practically all of its Romanesque and Byzantine characteristics and became entirely Gothic. Yet the new Gothic choir and apses had scarcely been completed in 1443 when it was resolved not only to alter the building yet again, but also to build a new one on an adjoining site. As sometimes happens, the two churches, instead of being juxtaposed, became partially joined, as the left nave of the older edifice was confused with the right nave of the newer one. These works, begun in 1458, continued for about a century. At the death of the architect Antonio Gambello in 1481, Coducci took over and introduced various Renaissance elements, though without fundamentally modifying his predecessor's design. The church was consecrated in 1543.

PAINTINGS AT SAN ZACCARIA. Among the many works preserved in the church is an altarpiece by Giovanni Bellini (second altar on the left), entitled *The Holy Converse*, 1505. In the CHAPEL OF SAN TARASIO are frescoes by Andrea del Castagno, along with altar pieces (1442–4) by Antonio Vivarini and his brother-in-law Giovanni d'Alemagna.

THE BENEDICTINES. From its earliest beginnings, San Zaccaria was controlled by the nuns of the neighboring Benedictine convent, which explains the number and importance of the alterations made to it over the centuries. As one of the most favored institutions of the Venetian nobility, the convent of San Zaccaria was exceedingly rich; its

nuns, many of whom belonged to the wealthiest families in Venice, brought substantial endowments when they entered the convent and left it large sums when they died. It is known that the nuns of San Zaccaria lived very freely. In the 18th century the convent was a haunt of the Venetian beau monde, where balls, masquerades and theatrical performances were held and members of both sexes met and mingled.

> «IT HAS HIGH SPIRITS OR LOW, IT IS PALE, OR RED,
> GREY OR PINK, COLD OR WARM [...] ACCORDING
> TO THE WEATHER OR THE HOUR.»
>
> HENRY JAMES

RIVA DEGLI SCHIAVONI

The RIVA DEGLI SCHIAVONI runs alongside the edge of the basin of San Marco. This 550-yard quayside area, which today is invaded by souvenir stalls, was named in honour of the merchants of Dalmatia. By decree of the Senate, it was enlarged and then paved with Istrian stone between 1780 and 1782 by the architect Tommaso Temanza, at which time it also became one of Venice's favorite promenades.

THE GRAND HOTEL DANIELI. The former Palazzo Dandolo, built in the 14th century, is today one of the world's most famous hotels. Constructed at a time when the Republic was encouraging people to build palaces that would demonstrate the power and wealth of Venice, this building has changed hands many times over the centuries and at the time of the fall of the Republic was shared by several families. In 1822 it was rented by Giuseppe Dal Niel, who transformed it into an hotel before buying it outright, floor by floor, and becoming its sole owner in 1840. Named after Dal Niel, the hotel attracted a host of kings, princes, politicians and writers throughout the 19th century, to whom it offered unparalleled surroundings and comfort. Among the Danieli's famous guests were Kaiser Wilhelm of Prussia, Dickens, Wagner, Balzac, Proust, Debussy, Cocteau, George Sand and Alfred de Musset. In 1948, the construction of the Danielino, a modern annexe between the main hotel and the prison behind, caused a considerable furore. Today, the Danieli belongs to a large Italian hotel chain. Along one side of the hotel runs the CALLE DELLE RASSE, with its series of overhanging houses. The name "Rasse" derives from *rassa*, or *rascia*, a woollen fabric from Raska in Yugoslavia which was used to cover the *felze* (cabins) ● *57*, ▲ *190* of gondolas.

IN THE FOOTSTEPS OF DE MUSSET
Alfred de Musset and George Sand ended their famous love affair at the Hotel Danieli in 1834. De Musset, seriously ill, found out that Sand was having an affair with his physician, Doctor Pagello, and returned by himself to Paris. After his death, Louise Colet traveled to Venice, where she had the owner of the hotel show her the room that was once occupied by the "sick young man with the blonde hair", an incident she recalls in *L'Italie des Italiens*.

The inscription on the plaque (right) on the south wall of the church in the Calle della Pietà is from Paul III's Papal Bull denouncing wealthy families who abandon their children at the Pietà (1548).

CLAUDIO MONTEVERDI Monteverdi was born in 1567 in Cremona.

LA PIETÀ AND RELIGIOUS MUSIC IN VENICE

THE CHURCH OF LA PIETÀ. In its present form, this church dates from the 18th century. It is the work of Giorgio Massari, who won a competition for its design in 1736. His plan, which can still be seen at the Correr Museum ▲ 246, also included the adjoining orphanage but only a part of this was completed. The oval interior contains three frescoes by Tiepolo, Piazzetta's altarpiece *The Visitation*, and a high altar graced with statues by Gianmaria Morlaiter.

Distinguishing features of La Pietà are the absence of a chapel, the wrought-iron choirstalls, the vaulted ceiling which gives excellent acoustic effects, and the narthex which cuts all sound from the street outside.

ENTHUSIASM FOR MUSIC. La Pietà fulfilled a double role as a place of worship and a concert hall. The church depended to a great extent on the orphanage next door, which from the 17th century onwards was a kind of conservatory in a city where, as Charles de Brosses noted, there was "an inconceivable passion for music", and whose primacy in the field was established by the masters of San Marco.

MUSICAL SUPREMACY. In 1527, the Fleming Adriaan Willaert was appointed as Master of Music at the chapel of San Marco. On first seeing the basilica, he is said to have been

He studied singing, the viola and musical composition. In 1590 he entered the service of the Duke of Mantua and, in 1613, was named Master of Music at the Chapel of San Marco, spending the last thirty years of his life in Venice. This was where he composed an immense body of religious music, of which little remains, as well as most of his operas. When he died in 1647, the city gave him a lavish funeral.

stupefied . . . and convinced that his music was unsuitable for such a place. The two side naves each had their own organ, which probably gave Willaert the idea for a double choir to match. This innovation was to predominate in Europe right up to the time of Bach's *St Matthew Passion*, and its stereophonic effect was developed by Willaert's successors, Andrea and Giovanni Gabrieli. The voices of the choirs were answered by pealing trumpets placed in different places around the church; and after the arrival of Monteverdi ▲ 263, the most famous of the masters of San Marco, the music achieved a quality that was maintained throughout the 17th century, at a time when Venetian opera was the rage of Europe.

OSPEDALI AND PUBLIC CONCERTS IN THE 18TH CENTURY.

The taste for music in Venice grew apace until the 18th century. In addition to the academies, and the private concerts which took place every night in one place or another around the city, the four *ospedali* ▲ *160, 322* also began to organize paying concerts, which were attended by select audiences; Jean-Jacques Rousseau attended a few of these during his stay in Venice in 1743–4. In Vivaldi's time, the Englishman Edward Wright wrote that ". . . every Sunday or feast-day, in the chapels of these hospices, concerts of vocal and instrumental music are given by the young girls of the institution; they stand in an upper gallery, and remain hidden from the view of their hearers by a grille of wrought iron. The organ and other instrumental parts are all played by these girls . . . " Each of these ensembles was composed of about forty inmates. They were trained to sing and play several instruments, and they were theoretically "cloistered like nuns" (de Brosses), but in practice the most gifted performers among them were permitted to sing outside their hospices, and even to teach music to the other girls. The success of such concerts was very considerable, and the profits they generated were so immense that the great masters such as Galuppi ▲ *263, 373* and Vivaldi welcomed the opportunity of directing them.

LA PIETÀ DURING THE 18TH CENTURY: VIVALDI'S OSPEDALE.

From 1703, Vivaldi taught at the musical seminary of La Pietà, where he was the violin master and occasionally also the choirmaster and resident composer. This collaboration raised the prestige of the Ospedale, which consequently acquired a reputation for unrivalled musical skill. The bulk of Vivaldi's work (apart from his operas) was written for La Pietà, and no fewer than sixty of his religious works, including both the *Judith Triomphans* and the *Stabat Mater,* have survived down the years. Nevertheless Vivaldi, like Monteverdi, made his most significant contribution in the field of non-religious music. An incomparable virtuoso himself, he was the author of approximately 250 violin concertos which made him an outstanding master of the concerto for solo instrumentalists. Although La Pietà survived all the other *ospedali* by a hundred years, when it was finally closed towards the end of the 19th century it had become only a shadow of the institution which it had been during Vivaldi's time.

CONCERTI
Sonati dalle Figlie dell'Ospedale della Pietà
SUA ALTEZZA REALE
di Sereniſſimo
FEDERICO CHRISTIANO
Principe Reale di Polonia, ed Elettorale di Saſſonia
DA
D. Antonio Vivaldi
Maeſtro de Concerti del ſudetto ospedale
In Venetia nell'Anno 1742.

ANTONIO VIVALDI
The son of a San Marco violinist, Vivaldi was born on March 4, 1678. His was a musical education, though he was destined for the priesthood and ordained in 1703. But the man nicknamed "Prete rosso" on account of his red hair (or because of the red uniform he wore) soon distanced himself from the ministry, devoting his time to composition. Named violin master at La Pietà, in 1705 he published his first work and made his opera debut with *Ottone in villa*. Discovering a vocation for theater, he became director of Teatro Sant'Angelo in 1714. The successes that followed did not prevent him composing pieces for his favorite instrument, the violin. In 1740 he left Venice to offer his services to Charles VI, but the king died before his arrival. He went to the grave as a forgotten pauper the following year.

▲ CASTELLO

THE BANDIERAS

After the violent repression of the 1844 uprisings in Italy, the brothers Attilio (1810–44) and Emilio (1819–44) Bandiera attempted a landing in Calabria with a small band of followers. As former officers of the Imperial Austrian

Navy, they had joined Mazzini's Young Italy movement. The forlorn gesture of the brothers was intended as an example to their compatriots. They were captured and shot near Cosenza on July 25, 1844, with the cry of "Long live liberty. Long live the Motherland!" Later Mazzini was wrongly held responsible for their deaths.

A window of Palazzo Gritti-Badoer.

SAN GIOVANNI IN BRAGORA

At the foot of the PONTE DEL SEPOLCRO stands PALAZZO NAVAGERO, which is famous for having been given to the poet Petrarch by the Republic between 1362 and 1365, in exchange for the gift of his manuscripts to the Libreria Marciana ▲ *254*. (Take the Calle del Dose across the Rio della Pietà.)

CAMPO BANDIERA E MORO. This square is a little way off the main promenades. It is named after the patriot brothers Attilio and Emilio Bandiera (who lived at Palazzo Soderini, number 3618 here), and their friend Domenico Moro. All three were shot by the Bourbons near Cosenza in 1844. PALAZZO GRITTI-BADOER, rebuilt in the 15th century on much older foundations, is now an hotel (La Residenza) and is distinguished from the other buildings here by its grandeur. The church, by contrast, stands slightly back from the campo.

THE CHURCH OF SAN GIOVANNI IN BRAGORA. The origin of the term *bragora* is much disputed. Some think it refers to a region of the Orient from which the relics of St John the Baptist are supposed to have come (the church is dedicated to him). Others believe it derives from two very ancient dialect words, *brago* (mud) and *gora* (stagnant canal), which describe the way the site probably looked in early times. Still others favor a derivation from *bragolare* (to fish), a simple allusion to daily life on the Gemini Islands which form the greater part of the sestiere. There is also a school of thought that traces it to the Greek *agora* (a town square). As to the church, local legend sets its foundation at the beginning of the 8th century, although the first document in which it is mentioned is dated 1090. It owes its outer aspect to works begun in 1475, with a façade reflecting the period of transition between Gothic and Renaissance. The interior was reorganized in the 18th century; today it has a ceiling designed like the hull of a ship, with vestiges of 15th-century frescoes on the walls of the naves. Paintings by Alvise Vivarini, Cima da Conegliano (a *Baptism of Christ*) and Palma the Younger are kept here, along with the record of Vivaldi's christening. The composer, who was born in one of the houses on the campo, was baptized in one of the 15th-century fonts here, the red marble of which was salvaged from an octagonal Gothic capital. As you go out, note the lip of the well with its fine head of John the Baptist.

SAN MARTINO

THE CHURCH OF SAN MARTINO. This building was founded some time between the 7th and 8th centuries. The original Venetian-Byzantine church was demolished in 1540 and rebuilt by

La Residenza

176

Sansovino, who altered its orientation by 90 degrees and made it much larger. This indicates that the church and surrounding district were growing in importance with the development of the Arsenal nearby. St Martin, to whom it is dedicated, is the patron of an annual festival held on November 11, when the children of the city go from door to door collecting coins and drumming on sauccpans. At Martinmas the pastryshops of Venice are filled with delicious cakes representing the saint on his horse, which are very

COMMYNES IN VENICE
"Afterward they shewd me their arsenal, wherein they keep

popular with Venetian children. Antonio da Ponte, the architect of the Rialto Bridge ▲ *282*, lived in this parish.

their gallcys and do everything ncedful for their navy, which Is the finest in the world today . . ." Thus Philippe de Commynes described the Arsenal in 1494,

THE ARSENAL

Until 1808, the mid-16th century church of SANTA MARIA DELL'ARSENALE stood on the Campo dell'Arsenale, and was much frequented by sailors and local workmen. This church, which has now vanished, was attached to one of the two towers overlooking the docks and resembled a small classical temple.

THE FIRST ARSENAL. Venetian power overwhelmingly rested on the city's mastery of shipbuilding and the use of naval and merchant vessels. Nobody knows when the first arsenal was constructed; the usually quoted date of 1104 is not supported by any document. However, it is certain that an arsenal serving as a depot for arms, oars and rigging existed here in the early 13th century, which made it possible to repair and construct galleys. This first arsenal seems to have been the onc described by Dante in the 21st canto of the *Inferno*: "For as at Venice, in the Arsenal, in winter-time, they boil the gummy pitch, to caulk such ships as need an overhaul; now that they cannot

when he stayed in Venice as councillor and ambassador of Charles VIII of France, and reported on the attempts made by the Republic to organize a secret coalition against the French in the eastern Mediterranean.

PLANS OF THE ARSENAL
In the plans shown on the right, which were traced by Maffioletti in 1797–8 after the fall of the Republic, there are four basins visible, in which galleys and galleasses were moored. The two great docks on the right, still separated by warehouses and communicating by the narrowest of canals, were later united to create a single basin.

THE TWO LIONS FROM GREECE
The statues of two lions still guard the entrance to the Arsenal. They were brought home from Athens as booty by Francesco Morosini after the reconquest of Morea in 1687. The seated one was once part of a fountain at Piraeus. The carved inscription in runic

characters probably refers to the brutal repression of the Greeks by the *vernighi* (Scandinavian mercenaries in the pay of Byzantium) in 1040.

sail – instead of which one builds him a new boat, one toils to plug, seams strained by many a voyage, others stitch canvas to patch a tattered jib or lug, hammer at the prow, hammer at the stern, or twine ropes, or shave oars, refit and make all snug."

(translated by Dorothy L. Sayers)

Despite the beginnings of centralization, naval construction at that time remained firmly linked to private initiative. It was handled by the *squeri* ● 69 at various points around the city. But the state fixed norms of construction and the Doge was able, if any pressing need emerged, to requisition carpenters and caulkers to work in the government shipyards.

A NEW ARSENAL. It was not until after 1320 that work commenced on the new Arsenal. Its area quadrupled in size and its role changed in consequence. Previously the Arsenal had been used for maintaining ships: now it was also expected to construct them. The "light galleys" (*galere sottili*) of the war fleet were built here, as were the larger merchant vessels (*da mercato*). These ships were chartered to merchants, but they always remained the property of the state which, when necessary, could integrate them into its war fleet. When they carried precious cargo, the ships travelled in convoys of eight to eleven vessels. Meanwhile, "round ships" continued to be built in the private shipyards, which still produced the main bulk of Venice's seagoing tonnage.

THE ARSENALOTTI. The *arsenalotti*, or arsenal workers, operated in teams. Each team was composed of a dozen carpenters, six sawyers, fifteen caulkers, their apprentices and one or two unskilled laborers; together, these men could float up to six large merchant galleys every two years. Every speciality had its foreman, and the work of the team was supervised by a general overseer. The management of the Arsenal was chiefly concerned with the materials and the quality of the finished product; it did not interfere with the practical process of shipbuilding. Constituting a kind of artisans' elite, the *arsenalotti* enjoyed huge prestige and benefits. Their skill as firefighters was much admired and they were always called upon when there was a fire in the city. The "Masters of the Arsenal" also formed the guard of honor at the Doge's Palace during the election of a new Doge, as well as manning the Bucintoro on major occasions. They constituted a reserve corps of non-commissioned officers, and many of them took part in sea-battles on the galleys they themselves had built. Lastly, they had rights to free or low-rent lodgings; this led to the construction of whole districts of houses in the vicinity of the Arsenal, which are among the earliest examples of "modular housing" attempted by mankind.

THE TANA. At the time of the expansion of the Arsenal in the early 14th century, a number of warehouses were built for storing and manufacturing ropes and cordage. These were incorporated into the Tana, which was 345 yards long by 22 yards wide, with 84 columns. The importing of hemp and tar was consigned to private entrepreneurs; inside the Tana, the hemp plants were carded and sorted, and the fibers separated. Once they had been spun, the fibers were either turned over to master-cordwainers who ran their own workshops, or else were made into ropes at the Tana itself.

THE ARSENALE NOVISSIMO. Faced with the Ottoman menace, and above all with the growing power of the Spanish fleet, in 1473 the Senate decided to build the Arsenale Novissimo, although the work was not completed until the beginning of the 16th century. With this addition, Venice was able to add a huge reserve to her existing stock of galleys. Some of these reserve vessels were kept afloat in the harbor and could be fitted for sea at only a moment's notice. Others stood in dry dock and could be relaunched after caulking. The process of building the galleys was not unlike an assembly line. The hulls were constructed in the new Arsenal and the Arsenale Novissimo before passing through a series of buildings in the old Arsenal where

PORTA MAGNA
The majestic gate of the Arsenal was the first piece of Venetian architecture to break with the Gothic tradition and imitate antiquity. Probably dating from about 1460, it was based on a drawing by Jacopo Bellini, and built by Antonio Gambello.

THE PELOPONNESIAC
Francesco Morosini ● *40* was the last Venetian to combine the offices of Doge and Supreme Commander of the Fleet. At the close of the 17th century, when Venice's status as a maritime power seemed to be undergoing a revival, Morosini won a series of battles against the Turks, and reconquered Attica and the Peloponnese, earning himself the sobriquet of "Peloponnesiac". Pictured above is a battle pitting Venetians against Turks in which "with a few galleys and four warships, Morosini put seventeen Turkish vessels to flight." He died while in office at Nauplis in 1694.

THE MERCHANT GALLEY

Although they were equipped with sails, the big Venetian merchant galleys continued to be largely propelled by oarsmen. Fast, fitted with ornaments like

warships, always traveling in convoy, but incapable of carrying heavy cargo, these vessels were usually reserved for the transportation of valuable goods. Given the cost of their armament, it was rare for single individuals to lease one of these galleys alone – as a rule, the merchants tended to form temporary associations in order to spread the cost.

they were fitted out with rigging, weaponry and victuals. Some parts of them, which were made according to very strict specifications, were interchangeable – these included the masts, spars, rowing benches and pulleys. In this way the size of Venice's reserve of warships doubled from twenty-five to fifty vessels at the close of the 15th century, and increased again to a hundred ships in the mid-16th century. This total then fell to about fifty by 1633. The activity of the Arsenal was at its height during the 1560's, at which time it employed an average of about two thousand workers. This number would rise to three thousand in times of emergency. In 1570, in order to counter the Ottoman offensive against Cyprus, a hundred galleys were built in the space of two months, and at the Battle of Lepanto ● 36, no less than half the Christian fleet which defeated the Turks consisted of ships that had been built in the yards of Venice. On this occasion the Venetians unveiled a brand new type of warship, the galleass, which was the first galley of its kind to carry cannon on both sides.

GALLEYS AND SHIPS. The Venetians remained faithful to the galley concept until the end of the 17th century, but by 1667 the Arsenal was already starting to turn out 70-gun ships of the line according to the English pattern. In 1794 production of a new type of ship, the 30- to 40-gun frigate, began in the Arsenal. At the same time, the yards continued to produce better-armed and larger sailing vessels than the traditional galleys, which were finally given up altogether in 1755. Despite her slow and steady decline, Venice remained the most active naval construction center in the Adriatic until 1797. The end of the Republic, brought about by the Napoleonic Wars and the Austrian occupation, also marked the collapse of the Arsenal.

THE ARSENAL TODAY. Line 52 of the vaporetto crosses the old Arsenal, which is currently occupied by the Italian navy. It is used mainly as a roadstead for large battleships and as an unloading dock. There are plans currently afoot to convert the site into a major cultural center.

THE NAVAL MUSEUM

Venice's Naval Museum occupies the upper floor of a warehouse annexe that is situated beside the Rio dell'Arsenale. Its predecessor was the Casa dei Modelli, which was built by the government towards the end of the 17th century in order to preserve models of the ships that were built in the shipyards of La Serenissima. Many of these models subsequently disappeared: first during the events of December 1797 and January 1798, when Napoleon's soldiers sacked the Arsenal and destroyed the Casa, and then again during the Second World War. Some of the Venetian maquettes may be seen today at the Musée de la Marine in Paris, while others, dating from the late 17th and early 18th centuries, have remained in Venice. The present museum was built on the initiative of the Austrian admiralty. It has about 25,000 objects on display, and these offer a microcosm of the history of the Venetian and Italian navies. Among other things there are collections of navigational instruments and uniforms, models of fortresses held by Venice throughout the Mediterranean, scale models of various types of vessels, such as the Bucintoro ● *38* and a 17th-century galleass. Among these scale models there is one particular curiosity: the *cammello*, which worked like a vise to grasp ships and raise them from the low waters of the Lagoon. However, the two *cortelà* (the decorated sides of a galley belonging to Lazzaro Mocenigo, which foundered by the Dardanelles in the 16th century) are unquestionably the most interesting exhibits here. (After the museum, take the Fondamenta dell'Arsenale which leads to Campo San Biagio, an area which has been considerably altered since the closure of the shipyard at the end of the 18th century.)

The emblem of the oar-makers.

TOWARDS VIA GARIBALDI

RIVA SAN BIAGIO. This wharf was originally used as an unloading and weighing area for imported goods. The original 11th-century Church of San Biagio situated here was, until the 16th century, the main sanctuary of Venice's Greek community ▲ *164*.

RIVA DEI SETTE MARTIRI. Built in 1937, the original name of Riva dell'Impero was changed to Riva dei Sette Martiri in memory of seven Venetians who were shot by German soldiers during the Second World War.

VIA GARIBALDI. At 57 feet wide, this is the broadest street in the whole of Venice. It was created by filling in the Rio del Castello, and was opened by Napoleon during his visit to the city in 1807. It was originally called Via Eugenia, in honor of Eugène de Beauharnais, the French Viceroy of Italy; then it was renamed after Garibaldi, the hero of Italian unification, in 1867. On the right, at the beginning of this arterial road leading towards San Pietro di Castello, there is a plaque indicating the house of the navigators John and Sebastian Cabot, who were born in Chioggia ▲ *361*.

THE GALLEY OARSMEN
The most difficult problem to solve was that of finding crews to man Venice's ships, and in particular the oars. In the 13th and 14th centuries, to be a *galeotto* was still considered to be an honorable calling, but later it became more and more difficult to find free Venetians who were prepared to do this work. First Dalmatian and Greek volunteers were recruited, and then, in the second half of the 16th century, convicts were finally drafted to the galleys and kept chained to the benches. This innovation was championed in 1545 by Cristoforo da Canal, the first Venetian captain to put to sea in a galley rowed by convicts.

"IL CORSO"
Every Sunday during Lent, until the start of Holy Week, the Venetians repaired to the Church of San Pietro di Castello, where pardons were awarded.

Following the completion of the religious ceremony, which also gave the women an excellent opportunity to display their finest jewelry, everyone feasted on *frittele* (fritters, the traditional holiday fare) and *zucca barucca* (grilled pumpkin), which they washed down with some Cypriot wine and Malvasia, while a *corso* was held on the canal. In front of a crowd which gathered to watch on the parvis of the church on the bridge, the silk-clad gondoliers would engage in a sort of contest, weaving their vessels to and fro and generally showing off their skills with the oar. Today's modern regattas have evolved from this very ancient game.

SAN PIETRO DI CASTELLO

A wooden bridge leads from here to the island of San Pietro. On this site, which has probably been inhabited since the 5th or 6th century, there used to be a fortress (*castello*) whose purpose was to protect the Realtine Islands from attackers approaching from the sea. It was this *castello* which gave the sestiere its name. Apparently there was also a line of

fortifications that stretched along the basin as far as Santa Maria del Giglio ▲ *264*, at which point a chain barred the entrance to the Grand Canal. From the 7th century until 1807, the island of San Pietro was the seat of religious power in Venice.

CAMPO SAN PIETRO. This campo is unusual for Venice in that it is green, very large, and directly adjoining the water. Opposite the canal stands the church and the PATRIARCHAL PALACE, whose entrance bears the arms of the Patriarch Lorenzo Priuli. The building was converted into a barracks at the beginning of the 19th century, by Napoleonic decree.

THE CHURCH OF SAN PIETRO. The Church of San Pietro was built during the 9th century. It played an important role for hundreds of years as the seat of the bishopric of Venice, which was subordinate to the Patriarchate of Grado. Finally, in 1451, Venice acquired her own patriarch, and the church became a cathedral. Thus it remained until 1807, when the title was passed to St Mark's. The Church of San Pietro had been modified several times before Andrea Palladio was commissioned to rebuild it in 1558. This operation was completed by Francesco Smeraldi and Giangirolamo Grapiglia who, as faithful disciples of Palladio, appear to have respected his plans to the letter. The monumental high altar was executed in 1649 by Clemente Moli, from a design by Baldassare Longhena, to whom we also owe the design for the chapel dedicated to Cardinal Francesco Vendramin (on the lower left side.) The church also contains the so-called CHAIR OF SAINT PETER, a marble throne said to have been used by the apostle in the Orient. Its back, curiously, consists of a Muslim funeral stele covered in Arab decorative motifs and verses from the Koran.

THE CAMPANILE. The construction of this campanile (1463–74) had just been completed when it was seriously damaged by lightning. The repairs were assigned to Mauro Codussi in 1482 and, when he finished eight years later, the result looked very different. The new campanile was covered with Istrian stone and sported a dome with a lead roof on a wooden structure.

CHURCH OF SAN PIETRO DI CASTELLO

PUBLIC GARDENS

BIENNALE GARDENS

CHURCH OF SANT'ELENA

LA CERTOSA

This
dome was
replaced by a
polygonal tambour
roof in 1670. Each Saturday,
Venice's oldest market was held in the Cathedral square, most
of the customers being sailors from the port of San Nicolò di
Lido. Today there is just a series of *squeri* ● 69 on the Canal
San Pietro, along with workshops, pontoons, sheds, buoys and
moorings for small fishing boats and other vessels. (Return to
Via Garibaldi by the Fondamenta Quintavalle, the wooden
bridge of the same name, and the unassuming Fondamenta di
Sant'Anna.)

Two hours

THE PAVILIONS OF THE BIENNALE
In the area of the public gardens occupied by the Biennale stand the pavilions of the various participating countries. Many of these were built by some famous architects, notably Josef Hoffman

(Austria 1934), Gerrit-Thomas Rietveld (Holland 1954), Carlo Scarpa (Venezuela 1954–6), and Alvar Aalto (Finland 1956). These pavilions have had the effect of transforming the gardens into a kind of resumé of modern architecture, illustrating the evolution of 20th-century taste. They come alive in the autumn, when the Biennale crowds return. Shown above are the American and Italian pavilions.

Poster of the first Venice Biennale.

THE PUBLIC GARDENS

Napoleon drained a section of marshland and demolished several churches to create these gardens, which became Venice's favorite park. Concerts were performed here, the central promenade was used for bicycle races (then a highly novel pastime), and there was even a balloon ascent. Today, most of the site is occupied by the Biennale. The main entrance was designed by Gianantonio Selva (1810), who also directed the rest of the works on the park. Opposite stands the MONUMENT TO GIUSEPPE GARIBALDI (1885). Giambattista Tiepolo was born in the Calle San Domenico, which runs alongside the Gardens.

THE BIENNALE

THE BIRTH OF THE BIENNALE. A decision taken by the communal administration of Venice, on April 19, 1893, decreed that an exhibition by Italian artists should be mounted every two years, and this became the catalyst for the creation of the Biennale. The decree was changed in 1895 to include the exhibiting of works by foreign artists as well, with certain restrictions. Invited artists could only show a single work; non-invited artists had to submit their creations to a jury. The gardens of the Castello sestiere were selected as the venue; an old merry-go-round and the stable block which contained Toni the elephant (a celebrated 19th-century attraction) were demolished in order to make way for the Biennale. The first exhibition, which opened on April 30, 1895, in the presence of King Umberto I and Queen Margherita, proved to be a huge success: 200,000 visitors came to see the pictures, no doubt encouraged by the specially cheap train fares and the free entry to the exhibition.

THE FIRST BIENNALES. At the first exhibition, a painting by Giacomo Grosso, *Il Supremo Convegno*, representing a corpse on a bier surrounded by five nude women, raised such a furore that the Patriarch of Venice (later Pope Pius X) had it removed. The first Biennales were so oblivious to new trends in art that, on April 27, 1910, a group of Futurist painters climbed to the top of St Mark's clocktower in order to scatter leaflets attacking Venice's addiction to the past and the Biennale in general. After the First World War, the Biennale became rather more receptive to modern art. The works of Cézanne were shown there for the first time in 1920, at an exhibition of Impressionists. Toulouse-Lautrec and Degas followed in 1924.

THE FASCIST PERIOD. In 1930, the Italian state took over control of the Biennale and divided it into several sections: cinema, theater and music. In June 1934, Adolf Hitler visited Venice and proclaimed his "disgust" with the degenerate art shown at the Biennale.

THE POST-WAR BIENNALES.

The first post-war Biennale took place in 1948 and was a crucial event. All the greatest artists of the day were represented: the Impressionists, the German artists banished by Nazism (notably Dix and Pechstein), Picasso, Klee, Schiele and Magritte, along with works from the Peggy Guggenheim Collection and the metaphysical painters (Carrà, Morandi and De Chirico).

THE BIENNALE AFTER 1960.

In 1964, it was America's turn to produce a revolution in art, with the great exhibition that introduced Pop Art to Europe. "New democratic status" was introduced in 1973; a rather tardy expression of the principles of 1968, this sought to make the management of the Biennale more open, and to deprive critics, who might have a private stake in certain types of art, of their monopoly. During the 1970's, the Venice Biennales were organized around specific themes. The "Ambiente e Arte" exhibition on the environment took place in 1976 and was followed in 1977 by the

celebrated Biennale dedicated to dissidents in the East. But the new rules tended to favor the creation of lobbies which, coupled with the total inadequacy of Italian state funding, compromised the validity of the Biennale's programming and the effectiveness of its organization. Since the 1980's a growing campaign has sought to abolish the Biennale's status as a government institution controlled by political parties.

THE GARDENS
Linked to each other by paths and separated by hedges, the Biennale pavilions stand in the public gardens in which Wagner and Taine used to take the air, and where Théophile Gautier went to contemplate the pretty Venetian girls walking arm in arm.

SANT'ELENA

Until the 19th century, Venice ended at the point of San Antonio – today's Public Gardens and site of the Biennale. The gardens are now connected by a bridge to the island of Sant'Elena, which owes its name to a convent and church containing the relics of the saint, brought from the East in the 13th century. The part of the Lagoon separating the island from the city was filled in during the last century. Modern Sant'Elena, which was developed only recently, has preserved plenty of green space by the water (the Rimembranze Park) and is the site of the Francesco Morosini Naval College and the football stadium.

THE CHURCH OF SANT'ELENA.

This church was founded in the second half of the 12th century. An Augustinian monastery was joined to it at a later date and, in 1439, works were begun to rebuild it in the Gothic

THE BOOK PAVILION
Just opposite the Italian pavilion stands the 240 square yard Electa Book Pavilion (left), which was built by the architect James Stirling. This brand new, glass-sided structure, with its copper roof, was inspired by naval architecture and looks like nothing so much as a monster vaporetto. Inside the pavilion, art books and catalogues are displayed under wooden beams and rafters.

BIENNALE POSTERS

In order to conform with the tastes of the period, and the wishes of the organizers, the posters for the first contemporary Biennale favored stereotyped images of Venice which were familiar all over the world. This choice of graphics was in accord with goals which the Biennale had set itself, namely the development of tourism in Venice (the new luxury hotels at the Lido were built at this time) by organizing events which had international connotations. Thus the posters were commissioned from artists who shared the same objective; as to their texts, these endeavoured to attract visitors by advertising special rail ticket reductions and free admittance.

Poster for the Biennale of 1936.

style favored by the Benedictines, to whom the complex had been ceded by Pope Gregory XII. The Renaissance portal, by Antonio Rizzo, originally came from Sant'Aponal ▲ 286 and was only added in 1929. The sculptures in the LUNETTE depict Vettor Cappello, a hero of the Venetian navy who died in action against the Turks; this warrior is shown kneeling before the Madonna. Nothing of the convent remains today but a wing of the cloister, whose brick arches support a gallery. The campanile was rebuilt very recently.

GRAND CANAL

 From Santa Lucia Station
to St Mark's Square

 From St Mark's Square
to Santa Lucia Station

Vaporetto stop

 Traghetto
(a gondola which
crosses the river)

▲ THE GRAND CANAL

The *Canalazzo*, as the Venetians call it, traces a broad, inverted "S" shape, two and a half miles long, through the centre of Venice. Today's great waterway was originally the thoroughfare for merchant vessels on their way to and from the Rialto. Although the traffic is less dense than it used to be, the *Canalazzo* is still Venice's main street, with an unbroken sequence of palaces and churches on either side. The main façades of all these buildings overlook the water, and the best way to see them is from a gondola or vaporetto. Nothing seems to have been left out of this miraculous open-air stage, set for Venice's great regattas and festivals.

This painting shows the Church of Santa Lucia, which was demolished to make way for the railway station. The relics of St Lucia, who was martyred in Sicily, were moved to the Church of San Geremia, where they were placed in a glass coffin.

PALAZZO DIEDO

The Church of Santa Lucia, along with many Gothic and Renaissance palaces, was demolished in order to clear the way for the new station.

Venice was one of the obligatory stages of the Grand Tour, and so it attracted well-to-do travelers, artists and intellectuals of all nations bent on discovering both the Renaissance and their own romantic image of Italy.

THE STATION In 1846 Venice finally broke her thousand-year isolation from the rest of the world, when the railway bridge planned by the Austrians was completed.

GATEWAY TO VENICE

Venice is divided into six districts (*sestieri* in Venetian). The station quarter is called CANNAREGIO, a name that probably derives from the *canne* (rushes) that once grew here.

THE CHURCH OF THE SCALZI

The exiled Roman Discalced Carmelites commissioned Baldassare Longhena to build a church here in 1656. Thanks to Longhena (who also designed La Salute) the Grand Canal begins and ends with Baroque buildings. The rich interior of the Scalzi included a fresco by Giambattista Tiepolo (1743) which was destroyed in 1915 – *Il Trasporto della Casa di Loveto*.

THE BRIDGE OF THE SCALZI

Miozzi's stone bridge (1934) replaced the original iron one linking the two sides of the canal, which was built at the start of the 19th century during the Austrian occupation. At its foot is the Church of the Scalzi, the only building to survive the construction of the station.

CHURCH OF THE SCALZI

FERROVIA

PALAZZO FOSCARI-CONTARINI

VENETIAN WINDOWS

The immense variety of windows in the buildings along the Grand Canal reflects the many different architectural styles of the palaces.

CHURCH OF S
SIMEONE PIC

CHURCH OF SAN SIMEONE PICCOLO

San Simeone Piccolo is an 18th-century imitation of the Pantheon in Rome, designed by Giovanni Scalfarotto. It has a copper dome and today is used as a concert hall.

189

« THE BUILDINGS LINING EACH BANK MADE ONE THINK OF NATURAL SCENERY, WITH THE DIFFERENCE THAT THE NATURE WHICH CREATED THESE POSSESSED A HUMAN IMAGINATION.»

MARCEL PROUST

PALAZZO CALBO CROTTA

Just after the Bridge of the Scalzi stands the first palace of the Grand Canal, Palazzo Calbo Crotta. Originally Byzantine in style, but many times restored, the Calbo Crotta family home was filled with beautiful furniture which is now on display in the CA' REZZONICO, the great museum of 18th-century Venice ▲ *333*. Today it is better known as the Hotel Principe.

PALAZZO CALBO CROTTA

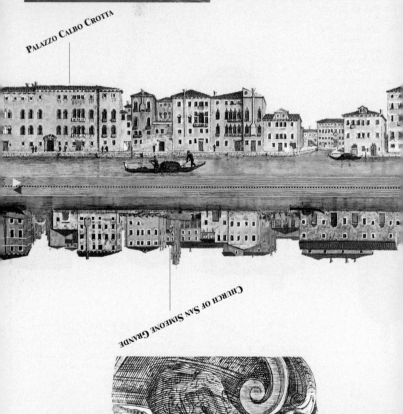

CHURCH OF SAN SIMEONE GRANDE

THE "FELZE"

Gondolas used to be closed in by *felze*, removable cabins with roofs like half-barrels. The *felze* also had a door with bas-reliefs and a small window at the side: very comfortable, with voluminous black fabric draped over their outsides, they were installed during the winter months and taken off every evening.

THE GONDOLAS

The special conditions of Venice led to the invention of the gondola – originally a richly decorated little craft. However an edict of the Seignory in the early 16th century limited their colour to black "with a view to avoiding unnecessary expense".

190

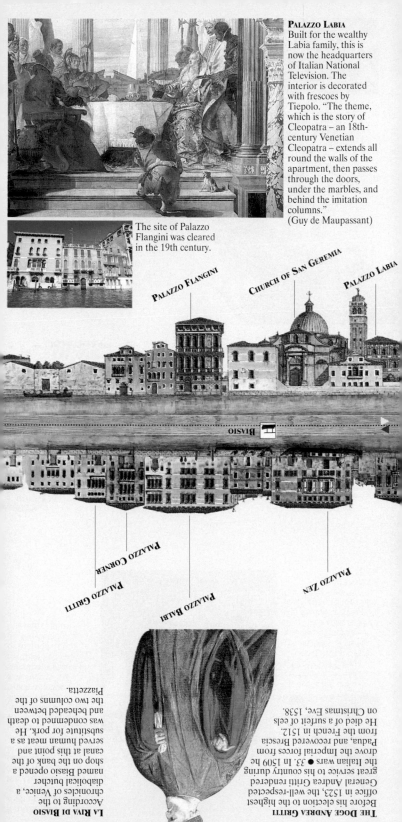

PALAZZO LABIA

Built for the wealthy Labia family, this is now the headquarters of Italian National Television. The interior is decorated with frescoes by Tiepolo. "The theme, which is the story of Cleopatra – an 18th-century Venetian Cleopatra – extends all round the walls of the apartment, then passes through the doors, under the marbles, and behind the imitation columns."
(Guy de Maupassant)

The site of Palazzo Flangini was cleared in the 19th century.

PALAZZO FLANGINI

CHURCH OF SAN GEREMIA

PALAZZO LABIA

BIASIO

PALAZZO CORNER

PALAZZO GRITTI

PALAZZO BALBI

PALAZZO ZEN

LA RIVA DI BIASIO
According to the chronicles of Venice, a diabolical butcher named Biasio opened a shop on the bank of the canal at this point and served human meat as a substitute for pork. He was condemned to death and beheaded between the two columns of the Piazzetta.

THE DOGE ANDREA GRITTI
Before his election to the highest office in 1523, the well-respected General Andrea Gritti rendered great service to his country during the Italian wars ● 33. In 1509 he drove the Imperial forces from Padua, and recovered Brescia from the French in 1512. He died of a surfeit of eels on Christmas Eve, 1538.

191

« THE FONDACO DEI TURCHI VANISHED BEHIND THEM, ITS IVORY SURFACE WONDERFULLY YELLOWED AND WORN, LIKE THE CRUMBLING PORTICO OF SOME RUINED MOSQUE. »

GABRIELE D'ANNUNZIO

PALAZZO CORRER-CONTARINI

Known as the "House of Hearts" because of their heart-shaped blazons, these two palaces were acquired by the Contarinis in 1768, and a century later they passed into the hands of one of Garibaldi's generals.

PALAZZO CORRER-CONTARINI

PALAZZO GIOVANELLI

Built in the first half of the 15th century, this Gothic palace acquired a large collection of paintings in the 18th century, including Giorgione's famous *Tempest* ▲ *307* (now in the Accademia ▲ *301*). Beside it, on a site which is now a garden, the sumptuous palace of the Bembo family once stood. It was demolished during the 19th century.

PALAZZO GIOVANELLI

« A man's life often resembles these palaces of the Grand Canal, which begin at the base with an array of stones proudly sculpted in diamond points, and end with the upper floors hastily cobbled together from dried mud. »

Paul Morand,
Venise

192

ALTANE

Many Venetian palaces have *altane* – wooden roof terraces – on which the ladies of the nobility used to sit bleaching their hair according to an ancient formula.

VENETIAN BLEACH

"Take a full measure of the soap used for bleaching silk, and boil it with a little alum . . . next add two ounces of burned lead and boil the mixture until a piece of white fabric dipped in it turns black. Allow to cool . . . then add two ounces of powdered Damascus soap and leave in the sun."

Marinello

PALAZZO MARTINENGO-MARTELLI

This former palace was completely altered during the 19th century.

PALAZZO GRITTI

PALAZZO MARTINENGO-MARTELLI

CHURCH OF SAN MARCUOLA

SAN MARCUOLA

CHURCH OF SAN GIOVANNI DECOLLATO

FONDACO DEI TURCHI

DEPOSITO DEL MEGIO

FONDACO DEI TURCHI

This Venetian-Byzantine building, one of the oldest in Venice, became the warehouse of the Republic's Turkish merchants in 1621 ▲ 347. In the mid-19th century, a misguided restoration left the Fondaco dei Turchi with two incongruous side towers. Today it is used as the city's Natural History Museum.

DEPOSITO DEL MEGIO

This was one of the Republic's grain and flour stores, maintained in readiness for times of famine.

PALAZZO VENDRAMIN-CALERGI

Now the winter quarters of the municipal casino, this was the home of the composer Richard Wagner during the last months of his life. After he died on February 13, 1883, Wagner's body was taken to the station by gondola in the middle of the night, then shipped to Bayreuth for burial.

This majestic Renaissance palace was built in the early 16th century by the great architect Mauro Coducci, and became the property of the Duchesse de Berry in 1844. She also bought the Palazzo Marcello, named after the musician Benedetto Marcello, who was born there at the end of the 16th century.

PALAZZO VENDRAMIN-CALERGI

PALAZZO MARCELLO

PALAZZO ERIZZO

PALAZZO SORANZO

PALAZZO EMO

PALAZZO BELLONI-BATTAGIA

PALAZZO TRON

PALAZZO TRON

A late 16th-century construction, this little palace belonged to the Trons, a patrician family which only managed to produce a single doge. One of its more distinguished members was Andrea Tron, known as El Paron (the master), who attempted to reform the declining economy of Venice during the 18th century.

PALAZZO BELLONI-BATTAGIA

This building was commissioned from Longhena by Borolo Belloni. His integration into the ranks of the Venetian patricians cost this wealthy merchant the sum of 150,000 ducats in 1647. Aside from their decorative function, the two *oculi* which stand above the palace signify the presence in the family of a *capitan da mar*, or admiral of the Venetian fleet.

PALAZZO GUSSONI-GRIMANI DELLA VIDA

The façade of this palace, built in the 16th century (probably by the architect Michele Sanmicheli) used to be covered with frescoes by Tintoretto.

PALAZZO DA LEZZE

GIOVANNI PESARO

Elected Doge on April 8, 1658, Giovanni Pesaro belonged to a patrician family that originated in Pesaro on the Adriatic Coast. At one time or another, members of the Pesaro family filled most of the state's important political, military and religious offices.

AZZO MOLIN-QUERINI

PALAZZO BARBARIGO

PALAZZO GUSSONI-GRIMANI DELLA VIDA

SAN STAE

CHURCH OF SAN STAE

PALAZZO PRIULI

CA' PESARO

CHURCH OF SAN STAE This church, said to have been founded in the 10th century, is dedicated to St Eustace (contracted in Venetian to *Stae*). On its left is a small red building, which was the headquarters of the brotherhood of the *tira e battioro* (gold wire drawers and spinners).

CA' PESARO ▲ 351 This palace, designed by Baldassare Longhena, today contains two museums, one of Oriental, the other of modern art. The latter, founded in 1897, has paintings by 20th-century artists from all over the world, including Matisse, Klimt, Chagall and many others.

195

THE FIFTH POPE
Carlo Rezzonico, who as Clement XIII was the fifth Venetian Pope, was born in 1693 in the 16th-century Palazzo Fontana.

THE CA' D'ORO ● 89
As the most beautiful Flamboyant Gothic building in Venice, the Ca' d'Oro is a place of great subtlety and refinement, full of Byzantine overtones and delicate touches that might have been borrowed from the art of the goldsmith. It owes its name (House of Gold) to the gildings which originally embellished its façade. In 1916, Baron Giorgio Franchetti, the last private owner, bequeathed the Ca' d'Oro and its great collections of furniture, medals and paintings to the city of Venice.

PALAZZO CONTARINI-PISARI

PALAZZO FONTANA-REZZONICO

PALAZZO GIUSTI

CA' D'O...

CA' CORNER DELLA REGINA

PALAZZO MOROSINI-BRANDOLIN

CHURCH OF SAN CASSIANO

CA' CORNER DELLA REGINA
Caterina Cornaro was born in this palace in 1454; later she became Queen of Cyprus through her marriage to James II of Lusignan ▲ 352. After his death she was forced to surrender the island to the Venetian Seignory in exchange for a domain at Asolo, a quiet town in the province of Treviso. Received in Venice with every honor in 1489, Caterina reigned for 20 years thereafter over a court of great refinement at Asolo, which included (among others) the 16th-century poet and man of letters Pietro Bembo. The present palace was built by Domenico Rossi in the 18th century.

Among the collections of the Ca' d'Oro are some fragments of frescoes which adorned the FONDACO DEI TEDESCHI ▲ 276. Artists involved in the project included Giorgione, who painted the side of the building facing the canal, and Titian.

PALAZZO MICHIEL DALLE COLONNE
This building is named after the portico on which its upper floors seem to rest so lightly. The Michiel family were famous for organizing lavish parties and spectacles – one of these involved a human pyramid balanced on boats anchored in front of their palace.

PALAZZO MOROSINI-SAGREDO

PALAZZO MICHIEL DALLE COLONNE

CA' D'ORO

Many Venetian merchants were ready to part with huge sums of money in order to join the governing patrician class of Venice.

PESCHERIA

PESCHERIA ▲ 285
This Neo-Gothic construction is the site of a daily fishmarket. From the earliest hours of the day, multi-colored fishing boats come in to unload their catches here.

I BACARI ▲ 285
Not far from the fishmarket are the *bacari*, typically Venetian wine bars which have served food and drink to local tradesmen ever since the 14th century.

« THE HOUSES OF VENICE ARE
NOSTALGIC FOR SHIPS – HENCE
THEIR GROUND FLOORS, WHICH
ARE SO FREQUENTLY AWASH.»
PAUL MORAND

Venetian-Byzantine detail of the
façade of the Ca' da Mosto.

CA' DA MOSTO
This 13th-century palace is one of Venice's oldest.
In 1432 the celebrated navigator Alvise da Mosto was
born here. Later he was to explore the west coast
of Africa in his caravelle.

PALAZZO MICHIEL
DAL BRUSÀ

PALAZZO MANGILI-
VALMARANA

CHURCH OF SANTI APOSTOLI

CA' DA MOSTO

Among the
street traders of the 18th
century was the vegetable and
pumpkin-seller.
"The Venetians love
pumpkins, and the
pumpkin-seller
displays her wares
like loaves of
yellow wax, and
slices them into
pieces."
(Théophile
Gautier,
Voyage d'Italie)

"Venice . . . is one of those places
which I know before I see them,
and has always haunted me most
after the East."
Byron

198

PALAZZO CIVRAN
Built in the 18th century on the site of a Gothic building.

PEACE IN A GONDOLA
According to legend, the daughter of the Doge Agnelo Partecipazio went on board a gondola in order to convince Pepin, son of Charlemagne, King of Italy, not to attack the Realtine Islands. The origins of the gondola must therefore go back at least a thousand years.

"These black gondolas slipping round the canals look like both coffins and cradles, the last and first resting-places of mankind."

Madame de Staël,
Corinne ou l'Italie

PALAZZO CIVRAN

FABBRICHE NUOVE

FABBRICHE VECCHIE

The construction of these two lengthy buildings answers a functional need: under their arched porticos were spaces for lines of shops, while the upper two floors were reserved for various magistratures.

MERCANTILE INSTITUTIONS
The institutions which administered the Republic's treasury and commerce were grouped in this part of the city. The FABBRICHE VECCHIE were built by

lo Scarpagnino for the offices of the tribunal, while the FABBRICHE NUOVE, built by Sansovino, were used for the trade ministry. Today the Fabbriche Nuove is the seat of the Venice assize court.

199

« THE RIALTO BRIDGE [...] IS LIKE A GREAT HORN POURING FORTH PLENTY FROM LAND AND SEA ALL OVER THE SURROUNDING WATERFRONT. »

GABRIELE D'ANNUNZIO

FONDACO DEI TEDESCHI
Before the central post office moved here, this palace was a warehouse used by the "German" merchants of Venice (that is the Germans, Hungarians, Austrians, and so on). In the 16th century its façade was covered in symbolic and allegorical frescoes by Giorgione and Titian ▲ 276.

FONDACO DEI TEDESCHI

CHURCH OF SAN BARTOLOMEO

RIALTO BRIDGE

PALAZZO DEI CAMERLENGHI

THE WATER BEARER
In the 18th century Venice lacked clean drinking water and the water-bearer was a familiar figure in the city's streets.

THE RIALTO BRIDGE
This bridge was originally made of wood, with a central section that opened to allow galleys – and the Bucintoro – to pass through. It was rebuilt in stone in 1588–91 by Antonio da Ponte, after a long battle for the contract between the greatest architects of the 16th century (Michelangelo, Palladio and Sansovino). Today, the bridge is 92 feet long with a single arch, and is covered in souvenir stands ▼ 282.

200

AROUND THE RIALTO

The Rialto area has been the heart of Venice and the city's commercial hub ever since the 9th century. For a thousand years now, this place has been aswarm with people shopping for vegetables, fish and flowers; grouped around it are Venice's most ancient buildings.

As it runs through the Rialto district, the Grand Canal is bordered by fondamente, which are quays along which one can walk and admire the palaces on either bank without taking a vaporetto.

PALAZZO BEMBO

RIALTO

PALAZZO BARBARIGO

FONDAMENTA DEL VIN

PALAZZO BEMBO

LA FONDAMENTA DEL VIN
Barrels of wine used to be unloaded along this quayside, but today it is mainly given over to tourist restaurants and souvenir stalls.

Multi-colored boats from the Lagoon bring fresh supplies to the Erberia and Pescheria markets every morning.

CA' LOREDAN AND CA' FARSETTI
These two palaces, built in the 13th century and extensively restored in the 16th, are now the offices of the Mayor of Venice. The salons of the Ca' Farsetti were a favorite haunt of the sculptor Antonio Canova.

ENRICO DANDOLO
The Doge of the Fourth Crusade ● 31 was born in a house that preceded the Casetta Dandolo, built in the 15th century.

PALAZZO CORNER-MARTINENGO-RAVA
(16th century)

PALAZZO GRIMANI
(16th century)

This imposing white marble house was built by Michele Sanmicheli for Girolamo Grimani, Procurator of San Marco. Palazzo Grimani is now the seat of the Venice Court of Appeals.

CASETTA DANDOLO

CA' LOREDAN

CA' FARSETTI

PALAZZO CORNER-VALMARANA

PALAZZO GRIMANI

SAN SILVESTRO

CHURCH OF SAN SILVESTRO

THE "PALO"
The *palo*, like the gondola, is a Venetian symbol. Used for tying up boats, the *pali* along the Grand Canal were painted in the individual colors of patrician families.

PALAZZO BUSINELLO AND BARIZZA
Though restored in the 17th century, these palaces (shown on the left, and above left) retain Venetian-Byzantine decorative elements, notably the 12th- and 13th-century capitals.
PALAZZO RAVA This Neo-Gothic building (above right) was built in the early 20th century on a site thought to be that of the palace of the Patriarch of Grado – the original bishopric to which Venice belonged.

PALAZZO CORNER-CONTARINI DEI CAVALLI AND THE TWO TRON PALACES

The first, built in 1445, owes its name to the horses on the family coat of arms. The second is 19th-century Neo-Gothic, and the third is 15th-century and heavily restored.

LORD BYRON
(1788–1824)
Lord Byron was an habitué of the Contessa Marina Querini Benzon's literary salon.

PALAZZO BENZON was rebuilt during the 18th century.

The Comte de Chambord stayed at the Palazzo Benzon during the 19th century.

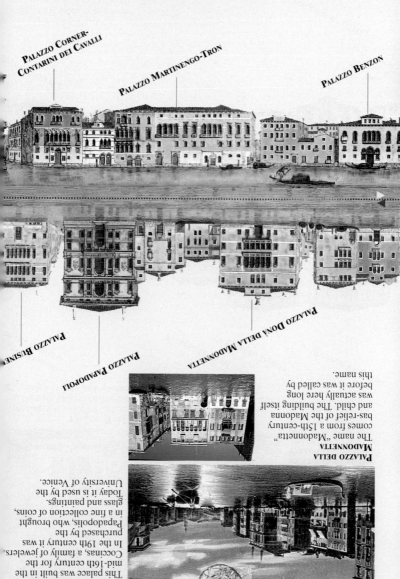

PALAZZO CORNER-CONTARINI DEI CAVALLI

PALAZZO MARTINENGO-TRON

PALAZZO BENZON

PALAZZO BUSINE

PALAZZO PAPADOPOLI

PALAZZO DONÀ DELLA MADONNETTA

PALAZZO DELLA MADONNETTA
The name "Madonnetta" comes from a 15th-century bas-relief of the Madonna and child. The building itself was actually here long before it was called by this name.

PALAZZO PAPADOPOLI
This palace was built in the mid-16th century for the Coccinas, a family of jewelers. In the 19th century it was purchased by the Papadopolis, who brought in a fine collection of coins, glass and paintings. Today it is used by the University of Venice.

PALAZZO CORNER-SPINELLI

Built by Mauro Coducci, this building incorporates a number of Renaissance elements, foreshadowing Palazzo Vendramin-Calergi ▲ *90, 194*. It belonged to Giovanni Corner, nephew of Caterina, Queen of Cyprus, before reverting to the Spinellis, a family grown rich in the silk trade. Today it is the headquarters of the RUBELLI fabrics firm.

TEATRO SANT'ANGELO

One of Venice's seven lyric theaters formerly stood on this site. Vivaldi created a number of operas there ▲ *175*.

PALAZZO CORNER-SPINELLI

PALAZZO GARZO...

SANT'ANGELO

PALAZZO BERNARDO

PALAZZO DUBOIS

PALAZZO GRIMANI

...AZZO BARBARIGO DELLA TERRAZZA

PALAZZO BERNARDO

This elegant 15th-century building has many decorative features in common with the Ca' d'Oro.

PALAZZO BARBARIGO DELLA TERRAZZA

This palace is so called on account of the broad terrace at one side of it. Up until 1850, it contained a magnificent collection of paintings, most of which were eventually purchased by Czar Nicolas II.

CA' MOCENIGO VECCHIA

This palace once belonged to one of Venice's greatest families, which produced no fewer than seven Doges. In the years 1591–2, Giovanni Mocenigo entertained the alchemist Giordano Bruno here, intending to find out his secrets. He later denounced Bruno to the Vatican, and the alchemist was burned to death in Rome.

It is said that, on certain nights, the ghost of Giordano Bruno haunts the Ca' Mocenigo Vecchia.

PALAZZO MOCENIGO

The building is 18th-century and constructed from Istrian stone. Lord Byron lived here in 1818–19 while he was writing *Don Juan*.

CA' MOCENIGO VECCHIA

PALAZZO MOCENIGO

PALAZZO PISANI-MOR-

PALAZZO TIEPOLO

PALAZZO PERSICO

In contrast with most other Venetian palaces, PALAZZO PISANI-MORETTA has not changed at all since it was built, and its interior décor remains intact. It still belongs to the heirs of the Pisani family.

TRAGHETTO DI SAN TOMA

The Grand Canal can be crossed by gondola at this point for a nominal fee.

"The Grand Canal in Venice is the most wonderful thing on earth. No other city can offer a spectacle so beautiful, so strange, so fairylike ... Every palace there has a mirror in which to admire its own beauty, like a lovely woman. The magnificent reality is duplicated by a charming reflection. The water laps at the feet of each fine façade, lit by the pale-gold light of Venice and swayed in a second sky. The little boats and larger vessels which wait upon the water seem to have been placed there deliberately to make a foreground for decorators and watercolorists.**"**

Théophile Gautier,
Voyage d'Italie

PALAZZO MORO-LIN
In the 18th century, two Gothic buildings separated by a calle were united to form this thirteen-windowed palace.

PALAZZO CONTARINI DELLE FIGURE
Built at the beginning of the 16th century, this building gets its name from the caryatids which hold up its balcony. It was commissioned by Jacopo Contarini, a great protector of artists and the patron of Palladio, architect of San Giorgio. At his death, Contarini left his fabulous art collection to the state.

PALAZZO CONTARINI DELLE FIGURE

CHURCH OF SAN TOMÀ

PALAZZO CIVRAN-GRIMANI

PALAZZO BALBI

PALAZZO BALBI
With its magnificent position right on the curve of the Grand Canal, this much-painted building was commissioned in the 16th century by Nicolò Balbi. In 1807 Napoleon watched a regatta from here. Palazzo Balbi is now the seat of the Veneto Regional Council.

"All the balconies are crowded with pots of flowers: the flowers of Venice, sprung from warm loam and blossoming in the humid air, have a special freshness, a richness of substance, and a special heavy langor.**"**

Georges Sand,
Lettres d'un voyageur

206

«Every boat had its lantern. And the gondolas, moving rapidly along, were followed by tracks of light, which gleamed and played upon the waters.»
WILLIAM BECKFORD

PALAZZO GRASSI ▲ *270*
The last great 18th-century building to be constructed on the Grand Canal, Palazzo Grassi was designed by Giorgio Massari. In the 19th century it was the premises of the celebrated Degli Antoni bath-house, and in 1984 was bought and restored by the Fiat Foundation for use as an exhibition centre.

PALAZZO MORO-LIN   PALAZZO GRASSI   CHURCH OF SAN SAMUELE

SAN SAMUELE

CA' FO...   PALAZZO GIUSTINIAN   CA' REZZONICO

CA' FOSCARI
This majestic Gothic palace on the corner of the Rio Nuovo was built for the Doge Francesco Foscari. Because of its convenient location on the canal, the Republic used it to accommodate distinguished visitors, such as the French King Henri III in 1574 ● *38*. It is now the university's Institute of Economics.

Wagner lived for seven months (1858–9) at PALAZZO GIUSTINIAN, where he composed the second act of *Tristan and Isolde*. He died in Venice in 1883.

PALAZZO GIUSTINIAN-LOLIN
This 17th-century building, designed by Baldassare Longhena when he was a young man, was the home of the Duchess of Parma. Her brother, Count Henri de Bardi, brought back from India, China and Japan a collection of more than thirty thousand objects, which later formed the basis for Venice's Museum of Oriental Art (which is now in the Ca' Pesaro).

PALAZZO FALIER
(early 15th century)

THE "LIAGHI"
Palazzo Falier has two romantic *liaghi*, or covered balconies, on either side of its central windows. In the 19th century these typically Venetian features were restored, but their original structure was faithfully preserved.

PALAZZO MALIPIERO

CA' DEL DUCA

PALAZZO FALIER

PALAZZO CONTARINI

PALAZZO MORO

PALAZZO LOREDAN

"Venice is not merely a city of marble and water: she also has her gardens, whose cloistered greenery is somehow more rare and unexpected than elsewhere."
Henri de Régnier, *Esquisses vénitiennes*

PALAZZO LOREDAN
"THE AMBASSADOR'S HOUSE"
In 1572, this palace became the Austrian ambassador's residence, hence its name. The Austrian government had to pay 29 years of rent in advance, plus maintenance charges.

« THEN MY EYES [...] TURNED BACK TO THE CANAL, WHERE THE BOATS WENT PAST, STEERED BY ADOLESCENTS IN PINK JACKETS AND PLUMED CAPS. »
MARCEL PROUST

DORSODURO ▲ 297
This district takes its name from the notably hard subsoil on which it is built; it is among the less populous areas of Venice.

PALAZZO GIUSTINIAN-LOLIN
This palace is now the Levi Foundation Music Centre.

THE ACCADEMIA ▲ 301
The galleries of the Accademia at the former SCUOLA DELLA CARITÀ possess an incomparable collection of Venetian paintings, including works by all the great masters of the city (the Bellini brothers, Carpaccio, Giorgione, Titian, Veronese, Tintoretto, the 18th-century painters Longhi, Guardi and Tiepolo, and the landscapists). Other parts of the building are used by the Fine Arts Academy.

PALAZZO GIUSTINIAN-LOLIN

ACCADEMIA

PALAZZO CONTARINI DEGLI SCRIGNI

PALAZZO GAMBARA

PALAZZO QUERINI

CARITÀ

PALAZZO GAMBARA
(late 17th century)

THE LEGEND OF SAINT URSULA
The Accademia contains the *Legend of St Ursula* cycle by the great Venetian painter Vittore Carpaccio ▲ 306. This series is made up of nine canvases tracing the life of the saint, eight in which portray scenes of the city in the 15th century, with its festivals, processions, palaces and interiors. A detail of the *Arrival of the Ambassadors*, c. 1500, is shown on the right. The scene is set in Brittany, but the sails, the gondolas skimming the Lagoon, the gentlemen's costumes and the design of the buildings leave no doubt that the artist was inspired by Venice.

PALAZZO BARBARO

This richly decorated group of palaces was built for the patrician Barbaro family, and purchased in 1885 by the Curtis family from Boston, USA. The Curtises, who were great art-lovers and collectors, made it a famous meeting-place for foreign artists and writers.

ROBERT BROWNING (1812–89) wrote poetry at Palazzo Barbaro.

HENRY JAMES (1843–1916) wrote his *Aspern Papers* there, featuring an American narrator searching for the papers in Venice. James' *Wings of a Dove* was also set in the Palazzo Barbaro.

CLAUDE MONET (1840–1926) and **JOHN SINGER SARGENT** (1856–1925) had studios in the palace, and **COLE PORTER** lived there before he opened his jazz club on a boat anchored in front of La Salute.

CHURCH OF SAN VIDAL

PALAZZO CAVALLI-FRANCHETTI

PALAZZO BARBARO

PALAZZO BRANDOLIN

ACCADEMIA BRIDGE

PALAZZO CONTARINI-POLIGNAC

PALAZZO BALBI-VALIER

THE ACCADEMIA BRIDGE It was intended that the wooden bridge would be replaced by a stone one, but the project has yet to come to fruition.

PALAZZO CONTARINI-POLIGNAC This building, with its magnificent Renaissance façade, has belonged to the Polignacs since the early 1900's. Its many famous guests included Proust, Sargent, Curtis and Picasso.

CASETTA DELLE ROSE

The Casetta delle Rose, a small palace standing slightly back from the Canal, was the poet Gabriele d'Annunzio's home during the First World War. His jealous mistress, the actress Eleonora Duse, is said to have lodged in a palace on the opposite bank, in order to keep an eye on him.

PALAZZO CORNER DELLA CA' GRANDE

This majestic palace, built for a wealthy family by Jacopo Sansovino, owes its name to its sheer size. Famous for its rich interior, notably a bedroom decorated in cloth of gold, the Ca' Grande was bought by the Napoleonic government in 1812, and later restored for the Austrian administration. Today it houses the Prefecture of Venice.

"The gondolas rock at their berths, with a rhythm of calm, slow breathing. And their dry hawsers utter little cries."

André Suarès, *Voyage du Condottiere*

PALAZZO CORNER DELLA CA' GRANDE

CASETTA DELLE ROSE

PALAZZO LOR...

CAMPO SAN VIO

PALAZZO BARBARIGO

PALAZZO DA MULA

CA' VENIER DEI LEONI

CA' VENIER DEI LEONI – THE PEGGY GUGGENHEIM FOUNDATION

This palace, with its unfinished ground floor, was bought by the wealthy American collector, Peggy Guggenheim, in 1951. On her death, it became the Guggenheim Foundation, containing one of Europe's greatest privately assembled collections of 20th-century art ▲ 316.

PALAZZO BARBARIGO

Lavishly decorated with mosaics by Carlini, this palace now belongs to a glass firm and is used to display its products.

SANTA MARIA DEL GIGLIO

At Santa Maria del Giglio there is a traghetto which plies from bank to bank of the canal. For the Festival of La Salute on November 21 ● *49*, ▲ *320*, a bridge of boats is set up at this point, so the processions can make their way across.

THE GRITTI PALACE HOTEL

John Ruskin and his wife Effie rented a suite of rooms here during their second visit to Venice. Later, the Gritti became Hemingway's favorite Venetian hotel.

The terrace at the Gritti is famous as a place for breakfast.

PALAZZO BARBARIGO

PALAZZO PISANI-GRITTI

SANTA MARIA DEL GIGLIO

PALAZZO DARIO

PALAZZO SALVIATI

PALAZZO DARIO

A Renaissance palace encrusted with polychrome marbles, the Palazzo Dario was the home of the French poet Henri de Régnier at the turn of the century. Despite a curse which is supposed to have been laid on it, the house was recently bought by the Italian magnate Raul Gardini.

PALAZZO SALVIATI

This palace now houses the exhibition rooms of the Salviati family, famous glassblowers from Murano.

CA' GENOVESE

In 1892, the second Gothic cloister of the San Gregorio Monastery was demolished to make way for this Neo-Gothic palace – one example of how little the artistic legacy of earlier centuries was valued during the 19th.

« THE MOORISH GOTHIC HOUSES, NARROW AS THE JEALOUS EYES OF OTHELLO, STAND DIRECTLY ON THE CANAL.»

LOUIS ARAGON

THE HOUSE OF DESDEMONA

According to legend, Palazzo Contarini-Fasan was the house of Desdemona, a noble Venetian lady who fell victim to the mad jealousy of her husband, a member of the Moro family. William Shakespeare made her the tragic heroine of his play *Othello*.

PALAZZO FLANGINI-FINI

PALAZZO CONTARINI

SALUTE

ABBEY OF SAN GREGORIO

BASILICA SANTA MARIA DELLA SALUTE

THE ABBEY OF SAN GREGORIO
(15th century)

"Like an old lady on crutches, Venice rests on a forest of pilings . . . it took a million of them to build La Salute." (Paul Morand, *Venises*) Indeed, most of Venice's buildings are founded on pilings, which are set in the layer of *caranto* (clay and sand) and have gradually hardened into mineral form ● 97.

THE BASILICA DELLA SALUTE

In 1630, plague struck Venice, and more than a third of the population succumbed to the "black death". On October 22, while the people were still counting their dead, the Senate commissioned Longhena to build a church in gratitude to the Virgin for bringing an end to the epidemic.

PALAZZO TIEPOLO
It is named after Bajamonte Tiepolo, who hatched a plot against the republic with Marco Querini in 1310. The plot failed and their houses were razed to the ground. In the 19th century, this palace was the Hotel Britannia. It is now the Regina e Europa.

PALAZZO GIUSTINIAN
During the 19th century this Gothic palace became the Hotel Europa. Verdi, Gautier and Proust all stayed there.

PALAZZO TREVES DEI BONFILI
The interior of this palace is redecorated throughout in the Neo-classical style.

PALAZZO TIEPOLO

PALAZZO TREVES DEI BONFILI

PALAZZO GIUSTIN

CHURCH OF SAN MOISÈ

SEMINARIO PATRIARCALE

CUSTOMS POINT

THE SEMINARIO PATRIARCALE
This building was constructed in the 1670's by Baldassare Longhena. Today it is the home of the Manfrediana art gallery.

THE PALA D'ORO
To replace the tower that once defended the entrance to the Grand Canal, a belfry was erected with a bronze globe supported by two atlases and a weathervane (a statue of Fortune) by Bernardo Falcone.

After the customs point, the Grand Canal opens onto St Mark's Basin, where the full grandeur of Venice becomes apparent with views of the Doge's Palace, Piazza San Marco and the island of San Giorgio Maggiore.

PROUST delayed going to Venice for many years, because for him cities, like women, were best confined to dreams. But when he finally arrived he was not disappointed. Indeed he described the city lovingly and at length in his *Albertine Disparue* (*The Fugitive*).

HARRY'S BAR Frequented by Hemingway, this is one of the world's most famous café-restaurants.

PALAZZO ERIZZO   HARRY'S BAR   PALAZZO DEL MAGISTRATO   ROYAL GARDENS

SAN MARCO VALLARESSO

MONASTERY OF THE CYPRESSES

SAN GIORGIO MAGGIORE

SAN GIORGIO MAGGIORE

This green island, once known as "The Isle of Cypresses," was the site of a Benedictine monastery from the 10th century onwards. In the mid-16th century, Andrea Palladio designed and partly completed the refectory, which was decorated with Veronese's *Marriage at Cana* (now in the Louvre); the church and the cloisters ▲ 340. The building is now owned by the Cini Foundation, which holds exhibitions there. The stunning view from the top of the campanile takes in the whole of Venice, the Giudecca and the Lagoon.

"Behind the rigid forest of ships riding at anchor, San Giorgio Maggiore appeared like a great pink galley, whose prow was turned to Fortune as she beckoned from her golden sphere."

Gabriele d'Annunzio, *Fire*

215

SAN MARCO ▲ 219

With its Byzantine basilica, Gothic palace and classical and Renaissance library, Piazza San Marco is a microcosm of differing styles. It is also a symbol of all earthly powers. Already a political and religious center, in the early 16th century it acquired a temple of culture, the Libreria Marciana, and a symbol of Venetian financial strength, the Zecca (Mint), looking on to the Lagoon.

THE ZECCA

CAMPANILE

CLOCKTOWER

THE PIAZZETTA

The high columns of red and grey granite standing on the Piazzetta mark the "gateway" to Venice, which could formerly be entered only by sea. At times when there were no state visitors, the space between the two columns became a free zone where gambling was tolerated.

THE DOGES

One hundred and sixteen Doges ruled the Serenissima from 726 AD to May 12, 1797, when the last Doge, Lodovico Manin, abandoned by his Council, gave his linen cap, worn under the ducal *corno*, to his valet. "Take it, I shall not be needing it again," he said.

❝The admirable square sets forth its forest of columns, its Corinthian capitals, its statues and the noble variety of its classical forms. ❞
Hippolyte Taine, *Voyage en Italie*

THE LION OF VENICE

Venice chose as her emblem the Lion of St Mark the Evangelist, her patron saint. As the incarnation of the majesty of state, the lion standing on its hind legs and brandishing a sword became the city's defender and the symbol of her warlike strength.

«AND AT NIGHT THEY SANG IN THE GONDOLAS, AND IN THE BARCHE WITH LANTHORNS; THE PROWS ROSE SILVER ON SILVER, TAKING LIGHT IN THE DARKNESS.»

EZRA POUND

THE BRIDGE OF SIGHS

Built in the early 17th century, the Bridge of Sighs linked the jails of the Doge's Palace (the "Leads" and the "Wells") to a more recently constructed prison block.

THE "LEADS" ▲ 252

Casanova made these prison cells famous by escaping from them on the night of October 31, 1755.

ST MARK'S BASILICA

DOGE'S PALACE

BRIDGE OF SIGHS

PRISONS

THE SCULPTURES OF THE DOGE'S PALACE

In the 14th and 15th centuries, both the Doge's Palace and the basilica were substantially altered. The palace was rebuilt in the Gothic style, with masterpieces of sculpture refining the effect produced by the fretwork of the façade. So that the basilica should not suffer by comparison, it was in turn covered with pointed features and sculptures in the new style.

THE DOGE'S PALACE

The Doge's residence, which formerly housed the administration of the Republic, was the heart of Venice for nearly seven centuries. The long history of the city is recorded in its richly decorated rooms ▲ 224.

CAFFÈ QUADRI

Opened in 1775 opposite Florian's, this café was one of the first in Venice to serve Turkish coffee.

SAINT MARK'S SQUARE

1. Procuratie Vecchie
2. Clocktower
3. Napoleon wing
4. Procuratie Nuove

Called *piazza* (square) rather than *campo* (field) in order to distinguish it from

1.

🕏 Half a day

3.

the other open areas in Venice, this "drawing room of Europe" (to use Napoleon's phrase) has been at the heart of Venetian life for more than a thousand years. In fact, the Piazza San Marco (St Mark's Square) became the focus of the major religious festivals ● *48*, games ● *50* and political activities of the Serene Republic at a very early stage. Like the Venetians themselves, for whom the square has always been a favorite haunt, tourists flock here in the thousands every year.

5.

**St Mark's Square
(11th century)**
At this stage the square was divided in two by Rio Batario.

**St Mark's Square
(12th century)**
The Rio Batario and the dock which reached almost to the foot of the basilica had been filled in.

The First Square

Having abandoned Malamocco for the Rialto ● *30*, the Doges installed themselves at the junction of the area's two primary waterways. The spot they chose became the administrative, political and judicial heart of the Republic, though at the time it looked very different from the San Marco we see today.
Rio Batario. A rio used to divide in two the space that is now occupied by the square, making the original piazza little more than the parvis of the basilica. The other side was taken up by the vegetable gardens of the monastery of San Zaccaria ▲ *171,* with the little Church of San Geminiano in the center.
The dock. A sheltered dock extended almost to the foot of the basilica, effectively separating it from the Doge's Palace. The basilica itself was flanked on its north-eastern side by the Church of San Teodoro, dedicated to the city's first patron saint, St Theodore.

Enlarging San Marco

The square was reorganized in the 12th century for the meeting of Pope Alexander III and the Emperor Barbarossa ● *30*, the foremost political rivals of the time. The Rio Batario was filled in, doubling the length of the square. In place of the dock, a smaller square was

2.

6.

laid out, on which the columns of Marco and Todaro (Venetian for Teodoro), the city's two patron saints ▲ 251, were erected. The Church of San Geminiano was demolished and then rebuilt opposite the basilica at the end of the new square, and work was begun on the first Procuratie. Other elements of the piazza remained unaltered. Towards the Lagoon a hospice, the Orseolo, was built to accommodate pilgrims on their way to or from the Holy Land. The BASILICA was crowned with the low, hemispherical domes typical of Byzantine churches, while the CAMPANILE (mostly used for scanning the sea-horizon) took the form of a spireless tower. The

4.

DOGE'S PALACE, with its lateral towers, resembled a turreted stronghold. All in all, square, church and palace remained faithful to the spirit of the Byzantine Empire's final years, and together constitute one of the last examples of the Roman *palatium*, which included a prince's lodgings (the Doge's Palace), a mausoleum (the Basilica) and a main square. The main square of St Mark's was paved with herringbone bricks at the end of the 13th century. It was the scene of Venetian state ceremonies until the fall of the Republic in 1797.

8.

7.

MORE CHANGES

In the 14th and 15th centuries, only the basilica and the Doge's Palace were substantially altered. The palace was gradually transformed into the ensemble we see today. To conform with the canons of Gothic style (and to bear comparison with the palace) the basilica was covered in pointed elements tending to

"St Mark's Square: polished and brilliant people have passed through here in successive epochs . . . all the techniques, all the materials have been used. Yet each new builder seems to have put his faith in his particular star."
Le Corbusier,
Propos d'urbanisme

"Around the buildings, the water, broad as a lake, weaves its magic setting of greenish and blueish hues, its mobile, crystalline sea-green. A thousand ripples glint before the breeze, with sunshine sparkling at their crests ... meantime the lustrous, luminous, enveloping sea penetrates Venice like a nimbus. And like a diamond in its setting, the Doge's Palace outshines all else.**"**

Hippolyte Taine,
Voyage en Italie

BULL-BAITING
It was the custom in Venice to greet important visitors with bull-baiting sessions ● *50* (right) on St Mark's Square. One such baiting session, which was held in 1740 for the heir to the throne of Poland, and the 1782 celebration in honor of the Czarevitch ▲ *169*, became legendary in the annals of Venetian history.

give an impression of greater height. At the turn of the 15th and 16th centuries it was decided to redesign the entire north side of the square, after which Mauro Coducci built the clocktower and rebuilt the Procuratie Vecchie, which had only two floors.

THE ARCHITECTS OF THE PIAZZA

At the start of the 16th century, the Republic launched a renovation programme to make St Mark's Square worthy of Venice's greatness and power.

SANSOVINO. The project was assigned to Jacopo Tatti (better known as Sansovino) who worked on it without interruption for more than thirty years, beginning in 1529, and becoming a model "State Architect" in the process. Sansovino completed the Procuratie Vecchie on the west side of the square, restored the basilica and the campanile, reconstructed the Zecca and the Church of San Geminiano, and built the Loggetta. Lastly he constructed the Libreria, with its arcades and loggias opposite the Doge's Palace, and made the Piazzetta "fit rival to Michelangelo's Campidoglio" (W Lotz).

SCAMOZZI. In the late 16th century the authorities committed themselves to the completion of Sansovino's Libreria and to rebuilding the entire south side of the Square. Vincenzo Scamozzi took charge of these works and erected the Procuratie Nuove; these were finished by Longhena, who attached them to the Church of San Geminiano. To make way for the new building, which was supposed "to give proper proportions to the square occupied by St Mark's Basilica, its principal element", the buildings of the Orseolo hospice were demolished because they were "too old and too ugly". When this was finished, St Mark's Square achieved its full magnificence, as Venice's "drawing room of Europe", public forum and theater.

THE FINAL TOUCHES

NEW PAVING. In 1723, Tirali was commissioned to change the paving of the square. He had just rebuilt the wall to the north of the basilica, placing two sculpted lions on either side of it – hence the name of Piazzetta dei Leoncini given to the little square adjoining it in 1722. He tore up the old brick pavement and replaced it with large slabs of trachyte, framed by bands of Istrian stone. His geometrical motifs follow the longitudinal axis of the square, heightening its effect of depth.

DEMOLITIONS AND RECONSTRUCTIONS. The only buildings which had not yet been tampered with were the 14th-century granaries (Granai di Terranova) next to the water after the Zecca. These were pulled down during the Napoleonic era to make way for the Royal Gardens (1808). A Napoleonic wing also displaced the Church of San Geminiano, and the Emperor's architects designed a new façade to the Doge's Palace on the Piazzetta dei Leoncini, which was completed between 1820 and 1843. A number of old houses were destroyed during this work, which radically altered the immediate area of the basilica.

THE THREE MASTS
"In the main square before the portal of St Mark's stand three tall ships' masts to which were attached three banners in red silk, picked out in rich gold, and at each side of the portal flew a lesser banner of like hue." (*Voyage to the Holy City of Jerusalem*, Anon, 1480.) On these three masts the banner of St Mark is still hoisted on feast days. the colors are still red and gold, but now they are surrounded by the colors of the Italian national flag. The masts stand on pedestals by Alessandro Leopardi. The one in the middle (1505) has a medallion with the effigy of Leonardo Loredan, Doge of Venice 1501–21.

❝Venice, which is not a civilization, is yet something more than a city – like Alexandria or Byzantium. Since Venice revelled longer than any other place, and died wearing a mask, we should perhaps linger there awhile.❞
André Malraux, *L'Irréel*

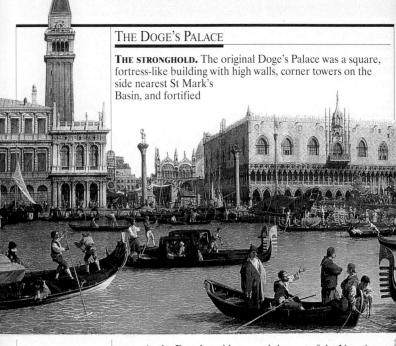

THE DOGE'S PALACE

THE STRONGHOLD. The original Doge's Palace was a square, fortress-like building with high walls, corner towers on the side nearest St Mark's Basin, and fortified

gates. As the Doge's residence and the seat of the Venetian government and magistrature, it contained armories, courtrooms and dungeons. Between the 14th and the 16th centuries, this huge edifice was transformed into the building which we see now, after succumbing to a series of fires. But above all changes in the palace were brought on by necessity, as Venice grew richer and her empire expanded. Each organ of power (such as the Grand Council, the Senate, the Seignory and the Council of Ten) had to have a seat worthy of its dignity. Hence, the need to supply the Grand Council with a new chamber for its deliberations was the first goal of the reconstruction.

THE DOGE'S PALACE. Rebuilt (respectively) in 1340 and 1424, the two wings of the palace bordering St Mark's Basin and the Piazzetta are among the finest examples of Gothic art anywhere in the world. They testify to an uncommon degree of architectural skill because, in a kind of reversal of equilibrium, an airily light gallery and arcade are made to support the overwhelming mass of the upper masonry. Moreover, the building is adorned with beautiful 14th–15th-century capitals and corner figures (such as Bartolomeo Bon's early 15th-century *Judgement of Solomon*). The PORTA DELLA CARTA, a masterpiece of Flamboyant Gothic (named after the scribes who used to sit copying out petitions, both here and in the vicinity of the State Archives), leads through to the

ACQUA ALTA ■ 26
Because it stands nearer to sea-level than the other quarters of Venice, St Mark's Square is frequently flooded at times of *acqua alta* (high tide) – as shown here during the winter of 1911. This phenomenon is a serious problem, for which a solution has yet to be found.

From the 17th century onwards, the myth of the Venetian government spread throughout Europe, and its institutions became an obligatory reference point in every area of political thought. Travelers, ambassadors and men of letters all admired the stability of a regime that appeared to be unaffected by the passing of time, and in the eyes of political thinkers the Republic was a harmonious combination of monarchical, aristocratic and democratic principles, in the form of the Doge, the Senate and the Grand Council.

THE PATRICIAN CLASS
The members of noble families who were inscribed in the Golden Book (which recorded births and marriages) all had a lifetime seat on the Grand Council.

THE SENATE
Created in about 1255, the Senate numbered sixty members selected from the Grand Council and elected for one year. To these were added sixty more members (LA ZONTA), also elected by the Grand Council, and various magistrates who did not all have the right to vote. The senators had to be more than thirty years old and were the only magistrates who could be re-elected at the end of their term. As a kind of council of sages (made up of hot-blooded younger men, old men rendered prudent by long experience, and men in the prime of mid-life, calm and sure of themselves) the Senate debated the measures that should be taken by the government, provided the state with most of its higher civil servants, performed administrative functions and recommended "its" candidates for election to magisterial offices. These candidates were then confirmed by the Grand Council.

THE "BROGLIO"
Venetian elections were subject to widespread fraud. Before ballots were cast, members of the Grand Council milled about in front of the palace, on the *broglio*, and the most powerful attempted to buy the votes of impoverished nobles – the *barnabotti*. This practice became known as *broglio* – hence the Italian expression *imbroglio* (entanglement).

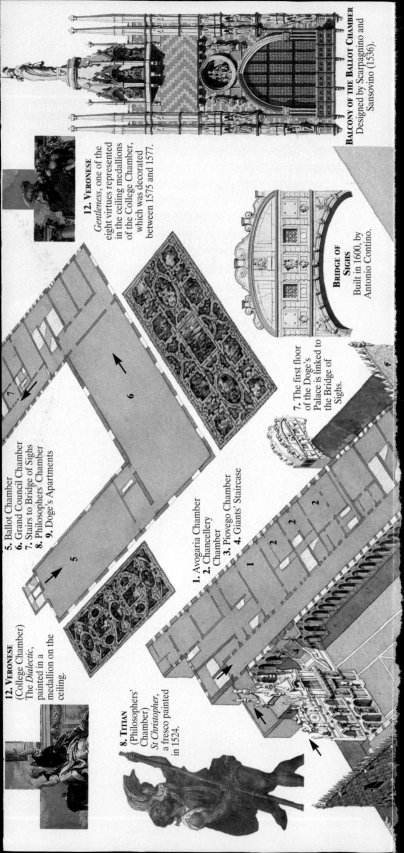

BALCONY OF THE BALLOT CHAMBER
Designed by Scarpagnino and Sansovino (1536).

12. VERONESE
Gentleness, one of the eight virtues represented in the ceiling medallions of the College Chamber, which was decorated between 1575 and 1577.

BRIDGE OF SIGHS
Built in 1600, by Antonio Contino.

7. The first floor of the Doge's Palace is linked to the Bridge of Sighs.

5. Ballot Chamber
6. Grand Council Chamber
7. Stairs to Bridge of Sighs
8. Philosophers' Chamber
9. Doge's Apartments

1. Avogaria Chamber
2. Chancellery Chamber
3. Piovego Chamber
4. Giants' Staircase

12. VERONESE
(College Chamber)
The *Dialectic*, painted in a medallion on the ceiling.

8. TITIAN
(Philosophers' Chamber)
St Christopher, a fresco painted in 1524.

▲ THE DOGE'S PALACE

The Grand Council and Senate made all the decisions about works to be carried out on the palace, clearly demonstrating that it was the property of the Republic and not of the Doge. While the names of the architects are not always known, the fame of artisans, decorators and, above all, painters who embellished the palace has long endured.

FAÇADE OVERLOOKING THE PIAZZETTA
The refined colors, as well as the play of light and shade on the Loggia Foscara and the Gothic arcades, make this façade a symbol of the majesty of the Venetian State.

14. VERONESE
(Chamber of the Council of Ten)
Youth and Age, painted in 1553–4.

14. CEILING OF THE CHAMBER OF THE COUNCIL OF TEN
Decorated by Giambattista Penchino and Veronese.

PORTA DELLA CARTA
The work of Giovanni and

10. Quattro Porte Chamber
11. College Antichamber
12. College Chamber
13. Senate Chamber
14. Chamber of the Council of Ten
15. Tre Capi Chamber
16. Inquisitors' Chamber

11. TINTORETTO
(College Antichamber)
The Discovery of Ariadne, Pallas and Mars; Mercury and the Graces; The Strength of Vulcan and Mercury and the Graces. These four canvases, painted in 1577–8, were originally intended for the square vestibule.

**BALCONY OF THE GRAND
COUNCIL CHAMBER**
The work of Dalle Masegne
(1404).

6. VERONESE
(Grand Council
Chamber)
Apotheosis of Venice,
painted in 1583.

6. TINTORETTO
(Grand Council
Chamber)
Paradise, painted 1588–94.
This grandiose work (23 x 72ft)
was commissioned to decorate
the walls of the chamber after the
ceiling was completed in 1584.

FOSCARI PORTICO and thence to the palace's magnificent inner courtyard. This area was closed off by a Renaissance east wing designed by Antonio Rizzo (1483), from the base of which rises the SCALA DEI GIGANTI (Giants' Staircase), which was the scene of the Doges' inaugurations. Also designed by Antonio Rizzo in 1485, this staircase was decorated by Sansovino in the second half of the 16th century with the statues of Mars and Neptune, symbolizing Venice's domination of land and sea. The SCALA D'ORO (Gold Staircase), also by Sansovino, leads from the loggia floor to the upper levels of the building, past a riot of stuccos and frescoes.

THE INTERIOR OF THE PALACE. The rooms of the Doge's Palace were intended to illustrate the entire history of Venice, painted by some of her greatest 16th-century masters. Their work here defines Venice's greatest triumphs, from her mythical foundation and her institutions to her military victories. But more striking perhaps than the pictures of these great historical events is the vivid sense one has of the daily bustle that once enlivened the palace. The first floor was occupied by several minor institutions, namely the AVOGARIA (which examined cases at law), the CHANCELLERY, the CENSORS and the PROVVEDITORI DELLA MILIZIA DA MAR (which was in charge of equipping Venice's galleys). The GRAND COUNCIL held its sessions on the second floor, in the largest chamber of the palace. Tintoretto's magnificent late 15th-century *Paradise* (23 ft x 72 ft) dominates this chamber, the walls of which are covered with works by Veronese, Palma the Younger and Bassano, all of which extol the martial prowess of the Serene Republic. The same theme prevails in the BALLOT CHAMBER, where the votes of the Grand Council were counted and where the committee met to elect the Doge. Just below the ceiling is a frieze containing the portraits of every one of Venice's Doges, whose apartments were also here. On the third floor, the SALA DELLE QUATTRO PORTE contains Tintoretto's ceiling illustrating the foundation of the city, *Jupiter leading Venice into the Adriatic*, 1577; after that is the SALA DEL COLLEGIO, where the Seignory met and foreign ambassadors were received. After the SENATE CHAMBER come the rooms used by the state security service – the COUNCIL OF TEN – which were decorated, like the SALA DEL COLLEGIO, by Veronese; the SALA DELLA BUSSOLA, with one of the boxes used for written denunciations which were formerly a common feature of the city; the SALA DEI TRE CAPI was the room used by the Council of Ten's "three heads", each of whom was chosen for a period of one month at a time; and lastly the room used by the STATE INQUISITORS. The tour ends with the palace's COLLECTION OF ARMS AND ARMOR, most of it captured from enemies.

PORTA DELLA CARTA
Recently restored, the elegant "paper doorway" to the Doge's Palace was made in the years following 1438 by the Bon brothers. The statues of Strength and Temperance in its lower section are attributed to Pietro Lombardo; those of Prudence and Charity are by Antonio Bregno. The statues of the Doge

Francesco Foscari and the winged lion, which were destroyed in 1797, were remade in 1885 by Luigi Ferrari.

BOSCH
In the TRE CAPI chamber hang several canvases commissioned from the Flemish painter Hieronymus Bosch.

THE GRAND COUNCIL

This body was intended to represent the whole city of Venice. But in 1297, with the "Closure of the Grand Council" (*La Serrata del Gran Consiglio*) ● 31, access to it was narrowed to life membership for the members of noble families only. The council, which numbered just over a thousand nobles in the 13th century, grew to twice that size in the 16th century. Extraordinary service to the Republic, or else the payment of a substantial sum to the government, could elevate certain commoners to membership of the Grand Council, with their names included in the Golden Book. The council could not initiate laws, but had the right to veto the more important ones. On the other hand, since it selected the members of future governments, it could also channel and legitimize an individual's political ambitions. The continuity of this self-perpetuating governing class was unique in Europe.

THE DOGE'S HATS

THE DOGE

The Doge of Venice personified the unity that existed in the Republic. Elected for life by the Grand Council, he was usually chosen from among the greatest Venetian families, and had to have attained a respectable age (often at least seventy). The Doge reigned rather than governed; his powers were limited and his actions severely controlled, even though in theory he had a say in all important decisions. He could not take any decision in the absence of his six councillors (one for each sestiere of the city). Indeed he did not even have the right to leave Venice, unless he was accompanied by two or more of these councillors.

THE "CORNO"

This hat, worn by the Doge, had a strange rounded peak and a broad band. It was covered in precious stones and was woven in cloth of silver and gold, on a base of velvet and damask.

...e Ballot Chamber
...ne Doge's Palace,
...e portrait of Falier
...s replaced by a
black veil.

HIC EST LOCVS MARINI FALETRI
DECAPITATI PRO CRIMINIBVS

MARIN FALIER
After entering government service as a very young man, Marin Falier ended his long and brilliant career, at the age of seventy-six, decapitated by the executioner's sword. In 1355, just after his election as Doge, Falier led a popular conspiracy. Betrayed by a follower, he was sentenced by the Council of Ten, which he had controlled at the age of thirty. He was executed on April 17, 1355, in the courtyard of the Doge's Palace, and his head was displayed on the Piazzetta.

THE APPORTIONING OF POWER WITHIN THE REPUBLIC
No single institution monopolized power, and no single decision making body could operate unchecked by another. The quick rotation of all offices -- except those of the Doge and the nine procurators of St Mark's (State Treasurers) – made it difficult for a single individual or faction to appropriate power. The opposition did actually have a place in the system and did not need to plot its downfall in order to make itself heard, since everyone had a hand in the decision making process and in the election of magistrates. Moreover, the complexity of the authorities above the Grand Council level rendered personal ambition more or less futile. This system survived until 1797 and ensured the existence of a government that was as stable as it was effective.

THE SEIGNORY
The Seignory consisted of the six councillors of the Doge and the three heads of the QUARANTIA (supreme tribunals which pronounced judgement in the civil and criminal appeal courts, and on the most serious penal offenses).

THE COUNCIL OF TEN
Set up in 1310 after the con⁵ Bajamonte Tiepolo ▲ *214*. council of sixteen membₑ Doge) was a permanenᵗ the end of the 14th cₑ

The Doge
procession. .
this 16th-cent.
is more than 13 .

The ballot ᵥ
secret with eₐ
voter slipping ᵢ
fist intᵥ
an
urn
to
cast
his
vote. To be
elected, a
candidate needed
to win a
minimum of
twenty-five
votes.

Wax counters of three different colors
were used as ballots, but then it was
realized that the wax melted in the hand,
so they were replaced by counters made
of canvas. The
counting was
done with little
modelled hands
made of
wood or
gold.

Its members, chosen by the Grand Council and
renewed a third at a time, were not permitted to
be related to the Doge since their function was
both to observe him and to work with him. The
Seignory determined the order of the elections to
the magistrature and made sure that they were
carried out correctly, but it had to answer for its
decisions to the Senate.

THE "BALLOTINO"

For the final election, two
nobles went to the basilica
and picked out a ten-year-
old boy from the crowd.
This boy distributed the
counters and added
them up after the
vote. He
then
remained
in the
Doge's
service.

he Council's competence was extended from
domain of crimes against the state to cover
ʳisions requiring absolute secrecy. Often
ᵈ as a despotic power ruling the city, its
ᵒn was to prevent the ambition of
ᵗizens from threatening the State.

SAINT MARK'S BASILICA ★

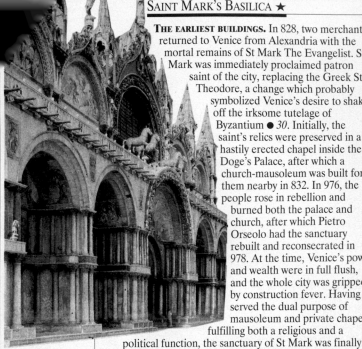

THE EARLIEST BUILDINGS. In 828, two merchants returned to Venice from Alexandria with the mortal remains of St Mark The Evangelist. St Mark was immediately proclaimed patron saint of the city, replacing the Greek St Theodore, a change which probably symbolized Venice's desire to shake off the irksome tutelage of Byzantium ● *30*. Initially, the saint's relics were preserved in a hastily erected chapel inside the Doge's Palace, after which a church-mausoleum was built for them nearby in 832. In 976, the people rose in rebellion and burned both the palace and church, after which Pietro Orseolo had the sanctuary rebuilt and reconsecrated in 978. At the time, Venice's power and wealth were in full flush, and the whole city was gripped by construction fever. Having served the dual purpose of mausoleum and private chapel, fulfilling both a religious and a political function, the sanctuary of St Mark was finally demolished along with the neighboring Church of St Theodore to make way for a third and last building in 1063.

THE BYZANTINE BASILICA. Venice was already the gateway between the Orient and the West, though she still acknowledged the cultural supremacy of Byzantium. For this reason the city of the Doges produced a cathedral that was completely oriental in aspect, modelled on two basilicas in Constantinople – the Church of the Holy Apostles (now destroyed), and St Sophia. With its centralized, Greek cross floor plan, and its choir slightly raised to make space for a crypt ▲ *239* below, the basilica, consecrated in 1094, appeared structurally foursquare and robust on account of its brickwork and the cluster of low domes.

THE FAÇADES. Between the 11th and the 15th centuries, the basilica's aspect changed with the addition of a mass of ornament to its façades. Each of the original low domes was covered with a second cupola in wood, with a lead skin topped by a lantern and a gilded cross. The brickwork was concealed behind marble patterns, while in front of the main façade rose a double line of small columns that were topped by capitals, also of rare marble from the East. Leaf-work, aedicules and spires were grafted on to the arcades as Gothic additions, while the main portal was decorated with bas-reliefs representing the various crafts, and the signs of the zodiac. Towards the present Piazzetta dei Leoncini, an arch was constructed (the Arch of Sant'Alippio). Some of these ornamentations were bought or captured in distant Orien~ countries by Venetian merchants, or else seized during ~ and crusades. This was the case with the two pilasters Acre, fine specimens of 6th-century Syrian art take~

The lame man gnawing his knuckles on the third arch is said to be a likeness of the architect of the basilica. Having fallen from the scaffolding in a transport of admiration for one of the domes, he is biting himself in rage because the church he built is not as beautiful as he hoped.

❝The five domes of the basilica reigned in the sky like enormous bishops' mitres glittering with precious stones.❞
Gabriele d'Annunzio

«ABHORRENT GREEN, SLIPPERY CITY, WHOSE DOGES
WERE OLD, AND HAD ANCIENT EYES.»

DH LAWRENCE

victory over the Genoese in the 13th century; and of the
TETRARCHS, an example of 4th-century Egyptian-Syrian
carving in porphyry which is still a part of the façade that
gives on to the Piazzetta.

**FIDELITY TO THE
ORIENTAL STYLE.** The
crowning of the
arcades, which allowed
the basilica to grow in
height and brought it
into harmony with the
Doge's Palace, was
really a concession to
Gothic art. The slow
process of covering the
façades led to a great mixture of styles. But perhaps the most
striking thing about St Mark's is its persistent Orientalism,
showing that although the balance of power between
Byzantium and Venice was changing in Venice's favor, the
Republic's taste in architecture was still Oriental. The city in
general, and St Mark's in particular, showed astounding
fidelity to Byzantium – or perhaps a desire to appropriate her
culture. This continuity is most evident in the use of mosaics, a
typically Byzantine trait; and the extravagant use of gold as
background, even on the façade. Thus the lunettes of the
upper register portray the *Deposition of Christ*, *Christ's
Descent into Limbo*, the *Resurrection*, and the *Ascension*; on
the lower register, the lunette of the main portal is filled by a
Last Judgement, and those of the side portals by pictures of
the transportation of the relics of St Mark. These decorations
were added quite late in the day, with the exception of the last
mosaic on the left (13th-century) representing the *Relics of St
Mark Transported into the Basilica*, which shows the building as
it was prior to the addition of its Gothic elements.

**THE PIETRA DEL
BANDO**
At the corner nearest
the Piazzetta is a
proclamation stone
(pietra del bando)
like the one at the
Rialto ▲ 283, made
from a piece of
porphyry brought
from Syria in the 13th
century. Government
decrees were
announced from here.

HIC·DEFERT·
OR·P·SSÇIM ARCI

THE GOLDEN SANCTUARY. You enter St Mark's through a narthex, which serves as a transitional space between the exterior portal (an open and light-filled area) and the interior, a place of serenity in which semi-darkness alternates with golden shafts of light. Far from revealing itself at a single glance, this secret, internalized space impinges very slowly on the consciousness. The first visual barrier you encounter is the iconostasis ▲ 165, like the narthex, a typical feature of Oriental churches. It is made of red marble with polychrome panels. Columns with capitals support its architrave, which is adorned with statues by the dalle Masegne that are masterpieces of 14th-century Gothic. Beyond these, on the high altar, glitters the PALA D'ORO, a 14th-century altarpiece of gold. About three thousand precious stones and eighty plaques of enamel, some from Constantinople, are set into a Gothic mounting, the work of a Siennese goldsmith in 1345. The upper register illustrates the principal festivals of the church. In the middle, Christ is conferring his blessing, surrounded by four prophets and the images of the Virgin, the Empress Irina and the Doge Ordelafo Falier (on the right). On either side are three tiers of angels, apostles and prophets. Apart from this altarpiece, the TREASURE OF ST MARK's comprises a collection of icons and sacred objects, most of which came to Venice after the sack of

Constantinople ● 31, and is displayed in what may have been a corner tower of the first Doge's Palace. The 12th-century PAVEMENT is of marble and mosaic with alternating animal shapes and geometrical designs, reflecting Byzantine taste ▲ 240.

MURAL MOSAICS. The work of decorating the inside of St Mark's proceeded for several hundred years until the building was covered in an astonishing 10,764 square feet of mosaic. Since this was intended to teach the faithful the rudiments of sacred history, the story is depicted on the walls of the church like a gigantic illuminated Bible. As in Byzantium, the figure of Christ has pride of place. Thus, beginning at the back of the basilica, the sequence is as follows: in the apse, Christ Pantocrator (11th-century, partially remade in the 16th century); in the first dome, Christ Emmanuel (the young Christ, 12th-century); at the crossing of the transept, the Ascension ▲ 240 (13th-century); and finally, the Pentecost (first hal' the 12th-century). Though they may have been executed by local craftsmen, all these mosaics Byzantine stillness, with figures bearing n individuality, and the general mass of su matter in perfect balance. While the d transept are dedicated to St John the and St Leonard, along the main ar

DETAIL OF THE PALA D'ORO. Apparently when the two Venetian merchants Rustico and Buono brought the remains of the martyred St Mark from Alexandria, they hid them under a layer of pork so Muslim officials would not investigate too closely.

of the central nave run a series of episodes from evangelical history, regulated according to Byzantine iconographic canons to illustrate the principal festivals of the Christian Church. Thus the Passion (mid-13th century) appears on the main arch between the Ascension and Pentecost. This scene, in which the participants bear witness to Christ, shows the first stirrings of a taste for more sophisticated effects, with some angels revealing only part of their bodies. Elements from the Western, Romanesque and Gothic traditions have crept in here, as in the scene from the lives of Christ and the Virgin (right-hand nave and left-hand transept). The vision of the artists is more animated and more fluid: we are coming nearer to the 15th century and the close of the first and greatest period of St Mark's. Henceforth, mosaic art sought increasingly to compete with painting, introducing painterly relief and perspective. After a final

Part of the treasure.

THE LEGEND OF SAINT MARK
"Pax tibi Marce Evangeliste meus."
"Peace be unto you, Mark my Evangelist." These were the words that were spoken by an angel to St Mark when he came to the

harmonious phase in the early 15th century, when they were influenced by Tuscan masters such as Paolo Uccello and Andrea del Castagno (see the four saints in the rear of the right transept), the mosaic artists were happy to copy cartoons supplied by the great masters of painting, applying canons that were ill-adapted to their technique. Nevertheless, there are other panels here that are well worth a look, notably the *Dance of Salome* (14th-century) in the baptistry, and a beautiful *Creation* (13th-century) in the Old Testament sequence that adorns the narthex.

Lagoon, thus apparently leaving the saint in no doubt that Venice would be his final resting-place. The theft of the relics was held to be justified, since it was considered to be no more than the fulfilment of a divine prediction.

237

SAINT MARK'S SQUARE
THE MOSAICS OF THE BASILICA

The relics, which were brought from Egypt by merchants, had been hidden in the column of San Giacomo, near the altar, in order to foil the claims of the clergy of Alexandria. After their discovery, they were lodged in the crypt of the basilica.

ST MARK TAKING A SH[IP] TO ALEXANDRIA (Zen Chapel, 13th century) The supple lines and motifs of this mosai[c] are in strong contra[st] to the hieratic stiffne[ss] of Byzantine art.

THE CRYPT OF THE BASILICA, with its central vaulting, harbored the relics of St Mark until 1811. Its heavy, archaic style is typical of the 11th century.

THE DISCOVERY OF THE BODY OF ST MARK, at which Doge Vitale Falier and a few members of the Seignory were present. This "miracle", which took place on June 25, 1094, is illustrated by a 13th-century mosaic on the west wall of the transept.

THE DANCE OF SALOME (baptistery). This fascinating image stands out from the rest of the mosaic cycle dealing with the life of John the Baptist (14th-century).

ST JOHN among the guardian angels of the Seven Churches of the Orient (detail of the arch of the Apocalypse, completed in the 16th century by the Zuccato brothers, after a drawing by Palma the Younger.

THE CREATION OF EVE This is the 15th of the 24 concentric motifs in the dome of the Creation (13th century) at the south end of the narthex.

The Gothic treatment of Salome – who seduced Herod and so obtained the head of St John the Baptist – is a graceful, lascivious contrast to the Byzantine rigidity of the kings.

DETAIL FROM THE ARCH OF THE APOCALYPSE

CROSS-SECTION OF THE BASILICA, SHOWN LENGTHWISE

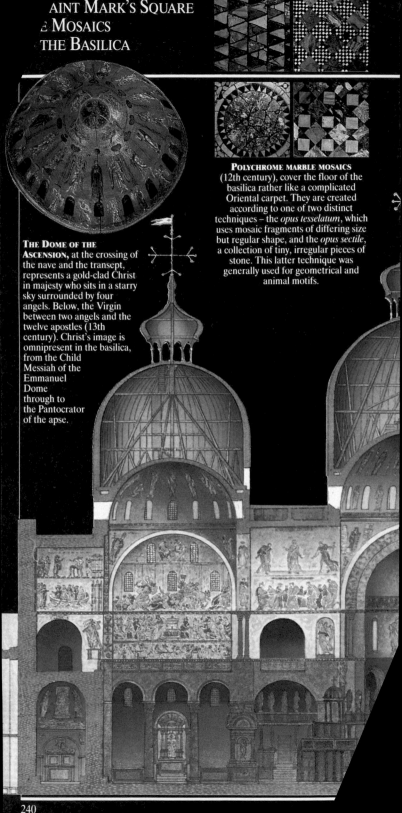

ʌINT MARK'S SQUARE
ʌ MOSAICS
THE BASILICA

POLYCHROME MARBLE MOSAICS
(12th century), cover the floor of the
basilica rather like a complicated
Oriental carpet. They are created
according to one of two distinct
techniques – the *opus tesselatum*, which
uses mosaic fragments of differing size
but regular shape, and the *opus sectile*,
a collection of tiny, irregular pieces of
stone. This latter technique was
generally used for geometrical and
animal motifs.

**THE DOME OF THE
ASCENSION,** at the crossing of
the nave and the transept,
represents a gold-clad Christ
in majesty who sits in a starry
sky surrounded by four
angels. Below, the Virgin
between two angels and the
twelve apostles (13th
century). Christ's image is
omnipresent in the basilica,
from the Child
Messiah of the
Emmanuel
Dome
through to
the Pantocrator
of the apse.

CHRIST'S ENTRY INTO JERUSALEM
This late 12th-century mosaic, which adorns the main arch of the south transept, is a faithful illustration of the texts of the Gospels. Children are shown crowding around the figure of Christ and spreading their coats under the hooves of his donkey.

ST MARK MEDITATING ON HIS GOSPEL
(North-west side of the Ascension dome.) The patron saint of the basilica is shown adopting the pose of a Byzantine scribe.

CROSS-SECTION OF THE BASILICA

According to a recent theory, the horses of St Mark's are Roman in origin, but with features borrowed from Greek art (the manes, for example) and dating from either the 2nd or 3rd century after Christ.

THE HEADLESS HORSES
The horse-statues were cast in a metal of extraordinary composition – almost entirely pure copper, much more difficult to melt than ordinary bronze, but also much easier to gild. Each statue was cast in two sections, with the joint concealed by the collar. Some people think that they may have been dissected for transportation from Constantinople, and then arbitrarily reassembled on their arrival.

THE HORSES OF ST MARK

In the LOGGIA DEI CAVALLI is a copy of this celebrated quadriga of horses in gilded bronze, which seems so lifelike that the animals might at any moment "neigh and stamp their feet", as Petrarch wrote. Stored in a safe place during the two World Wars, their originals were recently taken down from the basilica, victims of pollution. After restoration, they were reinstalled under cover in an exhibition room.

A SYMBOL OF VENETIAN FREEDOM. The origins of the horses are hotly disputed. Are they Greek or Roman sculptures from the fourth or third century BC, or are they from the time of Constantine (3rd century AD)? Another theory is that they were made by Lysippus, Alexander's court sculptor, but no-one now seriously believes the old contention that they came from Corinth. The most probable theory is that they once stood at the Hippodrome in Constantinople, while the only certainty is that they came to Venice in 1204 with other booty from the Crusades ● *31*. Fifty years later they were saved from oblivion by an anonymous ambassador from Florence, who saw them at the Arsenal. Subsequently it was suggested that they be placed on top of St Mark's, which was being repaired at the time. Once in place they quickly became the symbols of untrammelled Venice. But it seems to have been their destiny to be despoiled by occupying armies, for five centuries later they were once again removed, this time by Napoleon Bonaparte.

BONAPARTE AND THE HORSES OF SAINT MARK. In 1792, with all Europe in coalition against Revolutionary France, Venice opted to stay neutral, hoping the war would pass her by. The Republic was anyway no more than a shadow of its former self, and the city's fame only rested on the beauty of its palaces and churches, for Venetian military and naval power had vanished following the loss of Morea in 1718 ● *34*. The Doge Lodovico Manin and the Grand Council stuck to their neutral line until 1796, when the Directoire régime in France offered a full alliance; but ultimately the Republic could not prevent either Austrian or French troops from crossing Venetian territory. After his victory over the Austrians at Rivoli (January 14, 1797) Bonaparte decided to make peace with Vienna. Aware that his enemies would be reluctant to give up their positions on the left bank of the Rhine, he had the idea of offering them Venice in exchange. In the spring of 1797, French troops in the Veneto were attacked by

> «THE FOUR HORSES OF LYSIPPUS LEAPT INTO THE CLOUDS,
> ARCHING THEIR NECKS TO WHICH THE GOLD STILL CLUNG,
> PROUD TO BE YET IN THE SIGHT OF MAN.»
>
> PAUL MORAND

NAPOLEON IN VENICE
From November 29 to December 8, 1807, Venice entertained her sovereign, the Emperor Napoleon. Accompanied by Prince Eugène ▲ *181*, he was welcomed with enthusiasm (eight years of Austrian rule having softened the memory of six months' occupation by the French). Napoleon's entire visit was a succession of balls and celebrations.

the population, and Bonaparte, refusing the apologies of the Venetian Senate and demanding a change in the Republic's constitution, marched on the city. On May 12, the Doge and Grand Council resigned amid general panic. On May 16, a municipality was chosen in the name of the people, and a committee of public safety elected. At the request of this new government, Bonaparte's soldiers occupied the city, while Austria seized Istria and Dalmatia, Venetian territories allotted to the Empire at the Leoben negotiations before the Treaty of Campo Formio ● *34*. At the conclusion of this treaty (October 17, 1797) Bonaparte summarily informed the Venetian envoy of his country's fate. Thus, with a single stroke of a pen, and no discussion of her secular rights, one of Europe's oldest states was dismantled. Before surrendering Venice to the Austrians as the treaty required, the French systematically looted all that they could carry. Among the treasures they took (including paintings, the gilt of the Bucintoro ● *38*, and manuscripts) were the horses that had long been the symbol of Venetian liberty. Brought to Paris, they were "harnessed" to a chariot and installed in the Tuileries on the Arch of the Carrousel. Austrian troops entered Venice on January 18, 1798, to be greeted as liberators, so great was Venetian hatred for the nation that had betrayed them and pillaged the city.

But, on December 26, 1805, Napoleon imposed the Treaty of Presbourg on the Holy Roman Empire in the wake of his victory at Austerlitz. By this treaty, Venice and the Veneto were incorporated into the Kingdom of Italy. The city reverted to the French for seven years, before the final takeover by Austria and the return of the quadriga and other works of art in 1815.

THE TREE OF LIBERTY
In May 1797, a bay tree was planted on St Mark's Square, around which the populace danced the Carmagnole.

A savage caricature of Napoleon, with the face portrayed as a mass of corpses.

THE PROCURATIES

THE PROCURATORS OF THE REPUBLIC. The two long buildings of the Procuratie Vecchie and the Procuratie Nuove, which occupy the sides of St Mark's Square, formerly accommodated the offices of the Procurators of St Mark, the highest officials in the Republic, with the exception of the Doge. These magistrates and administrators of state property were nine in number, divided into teams of three: the *de supra* procurators, who attended the basilica and St Mark's Square, and the *de citra* and *de ultra* procurators, who looked after Venice's six sestieri.

THE PROCURATIE VECCHIE. In the 12th century, following the decision of the *de supra* procurators to install themselves near the basilica, the Procuratie Vecchie were constructed, only to be destroyed by fire and rebuilt in the 16th century. Bartolomeo Bon (seconded by Guglielmo dei Grigi) directed

INVESTITURE OF THE PROCURATOR
At this major event in Venetian life, the elected official gave bread to the poor and wine to the gondoliers, and threw parties for the nobility. He went in state to the basilica, where he swore an oath to do honor to his office before taking possession of an apartment in the Procuraties, which thenceforth bore his name.

the works, according to a design by Coducci. The project stressed the functional nature of this building, which was intended above all to house offices – as it does to this day.

THE PROCURATIE NUOVE. With the development of the administrative activities of the procurators, there arose a need for a second building, the PROCURATIE NUOVE, on the site of the Orseolo hospice, a venerable institution which figures in Gentile Bellini's painting of *The Procession of Corpus Christi* ● 48. The works began in 1586 under Scamozzi's direction. Interrupted by the death of the architect in 1616, the buildings were finally completed by Longhena in 1640. The Procuratie Nuove were a part of the general reorganization of the square, which had been under way for some time ▲ 222. Their aspect was rather more official and sober than that of the Procuratie Vecchie. They also contained lodgings for the Procurators, who moved in reluctantly, since they were having to leave their splendid palaces for what they considered to be poky cubbyholes.

> «EACH ARCADE SERVED AS THE ENTRANCE TO A COFFEE SHOP,
> WHICH WAS NEVER OTHERWISE THAN FILLED WITH PEOPLE.»
>
> CHARLES DE BROSSES

THE CAFÉS

THE BOTTEGHE DEL CAFFÈ. The first *bottega del caffè* opened under the Procuraties in 1683, and thereafter such cafés quickly multiplied. Many of them were similar to taverns, with low ceilings, no windows, poor lighting and the bare minimum of furniture. A century later, there were no fewer than twenty-four cafés situated on St Mark's Square alone, and they acquired such importance in Venetian life during the 18th century that Goldoni ▲ 291 had a café owner say in his *La Bottega del Caffè*: "My profession is necessary to the glory of our city, to men's health, and to the honest amusement of

people who need to breathe easy for a spell." In due course, people of all ages and walks of life came to relax in these public places. But affinities, professional or otherwise, often tended to play a part in the choice of one café as against another. Patrons played cards, a passion with Venetians, in these establishments; likewise the cafés became the

traditional meeting place of lovers, so much so that the government, which had long sought to impose its control, decided to make them off limits to women in 1767. Certain cafés also were known as the resort of men of letters.

FLORIAN'S. In 1720, an elegant new café was opened under the arcades of the Procuratie Nuove. It started out with a name that roughly translated as "Venice Triumphant", and which quickly reverted to the Café Florian in honor of its first owner, Floriano Francesconi. Venetian high society soon took the Florian to its heart: Goldoni was a regular habitué, as were the Gozzi brothers, Canova, and (a hundred years later) Balzac, who wrote of it: "Florian's is at once a stock exchange, a theater foyer, a reading room, a club, and a confessional, and it is so suited to the multiplicity of this nation's affairs that some Venetian women have no idea at all as to what kind of business their husbands conduct, because whenever a man has a letter to write, he goes to this café for the purpose." Today, as in the past, a half-hour spent on the terrace of Florian's, or in one of its magnificent coffee-rooms, is one of the greatest delights to be found in Venice.

AN ORIENTAL BEVERAGE
In 1585, the Venetian ambassador to Istanbul described before the Senate the customs of the Turks, who "drank a species of blackened water, drawn from a grain called *kahave*, which doth keep them awake." This grain, roasted and ground and viewed as a form of medicine, was sold in Venice from 1638

onwards at a very high price. But by 1676 it had become so popular that the Senate decided to impose a higher duty on its importation.

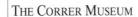

"DAEDALUS AND ICARUS"
This marble group (right) stands in the Throne Room and dates from 1778–9. It signals Canova's arrival as a sculptor and his passage from the Mannerism of the 18th-century to the Neo-classical style.

THE QUADRI. Opened in 1775 by Giorgio Quadri, a native of Corfu, this café, situated opposite Florian's was one of the first in Venice to serve real Turkish coffee. It would seem that Quadri enlarged and converted an older premises in order to make it rather more elegant. Nevertheless, for many years, his café had a bad reputation, its owner being constantly beset by creditors. Only in 1830 did the Quadri finally begin to attract the kind of elegant clientèle which may still be seen there today.

THE CORRER MUSEUM

FRANCESCO FOSCARI
Doge of Venice 1423–57.

SAN GEMINIANO
Sansovino completed the façade and dome of this church, which was begun in 1505 on far older foundations.

THE NAPOLEONIC WING. The construction of a building to close off the end of St Mark's Square began in about 1810, after the demolition of Jacopo Sansovino's 17th-century Church of San Geminiano. The new building not only replaced this church but also the respective wings of the Procuratie Vecchie and Nuove. It was designed by Giuseppe Maria Soli for the Napoleonic court, and it is clearly inspired by the Neo-classical Libreria Marciana, with a top floor that is adorned by statues and bas-reliefs glorifying Napoleon Bonaparte.
THE MUSEUM OF VENETIAN CIVILIZATION. The entrance to the Correr Museum is located at the top of the formal staircase which formerly led to the reception rooms of the Napoleonic wing. The latter only contains a part of the collections, the rest being exhibited in the Procuratie Vecchie. The museum itself owes its name to Teodoro Correr, a Venetian gentleman, who on his death in 1830 left his entire rich collection to the city of Venice. Opened in 1922, this "Museum of the City and Civilization of Venice" is made up of three main sections. On the first floor, after a suite of Neo-classical rooms, is the HISTORY SECTION. Beyond the Napoleonic loggia, frescoes by Giuseppe Borsato in the throne-room offer a fitting backdrop to the works of Antonio Canova, who was the greatest Italian exponent of the Neo-classical style. Among his sculptures that are shown here are a fine rendering of *Daedalus and Icarus* and a terracotta group entitled *Eros and Psyche*, a rough cast for the marble masterpiece at the Louvre. In the richly decorated former dining room are a series of views of Venice and Milan, among them a picturesque Piazza *San Marco at High Water*. Here begins a

The Napoleonic wing, seen from the Basilica. The cornice bears images from mythology and statues by Domenico Banti and Antonio Bosa. Below, the monumental main staircase, designed by Giuseppe Maria Soli.

journey that travels through the history of Venice. The visitor has barely had time in which to admire the marble effigies of the Lion of St Mark, before the figure of the Doge appears (represented by the *corno*, oath and election to that office ▲ *231, 233*). After this comes a representation of the principal feasts of Venice ● *48* (Ascension, the Feast of the Redeemer ▲ *339* . . .), which is followed by an evocation of the great offices of the Republic by way of a display of the costumes that were worn by its dignitaries – including the gown of mourning that used to be worn by the Doge on Good Friday. Coins, representations of the Bucintoro ● *38*, the Battle of Lepanto ● *36* and a collection of arms and armor (in the Morosini Room) all testify to the former vitality and grandeur that was such a feature of Venice.

The Man in the Red Cap, by Carpaccio.

THE PAINTINGS SECTION. On the second floor, the picture gallery demonstrates the great wealth of Venetian painting that existed between the 13th and 16th centuries. After sculpture's adoption of a more realistic style (as demonstrated in the 14th-century *Doge Antonio Venier*, by J delle Masegne), the painters followed suit; hence Paolo Veneziano's Byzantine art ▲ *302* (*Six Saints*, late 14th-century) is close to Gothic, as in *Jesus Giving St Peter the Keys of Heaven* (1369) by Lorenzo Veneziano. But Byzantine art was soon to yield altogether, for by the 14th century the problems of rendering space and light in paint had been largely solved by the Renaissance. Each artist was now able to express himself in his own idiom, above all chromatically. There is a noteworthy contrast, for example, to be found between the poignant tension of the *Pietà* by the Ferraran Cosmè Tura (c.1468) and the golden atmosphere and miniaturistic, rustic backdrop of the *Pietà* of Antonello da Messina (1475–6). The room dedicated to Bellini ▲ *304* contains some of the treasures that were bequeathed by one of the most prolific of Venice's artistic families, among them a *Transfiguration* (1455–60) and a *Madonna and Child* (1460–4) in which the delicate light suffusing the work of Giovanni Bellini lends great force to the serenity and poetry of his art. Further on, with Carpaccio's *Courtesans* (1510–15), the colors take on a new gaiety and brightness. The paintings section of the museum ends with Lorenzo Lotto's *The Madonna with the Christ Child at her Breast*, c.1525, a canvas that is full of tormented realism.

In his *Eurydice* (1775) Antonio Canova gives proof of his interest in the Baroque style; there is no indication here of Neo-classicism, of which he was to become one of the greatest exponents.

MUSEUM OF THE RISORGIMENTO. Here the collections of paintings and objets d'art reflect the difficult period between the fall of the Republic in 1797, and Venice's annexation to the Kingdom of Italy in 1866 ● *35*.

THE CAMPANILE

THE MASTER OF THE HOUSE. From Coryate to Goethe, writers have advised visitors to Venice to climb the steps of St Mark's Campanile for its sublime view across the city and Lagoon. Standing where the Piazza meets the Piazzetta, this campanile is a full 315 feet high. It was built in the 8th century to serve as a guard tower for the dock ▲ *220*, the *paron di casa* (master of the house) as it is known to Venetians. It was then reconstructed, heightened and modified during the 12th, 14th and 16th centuries. It is crowned by a pyramid-shaped spire with a golden angel weathervane that turns with the wind. The campanile also contains the five bells of St Mark's, which can be heard across Venice tolling out the hours. In the time of the Republic, each bell had its own name: the big one was called Marangona (from the term for the widespread profession of carpenter, which was virtually a synonym for "worker" in Venice). Marangona was tolled morning and evening, to mark the beginning and end of each working day. The smallest bell, il Maleficio, announced death sentences, and La Nona marked the hour of the nones, while the Pregadi bell was rung to summon senators to the Doge's Palace. Finally, it was to the sound of La Trottiera that the magistrates made their way to the palace until the 14th century, no doubt trotting on horseback. On July 14, 1902, at 10 o'clock, the old campanile collapsed. Nobody was injured, but it totally demolished the nearby Loggetta of Sansovino. The decision was taken to rebuild the campanile "where it was, and like it was", using the original materials. The same applied to the Loggetta.

THE LOGGETTA. This building replaced a *ridotto* ▲ *259*, which had itself supplanted some wooden shops. It was built by Sansovino between 1537 and 1549, and was completed by a terrace and balustrade in 1663. From 1569 the Loggetta was the barracks of the Guard of the Doge's Palace. With its three arcades separated by double columns, this building's small façade covered in mottled marble and allegorical figures representing Good Government (Apollo, Peace, Mercury and Minerva), made it possible to integrate the campanile with the rest of the piazza's architecture.

«AND THE "MORI" OF THE CLOCKTOWER RANG OUT THE HOURS,
OBEDIENT TO THEIR ANCIENT DUTY OF MEASURING
THE PASSAGE OF TIME.»

ALEJO CARPENTIER

THE CLOCKTOWER ● 98

The clocktower stands on the north side of the square; the
Merceria, Venice's principal shopping street, begins on
the far side of its arch, to the left. A Renaissance building,
the clocktower was constructed towards the end of the
15th century by Mauro Coducci. Later, in 1755, terraces
were affixed to it by Giorgio Massari. The central corpus
of the clocktower, which has remained unchanged since
its construction, has three different registers directly
above the arch. Each of them is heavily ornamented with
colored décor and gilt. Immediately above the arch is the
clock itself, a huge object made of gilt and blue enamel
that rather resembles an eye watching over St Mark's Basin.
In addition to the time, it also records the phases of the moon
and of the zodiac. This clock is contemporary to the tower
itself and was designed in order to assist people planning sea

voyages, providing information about the
tides and the most favorable months for
navigation. Higher up the façade, on
either side of a niche containing a statue
of the Madonna, are two little doors
through which, at Ascensiontide ● 38,
carved figures of the Three Kings were
made to process. In the upper register
stands a lion of St Mark against the
backdrop of a starry sky. Finally, the
whole tower is crowned by a celebrated
pair of bronze figurines that are known as "The Moors", on
account of their dark color. These automata, driven by a
complex mechanism, indicate the hour of the day by striking a
large bell.

THE CLOCKMAKERS
Paolo and Carlo
Rainieri, who
invented the
mechanism which
moves both the clock
and the automata,
were well rewarded
by the Republic for
their pains.
Nevertheless, a later
rumor had it that
their eyes were put
out, to prevent them
reproducing a similar
masterpiece
elsewhere.

THE PIAZZETTA

The Piazzetta dei Leoncini is directly adjacent to St
Mark's Square. It occupies the site of a dock that
was here in the early days of the Republic ▲ 220,
whose waters used to lap at the base of the
campanile, and somehow it gives
the illusion of being

The lions of the Republic

The lion, one of the four winged creatures that appeared to the prophet Ezekiel, was taken as the sign of St Mark the Evangelist. In placing herself under this saint's protection, Venice adopted his symbol for her emblem. Thus the Republic secured a religious raison d'être and the winged lion became an omnipresent feature in the city – there are fourteen such lions to be counted on St Mark's Square alone. In sculpture, painting, manuscript illumination and ships' ensigns, the emblem of the Republic became famous throughout the known world. Its two principal attitudes were the *leone in moleca* (sitting) and the *leone andante* (walking). The hieratic position of the former represented the majesty of the state. The latter sometimes appeared with two feet on water and two on land, symbolizing the sovereignty of Venice over both elements. Portrayed with the open Bible – the Book of Wisdom – and the inscription *Clementia augustae*, it indicated the peace which Venice imposed within her territories. Finally, a lion with sword in paw and closed book signified the defender of the city in time of war. This was the symbol of Venice's military power, hence the inscription *Forteria leoni*.

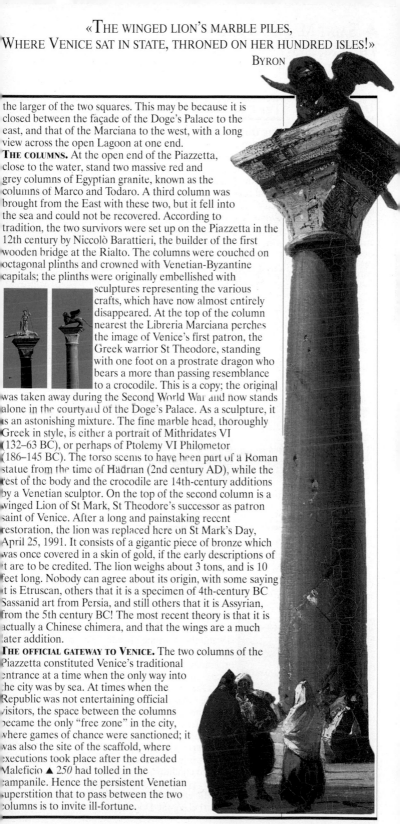

the larger of the two squares. This may be because it is closed between the façade of the Doge's Palace to the east, and that of the Marciana to the west, with a long view across the open Lagoon at one end.

THE COLUMNS. At the open end of the Piazzetta, close to the water, stand two massive red and grey columns of Egyptian granite, known as the columns of Marco and Todaro. A third column was brought from the East with these two, but it fell into the sea and could not be recovered. According to tradition, the two survivors were set up on the Piazzetta in the 12th century by Niccolò Barattieri, the builder of the first wooden bridge at the Rialto. The columns were couched on octagonal plinths and crowned with Venetian-Byzantine capitals; the plinths were originally embellished with sculptures representing the various crafts, which have now almost entirely disappeared. At the top of the column nearest the Libreria Marciana perches the image of Venice's first patron, the Greek warrior St Theodore, standing with one foot on a prostrate dragon who bears a more than passing resemblance to a crocodile. This is a copy; the original was taken away during the Second World War and now stands alone in the courtyard of the Doge's Palace. As a sculpture, it is an astonishing mixture. The fine marble head, thoroughly Greek in style, is either a portrait of Mithridates VI (132–63 BC), or perhaps of Ptolemy VI Philometor (186–145 BC). The torso seems to have been part of a Roman statue from the time of Hadrian (2nd century AD), while the rest of the body and the crocodile are 14th-century additions by a Venetian sculptor. On the top of the second column is a winged Lion of St Mark, St Theodore's successor as patron saint of Venice. After a long and painstaking recent restoration, the lion was replaced here on St Mark's Day, April 25, 1991. It consists of a gigantic piece of bronze which was once covered in a skin of gold, if the early descriptions of it are to be credited. The lion weighs about 3 tons, and is 10 feet long. Nobody can agree about its origin, with some saying it is Etruscan, others that it is a specimen of 4th-century BC Sassanid art from Persia, and still others that it is Assyrian, from the 5th century BC! The most recent theory is that it is actually a Chinese chimera, and that the wings are a much later addition.

THE OFFICIAL GATEWAY TO VENICE. The two columns of the Piazzetta constituted Venice's traditional entrance at a time when the only way into the city was by sea. At times when the Republic was not entertaining official visitors, the space between the columns became the only "free zone" in the city, where games of chance were sanctioned; it was also the site of the scaffold, where executions took place after the dreaded Maleficio ▲ 250 had tolled in the campanile. Hence the persistent Venetian superstition that to pass between the two columns is to invite ill-fortune.

TURNER ● 109 AND VENICE
Light and water combine in Venice to create a restless magic. Whether veiled in mist, reddening at sunset, or ghostly under moonlight, all borderlines between dream and reality, present and past, are eradicated. It was this atmosphere of unearthliness that fascinated Turner, who in painting it rejected the representative style in favor of one approaching Impressionism.

The Italian comic actor Alberto Sordi, in *Venezia, la luna e tu*

THE PRISONS

THE DOGE'S DUNGEONS. At the time of the birth of the Venetian Republic, when the Doge's Palace was still no more than a fortress ▲ *224*, some space was naturally reserved there for prisoners. The later Gothic palace continued this tradition. But from the 14th century onwards the palace's tiny foetid cells, in which countless prisoners had both languished and died, were no longer sufficient to house all of the Republic's convicts. The government resolved to remedy this situation by adding some new cells, and eventually by building other prisons elsewhere. Although several attempts were made during the course of the 15th century to set up prisons outside the palace, it was not until the end of the following century that the idea finally came to anything. In 1580, it was resolved that new prison buildings should be built beyond the rio running alongside the Doge's Palace, close to the La Paglia bridge. The works were consigned to Antonio da Ponte, and then on his death in 1597, to Antonio Contin. By 1610 the job was finished, along with a bridge that linked the new prison to the Doge's Palace.

THE BRIDGE OF SIGHS

THE LEGEND. It was not until the romantic 19th century that this famous bridge actually became known as the "Bridge of Sighs". One is supposed to look at it and at the same time imagine the "sigh heaved by a prisoner fresh from the courtroom of the palace, who crosses the canal by this bridge on his way to serve a long sentence in a foul, dank dungeon; through the lattice window the wretch catches sight of the Lagoon, of the Island of San Giorgio, of the sky and the sunshine outside." This covered bridge, built in Istrian stone, with its frankly Baroque ornamentation, is made up of two corridors that are separated throughout their length by a partition wall. One of these corridors led to the courtrooms, and the other one to the Chamber of the Avogaria. In addition, these two corridors were also linked to the service staircase that leads from the "Wells" to the "Leads".

THE WELLS AND THE LEADS. The construction of the new prisons answered some of the need to improve conditions of detention in Venice, given that the government had decreed that there should be sufficient space, air and light in the cells. Nevertheless, the Doge's Palace still contained

« THE UPS AND DOWNS OF VENICE, WHERE HUMAN LIFE OSCILLATED FOR SO LONG BETWEEN TWO EXTREMES, BETWEEN *PIOMBI* AND *POZZI*, THE LEADS ABOVE AND THE WELLS BELOW.»

PAUL MORAND

dungeons in which prisoners' lives can only be described as miserable beyond belief. The nineteen cells of the WELLS were on the ground floor of the building, under the Chamber of the Avogaria. The Wells were narrow, dark, dank (on account of the nearby canal) and airless – hence their name. They were used from the 1530's until the end of the 18th century. The LEADS, by contrast, were situated just beneath the lead-covered roofs of the palace, just beside the TORTURE CHAMBER (*camera del tormento*). Probably built in the second half of the 15th century, they consisted of six or seven cells, in which were incarcerated special prisoners of the Council of Ten or of the Inquisitors, who were either awaiting judgement or else had already been convicted of minor offenses. These jails are assumed – perhaps wrongly – to have contributed to the dismal reputation of Venetian justice; in any case they aroused the indignation of many writers, particularly during the 19th century. Their fame is largely due to the celebrated adventurer and libertine, Giovanni Giacomo Casanova de Seingalt, who described in his *Story of my Escape from the Leads of Venice* both the jail itself and the incredible manner of his getting out of it.

CASANOVA

Cross-section of the prisons, showing the celebrated Wells and

CASANOVA'S ESCAPE. Following his arrest on July 26, 1755, Casanova was immediately locked up in a cell inside the Leads. Manuzzi, a right-hand man of the State Inquisitor, had accused him of living a dissolute life, and of spreading anti-religious propaganda. Languishing in his tiny cell, in which there was no room even to stand up, Casanova quickly fell ill – but this did not stop him hatching his first plan of escape. On August 25, however, he was moved to a different cell, and so this plan was foiled. Undaunted, he worked out another scheme with the complicity of one of his cellmates, Father Balbi; his idea this time was to escape across the rooftops. During the night of October 31, he managed to slip out of his cell and onto the roof, afterwards climbing down through a skylight into an attic. From here he crossed through a number of small rooms on his way to the square room (SALA QUADRATA) that adjoins the Scala d'Oro. At this point he leaned out of a window and was seen by a guard who, taking him for an official left behind in the palace, opened the gates and let him out through the Porta della Carta. Hailing a gondola, Casanova made good his escape to the frontier, and then on to Munich and finally Paris. Twenty years later he returned to Venice once more, only to leave her again forever.

Leads. One can still see the two *bocci dei leone* in the Doge's Palace. One is in the courtyard, the other

in the Bussola chamber ▲ 225.

The walls of the Venetian prisons are covered in prisoners' graffiti, such as this example by Francesco Sforza.

The Libreria Marciana is one of Italy's largest libraries, containing more than a million volumes, priceless manuscripts, beautiful nautical charts and the famous 15th-century planisphere

The Libreria Marciana

The origins of the Library. The gift of Petrarch – who bequeathed his library to the Republic in the 14th century – was followed, in 1468, by that of Cardinal Bessarion ▲ *164*, which included more than a thousand manuscripts. These two bequests formed the core of a huge state library for Venice, which subsequently became (along with the Library of Padua University) a depository for all books that were published in

the Venetian state. As the collection grew, so also did the need for a much larger building in which to house it. A site was duly chosen and the Libreria Marciana was built opposite the Doge's Palace.

by Fra Mauro ▲ *154*. It also contains the exquisite GRIMANI BREVIARY, a masterpiece which is illustrated with 110 Flemish miniatures (15th–16th century). At the entrance to the library stand two colossal caryatids (1553–5) by Alessandro Vittoria.

Venice's state architect. The work began in 1537 and continued until 1554, directed by Jacopo Sansovino. This Tuscan architect, who escaped from Rome in 1527, became the principal exponent of the Republic's architectural and urban development aspirations. He had already been commissioned to complete the rearrangement of St Mark's Square, a prestigious exercise by which the state hoped to affirm its political clout. By rediscovering the architectural manner of the ancients and developing a grandiose "Roman" style that suited Venetian tradition, Sansovino fulfilled the wishes of the Serene Republic; he created around San Marco not only the Libreria Marciana, but also the Zecca, the loggia of the campanile and the Church of San Geminiano (since demolished). The Libreria, in particular, represents an essential element of his new style, with the Doric arcades of its ground floor, the series of windows adorning the loggia of its first floor, and its terrace, which appears as a counterpoint to the crenellations of the Doge's Palace. Despite a number of problems during its construction – the "Roman" arch collapsed in 1545, and Sansovino was arrested and obliged to rebuild the roof at his own expense – the Libreria remains one of his most sublime creations. He solved the problem of adapting his architectural tenets to the site without upsetting its original balance.

Exaltation of knowledge. The decoration of this temple of culture, originally meant to house a school of philosophy and rhetoric, exalts human knowledge in general and Venetian civilization in particular. The sculptures on the façade are by (among others) Minio, Vittoria and Ammanati, while the frescoes on the main staircase are by Battista Franco and Battista del Moro. The allegorical paintings in the main hall and vestibule (see Titian's *Wisdom* on the ceiling), represent a thoroughgoing manifesto of Venetian Mannerism.

MUSEUM OF ARCHEOLOGY

The collections of the Museum of Archeology are displayed in sections of the Libreria Marciana and the Procuratie Vecchie. Its two main resources come from donations that were made during the 16th century. In 1523, Cardinal Domenico Grimani, a celebrated humanist and theologian, presented the Seignory with his collection of Greek marbles, along with a magnificent library; and in 1593 his nephew Giovanni, the patriarch of Aquileia, made another significant bequest of original Greek art. Other donations were made during the 17th century, until eventually the museum's collection was acknowledged as one of the richest in the whole of northern Italy. With their Greek originals and Roman copies (which in many cases constitute vital evidence of works that have long since vanished) the museum's display rooms not only offer an overview of Greek art, but they also give us an insight into the tastes of past collectors. The room containing the Grimani statues, for example, is a monument to the admirable artistic sensibility of Giovanni Grimani, who somehow contrived to assemble a hoard of minor masterpieces dating from the 6th and 5th centuries before the birth of Christ. In addition to these works the museum also possesses an intriguing collection of medals and some splendid cameos – among them a Hellenic *Zeus with his Shield*. There are also some very fine portraits, an area in which ancient Rome excelled. Among the various busts on display, note especially the one entitled *Vitellius*, which is so realistic that for many years it was assumed to date from the Renaissance period.

The balustrade on top of the Libreria Marciana (above) is decorated with statues of mythological deities; there are three obelisks at the corners. This statuary is mostly by sculptors of the second half of the 16th century.

Among the painters chosen by Sansovino and Titian to decorate the Libreria Marciana were Veronese, Battista Franco, Andrea Meldolla, called lo Schiavone, and Giuseppe Porta, called Salviati. Each worked according to his own lights, and the result reflects the wealth and variety of Venetian Mannerism.

THE MINT

LA ZECCA. The 9th-century mint in which the first Venetian coin was struck was located at San Bartolomeo, near the Rialto ▲ 276. It was not until the end of the 13th century that a *zecca* (mint) was installed on St Mark's Square. The Zecca

255

VENETIAN COINS
Of the 53 Doges, only Niccolò Tron in 1471 had coins struck with his effigy. Otherwise, the Doge's portraits did not appear on Venetian money; although the names were marked, the head was without individual features, a sign that Venice set more store by the Doge's office than by his person. The gold sequin bore the image of St Mark presenting a banner to a kneeling Doge, and on its reverse a Christ figure against a starred background. Other coins showed the Lion of St Mark, the Madonna, St Justine or an allegory of Justice. Under Doge Andrea Grimani (1521) a strange medal was struck, the *osella* ● *38* (derived from *osello*, the Venetian form of *uccello*, which means a bird). It was intended to replace the game with which the Doge used to regale Venice's more prominent citizens during certain festivals.

produced a coinage that was readily exchanged everywhere, because it originated in the richest city-state in Italy. On the other hand, it was a trifle drab to look at by comparison with the coinage of some other Italian states, which excelled in the realistic portraiture of princes – as in the Florentine florin. The most widespread coin, even after the appearance in the 16th century of gold ecus and heavy silver ducats, was always the sequin (called a ducat until 1540). The sequin came either in gold or in silver. The Zecca continued to function until 1870, some time after the collapse of the Venetian Republic. In the 16th century its old premises were replaced by the present building, designed by Sansovino. On the ground floor are a series of embossed arcades; on the upper floors, the façade is balanced throughout its length by windows, which lend emphasis to its ringed half-columns and imposing cornices. Since 1905, the mint building has been a part of the Libreria Marciana, its inner courtyard being covered over and used as a public reading room.

THE ROYAL GARDENS. These gardens were born of the Emperor Napoleon's wish to see a broad view from the windows of the Procuratie Nuove, which he had converted into a royal residence. To allow this view, the four huge, crenellated buildings of the Granai di Terranova (14th-century) were demolished in 1807. With these buildings, which formerly stood on the quayside beside the Zecca, vanished what had once been one of the largest grainstores in Europe.

SAN MARCO

PALAZZO GRASSI
CHURCH OF SAN SAMUELE
FORMER CHURCH OF SAN VITALE
HOUSE OF VERONESE
PALAZZO LOREDAN
PALAZZO PISANI
PALAZZO MOROSINI
CHURCH OF SANTO STEFANO
PALAZZO PISANI TREVISAN
CHURCH OF SAN MAURIZIO
PALAZZO FORTUNY
CHURCH OF SANTA MARIA DEL GIGLIO
LA FENICE THEATER
CHURCH OF SAN BENE[...]
CHURCH OF SAN [...]

⏳ Half a day

CASINO VENIER ★
At the heart of the Merceria, this small apartment with its stuccos and marble floors has preserved the atmosphere of the original casini, where masked Venetian nobles came for entertainment. Casino Venier belonged to Elena Priuli, the wife of the procurator Federico Venier.

Small though it is by comparison with the other districts of Venice, the sestiere of San Marco, at the heart of the city, plays a crucial rôle in its cultural life, retaining considerable importance because of its position between the Rialto ▲ *279* and St Mark's Square ▲ *220*. Because it is so central, and because it is semi-enclosed by the southern loop of the Grand Canal, this area was constantly being altered until the beginning of the 19th century. In the past, construction, demolition and reconstruction work was always in progress in the vicinity of St Mark's Square; today its maze of calli (alleyways) is still packed with stalls and workshops, magnificent patrician houses, museums, libraries and theaters. Beyond these lie the broad light-flooded spaces of the Campo Santo Stefano and the Campo Sant'Angelo, the liveliest part of Venice's center, where the big hotels, banks, travel agencies, antique shops, art galleries and booksellers are all concentrated. (From the Piazzetta, take the Fondamenta delle Farine to Calle Vallaresso).

HARRY'S BAR

SESTIERE DI ⋂ S.MARCO

This celebrated restaurant and bar was founded by Giuseppe Cipriani, who ran it at the time Ernest Hemingway was staying in Venice. You can sample exquisite *tramezzini* (sandwiches) and sip the famous Harry's Bar

ARSETTI AND CA' LOREDAN
CA' CONTARINI DEL BOVOLO
RIALTO BRIDGE
CHURCH OF SAN BARTOLOMEO
CHURCH OF SAN SALVADOR
CHURCH OF SAN MOISE

SAINT MARK'S SQUARE

SAN MICHELE

cocktails
of fruit juice
and champagne, each
named after one of
Venice's great masters: for example, a
Bellini (peach juice) or Tiziano (grape and pomegranate).

PALAZZO DANDOLO

A CELEBRATED RIDOTTO. In 1638, Marco Dandolo
opened a public gaming room in his palace,
which the Grand Council later described as a
place of "solemn, continuous, universal and
violent gambling". This *ridotto* was much
frequented during carnival, when games of
chance like *bassetta* and *faraone* were
permitted. Ten rooms of the palace were
devoted to this function; anyone might
enter, but men were expected to wear the
auto ● 53. In 1758, the Dandolo family
commissioned the architect Bernardino
Maccaruzzi and the painter Jacopo
Guarana to renovate the old palace. Six
smaller gaming rooms were built around
the main hall: a pair of these were for
dining, with wine, cheese, sausage and fruit
in one, and tea, chocolate and coffee in the
other ▲ 245. On November 27, 1774, the
Grand Council ordered the closure of the
premises, because several families had been
completely bankrupted there. The *ridotto* reopened
under the French régime and was closed again by the
Austrians. At the beginning of the 20th century one of

**AN ESCORT TO THE
RIDOTTO**
The noblemen on
their way to the
ridotto wore the *bauto*
and the white mask
● 53 so that they
could go about the
streets of Venice
incognito. They took
a lantern-bearer, or
codega, who
walked ahead of
them.

259

This famous painting by Francesco Guardi shows a crowd of masked noblemen in the main hall of the Dandolo *ridotto*.

the most beautiful gaming rooms of the Palazzo Dandolo was turned into a cinema, and then converted into a theater in 1947. As such, it made a significant contribution to Venetian drama during a difficult period.

CASINI IN VENICE. The Grand Council's decision to close the *ridotto* on November 27, 1774, aroused strong protest, and the

THE LOTTERY
Introduced to Venice in 1522 by a certain Geronimo Bombarara, the idea of a lottery quickly spread among ordinary people, who were banned from the *ridotto*. In 1644 the government imposed a tax on the *loto*, and in 1734 it finally became a public institution.

gamblers simply decamped to resume play elsewhere. In theory, there had been free access to the *ridotto* for all, but in practice the stakes there were far too high for the gondoliers, artisans and servants to contemplate. As a result, ordinary people went to taverns to play cards or bet on the lottery; then, after the closure of the *ridotto*, the Venetian nobles duly followed suit, gravitating towards the city's cafés and casini. Casini were originally small apartments rented by patricians around St Mark's Square. Since they often had to attend Grand Council meetings, the patricians were obliged to wear their black robes constantly. This created a need for apartments near the palace where they could change clothes and relax – and they solved this problem by renting casini, under the arcades of the Procuratie ▲ 244. The casini began as places of relaxation, but this soon changed and they became elegant bachelor apartments where people gathered to listen to music. With the 18th-century fashion for chinoiserie ● 45, the décor and furnishings of the casini took on a strong flavor of the exotic and later, when gaming tables were installed, began to proliferate in earnest. The nobility had their own gaming houses, such as the CASINO DEI NOBILI at San Barnaba ▲ 334, as did the ordinary people, who tended to favor casini outside Venice in places where there was also space to play ball games. From their beginnings around St Mark's Square, the casini spread through the neighboring parishes and beyond. The magistrates, forced to acknowledge their inability to prevent gambling, instead began regulating and exploiting it with official gambling houses. (From Calle Vallaresso, take two lefts onto Calle del Ridotto.)

PALAZZO GIUSTINIAN

This Gothic palazzo (c.1474) fronting the Grand Canal is now the headquarters of the Venice Biennale ▲ 184. For a while (c.1432) it was the home of the patriarch of San Pietro di Castello ▲ 182, Lorenzo Giustiniani; later it passed to the Morosini family during the 17th century. It was then restored, and extensive additions were made to its façade. The interior still retains part of its original 17th-century decoration. (Return to the salizzada.)

SAN MOISÈ

THE CHURCH OF SAN MOISÈ. This church, originally dedicated to St Victor and probably founded in the 8th century, was rededicated to Moses after Moisè Venier paid for it to be rebuilt in the middle of the 9th century. A second rebuilding took place in the first half of the 11th century, after the church was destroyed by fire. It was not touched again until 1632, when the structure was completely changed. The present façade was built in 1668 by Alessandro Tremignon and paid for by a bequest from Vincenzo and Gerolamo Fini, who wanted their effigies placed within the church. Thus San Moisè became a kind of lavish mausoleum, filled with sculptures by the Flemish artist Meyring, a disciple of Bernini: many of these sculptures were removed in 1878. Today the interior is notable for its painting of *La Lavanda dei Piedi* by Tintoretto, and a *Last Supper* attributed to Palma the Younger. The celebrated courtesan Veronica Franco died in this parish in 1591, and is buried here. On the campo is one of Venice's better-known hotels, the BAUER GRÜNWALD. (Take the Calle Barozzi as far as the Corte del Teatro.)

SAN MOISÈ THEATER COURTYARD. This courtyard was the site of the first theater in Venice. Built in 1620 as a venue for comedies, the theater turned to opera a few years later with a performance of Monteverdi's *Arianna* ▲ 174, 263. In the 18th century, several works by Vivaldi, Albinoni and Galuppi were performed there (the latter with librettos by Goldoni). A century later, the theater first premièred Rossini. Closed in 1820, it was reopened in 1871 as a puppet theater, before becoming a cinema and finally a private house.

PLAYING CARDS
They were kept in small lacquered wood boxes, and decorated with chinoiserie patterns ● 45.

VERONICA FRANCO
This poetess and courtesan, who died age forty-five in the parish of San Moisè, left money to permit two ladies of her profession to marry or take the veil; if none were forthcoming, the cash was then intended to serve as a dowry for two young girls.

261

THE THEATER OF LA FENICE

THE BIRTH OF LA FENICE. In 1774, the San Benedetto Theater, which had been Venice's leading opera house for more than forty years, was burned to the ground. No sooner had it been rebuilt than a legal dispute broke out between the company managing it and the owners, the Venier family. The issue was decided in favor of the Veniers, with the result that the theater company decided to build a new opera house of its own on the Campo San Fantin. From the twenty-nine architectural plans which were submitted, the one by Gian Antonio Selva was chosen. The building works began in June 1790; by May 1792 the auditorium was completed. It was named *"La Fenice"* (The Phoenix), in an allusion to the

In 1808, when the French had been back in Venice for two years, Selva completed the Imperial box at La Fenice.

"SENSO"
The opening scenes of Visconti's *Senso* (center) based on the *Secret Journal of Countess Livia,* take place at La Fenice on May 27, 1866, during the Austrian occupation. Towards the end of the third act of Verdi's *Il Trovatore*, the Italian patriots throw leaflets and tricolored cockades onto the stage and into the stalls, shouting "Viva Verdi"! (Viva Vittore-Emmanuelle, Rei d'Italia).

company's survival, first of the fire, then of expulsion from its former base. La Fenice was inaugurated on May 16, 1792 with an opera by Giovanni Paisiello entitled *I Giochi di Agrigento* (*Distractions of Agrigento*). The libretto was written by Alessandro Pepoli.

THE FAME OF LA FENICE. From the beginning of the 19th century, La Fenice acquired a European reputation. Rossini mounted two major productions in the theater and Bellini had two operas premièred there. Donizetti, fresh from his triumphs in Milan and Naples, returned to Venice – and La Fenice – in 1836, after an absence of seventeen years. Thus the three greatest Italian composers of the period each affirmed the theater's pre-eminence, but in December 1836 it was tragically burned down yet again. The following year Giambattista and Tommaso Meduna were commissioned to design a new theater, with décor by Tranquillo Orsi. La Fenice rose once again from its ashes on the evening of December 26, 1837.

VERDI AT LA FENICE. Verdi's association with La Fenice began in 1844, with a performance of *Hernani* during the Carnival season. Over the next thirteen years, the world premières of *Attila*, *Rigoletto*, *La Traviata* and *Simon Boccanegra* all took place there.

LA FENICE IN THE 20TH CENTURY. After a period of closure during the First World War, La Fenice again became the scene of intense activity, attracting the world's greatest singers and conductors. In 1930, the Biennale ▲ 184 initiated the First International Festival of Contemporary Music, which brought composers like Stravinsky and Britten, and more recently Berio, Nono and Bussotti, to write for Fenice. Latterly, as part of the theater's bicentenary celebrations, La Fenice has put o series of revivals of some of its greatest trium

The phoenix, symbol of the theater, was a mythological bird reputed to rise from its own ashes: in the case of the theatre which bore its name, this happened twice.

MONTEVERDI: THE FIRST GOLDEN AGE OF OPERA.

In 1607, Monteverdi's *Orfeo* was performed before the court of Mantua. The Florentines Peri and Caccini had previously sought to subordinate music to dramatic expression, with sterile and mechanical results. But with Monteverdi, the libretto remained intelligible, yet gained new meaning from the music, which the composer based entirely on emotional expression and the seductive power of the human voice. "With Monteverdi," wrote the French commentator Romain Rolland, "the cause of opera was won."

THE FIRST OPERA HOUSES.

In 1637, the San Canciano Theater performed Europe's first opera before a paying public. The final works by Monteverdi were, of course, shown in Venice. Opera had at last emerged from the closed world of princely courts; it became a fiercely competitive business for several of the city's great families, who opened their own opera houses. Each year they

THE BURNING OF LA FENICE
At 3am on the night of December 12–13, 1836, the alarm was sounded by the bells of the San Marco campanile ▲ *248* – the theater of La Fenice was in flames. Firemen and Austrian soldiers fought the blaze, but by morning the theater's interior was completely destroyed.

mounted one or two seasons, hence the need for a constant renewal of the repertoire. This explains why the 17th-century Venetian school, represented by composers like Pier Francesco Cavalli and Marc'Antonio Cesti, was so prolific.

GRANDEUR AND DECADENCE.

From the early 18th century, Venice gradually yielded operatic primacy to Naples, where Alessandro Scarlatti, the pioneer of *opera seria*, was making his mark and comic opera began to emerge in about 1730. This loss of primacy did not cause a decline. On the contrary, ̇he new Venetian genre was represented by Galuppi ▲ *̇1*, who set to music twelve libretti by Goldoni ▲ *291*. ̇valdi ▲ *175* became director of the Sant'Angelo ̇eater and composed a number of operas, most of ̇h are now lost. Venice still attracted composers, ̇s public grew fickle. In a city which saw the ̇on of 1,274 operas in little over a generation, ̇tions were as quickly forgotten as made.

THE CURTAIN
In 1878, La Fenice commissioned a new curtain with a historical theme from the painter Ermolao Paoletti, because the first one dating from 1850 had by now deteriorated. Paoletti chose a famous episode from Venetian history: the official welcome in front of the Doge's palace of the force that crushed the Turkish armada at Lepanto ● *36*. But time, damp and constant use damaged this painting too, and it has just been restored.

SAN FANTIN

THE CHURCH OF SAN FANTIN. This church stands opposite the entrance of La Fenice. Founded during the 9th century, and then reconstructed after a "miraculous" image of the Virgin was brought here from the Orient, the original sanctuary was demolished in 1506 along with its campanile. The following year the architect Scarpagnino began work on the building that we see today. The church was still unfinished when Scarpagnino died, but was completed by Sansovino in 1564. His contribution included the choir, with a dome resting on four grandiose Corinthian columns. On the walls, with their surface of white marble, hang two paintings by Palma the Younger, a *Deposition of Christ* (on the right-hand side) and *The Doge Luigi Mocenigo Kneeling in Gratitude for the Victory at Lepanto* (on the left).

THE SCUOLA. Built in 1471, the Scuola was redesigned at the close of the 16th century by Alessandro Vittoria. After the suppression of the guilds, in 1812 the building became the headquarters of the Ateneo Veneto (the Venetian Academy of Letters and Sciences). The ground floor gallery contains fourteen canvases by Palma the Younger, depicting the souls of the dead in purgatory. The reading room on the first floor, which has a ceiling decorated by the same artist, also contains a painting by Tintoretto entitled *Saint Jerome Receiving the Gifts of the Merchants*. (Rejoin the Calle XXII Marzo and then continue along the Calle dei Ostreghi).

TOWARDS THE CAMPO SANTO STEFANO

The Church and Campo San Maurizio.

SANTA MARIA DEL GIGLIO. This area is also known as Santa Maria Zobenigo, a name which has been distorted from that of a Slavic family, the Jubanicos, who once owned a sumptuous palace on the site. During the Festival of La Salute ● 49, ▲ 320 a wooden bridge is erected from the campo across the Grand Canal. At other times of the year one can cross the water on the traghetto ● 57, which has plied to and fro along this route ever since the 14th century. The CHURCH OF SANTA MARIA DEL GIGLIO owes its name to the lily which the Archangel is said to have carried at the Annunciation. It is also known as Santa Maria Zobenigo because the Jubanico family contributed generously to its foundation in the 10th century. It was completely rebuilt in the second half of the 17th century, at which time Antonio Barbaro, a high official i Dalmatia, commissioned Giuseppe Sa to design the façade, donating thirty thousand ducats for the purpose. Ins the sanctuary are a number of paint

THE FAÇADE OF THE CHURCH OF SANTA MARIA ZOBENIGO
This is one of the most important examples of the Venetian Baroque style, with statues of the four Barbaro brothers (the one of Antonio Barbaro is by the Fleming Josse Le Court), and the allegorical figures of Glory, Fame and Wisdom extolling civil and military virtues. The base of the columns is carved with bas-reliefs representing naval battles, and maps of Zara, Candia, Padua, Rome, Corfu and Spalato (above). These allude to the military expeditions undertaken by the Barbaro family on behalf of Venice.

notably some portraits by Palma the Younger, Tintoretto's Evangelists (*Mark and John; Matthew and Luke*), and a *Virgin and Child with St John*, which has been attributed to Rubens (above). The 13th-century campanile fell down in 1775; it was never rebuilt, and today its base is occupied by shops.

CAMPO SAN MAURIZIO. This charming campo, which is dominated by the Church of San Maurizio, lies on the route between St Mark's Square ▲ *220* and the Grand Canal ▲ *187*. Founded in the 11th century, it was rebuilt in 1580 so that its façade overlooked the campo. In 1806, the church was demolished and rebuilt again by the architects Antonio Diedo and Giovanni Antonio Selva. To the right is the old SCUOLA DEGLI ALBANESI, the façade of which (1531) is decorated with classically inspired Renaissance bas-reliefs. Opposite the church is the PALAZZO BELLAVITE, built by a rich oil and flour merchant, Dionisio Bellavite. Because he wanted his façade to be as lavish as possible, no expense was spared, particularly with regard to the delicate working of the stone, which forms a lovely contrast to the frescoes by Veronese (c.1555) and a series of monochrome friezes of chubby cherubs and other allegorical figures. The poet Giorgio Baffo (1694–1768) lived in this palazzo at one time. He was famous for his lewd poems written in the Venetian dialect. Another famous occupant, in 1803, was the writer Alessandro Manzoni. (Continue along the Calle del Pivan and the Calle del Spezier.)

THE ANTIQUE MARKET
For those interested in antiques, there is a small market held in the Campo San Maurizio at various times of year, particularly at Easter and on All Saints' Day.

This was the origin of the Venetian expression "to go to the *liston*" (to go for a walk).

CAMPO SANTO STEFANO ★

Officially known as CAMPO MOROSINI, this open area lies at the heart of the most fashionable quarter of the city. At its center is a large STATUE (in itself a rarity for Venice) of Nicolò Tommaseo, the writer, patriot and leader of the Venetian uprising ● 34 ▲ 275 in 1848.

PALAZZO LOREDAN. In 1536, the Loredan family commissioned the architect Scarpagnino to rebuild this palazzo, which until that time had belonged to another great Venetian family, the Mocenigos. The long façade, with its broad, many-arched window, was once decorated with frescoes on Roman themes by Giallo Fiorentino and Giuseppe Porta. The palace was enlarged in 1618, a substantial reception hall being added on one wing. This new wing was adorned with a façade in Istrian stone, attributed by some to Palladio, although it is more likely to have been the work of his assistant, Giovanni Girolamo Grapiglia, who was the Loredan family's architect. In 1809 General d'Illiers, the first French governor of Venice, lived in the Palazzo Loredan. He had the reception hall decorated with frescoes, which were obliterated when the Austrians resumed control of the city. In 1840 Ferdinand I, Emperor of Austria, founded the Istituto Veneti di Scienze, Lettere ed Arti (the Venetian Institute of Science, Arts and Letters); the Palazzo Loredan became this institute's headquarters and has remained so ever since. It maintains a rich library, with one of the largest collections of periodicals in Italy.

PALAZZO MOROSINI. The Morosini family acquired this 14th-century palace in 1648. Its façade, then decorated with frescoes of scenes from antiquity by Antonio Aliense, was covered with stone to fit in with contemporary taste. At the close of the 17th century, Francesco Morosini ● 40 commissioned the family's architect, Antonio Gaspari, to undertake a fresh restoration (1688–94).

In the second courtyard of Palazzo Pisani – designed in the 18th century by the Paduan architect Girolamo Frigimelica – stands the mysterious statue of a veiled woman, whose identity has never been discovered, despite the best efforts of many researchers.

As a tribute to the owner's naval triumphs, a sea-horse's head was sculpted over the main doorway, with sea monsters above the side entrances. The illustrious client and his architect devised a project to unite the palace with a neighboring building belonging to the Morosini. The two houses shared a large courtyard, but their floor levels did not match; Gaspari corrected this, enriched the interiors with stucco, paintings and sculptures, and set aside a gallery in which the armor and war trophies of the Morosini family could be exhibited. At the end of the 18th century a further modernization was carried out by Gianantonio Selva, who removed the more baroque

The inner courtyard of Palazzo Pisani, now the Conservatory of Music.

elements from the façade. In 1894 the Counts of Gattemburg (from Salzburg), who had inherited the palace, sold its precious collections at auction. The city of Venice acquired the collection of arms and armor, the archives and objects which had belonged to Francesco Morosini himself (now exhibited at the Correr Museum ▲ 246), and lastly a series of paintings by Pietro Longhi, now at the Ca' Rezzonico ▲ 332.

PALAZZO PISANI. This palace overlooks the Campiello Pisani, a delightful square in which lyrical plays and ballets are performed in summer. The building itself is one of the biggest in Venice, a charming mass of LOGGIAS, staircases, porticos and labyrinthine courtyards. Built in 1614–15, the Palazzo Pisani was designed around a splendid main courtyard surrounded by loggias, one above the next. In 1688 and 1716 the Pisanis acquired

The campanile and the galleried clocktower ● 85, rising over the sacristy of the Church of Santo Stefano and the rooftops of one of Venice's busiest campi.

adjacent properties and enlarged their palace to plans by the Paduan architect Frigimelica. The result was completely faced with Istrian stone, and included a second main floor with a ballroom and library. The interior was decorated by the most prominent painters of the time – Guarana, Amigoni, Ricci, Pittoni and Tiepolo. In 1793 it was modernized by Bernardino Maccuruzzi, who added many more stucco features, particularly on the mezzanine floor. In 1880, after the death of Almoro, the last of the Pisanis, the palazzo became the headquarters of the BENEDETTO MARCELLO MUSIC

CONSERVATORY, an institute which owns a number of autographed manuscripts by Venetian composers.

THE CHURCH OF SANTO STEFANO. The façade of this church is immediately striking on account of its huge rose window and long side windows. However, the sculptures over the main portal, created in the workshop of Bartolomeo Bon, are its chief glory. Founded at the end of the 13th century by the Augustinians, and financed in part by the Republic, this Gothic church was altered in the early 18th century, when it was considerably lengthened. The apse was extended beyond the Rio

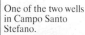

One of the two wells in Campo Santo Stefano.

del Santissimo di San Stefano, which was never filled in, so one can still pass beneath the church by boat, although there is little headroom. Inside, the principal feature is the ceiling, which looks like a richly decorated inverted ship's hull and is one of the few of this type still intact. The CORO DEI FRATI (monks' stalls) which faced the choir were dismantled in the 16th century and replaced in part behind the main altar. The church also boasts remarkable Lombard sculptures, and paintings by Bartolomeo Vivarini, Palma the Elder, Marieschi and Tintoretto, which were brought here over the centuries. Santo Stefano is the burial place of a number of people who performed great services to the Republic, foremost among them the Doge Francesco Morosini ● *40*. The church's convent buildings, which stand between it and the Campo Sant'Angelo, are built around a cloister restructured by lo Scarpagnino.

The façade of the former Scuola dei Laneri still boasts a small 15th-century bas-relief in which the guild is seen gathered in adoration around the figure of Stephen, their patron saint.

SCUOLA DEI LANERI. This building opposite the main entrance to the church was built with help from the Augustinians in 1437, then enlarged in 1473. The former Scuola di Santo Stefano, founded on March 3, 1298, became the Scuola dei Laneri di Santo Stefano after it was taken over in 1506 by an influx of merchants and artisans trading in woollen goods (*laneri*). At this time the scuola acquired five canvases (1511–20) by Carpaccio representing episodes in the life of St Stephen; one of them was lost and the other four were dispersed during the 19th century. In

the second half of the 18th century, the corporation went through a deep crisis in which the scuola had to lease its chapel to a cheese merchant to survive. By the time of its abolition by Napoleonic decree in 1806, it had effectively ceased to exist. Today, heavily altered and two floors taller than before, the old building is occupied by a restaurant.

THE FORMER CHURCH OF SAN VITALE. This church was founded in 1084 under the Doge Vitale Falieri and was restored many times before being completely rebuilt in 1696 by the architect Antonio Gaspari. Its façade was originally designed to celebrate the exploits of Francesco Morosini, but was ultimately executed in the Palladian style by Andrea Tirali, who added a row of Corinthian columns. Inside, on a wall at the far end of the nave, hang two later works by Carpaccio: *Saint Vitale on Horseback* and *Four Saints Adoring the Virgin*. No longer used for worship, the church is now the headquarters of the Unione Cattolica dei Artisti Italiani, which holds exhibitions of its members' work. On St Vitale's day, the clergy of the parish used to go in

On the small Campo San Vitale, opposite the galleries of the Accademia ▲ *301*, there stands a charming brightly colored palazzo, which is now the German Embassy.

procession to the ferry pier, where they met the clergy of neighboring San Trovaso ▲ *324*, presented them with a bouquet of flowers, and accompanied them back to San Vitale to say mass. This courtesy was returned by the San Trovaso clergy every June 16, on the feast day of San Gervasio and San Protasio.

Towards San Samuele

CAMPO SANT'ANGELO. This campo owes its name to a church, dedicated to St Michael the Archangel, which was demolished in 1837. In the ORATORIO DELLA SANTISSIMA ANNUNZIATA is an *Annunciation* by Palma the Younger and a 16th-century wooden crucifix. The quarter was mainly inhabited by nobles and their palaces may be seen round the campo. Among these is PALAZZO DUODO where the musician Domenico Cimarosa (formerly Catherine the Great's Master of Music at her chapel in St Petersburg) died in 1801. There is also the 15th-century PALAZZO GRITTI, with its façade presaging the Renaissance style, and PALAZZO PISANI. Originally built for the Trevisan family, the latter passed to the Pisanis in the second half of the 17th century. In terms of style it belongs to the period just after Longhena, who was its original architect. A series of details (heads on the keystones of arches, balustrades and the general handling of the stonework) suggest the work of Domenico Rossi, or at least of his school. The interior of the palace has remained unaltered, but its original sumptuous furnishings have now vanished.

THE HOUSE OF VERONESE ▲ *310*. At 3338 Salizzado San Samuele stands the reddish building in which the "magician of color" (to borrow a phrase from Giulio Lorenzetti) lived from 1583 until his death. Paolo Caliari, who was probably a native of Verona (hence his surname of "Veronese"), arrived in Venice in 1553. In the spring of 1588, while walking in a religious procession through Treviso, he went down with a violent fever. He was immediately taken to Venice, where he died a week later on April 19. Veronese is buried in the Church of San Sebastiano ▲ *326*, at the foot of the organ which he had decorated.

"Flag stones, walls, paved enclosed courtyards; all around are closed-up houses, making triangles or squares bulging outward in obedience to the need for more space, and to the flukes and accidents of building; and in the center is a delicately worked well-head with sculpted lions and naked figurines disporting themselves at its rim."
Hippolyte Taine, *Voyage en Italie*

On the *altane* (wooden terraces) "balanced on the rooftops with the lightness and sureness of birds' nests" (Pier-Maria Pasinetti), the ladies of Venice would sit bleaching their hair blond using the ancient mixture of unguents

based on sulphur or lead mixed with alum.

CAMPO SAN SAMUELE. The sculptors Giulio Tullio and Antonio Lombardo once lived in this parish, Titian's studio was here, and Casanova was born within its boundaries. The campo overlooks the Grand Canal, and its late 12th-century Venetian-Byzantine campanile (with a characteristic pyramidal spire covered in lead) has not changed since that time. This in itself is sufficient to make San Samuele a typical corner of old Venice.

TEATRO SAN SAMUELE. This theater, which was demolished in 1894, stood on the Rio del Duca, between Campo San Samuele and Campo Santo Stefano. It was opened in 1655 by the Grimani family ▲ *255*, who equipped it with a gaming room to make it more profitable.

Here Goldoni underwent his apprenticeship, and here Gozzi saw his fables acted ▲ *291*. The Teatro San Samuele turned out to be the fashionable Venetian venue for comedies, although it was also used for operatic productions after 1710, and at one time made an attempt to specialize in comic opera. There was no real distinction in Venice between comedy and opera theaters, and if some appeared to specialize in a particular genre, they did so only to keep up with their competitors. The Venetians loved both forms impartially, and were said to be willing to swim across the Grand Canal just to see a theater performance.

"The light here is truly an enchantress of great power, and with due respect to Titian, Veronese and Tintoretto, is a greater artist than any of them . . . the sea and the sky seem to meet one another halfway, to mingle their hues in a gentle iridescence, a glimmering blend of ripples and clouds, a hundred indefinable

PALAZZO GRASSI

THE LAST OF THE GREAT VENETIAN PALACES. Palazzo Grassi was built for the powerful family of that name, who came from Chioggia, though their origins were Bolognese. In 1718, the Grassi joined the ranks of the patricians of Venice after contributing sixty thousand ducats to the final war against the Turks ● *34*. Their palace remains an important example of 18th-century civil architecture and is, chronologically, the last in the long line of great Venetian mansions. To build it, the Grassi commissioned the architect Giorgio Massari, who had just successfully completed the Ca' Rezzonico on the other side of the Grand Canal ▲ *332*. Massari, a pupil of Longhena, anticipated the rise of Neo-classicism with his plan for an imposing, stylistically perfect but somewhat cold building. A majestic staircase leads from the entrance hall to the main salon on the *piano*

points of light, and then to cast this fine weave upon all visible objects.**"**

Henry James

nobile, then on to various other rooms on succeeding floors. The walls are decorated with frescoes by Michelangelo Morleiter, in which picturesque groups of figures dressed in 18th-century costume lean over a trompe l'oeil balcony. Some of the rooms still have their original décors of stucco and fresco done by the school of Tiepolo. Elsewhere, Fabio Canal's work glorifies the Grassi – who eventually died out in

«BETWEEN THE STILL-SLUMBERING WALLS OF BRICK AND MARBLE, BENEATH THE RIBBON OF THE SKY, MORE AND MORE BRIGHTLY GLEAMED THE RIBBON OF THE WATER.»

GABRIELE D'ANNUNZIO

THE SECRET STAIRCASES
Giorgio Massari, who designed the Palazzo Grassi (the last major building on the Grand Canal), is said to have added a number of secret staircases, in which lovers could conceal themselves.

the 1830s, leaving their palace to the Counts Tornielli. Later it was sold to the celebrated operatic tenor Poggi, then served a while as a hotel before being turned into the celebrated degli Antoni bathhouse – drawing its water from the Grand Canal. For a number of years thereafter it was the headquarters of the International Art Center, which mounted performances in the palace's 18th-century open-air garden theater.

THE RESTORATION OF PALAZZO GRASSI. After surviving several more owners, the palace was bought by Fiat in 1984, with a view to setting up a center for cultural, artistic and scientific activities. For this purpose, the company had the building radically restored by the architects Gae Aulenti and Antonio Foscari. Their work was guided by three imperatives: to re-establish a sound structure for the palace, to respect its innate character, and to make it more suitable for exhibitions. It was designed so that light would flood in everywhere and the central courtyard was covered by a glass roof. Color, too, was freely used – pink for the walls, pale green for the *boiseries*. In the stairway, as in the first-floor rooms, the frescoes and painted ceilings have been preserved in their original state.

MAJOR EVENTS AT PALAZZO GRASSI. The restored palace was inaugurated in May 1986 with an exhibition entitled "Futurisms". A year later came an exhibition on Arcimboldo and the transformation of the human face in art between the 16th and 20th centuries. Since then, Palazzo Grassi has

hosted exhibitions dedicated to Modern Art, the Phoenicians, and Italian Art 1900–45, along with retrospectives on Andy Warhol, the Celts, and Leonardo da Vinci and Venice. The works of Marcel Duchamp were shown there in 1993. (Return via the Campo Santo Stefano, then along Calle dei Frati; at the end of Campo Sant'Angelo, turn left into Calle degli Avocati, then take the Calle Pesaro on the right.)

Since the restoration of the Palazzo Grassi, a wide variety of major exhibitions has been organized there every year.

TOWARDS THE RIALTO BRIDGE

PALAZZO FORTUNY, OR PESARO, OR DEGLI ORFEI. (Number 3958 on Campo San Benedetto.) This imposing building was originally the property of the Pesaros, a rich merchant family which supplied Venice with a succession of politicians and admirals ▲ *195*. The palace dates from the end of the 15th century and is a superb example of Decorated Gothic, enriched with Renaissance elements. The building is arranged around two inner courtyards which are so huge that, in the 16th century, theatrical performances were regularly held in them. Its façades, which overlook the campo and Rio di Ca' Michiel, contain two rows of gemelled windows, with balconies supported by lions. The first and second floors each have their own *portego*, a salon which measures no less than 51 feet in length. The palace is also known as PALAZZO DEGLI ORFEI (Palace of the Orpheans) because, after the Pesaro family had departed to the new quarters which they had built at San Stae ▲ *351*, it became the headquarters of a famous philharmonic society called the Orphean Academy, which organized balls and concerts. Later, the palace came into the hands of the Apollinea Academy, which subsequently moved to La Fenice ▲ *262*. At the end of the 19th century the building was finally purchased by MARIANO FORTUNY Y MADRAZO (1871–1949), painter, photographer, fabric designer, couturier and inventor of genius. Fortuny was born in Granada. Following the death of his father, a famous painter and collector of fabrics, he moved to Venice in 1889. Ten years later he took over Palazzo Pesaro, divided up the space with hangings, covered the walls with fabrics, and then set up a workshop on the first floor, which he filled with works of art. The second floor was reserved for his studio; an excellent physicist and chemist, Fortuny worked constantly at his many inventions. He devised new lighting systems for the theater, and also a reflective moveable dome, which helped to give a sky-like illusion of depth. It was also for the theater that he created his first female dancers' costume, the "Knossos scarf", in 1906. The following year he introduced his first "Delphos dress" (facing page), in pleated silk. Its name was a homage to the statue of the *Charioteer of Delphi*, and the dress was inspired by the linen *chitons* of ancient Greece. The pleating was done by a process which was patented by Fortuny in 1909, in which the folds were set by hand into moistened fabric, then sewn in place and finally sealed with a hot iron.

On February 19, 1515, the Compagnie della Calza degli Immortali put on a performance of Plautus' *Miles Gloriosus* in the main courtyard of Palazzo Pesaro, which was hung with rich fabrics for the occasion. Among the audience that day were the family of Doge Leonardo Loredan, the Ambassador of the King of France, and many noble ladies.

«Fortuny's dresses, which combine originality with fidelity to the past, bear decorative witness [...] to Venice's debt to the Orient.»

Marcel Proust

The dresses were weighted with corded pearls of Murano blown glass ▲ 366. In order to keep its pleats in place, a Delphos would be wound in a skein, and then wrapped in tissue paper and stored in a small box. The Delphos had to be put on over the head, and it only took form when draped on a human figure. All in all, it represented Fortuny's contribution to the liberation of the body, and to the 20th-century revolution in women's clothes – an undulating garment worn with a top of silk velvet or slightly ribbed gauze. Fortuny used only natural colors, and the patterns of his fabrics were taken from the paintings of Carpaccio ▲ 306 and Memling, as well as from his private textile collection. He favored the Renaissance as well as Chinese, Japanese, Persian and Arab motifs. He also imitated Renaissance brocade, embroidery and lace designs, which he manufactured following his own techniques. In practice, all Fortuny's fabrics were stencilled, using wooden Japanese stamps (*katagami*) or a silk screen process that he invented, which was based on photographic methods. His velvets, which came unbleached, were prepared by applying colors with a brush, one after another, from front to back, until a patina emerged. Then, he applied gold, silver or some other color on a support washed with Chinese eggshell white in the areas reserved for the motif. His stencilled color patterns also left the fabric with just a hint of starchiness, since they penetrated so deeply into the weave of the fiber. To start with, Fortuny sold his fabrics at the Palazzo factory and, through couture designer Poiret; he later opened his own shops in Paris and New York. After the death of "Don Mariano", his widow Henriette left the Palazzo Fortuny to the city of Venice (in 1956). Still more of a secret garden than a traditional museum, the building is now used as a venue for exhibitions and other cultural events. While the Fortuny factory on the Giudecca ▲ 338 continues to produce cottons of fine relief and delicate coloring, the tradition of pleated material has been revived since 1984 by a small group of enthusiasts called the Venetia Studium. These artists also make diaphanous silk lampshades, which they hand-paint with Fortuny patterns.

Pleated silk and Fortuny lamps
To make these fragile objects, the silk is attached to a brass framework, then carefully hand-painted with a mixture of silver, oil and color; after that its edges are trimmed with Murano glass beads. A single one of these lamps can represent a week's hard work for ten people.

IL BOVOLO
The semicircular arches of this spiral staircase give it an airy quality; its construction appears to reproduce the classic Byzantine stairway-tower, in the style of the period. It is said to be Renaissance in its columns, Gothic in its method of construction, and half Venetian-Byzantine, half Renaissance in its form. It is thought that Giovanni Candi was the architect.

THE CHURCH OF SAN BENEDETTO. The present building dates from 1685. On the lower left-hand side of the aisle hangs Giambattista Tiepolo's *Saint Francis de Paule*, which has been heavily restored. (Take the Salizzada del Teatro, then Calle San Paternian.)

CAMPO MANIN. This campo received its name after 1875, at the suggestion of the patriot Giorgio Casarin, to honor the memory of Daniele Manin, leader of the 1848 Venice uprising ● *34*. The Savings Bank building here is one of the very few modern constructions in Venice (1968).

CA' CONTARINI DEL BOVOLO. This palace, which is a mixture of Renaissance and Gothic, could not be confused with any other. In the late 15th century, with a view to enlarging his home, Pietro Contarini added a series of loggias to it, which were linked together by a round tower with a spiral staircase. This tower so caught the imagination of the Venetians that they nicknamed the palazzo "Contarini del Bovolo" (of the snail). It was later converted into an hotel during the 19th century, then converted back to private use again. Today it is the headquarters of an organization which oversees the city's educational foundations. (Return to Campo Manin, then follow the Ramo della Salizzada.)

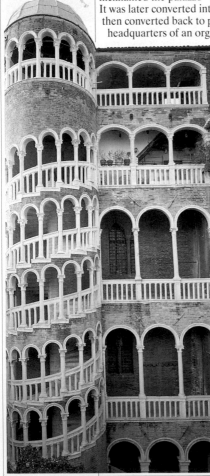

THE CHURCH OF SAN LUCA. San Luca features an altarpiece by Veronese, *The Virgin Appearing to Saint Luke*, at its high altar, and a *Virgin and Saints* by Palma the Younger. The writer Aretino is buried in this church. He is said to have died laughing, having been provoked by an obscene remark made about his sister (1556).

CAMPO SAN LUCA. This campo is a popular and lively meeting place for the city's young people. The marble plinth in the middle of the square is supposed to mark the exact center point of Venice; since it bears the arms of the Scuola della Carità and of various painters, it may refer to Bajamonte Tiepolo's conspiracy ▲ *214*, which his colleagues contrived to foil. (Continue along Calle del Forno, Calle del Teatro and Calle dell'Ovo.)

THE CHURCH OF SAN SALVADOR. No more can be seen of this church than the façade and part of the apse, because it is otherwise blocked by the adjacent monastery, whose monks were once notorious for their "licentiousness". Legend has it that a pre-8th century chapel once stood on this spot, but no church or monastery is mentioned

During the period of the Republic, Venice was subdivided into about seventy different parishes (*parrocchie*).

before the 11th century. The church was consecrated in 1177 by Pope Alexander III in person, when he came to Venice in order to conclude the peace treaty with the Emperor Barbarossa ● *30*. The architectural ensemble was restructured at the start of the 16th century. Begun by Giorgio Spavento in 1506, the works were continued under the direction of Tullio Lombardo. Finally Jacopo Sansovino added the two cloisters at the end of the Calle dell'Ovo and completed the main church between 1530 and 1534. San Salvador, which was much admired at the time for its modernity, has one grave defect, namely its lack of light. To compensate for this, Scamozzi placed a lantern in each of its domes (1569). The three-part façade, with its matching doorway, was designed by Giuseppe Sardi. Among the many monuments inside is that of the Doge Francesco Venier by Sansovino. He also contributed the altar in the CHAPEL OF ST AUGUSTIN which harbors Titian's retable, *The Annunciation*.

SCUOLA DI SAN TEODORO ● *87*. This building is said to date back to the time when St Theodore was still the patron saint of Venice ▲ *251*. But the first real mention of it does not come until 1258, at which time it was attached to the Church of San Salvador. With its pupils increasing in number, the scuola moved into a part of the monastery, but when the monks decided to restructure their building, the members of the scuola were obliged to move once again. On April 8, 1551, the scuola took possession of its new premises, and in December of that same year it was assigned an altar (to the left of the high altar) in the church. Then, in 1552 the guild was designated a "Scuola Grande" ▲ *295*, and so needed a building worthy of the new title. Several contiguous sites were bought and, in 1576, Antonio Sardi and his son Giuseppe won a competition for the architectural contract. Longhena then completed the second floor of the façade, which looks out on to the Calle dell'Ovo. After its suppression in 1806, the scuola was stripped of many of its art treasures, but it did retain its ceilings by Giovanni Segala and Giacomo Filippo Parodi. The building subsequently went through a number of successive identities as a repository for archives, an antique shop, a cinema and then a furniture warehouse, before the scuola was finally reconstituted in 1960. Today, the guild is responsible for running the building once again, and uses it to stage commercial and cultural exhibitions. (Take the Calle Larga Mazzini towards the Grand Canal, passing in front of Palazzo Dolfin-Manin, which was once the property of Ludovico Manin, the last Doge of Venice, and is now a branch of the Bank of Italy. From here, continue along the Riva del Ferro.)

DANIELE MANIN ● *34*
Born in Venice on May 13, 1804, Manin became a lawyer after completing his studies in Padua. In 1840 he began to take an interest in the

politics of the Republic, and in January 1848 he was arrested with Nicolò Tommaseo ▲ *266*. Two months later he was set free by the insurgents, who occupied the Arsenale. In the evening of March 22, the Austrians surrendered, and Manin became President of the short-lived Republic. An advocate of all-out resistance to the powerful Austrian forces, he was given full powers in August; but Austria was determined to reconquer Venice and on August 24, 1849, Manin's government was forced to capitulate: He died in exile in Paris, in 1857.

On December 20, 1883 a monument to Carlo Goldoni ▲ *291* was erected on Campo San Bartolomeo. The cast, of bronze, was made by the sculptor Dal Zotto.

CAMPO SAN BARTOLOMEO. Originally a market area, this campo is still a popular meeting place for Venetians. During the 9th century a little church dedicated to St Demetrius stood here, which was rebuilt in the 12th century and given the name of San Bartolomeo Apostolo. With the development of the Rialto quarter ▲ *279*, the church gained in importance, but it remained half-hidden by new construction; today we can only see its side entrance and campanile. It was not until some radical restoration work had taken place in 1723 that San Bartolomeo assumed its present form. For a while the church possessed a painting by Albrecht Dürer, *The Feast of the Rosary*, which was commissioned from the artist by the German community in Venice. This passed into the collection of Emperor Rudolph II in 1606, and is now at the National Museum in Prague. San Bartolomeo is now deconsecrated and is used as a site for temporary exhibitions.

FONDACO DEI TEDESCHI. The term *fondaco* or *fontego* comes from the Arabic word *fonduc*, which means an inn, a warehouse, or a place for commercial transactions. Built in 1228, this building was occupied by the accountants and experts who oversaw the commercial activity of the Rialto. When trade with northern Europe became vital to Venetian interests, it was reserved for the use of German merchants. At about this time the *fondaco* was transformed into a market and, when the original building was destroyed by fire, the city replaced it between 1506 and 1508 with the huge two-hundred-room building which we see today. Its coping, portico and two small corner-towers (destroyed in 1838) were all copied from older Venetian-Byzantine models, while its overall plan and façades are both clearly Renaissance in style.

Giorgione and the young Titian decorated the latter between 1508 and 1509. It would appear that the two painters' cycle of frescoes alluded to the solidity and stability of the Republic of St Mark, which was founded on the twin principles of peace and justice. Giorgione painted the allegory of peace on the main façade, while Titian took care of Justice, producing an allegory of *Judith*. Only a few restored fragments of these works survive today, and they can be viewed in the Ca' d'Oro ▲ *148, 196*. In 1806, Napoleon put an abrupt end to the activities of the Germans in the *fondaco* and turned the building into a customs house. Since 1870, it has served as the city of Venice's Central Post Office.

SAN POLO

CHURCH OF SAN PANTALON
CHURCH OF SAN ROCCO
SCUOLA DI SAN ROCCO
CHURCH OF SANTA MARIA GLORIOSA DEI FRARI
SCUOLA DEI CALEGHERI
CHURCH OF SAN TOMÀ
PALAZZO CENTANI
PALAZZO CORNER-MOC
CHURCH OF SAN

URBAN DEVELOPMENT
During the 9th and
10th centuries, the
Rialto area consisted
of little more than a
cluster of small
islands
which
were
set in
the midst of
sandbanks and
marshland. Then,
between the 10th and
11th centuries, the
land was
progressively drained
and a new
commercial center
grew up beside the
Grand Canal,
crisscrossed by
numerous footpaths.

Enclosed by the wide loop of the Grand Canal, the 84-acre sestiere of San Polo is Venice's smallest district. To the east it includes the Rialto, one of the city's livelier zones and certainly one of its most ancient; indeed the very name "Rialto" harks back to Venice's remote origins. In the 9th century there was a small settlement in the middle of the lagoon, called *Rivoaltus* (upper bank) because the land there was higher than elsewhere and thus less prone to flooding. After the year 810, the Doge moved his residence to Malamocco ● *30*, which became the heart of the new state. It extended over a cluster of small islands (the Realtine Islands) and at its center was the Rio Businiacus, the future Grand Canal, and the two sestieri known to us today as San Marco and San Polo. Only the left bank was to retain the name of "Rialto" when the city of Venice was undergoing its greatest expansion two centuries later. Another century passed; then, in 1097, the main market which had been located on the right bank was moved to the island opposite, to a site beside the waterway. During the 12th century, a pontoon of boats was thrown across the Grand Canal to link the two banks together; it was subsequently replaced by a wooden bridge some time between 1200 and 1260. At that time a major

PALAZZO BERNARDO
PALAZZI SORANZO
PALAZZO ALBRIZZI
PALAZZO TIEPOLO MAFFETTI
CHURCH OF SANT'APONAL
CHURCH OF SAN CASSIANO
CHURCH OF SAN SILVESTRO
PESCHERIA
FABBRICHE NUOVE
CHURCH OF SAN GIACOMO DI RIALTO
PALAZZO DEI CAMERLENGHI
RIALTO BRIDGE

✺ Half a day

commercial zone grew up around the market, and the Rialto became the hub of a great trading city. In time the urban fabric of the sestiere grew denser, the buildings taller, and new structures filled surrounding empty spaces. By the end of the 15th century, the quarter had acquired strong individual characteristics. On January 10, 1514, a fire reduced most of the Rialto to ruins; but the magistrates refused to abandon the area and commercial life quickly recovered. New houses were built on the foundations of old ones, a process that took more than eighteen years to complete. The east side of the district, where palaces stand beside humbler dwellings and churches are set on little campi, was complemented (to the west of the Rio di San Polo) by a more open area boasting major religious edifices and scuole – the Frari, San Rocco and San Giovanni Evangelista.

THE RIALTO, HOME OF COMMERCIAL VENICE

THE HEART OF THE BUSINESS DISTRICT. As well as its wholesale and retail traders, its workshops and stores selling luxury products (especially spices and fine fabrics), between the 13th and 15th centuries the Rialto area also contained the city's main trade-related legal authorities, private and public banking houses, marine insurance agencies and even a kind of commodity stock market. From dawn till dusk, the area was a hive of commercial activity. Men of all nations met and mingled beneath the Rialto's arcades, in the *fondachi* ● *89* or else in one of the myriad of picturesquely-named *osterie*.

THE BURNING OF THE RIALTO
The chronicle of Marin Sanudo, a learned patrician who owned an *osteria* on the Rialto, relates

how a fire ravaged the district during the night of January 10, 1514. The flames were spread by the high winds; the lumber stores, which were stacked high with wood, were destroyed one after another, while "certain citizens" took advantage of the chaos to loot the premises of others. Only the little Church of San Giacometto escaped unscathed from the flames.

279

Emblems
of the merchants.

A colony of the
Serene Republic.

The moneychangers,
and then the bankers,
set up shop at the
Rialto. The area was
policed day and night,
with extra protection
when funds were
moved from the
Banco di Giro to the
Zecca ▲ 255: at such
times, shopkeepers
armed themselves
and stood guard in
front of their shops.

Every form of business and barter was
conducted here. Quantities of grain were
bought and sold on a daily basis, as were
slaves, despite a series of strict bans on
the slave trade. In addition the Rialto
had its own corps of artisans, among
them jewelers, woodcarvers and
madonneri (painters of madonnas).

THE MAGISTRACIES. In the mid-13th
century, a magistracy was created in
order to oversee the affairs of the Rialto
district. Its officers had to swear an oath
not to yield to any form of pressure, and
to think only of the best interests of the
Seignory when they granted leases on
warehouses, shops and stalls. Additional
magistracies were set up until the 15th
century – notably fiscal and financial
organizations and offices assigned to
regulate the various professions and
corporations.

THE BANKS. The necessities of commerce
prompted the creation of banks, which
naturally enough began to cluster around
what had become the main trading
quarter of Venice. The first banks to
appear (in about 1157) were private ones,
and thereafter the banker's calling remained a prerogative of
the nobility until the great wave of bankruptcies in 1584. The
first state bank, the Banco di Piazza, was founded four years
later. The Banco di Giro (deposit bank), which stood beside
the Church of San Giacomo, appeared in 1619.

FOREIGNERS IN THE RIALTO. As a major port and crossroads
between East and West, Venice was a cosmopolitan city. It
was in the Venetian interest to welcome foreigners, since they
made such an obvious contribution to the city's prosperity,
and the Republic instituted highly tolerant laws in respect of
them. While foreigners had to submit to Venetian law in
matters such as taxation, merchants of the Rialto had the
freedom to manage their premises as they liked, whether they
were Venetians, Turks, Germans or any other nationality.

THE ERA OF TRADE. With her attention still firmly fixed on the
Orient, Venice grew bolder as her power increased. Although
the Venetians benefited from immense privileges within the
Byzantine Empire, and had taken advantage of the Crusades
to open new outposts throughout the Mediterranean,
unbounded greed eventually drove them to seize a quarter of
the Emperor's territories in 1204 ● *31*. However, the
Byzantines reconquered Constantinople in 1261; after
banishing the Venetians, they transferred their former
privileges to the Genoese. This setback did not discourage
the merchants of Venice, as the exploits of the Polo
family show. Full of confidence and enterprise, the
Polos set out from Venice to penetrate deep into the
East; clearly, the relative peace which existed in Asia,
unified by Genghis Khan, and the high taxation
on merchandise transported through Muslim countries,
were enough incentive for merchants to go to the Far
East on their own account.

> «AS SAILORS AND MERCHANTS, TOWN-BUILDERS AND POLITICIANS,
> THE VENETIANS WERE THE FORERUNNERS AND THE YOUTH OF
> TODAY'S CIVILIZATION.»
>
> LE CORBUSIER

Il Gazzettino Illustrato

MARCO POLO

FIRST VOYAGE OF THE POLOS (1265).
Niccolò and Maffeo Polo set out on
their first voyage in a vessel full of
merchandise for Constantinople; like
many of their fellow citizens, they
maintained a trading house there.
They then sailed on into the Black
Sea, where they bartered their goods
for Russian and Turkish products
before penetrating the lands of the
East, where they met the Great
Khan. After this they returned to Italy before setting out
again, this time taking the young Marco Polo with them.

MARCO POLO IN CHINA (1271–95). The three men completed
the long journey out almost entirely by land, and presented
themselves to the Mongol Emperor on arrival in northern
China. Genghis Khan made friends with Marco, appointing
him governor of the Yangzhou region. Though the
commercial goal that had motivated his family was mostly
put aside from this time on, Marco continued to observe
China with the practised eye of a merchant and of an
excellent administrator. He was amazed by the variety
and abundance of the products available in Quinzai,
now known as Hangchow. He chronicled the imports
and exports, the taxes levied, and the city's methods
of administration. His attention was also drawn to
products readily available in China, which he
thought vital to the West: sugar, spices (especially
pepper, which was abundant), silk and cotton, the
trade in which had so enriched his native Venice.

**THE RETURN OF
MARCO POLO**
After 25 years in
China, Marco Polo
returned to Venice in
1295 and lived there
largely unknown to
his fellow citizens. He
had left his native city
at a very early age
and now, though he
spoke many other
languages, had
trouble expressing
himself in his mother
tongue. We would
probably never have
heard of Marco Polo
had he not been
imprisoned for a spell
in Genoa, where he
related his
adventures to a
cellmate,
Rusticello
of Pisa
▲ *150*.

THE RIALTO

THE RIALTO BRIDGE. This was the first construction to span the Grand Canal, and it remained the only link between the two sides of the waterway until the 19th century. The first boat-bridge, which appeared around 1172, was superseded by a wooden construction between 1200 and 1260. But, after three successive wooden bridges collapsed, it was decided in 1524 that a permanent stone bridge should be erected. In 1557 the Republic launched a competition for the building contract, in which Palladio, Vignola, Sansovino, Scamozzi and Michelangelo all took part. But the project was endlessly delayed by a shortage of money and disagreements about the form that the bridge should take: how many arches should it have? Five, three, or one? Finally, in 1588, a one-arch bridge was settled upon, following a design submitted by an architect, Da Ponte, whose name seemed to predestine him for the work. The subsequent construction work was difficult, given the instability of the site and the height (25 feet) required to allow galleys to pass safely beneath. In 1591, the work was completed and the bridge finally opened. The overhanging portico is a later addition, and shelters two rows of luxury boutiques which are much favored by tourists today. In 1977, the Rialto Bridge was entirely restored by the Venezia Nostra Committee.

PALAZZO DEI DIECI SAVI. This palace, which stands on the left at the foot of the bridge, was built in 1521 by Antonio Abbondi (Lo Scarpagnino). Formerly the city's main tax office, it is now occupied by the municipal waterboard.

PALAZZO DEI CAMERLENGHI. Between 1525 and 1528 Guglielmo dei Grigi, who belonged to a family of Lombard master-builders, constructed an elegant palace by the Rialto; today, unfortunately, it is no more than a shadow of its former self. The *camerlenghi* (magistrates responsible for collecting state taxes), had their offices in this building, hence its name. The first floor was occupied by the Republic's treasury, and on the ground floor were the cells in which tax-evaders were imprisoned. The paintings of the Palazzo Camerlenghi were dispersed during the Napoleonic occupation and are now mostly to be found at the Cini Foundation on the island of San Giorgio ▲ *342*.

THE BRIDGE OF WOOD
The first wooden bridge at the Rialto was burned down during a rebellion in 1310 by retreating supporters of Bajamonte Tiepolo ▲ *214*. Its successor collapsed in 1444 under the weight of a crowd that had come to attend the marriage of the Marchioness of Ferrara. So a third bridge was built, a magnificent, solidly-based piece of construction with two central spars that could be raised to allow the passage of tall ships. This bridge was included by Carpaccio in his *Miracle of the True Cross* (opposite). At the start of the 16th century, it was in such bad shape that it had to be partly restored – in vain, for it later collapsed entirely.

RUGA DEGLI ORESI. This alley was formerly occupied by a number of gold and silver workers (*oresi*, in the Venetian dialect). The Sottoportico di Rialto, which adjoins it, is still full of jewelry stores.

THE "GOBBO DI RIALTO"
This little statue, sculpted by Pietro da Salo in 1541, shows a man holding up a flight of stairs. The figure was known as the "hunchback" (*gobbo*) though he is

merely bent beneath his burden, seen as an allegory of the heavy taxes imposed on Venetians. Nearby is the Pietra del bando, a pink granite podium from which government decrees were proclaimed.

A WARNING TO MERCHANTS
As Venice's commercial activities were mostly clustered around the Church of San Giacomo di Rialto, the outer wall of the apse was inscribed with an exhortation to merchants to be honest, not to cheat on weights and measures, and to draw up fair contracts.

THE CHURCH OF SAN GIACOMO DI RIALTO. Affectionately known as "San Giacometto" because it is so small, this church in the form of a Greek Cross is the oldest in Venice. According to legend it was founded in the 5th century, but a date somewhere between the 11th and 12th centuries would probably be nearer the truth. In 1587 its floor was raised and the dome and arches restored, but the Doge, who traditionally worshipped there once a year on Ash Wednesday, ordered the builders on no account to meddle with the form of the sanctuary. Of the original church, only the Greek marble columns of the naves and the chapters ornamented with sculpted foliage remain. These probably derive from other more ancient Venetian-Byzantine structures. The façade, which is dominated by an arcaded clocktower ● 85 in Istrian stone, is the product of many alterations: since the 14th century it has had a large clock in its center (rebuilt in 1749). As for the wooden portico, this was added in the 17th century and restored in 1758.

In the last century, people came from many miles around in order to buy the aromatic or medicinal herbs, flowers and fruit on the stalls of the Erberia market.

THE FABBRICHE VECCHIE. This arcaded building (1520–2) was completed by Scarpagnino at the same time as his reconstruction of the entire district following the great fire of 1514. Formerly the seat of the trade, navigation and food supply administrations, it is now Venice's main tribunal.

SOTTOPORTICO DEL BANCO DI GIRO. Merchants used to gather for business under this portico, which adjoined the offices of the Banco di Giro. The giro system allowed people to transfer money from one account to another without

The seller of *bussolai* ● 76 and other sweetmeats: hers was one of many street trades plied in Venice in the 18th century.

having to carry it on their person. The sums involved would be inscribed on the banker's register as an order of payment, which would have to be presented by the party himself; the money would then be "transferred" to the account which was to be credited. Since the bank register was an officially notarized document, no receipt was required.

THE ERBERIA. Casanova, in his 18th-century autobiography, had this to say about the Erberia: "It is so-called because it is positively the market for herbs, fruit and flowers. Those who go there early in the morning say they do so for the innocent pleasure of seeing the arrival of all kinds of green herbs, and of fruits and flowers in season. These are brought in by the inhabitants of the little islands surrounding the capital, and are sold at low prices to the main retailers." Nowadays there are still both wholesale and retail markets on the site. These are so delightful, even out of season, that they always attract large crowds of people. Between 8.00am and 9.00am the wholesalers take possession of the Erberia; they are followed by the retailers, between 9.00am and 11.00am. The prices of goods are much lower here than elsewhere and this is a fact of some importance in an island city like Venice, where produce is necessarily expensive due to the considerable cost of transport.

THE FABBRICHE NUOVE. This long building stands on the curve of the Grand Canal. Built between 1553 and 1555 by Sansovino, it used to be the headquarters of the trade administration and it is now the Assize Court.

CAMPO DELLA PESCHERIA. There has been a fish market on this site for a thousand years. The sunlight has barely begun to glimmer on the canal and on the still-wet pavement of the market, when the first brightly painted boats arrive and the air fills with the fishermens' shouts. The *bragozzi* ▲ *360* and

the *topi* ● *73* tie up at the fondamenta in apparent confusion, though in fact every mooring is strictly allocated. Then the fishermen bring their catch ashore, swapping banter in the strange dialect of Venice, with its bitten-off vowel sounds and musical cadences that differ depending on which sestiere one comes from. After the fishermen come the lighters, filled with fruit and vegetables for the Erberia. By 8.30am the stalls are laid out and ready for business: by 12.00pm the stallholders are packed and gone, and the marketplace is left to the cats. On summer evenings, concerts and theatrical performances are often held here, or near the ferry landing stage. The Campo della Pescheria is one of the few points at which one can walk along the bank of the Grand Canal. To do so, take the RIVA DELL'OLIO, so named because oil used to be brought ashore there. Other names for this stretch are the Fondamenta dei Sagomatori (a reference to the measures used for casks of oil), or the Fondamenta del Legno, because wood was also unloaded at this wharf. (Return to the Campo della Pescheria and turn off down the Calle delle Beccarie.)

CAMPO DELLE BECCARIE. This area, which once housed the public abattoirs, is now full of traditional Venetian *bacari*, and is much favored as a rendezvous by the local tradesmen. In fact anybody in Venice with someone to meet for an aperitif could well invite them into one of the wine bars here to share an *ombra*. This strange expression for a glass of wine – white wine, for preference – is said to have originated in St Mark's Square, where wine from the barrel used to be sold at the foot of the campanile. As the sun moved across the sky, the trestle-tables, demi-johns and kegs would all be moved in concert, to keep the wine cool and in the shade. Another school of thought believes that the phrase means the "shadow of a litre", in other words a ̄mall quantity of wine. The local habit is ̄ drink one's *ombra* with *cicchetti*, or ̄acks. Of these there is a wide range, ̄ably meatballs (*polpettine*), portions of fried fish or ̄etables, hard-boiled eggs, or creamy fish paste on toast. ̄e delicacies are generally eaten while standing up. (After ̄idge and the Campo delle Beccarie, turn left along the ̄lei Botteri, and then right into Calle Corpus Domini

FONDACO DEI TEDESCHI
Located in the San Marco sestiere, but visible from the Rialto Bridge, this former warehouse of Venice's German merchant community is now the city's central Post Office ▲ *200, 276*.

The Pescheria and the landing-stage for the ferry to Campo Santa Sofia ▲ *149*.

Campo San Giacomo di Rialto, with its market. At the far end, the Church of San Giacometto, with its characteristic galleried clocktower.

CAMPO
S. POLO

Florentine, the Venetian aristocrat Bianca Cappello married Francesco dei Medici in 1578. Venice was delighted with the match, giving her the title of "Daughter of the Republic"; in return, Bianca served her country well. Nevertheless when she and her husband were poisoned by Cardinal Ferdinand di Medici in 1587, Venice bowed to Florentine pressure and forbade citizens to wear mourning. In Florence the "traitor" Cardinal refused to allow Bianca to be buried in the Medici family vault.

RIVA DEL VIN

FROM THE RIALTO TO CAMPO SAN POLO

CAMPO SAN CASSIANO. This zone developed independently of the Rialto market, and was not directly linked to it until 1436. A few wealthy families pooled their funds to build the CHURCH OF SAN CASSIANO at the start of the 9th century, on the site of an oratory dedicated to St Cecilia. All that remains of this Venetian-Byzantine sanctuary is the pair of marble pilasters in the doorway; inside are several paintings by Tintoretto. There used to be two "very beautiful theaters" in the vicinity, "which were large enough to contain great concourses of spectators, and in which comedies were played at carnival time, as is the custom of this city" (Sanudo). One became the first paying theater in Europe open to the general public, by a decree of the Council of Ten in 1636. It was demolished in 1812. (Return to the Campo delle Beccarie, then take the Ruga degli Speziali and the Ruga Vecchia San Giovanni; turn left into Calle Toscana, then left again into Calle dei Preti.)
THE CHURCH OF SAN GIOVANNI ELEMOSINARIO. The Church of San Giovanni was founded towards the end of the 9th century, then reconstructed to plans by Scarpagnino after the fire of 1514. The interior, shaped like a Greek Cross, has the sobriety of the high Renaissance. The choir contains an altarpiece by Titian, *San Giovanni Elemosinario* (c.1545). In the CAPELLA DEI CORRIERI is one of Pordenone's greatest works, *Saint Catherine, Saint Sebastian and Saint Roch*. This church was formerly under the special protection of the Doge, who went to Mass there every Wednesday. Thus it is no surprise that the arms of the Doge Michele Steno are engraved on its campanile. (Continue straight on along the Ruga Vecchia San Giovanni.)
THE CHURCH OF SANT'APONAL. Built by a family from Ravenna in the 11th century, this church was dedicated to the patron saint of that town, St Apollinarius, and was totally rebuilt in the 15th century in the late Gothic style. Deconsecrated in 1810, it was used successively as a mill, a

night-shelter for the poor, and a prison: for the latter purpose, four large windows were knocked through its façade. Finally, the building was put up for auction and repurchased for Christian worship, and it was reopened in 1851. At that time, it still possessed the 13th-century bas-relief which stood over the little door of its campanile: a "Leone a moleca" (a lion clutching a closed Bible). Today it is closed again. (Continue into the Calle del Luganegher.)
CAMPO SAN SILVESTRO. Though now no more than a thoroughfare, this campo was once full of stalls and workshops, and was directly linked to the Grand Canal by rio (since filled in). The present CHURCH dates from the century, when it replaced a building founded in the 9th

Coat of arms of the Molin family.

century, of which the only remaining trace is a fragment of a column topped by a Venetian-Byzantine capital that has been incorporated into the outer wall facing the rio terrà. Inside is a *Baptism of Christ* by Tintoretto: facing the porch is the CA' VALIER, which was formerly decorated with 17th-century frescoes by Taddeo Longhi. This may have been the home of the painter Giorgione, unless (as some say) he lived at number 1099. (Continue along Sottoportico del Traghetto.)

RIVA DEL VIN. This fondamenta is one of the rare stretches of walkway beside the Grand Canal (along with the Riva dell'Olio and the Riva del Carbon opposite). It is so named because it was once an unloading point for wine barrels on their way to the various warehouses and *bacari* of the district. (Return to Campo Sant'Aponal. Take the Calle Bianca Capello – named after the famous noble Venetian lady who was born here – continue to PALAZZO MOLIN-CAPELLO, then take the Calle Banco Salviati).

PALAZZO ALBRIZZI. Belying its very sober exterior, on the inside the Palazzo Albrizzi is one of the most sumptuous houses in the whole of Venice – a maze of white-and-gold rooms filled with voluptuous stucco. The Albrizzi family came to Venice from Bergamo in the 16th century and acquired great wealth by trading in oils and fabrics. In 1648 they began purchasing this palace, floor by floor, embellishing it as they went. The final section of it passed into their hands in 1692. It was in this house that Isabella Teotochi, with whom the poet Ugo Foscolo was infatuated during his stay in Venice, held her literary salon at the start of the 19th century following her marriage to Count Albrizzi ▲ *171*. Here Isabella regularly received Pindemonte, Alfieri and Canova, who in 1812 sculpted her for a *Head of Helen*, which is still to be seen in the palace.

FONDAMENTA DELLA TETTE. One may be forgiven for wondering just how this fondamenta and the bridge nearby acquired their peculiar name, since *tette* is a slang Italian term for breasts. The reason is simply that the fondamenta marked the limit of the area in which prostitutes were authorized to solicit customers, which they did by exhibiting their breasts from the balconies. If local legend is to be believed, a law against homosexuality and transvestism lay at the root of this custom.

THE PROSTITUTES OF VENICE

In a city as rich as Venice, all the pleasures of the flesh were bound to be readily available, and the repressive laws of the Republic had little or no effect on the matter. According to Marin Sanudo, at the beginning of the 16th century there were no fewer than 11,654 prostitutes working in Venice, a considerable number in view of the total population of 100,000. The prostitutes lived close by the Rialto. Their highest category, the courtesans, lived in sumptuous apartments, dressed with elegance, were accomplished musicians and were familiar with the wealthiest patrician families.

CAMPO SAN POLO
As in Venice's other
major piazzas, bull-
baitings were
frequently held in the
Campo San Polo ● *50*
and were very

AROUND CAMPO SAN POLO

THE CAMPO. Campo San Polo, with its brick paving, is one of
the oldest and widest squares in the whole of Venice. In the
past it must have looked somewhat different, because the
Canal Sant'Antonio formerly lay in front of the buildings

which now divide it from the Soranzo
Palazzi. This watercourse was filled in
between 1750 and 1761, and the little
bridges which once gave direct access to
the palaces were subsequently
demolished. Because it is situated at the
heart of this crowded quarter, the campo
was formerly the scene of religious and
lay ceremonies, of preachings, bull-
runnings, balls, banquets, theatrical
performances and masked galas during
Carnival time. Since 1977, this function
has been resumed and now Campo San
Polo is not only one of the principal
Carnival venues, but it is also used as a
venue for screening films during the
Venice Film Festival ▲ *356*.

PALAZZO MAFFETTI-TIEPOLO (number
1957). Built during the 14th century, this
palace was reconstructed in the baroque
style by Massari during the 18th century.
A staircase decorated with stucco, multi-

popular. The
Compagnia della
Calza (literally, the
company of the
stockings), jovial
bands of young men
who were identified
by the different
emblems on their
hose, were
responsible for
organizing these
events, which usually
took place over
Carnival. Oxen were
generally used
instead of bulls, so as
to keep accidents to a
minimum.

colored marble and faded frescoes, along with bas-reliefs and
garlands over the doors, give some idea of what the
decoration by Domenico Rossi must have been like.
THE SORANZO PALAZZI. These two palaces, fused into one by
the Soranzo family, are the principal buildings on the campo.
Looking at the geminate window on the first floor, one is
tempted to date the palace on the left somewhere around the
mid-14th century; yet its two doorways with their sculpted
lintels seem older. The right-hand palace, with its eight-
arched window, has features that clearly indicate the 15th
century. Tradition has it that frescoes by Giorgione once
adorned the façade but, if so, no trace of them remains today.
Casanova entered this house as a humble violinist and came
out of it ennobled, having been adopted within by a sick
senator to whom he had rendered a service.
PALAZZO CORNER-MOCENIGO (number 2128). Palazzo
Corner-Mocenigo was built for Giovanni Cornaro
by the architect Michele Sanmicheli, in

order to replace a palace that was destroyed by fire in 1535. Although it was described at the time as "magnificent and very rich", the structure has always been considered a trifle big for Venice, at six storeys high. Today it houses the Guardia di Finanza.

THE CHURCH OF SAN POLO. Rebuilt several times, this building is now a hotchpotch of different styles. The two openings in the façade, and the fragments of cornices and pilasters on the same side as the entrance, are vestiges of the primitive church that stood here in the 9th century. The wooden ceiling (uncovered recently during renovation work), the rose-window and the side portal, are obviously the result of work undertaken in the 14th and 15th centuries to graft Gothic elements on to the original Byzantine building. The arrangement of the interior again reveals a Byzantine concept of space, despite the alterations made by Davide Rossi in 1804 with a view to adapting the church to Neo-classical canons. There are paintings by Tintoretto (including a *Last Supper*), Veronese, Palma the Younger, and Giandomenico Tiepolo (fourteen canvases of the *Way of the Cross*). The CAMPANILE (1365) stands in front of the church in the Salizzada di San Polo. Two face-to-face stone lions stand over the church entrance: one clutches a serpent in its claws, the other a man's head. This is said to be an allegory on the condemnation to death of Doge Falier.

PALAZZO BERNARDO. Standing slightly apart in the Calle Bernardo is this fine example of flowery Venetian Gothic (1422). Do not miss the magnificent spiral staircase in the inner courtyard. (Continue straight on, then turn left along the Rio terrà San Secondo.)

THE PRINTING HOUSE OF ALDO MANUTIUS THE ELDER. Apparently number 2311 of this rio terrà was where the humanist Aldo Manutius the Elder founded his printshop at the turn of the 16th century; and here the Aldine Academy met to decide what texts they should print, Erasmus himself being among their number. Manutius left the quarter towards the end of his life. He went to live at San Paterninio, where he is buried, and where Paola and Aldo the Younger carried on his work. (Take the Rio terrà Primo, turn right and continue along the Calle San Boldo.)

CAMPO SAN BOLDO. Built in the 18th century, PALAZZO GRIMANI has rather strangely engulfed the tower of the campanile. Though converted into a part of the house, it remains the last vestige of the church which was destroyed in 1826. On the other side of the rio one can hire boats of different types for reasonable prices. (Go back to Campo San Polo, then along Salizzada di San Polo and Calle dei Saoneri, then turning left and then right.)

L'ARTE
DELLA
STAMPA
NEL
RINASCIMENTO ITALIANO
VENEZIA

ALDVS·PIVS·MANVTIVS·R·

VENEZIA MDCCCXCIV
FERD. ONGANIA, Editore.

Chamber music at the Ca' Goldoni.

In the beautiful courtyard of the Palazzo Centani (the other name for the Ca' Goldoni) there is an open staircase that dates from the 15th century. At the center of the courtyard is a traditional well.

THE HOUSE OF GOLDONI ★

This 15th-century building, with its elegant Gothic façade overlooking the Rio San Tomà, was the birthplace of Carlo Goldoni. Goldoni, who has often been called the "Italian Molière", stated that he was born during the Carnival "in the year 1707, in a great and beautiful house between the Nomboli and Donna Onesta bridges, on the corner of the Calle della Ca' Centani, in the parish of San Tommaso". The house, which was bequeathed to the city in 1931, has been used as an institute of dramatic studies and a museum since 1952.

THE COMMEDIA DELL'ARTE.

From the mid-16th century onwards, a new theatrical genre began to develop which was much more focused on stagecraft than had been the case hitherto. The actors learned to combine the skills of acrobats, mime artists and singers, and they improvised their parts each night on the basis of a simple plot (the *canevas*) and a "formula" of tirades, soliloquies and *lazzi* – scene substitutions, mimicry and jokes which could be adapted to suit any comedy. The plots, which were generally inspired by classical comedy, in time became very similar to one another. In fact the great novelty of this comedy of improvisation – and one of the reasons for its huge success – was the introduction of "fixed" rôles, played by actors with masks. In other words, each actor gave up the pretence of renewing his part every night, instead limiting himself to a single character. Before long, the actors became known by the names of their masks alone.

> «I HAVE NEVER WITNESSED SUCH AN ECSTASY OF JOY AS THAT SHOWN BY THE AUDIENCE WHEN THEY SAW THEMSELVES AND THEIR FAMILIES SO REALISTICALLY PORTRAYED ON THE STAGE. THEY SHOUTED WITH LAUGHTER FROM BEGINNING TO END.»
>
> GOETHE

THE MASKS. In Commedia dell'Arte the same roles occur again and again. First of all, there are the two manservants, or *zanni* (from the name "Giovanni" ● 42), who are HARLEQUIN AND BRIGHELLA. At the beginning of the piece, both are equally coarse, lazy and greedy. Before long, however, Brighella becomes crafty, skilled at setting up traps and stratagems. Harlequin, who starts out dressed in white, is the acrobat of the troupe who makes everyone laugh with his antics: he is often the butt and victim of Brighella. "His garments are those of a poor wretch who picks up odds and ends of rags to clothe himself" (Goldoni). Then come the two "dotards": PANTALON ● 42, an old Venetian merchant whose function is to obstruct the aspirations of the young lovers and the plots of the servants, and BALANZON, a doctor-at-law who is his complement.

Balanzon is a pedant who lards his speeches with hopelessly muddled quotes and Latin tags. These "masks" are accompanied by lovers and servants, whose characters all derive from traditional comedy.

CARLO GOLDONI'S REFORMS. After studying law, Goldoni came to practise in Venice, continuing to do so off and on until 1748. As a young man he was enchanted by the theater, and began to write tragi-comedies and burlesques soon after meeting Giuseppe Imer, who was acting at the Teatro San Samuele in 1734. By the time Goldoni met Girolamo Medebach in 1745, his apprenticeship was complete. He had just written *The Servant of Two Masters*; Medebach, who had become director of the Teatro Sant'Angelo, engaged him as a full-time author for his theater troupe. As it turned out Goldoni became one of the first authors to make a living from his writing. Little by little, he was able to "reform" the Commedia dell'Arte which, since it depended purely on the skills of the actor, was at the mercy of any weakness he might exhibit. Goldoni returned to the written text: "I quietly sought the freedom to write whole plays of my own, and despite the hampering effect of the masks I quite quickly succeeded in doing so." His method was to describe in detail the daily life of Venice and to satirize the manners of his time. In 1753, he produced *La Locandiera*, then left Medebach to work for the Teatro San Luca. Gradually he gave more importance in his plays to ordinary individuals, satirizing the laziness of the aristocracy. In 1757, he quarrelled with CARLO GOZZI, who saw in Goldoni's work an "instrument of social subversion". Meanwhile Goldoni constantly renewed his repertoire to compete with other theaters. This was the period of his greatest success: *I Rusteghi* (1760), the trilogy of *La Villegiatura* (1761) and *Le Baruffe Chiozzotte* (1762). In 1762 he was invited to Paris by the Comédie Italienne; bidding farewell to Venice with *Una delle ultime sere de Carnevale* (One of the Last Nights of Carnival), Goldoni left for the French capital, where he wrote practically nothing but *canevas* comedies. He taught Italian at the royal court and received the king's protection; but the Revolution deprived him of his pension, which was only restored to him on February 7, 1793 – the day after his death.

CARLO GOZZI
Born in Venice on December 13, 1720, Gozzi grew up in a highly literate family. From the mid-century onwards, he pursued a career in the theater, declaring his total opposition to the innovations of Goldoni. In his early work, this quarrelsome polemicist set out to show that he could arouse the interest of the public with simple plots relying on improvisations within the Commedia dell'Arte framework. Later, he reduced his emphasis on improvisation, offering an approach to theater that was based on imagination and wonder, as opposed to Goldoni's realism. In 1761 he mounted *The Love of Three Oranges* at the Teatro San Samuele, a play holding Goldoni up to ridicule. A conservative in art and politics, Gozzi witnessed the decline and fall of Venice, dying at the age of eighty-six in 1806.

A picturesque house which looks on to the Campo Castelforte, with windows and balconies decorated with weathervanes.

THE LETTUCE OF THE FRARI
The Oratorio della Lattuga (lettuce) was founded in 1332 by Niccolò Lion who, if tradition be believed, built it after he was miraculously cured by a lettuce. Gravely ill, he suddenly craved one in the middle of the night, and it was found in the Frari's kitchen garden.

CAMPO SAN TOMÀ. THE CHURCH OF SAN TOMÀ has existed since the 10th century and took its present form in 1742. The 14th-century CAMPANILE was demolished because of its faulty foundations, and the present smaller one erected in its place. Opposite the church stands the old SCUOLA DEI CALEGHERI (shoemakers). Note the bas-relief over the doorway and the "lunette" containing Pietro Lombardo's *Saint Mark Healing the Shoemaker Aniano*. The shoemakers' guild, which acquired the building in 1446, had more than 1,500 members in the 18th century and operated in 400 workshops.

SANTA MARIA GLORIOSA DEI FRARI ★   ● 82

THE FRANCISCAN CHURCH. Around 1222, the Franciscans established themselves in Venice. They lived on charity and occasional jobs, sheltering in churches and convents until the state presented them with a former Benedictine abbey. In 1236, a site adjoining the abbey was given to the Franciscans, along with a handsome donation from the Doge Jacopo Tiepolo. Here they built the Convent and Church of Santa Maria Gloriosa, known as the Frari (a distortion of *frati*, brothers). Work on the church began in 1250 and was completed about 1330; the result was a building which was smaller than the future basilica, and oriented in a different direction. Donations from great Venetian families made it possible to enlarge and embellish this structure in the mid-14th century; it was then demolished at the start of the 15th century, to make way for the new basilica, a huge mass of brick punctuated by features of white marble.
THE INTERIOR. The Frari is a pantheon of the glories of Venice, the city's largest place of worship and one of the largest ever built by a religious order. At the center of the church is the ancient CORO DEI FRATI, a choir of 124 wooden stalls sculpted by Marco Cozzi (1468). Preserved intact, these stalls form an ensemble that has no equal in Venice. At the bottom of the central apse, framed by the arch of the high altar, hangs Titian's *Assumption* (1516–18). On either side are six smaller apsidal chapels, reserved for certain guilds and noble families, who decorated them at their own expense. On the left side of the transept is the CAPELLA CORNER (c.1420), dedicated to St Mark the Evangelist. On the altar here stands a triptych of *Saint Mark and Three Saints* (1474) by Bartolomeo Vivarini.

«THE "TOMB OF CANOVA", BY CANOVA, CANNOT BE MISSED; CONSUMMATE IN SCIENCE, INTOLERABLE IN AFFECTATION, RIDICULOUS IN CONCEPTION, NULL AND VOID TO THE UTTERMOST IN INVENTION AND FEELING.»

JOHN RUSKIN

Above the font is a fine wooden statuette of St John the Baptist, by Sansovino; and in the chapel to the side is the tomb of Monteverdi, ▲ *174, 263*. There is another wooden statuette of St John the Baptist in the chapel adjoining the high altar, which is the only work of the Florentine master

Detail of the frescoes in the basilica (opposite and below).

Donatello to be found in Venice. By way of the sacristy, at the end of the right-hand extension of the transept, one can reach the Capella Pesaro, which contains a glorious triptych by Giovanni Bellini. In the chapter-house some of the treasures of the basilica are exhibited, along with a *Virgin* by the great 14th-century master Paolo Veneziano; and in the nave, above the PESARO ALTAR, is a masterpiece by Titian, the *Ca' Pesaro*

Altarpiece. Further on is the MONUMENT OF ANTONIO CANOVA, who died in Venice in 1822. This Neo-classical pyramid was designed by the artist himself in honor of Titian, but was never realized in the sculptor's lifetime. It was finally executed by his pupils in 1827 and contains Canova's mummified heart in an urn of porphyry. In front of this is the MONUMENT TO TITIAN, who died of the plague in 1576 after asking to be buried in the Frari. This, too, was erected by Canova's disciples. In addition to these, the basilica contains a number of monuments to various Doges, notably Francesco Foscari, who is portrayed lying beneath stone drapes held by two knights bearing the dead man's coat of arms.

Detail of the portal of the basilica.

THE CAMPANILE. Situated at the junction of the transept and the left-hand nave, the 262-foot campanile of the Frari was constructed between 1391 and 1396 according to plans by Jacopo Celega. It is one of the tallest in Venice.

THE "ASSUMPTION" ★ by Titian.

THE ARCHIVES. The city's archives occupy both the former convent of the Frari and the old oratory of San Niccolò della Lattuga. The immense convent, a center of sanctity, faith, science and the arts in Venice, had by the 16th century achieved a size commensurate with the role played in the life of the city by the Franciscan community. As an architectural complex, it is focused around two cloisters. The CLOISTER OF THE HOLY TRINITY, with its 17th-century portico, was renovated in 1713 by Father Antonio Pittoni, who erected a monumental Baroque well at its center. The CLOISTER OF SAINT ANTHONY was designed by the school of Sansovino. The convent, which was closed by a Napoleonic decree in 1806, was used as a barracks until 1815, when it became a repository for the State Archives. In its three hundred-odd rooms are packed about fifteen million volumes, which record the entire history of La Serenissima.

SAN ROCCO

During the 14th century and after, San Rocco was venerated throughout Europe as a protector against the plague, but especially so in Venice, which was a frequent prey to epidemics. Having concluded that the plague of 1575–6 was brought to an end by his intercession, the state decreed that the feast of San Rocco (August 16) should be marked with a great ceremony in his church. On that day, paintings were exhibited in the piazza outside, which the Doge would admire after attending Mass.

THE CHURCH. San Rocco was built in about 1489 by Bartolomeo Bon, an architect who worked in the Renaissance style of Coducci. Its present appearance is the result of two major 18th-century modifications, when the façade with its bas-relief by Gianmaria Morleiter (*San Rocco Tending the Sick*) was rebuilt. Tintoretto painted an *Annunciation* and several episodes in the life of the saint which are now in the church, notably *Presentation of San Rocco to the Pope*.

THE SCUOLA GRANDE ★, ● 87. The Scuola di San Rocco, which gave great help to the sick during times of plague, was declared a Scuola Grande by the Council of Ten in 1489. In the same year, Bartolomeo Bon was given the task of constructing the scuola's first headquarters; not long after, as the scuola continued to prosper, a second building was commissioned from him. After 1524, Bon's work was continued by a series of architects, among them Sante Lombardo, Lo Scarpagnino and Giangiacomo dei Grigi. Despite all these contributions, the façade gives a remarkable impression of homogeneity.

Fortunately San Rocco was spared when Napoleon closed the other scuole in 1806, and today is chiefly famous for its interior décor, which includes about fifty works executed by Tintoretto between 1564 and 1587. In the LOWER GALLERY are episodes from the life of the Virgin. The pictures in the MAIN UPPER GALLERY illustrate the links between Old and New Testaments, while exalting the activities of the scuola. On the ceiling of the ALBERGO ROOM are allegories of the Scuole Grande around *San Rocco in Glory*. The side walls are painted with the figures of two prophets: one has his eyes turned toward the *Crucifixion* on the wall at the end of the room, while the other

«IT IS NOT IMMORTALITY THAT WE BREATHE AT THE SCUOLA DI SAN ROCCO, BUT CONSCIOUS, RELUCTANT MORTALITY.»

HENRY JAMES

Tintoretto's *Annunciation* (ground floor gallery). Here the beams of light draw the eye to the face of the Virgin, which is the focal point of the entire scene.

COMPETING MASTERS
Once the decision had been made to decorate the ceiling of the Albergo's main hall with a scene of *Saint Roch in glory*, a competition was launched in 1564 in which all the greatest painters of Venice took part. Tintoretto won by a stratagem: apparently he presented the jury with a completed work, which (against all the rules) he unrolled on the ceiling, proclaiming that this was his way of going about his work, and that if the other competitors had been honest, they would have done likewise. Not surprisingly there was an outcry, upon which Tintoretto offered his work free of charge to San Rocco, as a gesture of devotion. The competition was cancelled, and the contract to decorate the hall was given to Tintoretto. In three years, he completed all of the canvases now to be seen on the walls and ceiling. After making a number of other donations, he proposed in 1577 to decorate the entire building against a life annuity of a hundred ducats. By 1581 he had completed the paintings in the upper room; then, between 1583 and 1587, he added the eight paintings in the lower rooms.

contemplates three episodes from the Passion of Christ to the left.

SAN GIOVANNI EVANGELISTA. Behind the Frari, facing the CHURCH OF SAN GIOVANNI EVANGELISTA, is the scuola of the same name. The members

of this guild were established here from 1307. They enlarged their building in the 15th century. It still has a superb Renaissance portal in marble by Pietro Lombardo (1481), and its "lunette" is crowned by an eagle, the symbol of St John the Evangelist. In 1512 the church was restructured by Coducci, who rebuilt the façade and created the monumental staircase.

THE SCUOLE ● 86

The term *scuola* (from the Latin *schola*, a corporation or guild) in Venice designates a form of association between lay citizens. The scuole were corporations that combined devotion and mutual assistance; sometimes they were linked to professions. Their members met in churches under the protection of a patron saint, worshipping and participating in public ceremonies together. At the beginning of the 16th century, five of these guilds had the title of scuola grande: Santa Maria della Carità ▲ 300, San Giovanni Evangelista, Santa Maria in Valverde, San Marco, and San Rocco. In 1552, the Council of Ten accorded this title to a sixth guild: that of San Teodoro ▲ 275. Each of these main scuole had between five and six hundred members; the smaller ones, of which

Emblems of scuole grandi San Giovanni Elemosinario and Santa Maria della Misericordia.

In Gentile Bellini's *Procession of Corpus Christi* ● *48*, the scuole grandi walk in procession with their holy relics. In the foreground are the members of the Scuola San Giovanni Evangelista, who commissioned this painting.

there were about a hundred, had far fewer. The origins of all – and especially of the scuole grandi – went back to the 13th-century movement of the Flagellants, who castigated themselves in public to expiate the sins of the world and appease the wrath of God. The Flagellants, who appeared in Italy around 1260, quickly gained influence among the brotherhoods which the mendicant orders established among the lay populations of the cities. In Venice, the oldest scuola was that of Santa Maria della Carità, whose statutes (*mariegole*) went back precisely to the month of December 1260. The other scuole grandi appeared a little later. Apart from their religious function, the scuole fulfilled a role of mutual assistance: members knew that their scuole would procure them free lodging or money for their daughters' dowries, should they stand in need of such assistance. Some scuole even paid the doctors who visited the indigent sick, to whom they gave medicines free of charge. Thus even the poorest could obtain work or count on a regular distribution of alms. This social activity meant that the scuole played an important part in the life of the city. In effect, while politics as such had been the exclusive province of patricians ever since the closure of the Grand Council ● *31*, the direction of the scuole was barred to them; only merchants, artisans, state functionaries, advocates, notaries or doctors could occupy a position of responsibility in a scuola. Moreover, the scuole received immense donations, which they regularly invested in state loans or property development. So rich and powerful did they become that in the military and financial domains they amounted to a state within a state, with responsibilities ranging from recruiting men to row Venice's galleys, to financing her military expeditions. Thus the scuole gave citizens a way of influencing political events, while forming a link between the wealthier sectors of society and the lower orders. As such they were a highly effective instrument of social cohesion.

DORSODURO

CHURCH OF L'ANGELO RAFFAELE
PALAZZO ARIANI
PALAZZO ZENOBIO
CHURCH OF SANTA MARIA DEL CARMELO
CAMPO SANTA MARGHERITA
CHURCH OF SAN PANTALON
CHURCH OF SAN BAR...
CA' REZZONI...
CA' FO...

CHURCH OF SAN NICOLÒ DEI MENDICOLI
CHURCH OF SAN SEBASTIANO
CHURCH OF THE OGNISSANTI
SQUERO SAN TROVASO
CHURCH OF SAN TROVASO
CHURCH OF SAN TROVASO
CHURCH OF TH...

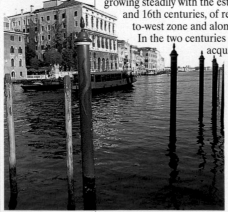

✺ One day

The sestiere of Dorsoduro covers Venice's southern flank; as an administrative area, it occupies 230 acres, including the island of Giudecca. The name means "spine" (hard back) and refers to the quality of the soil, which is higher above sea-level and more stable than that in the other quarters of the city. Although it is apart from the main orbit of the Rialto ▲ 279 and San Marco ▲ 220, Dorsoduro contains a number of monuments which rank among the most interesting in the whole of Venice. Building in this area began on the western side, with the first two poles of attraction forming during the 7th century around the Churches of l'Angelo Raffaele and San Nicolò dei Mendicoli. During the 11th century, new urban nuclei emerged in the central part of Dorsoduro, growing steadily with the establishment, between the 13th and 16th centuries, of religious complexes in the central-to-west zone and along the banks of the Grand Canal. In the two centuries that followed, Dorsoduro acquired both dignity and status, with the lavish rebuilding of many of its churches and the construction of magnificent palaces. The skyline was radically changed by the building of La Salute and the Zattere. During the 19th century, after the establishment of the Accademia at La Carità, and the construction of a new bridge, the sestiere became one of the areas most favored by wealthy foreign residents; later,

THE ACCADEMIA
CHURCH OF SAINT GEORGE
PALAZZO VENIER DAI LEONI
PALAZZO DARIO
CHURCH OF SAN GREGORIO
CHURCH OF THE CATECUMENI
RIALTO BRIDGE
CEMETERY OF SAN MICHELE

CHURCH OF SANT'AGNESE
CHURCH OF SAN VIO
OSPEDALE DEGLI INCURABILI
CHURCH OF SPIRITO SANTO
MAGAZZINI DEL SALE
BASILICA SANTA MARIA DELLA SALUTE
CUSTOMS POINT

n the second half of the century, the construction of the merchant shipping docks galvanized industrial development on the western end of the sestiere.

THE ACCADEMIA

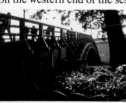

PONTE DELL'ACCADEMIA. From 1488 onwards, Venetians cherished the hope that a stone bridge might one day be built between Campo San Vitale ▲ *268* and Campo della Carità. But it was not until the 19th century and the time of the Austrian occupation ● *34* that the English architect Neville was able to realize his plans for a steel bridge. This was inaugurated on November 20, 1854, then demolished during the Fascist era and replaced, after a national contest, by a wooden bridge. The wooden bridge deteriorated rapidly, however, and another contest was held in 1985. But, although a wide variety of architects came up with some original ideas (one being a transparent bridge which was supposed to minimize the impact on the surrounding area), in the end the municipality decided to duplicate the previous design.

Along the Dorsoduro stretch of the Grand Canal, there stands an uninterrupted series of sumptuous palaces.

CAMPO DELLA CARITÀ
This was once an off-the-beaten-track campo, bordered on two sides by water and closed in on the third by now-demolished buildings. It was an isolated place of prayer and pilgrimage. But the arrival of the Accademia in 1807 changed both its function and its atmosphere; and the construction of the bridge in 1854 created a direct link to the center of Venice. The filling in of the Rio della Carità (1839) and the Rio di Sant'Agnese (1863), along with the appearance of a vaporetto line (1881), completed this development. Today the campo is very busy in the daylight hours, with students attending courses at the Academy of Arts and visitors coming to the museum; at night it falls silent, since nobody lives here.

CAMPO DELLA CARITÀ. The Academy of Fine Arts and its museum overlook this square. They occupy the former monastery of the Lateran Canons, the Church of Santa Maria della Carità and the scuola of the same name. The entrance to the faculty is by way of a portico linking the church to the scuola, and the entrance to the museum is through the door of the scuola.

THE CHURCH OF LA CARITÀ. Founded in the 12th century, this church (like the monastery adjoining it) was rebuilt in the years immediately following 1441, with a single nave and polygonal apses. One would hardly guess from the way it looks now that La Carità was once one of the most interesting examples of Gothic architecture in Venice. The truth is that it has been spoiled several times, notably when it became the seat of the Academy, and its interior was divided into two floors to create class and exhibition rooms.

THE CONVENT OF LA CARITÀ. This convent was founded in 1134 by the Lateran Canons when they first established their order in Venice. With the election of a Venetian Pope in 1434, new opportunities were opened to the Canons, and they became sufficiently wealthy to employ Palladio to rebuild their convent. In 1555–6 the architect submitted his project, which included an atrium leading to a cloister with a Doric portico and Corinthian loggia; stone bases and stone capitals were used for the columns to enhance the brick structure. But lack of funds prevented the work from being completed, and in 1630 the building was partly destroyed by fire. Finally the operations carried out in the 19th century left nothing of the original building save the right-hand side of the cloister.

SCUOLA DI SANTA MARIA DELLA CARITÀ ● 87. The Scuola Santa Maria, in existence since 1260, was one of the earliest guilds to receive the title of Scuola Grande ▲ 295. Its members first met on the Giudecca, and then in the Cannaregio district, before they acquired these premises close to the monastery of La Carità. Later on, the monks found themselves short of money and in 1344 were persuaded to part with the piece of land on which the scuola was built. In 1442 the order received the pope's financial aid and sought to enlarge its church; but the scuola resisted stoutly and undertook an expansion of its own, at the same time renovating the interior of its existing building. Thereafter the scuola remained unaltered until the mid-18th century, when it was given a new façade designed by Giorgio Massari and built by Maccaruzzi. Finally, when the Academy was installed there in the mid-19th century, the entire premises were adapted to this new function. Part of the artistic heritage of the scuola has remained, notably a *Madonna and Saints* by Antonio Vivarini and Giovanni d'Alemagna, and a *Presentation of Mary in the Temple* by Titian. The latter is an allegory of the duty the old scuola set itself, which was each year to supply dowries to twenty poor girls of an age to marry.

THE ACCADEMIA GALLERIES. The Academy of Fine Arts was created by a decree of the Senate on September 24, 1750, and placed under the responsibility first of Giambattista Piazzetta and then of Giambattista Tiepolo. In 1807 it was reorganized with an art gallery of its own. This gallery had a dual function: to provide examples to the pupils, and to house the artistic heritage of the public buildings dispersed by the fall of the Republic ● *34*, as well as the treasures of the convents, monasteries and churches recently suppressed by Napoleonic decree. The Academy was established at La Carità. On August 10, 1817, its galleries were opened to the public and thereafter its exhibition space grew steadily. At the end of the Second World War the great architect Carlo Scarpa ▲ *346* redesigned the Academy with the collaboration of the curator, and today it offers the most complete panorama of Venetian painting in existence. The original kernel of its collection, which consisted of pictures given to the Academy by the artists themselves in the late 18th century, along with a few works that formerly belonged to the Republic, has been enriched beyond measure by religious treasures, private legacies, restitutions and purchases. Among its collection of primitives are pieces by Paolo and Lorenzo Veneziano and Michele Giambono. The 15th century is represented by Giovanni Bellini and Carpaccio; and the 16th by Giorgione, Titian, Tintoretto, Veronese, Bassano and Lorenzo Lotto, as well as many other remarkable (if not so famous) painters. Equally well represented are the 17th and 18th centuries, with paintings by Tiepolo, Piazzetta and Longhi, and many delicate pastels by Rosalba Carriera. The collection of drawings includes several masterpieces by Leonardo da Vinci and an entire sketchbook by Canaletto. The pages that follow show a selection of major works by some of these painters which can be seen at the Academy; some of these illustrations are accompanied by other pictures by the same artists which are still kept in the churches and scuole of Venice, and which may help to give a more comprehensive idea of each master's style.

THE DOOR OF THE ACCADEMIA
Sculptures of St Leonard and St Christopher, the patrons of the brotherhood of La Carità, stand on either side of this door. In the niche above it sits the Madonna, surrounded by members of the guild.

Beyond the portico of the Academy is an inner courtyard, which was once shared by the scuola and the convent. There is a carving on the well of a cross held by two figures: this is the emblem of the Scuola della Carità, which also recurs in several other places around the courtyard and on the walls of the building.

301

LORENZO VENEZIANO
was active between 1357 and 1372. Apprenticed to Paolo Veneziano (no relation) he later moved to Bologna and Verona, where Gothic art was flourishing.

PAOLO VENEZIANO
(c.1290–c.1360) was the principal figure in 14th-century Venetian art. He is thought to have been responsible for introducing the taste for polyptychs to Venice. The replacement of mural mosaics by polyptychs is a major phenomenon of Venetian art; no longer would sacred images be inaccessibly placed on high walls and vaultings – they would instead be visible at eye-level. This implied a completely different relationship between man and things sacred. Venetian art was progressively breaking loose from the influence of Byzantium, which was more hieratic in its outlook. The works of Paolo are especially striking for their radiant colors, as in his *Coronation of the Virgin* (above, detail). The sweetness of the figures' expressions is only matched by their refinement and elegance.

MICHELE GIAMBONO,
whose career lasted from 1420 until 1462, was unmoved by the new influences of the Renaissance, preferring instead to raise his own archaic style to near-perfect levels.

«HERE, AS EVERYWHERE ELSE, THE NEW
ART WAS BORN OF THE BYZANTINE
TRADITION.»

HIPPOLYTE TAINE

His style has more relief than that of his
master, for Lorenzo is already more distant
from the Byzantine tradition. His figures'
clothes are realistic and enveloping, with the
suggestion of physical density that is actual,
though still stylized. In this there is a clear
reference to the Franciscan manner of
devotion, which was always at pains to
present sacred figures in a familiar
light. Otherwise, Lorenzo was a
precursor of the Gothic
style in his use of light
colors and sinuous
rhythms.

JACOBELLO DEL FIORE (c.1370–1439)
evolved a poetical manner of painting,
whose exquisite colors and narrative
verve have much in common with
international Gothic trends. The saints
shown above are taken from his
Coronation of the Virgin (1438), an
unusually incisive composition.

GIOVANNI BELLINI

Without breaking his ties with tradition, Giovanni Bellini revitalized Venetian painting, first by placing his figures in precise perspectives and then by opening up their backgrounds to include landscapes and clear rocky vistas. In his carefully framed altarpiece at San Giobbe (c.1487), a major work completed at the height of his career, Giovanni heightens his perspective with a coffered ceiling resting on pillars that are identical to those of the altar itself. Behind the group of figures is a niche-like apse which fades into the shadows. Giovanni saw this picture as an extension of real space, occupied by figures that were not only majestic but also aglow with human warmth. Yet the Virgin herself somehow remains aloof from the rest of the scene, and this icon-like detachment bears the stamp of Venice's Byzantine legacy.

The work of Giovanni Bellini (c.1433?–1516) is peopled by Madonnas, infant Christs and pietàs, all permeated by a sense of deep human melancholy.

"LA PIETÀ"
Here Bellini's interest in landscape is evident. Against the backdrop of a walled city (Vicenza) he places the body of Christ in the arms of the Virgin, whose face is worn with age and suffering.

«BELLINI'S VIRGINS ARE CERTAINLY THE LOVELIEST,
THE MOST HUMAN, THE TENDEREST AND
MOST DELICATE KNOWN TO MAN.»

MARCEL BRION

GENTILE BELLINI
Gentile, brother of Giovanni, became a portraitist and painter of Venice's ceremonies. At the same time, he was also adept at the traditional Venetian art of story painting, usually on a huge canvas, which was commissioned by one of the scuolas to tell the story of a saint, or of some miracle wrought by a relic.

Miracle of the Cross at the Bridge of San Lorenzo, by Gentile.

In the *Altarpiece of San Zaccaria,* the forms are relaxed and supple and the colors dazzling.

"ALTARPIECE OF SAN ZACCARIA"
▲ *171* Here Giovanni (then aged 75) developed and deepened his investigation of the relationship between color and light. The composition is basically the same as that of his San Giobbe altarpiece, except insofar as the architecture is opened up at the sides to admit light and reveal a background landscape.

THE SAINT URSULA CYCLE ★
Painted for the Scuola di Sant'Orsola between 1490 and 1500, this is Carpaccio's most extensive series. In these nine canvases, he was freely inspired by 15th-century stories of the life of St Ursula, a Breton princess who agreed to marry an English prince on condition that he convert to Christianity and go with her on a pilgrimage to Rome accompanied by ten thousand virgins. The entire group was massacred by the Huns at Cologne on the return journey.

"THE TRIUMPH OF SAINT GEORGE" ▲ *163*
A second cycle of paintings, partly devoted to the Dalmatian St George, was created by Carpaccio for the Scuola di San Giorgio degli Schiavoni.

Vittore Carpaccio was born in Venice in about 1465 and died c.1526.

"THE TEMPEST"
The spendours of nature and man's harmonious, poetic relationship to it are the true subjects of Giorgione's canvas.

"LA VECCHIA"
A symbolic representation of the passing of beauty, this painting is an explicit invitation to ponder mankind's destiny. The inscription reads "With time".

GIORGIONE
Born c.1478 at Castelfranco Veneto, Giorgione died in Venice in 1510. He perfected a way to extract undreamed-of luminosity from paint glaze, which created effects of atmospheric transparency. His themes were largely humanist in inspiration.

"THE ARRIVAL OF THE AMBASSADORS" shows Carpaccio's prodigious ability to encapsulate a story in paint.

The Presentation of Mary at the Temple (1539) was Titian's sole concession to the genre of story painting, which had been epitomized by the work of Gentile Bellini and Vittore Carpaccio, and which had largely fallen into disuse by the 16th century. Conforming to the aesthetic ideals of the Venetian school, Titian gave priority to color, using its power to stress the monumentality of his images.

THE DEATH OF TITIAN

This painting by Alexandre Jean-Baptiste Hesse, now at the Louvre, is a homage to the great master. In July 1576, Titian's son Orazio fell sick with the plague and was removed to the *lazaretto*. Left alone, Titian died on 27 August of "high fever", which may also have been the plague. However, he was spared the common grave used for victims of the epidemic, and interred at the Frari.

«[TITIAN] WALKS IN STEP WITH NATURE: HENCE EACH
ONE OF HIS FIGURES IS ALIVE AND IN MOTION,
WITH FLESH THAT QUIVERS.»

GIORGIO VASARI

"LA PIETÀ" (1576)
Titian intended this Pietà, the last of his works, for his own tomb, but he never had time to finish it, and this task fell to Palma the Younger. The large niche which encompasses the scene is a homage to Titian's former master, Giovanni Bellini. Like most of his other later works, this picture is infused with a dramatic, tragic questioning of the origin and purpose of human existence. The faint light from above makes the theme appear all the more anguished: the figures seem crushed between the solid masses of the arch. Christ's limp body magically absorbs the light, and is clasped by a motionless Virgin and a Nicodemus filled with pathos, Titian's last self-portrait. All trace of the original sketch has vanished; Titian has rendered this painting with broad, forthright strokes of color. In the *ex-voto*, the master and his son Orazio are shown kneeling before the Virgin. This detail may be a reference to the terrible plague epidemic of 1576 which claimed the life of Orazio, his son.

Born in the Veneto c.1490, Titian died in Venice in 1576. He began as an apprentice with the Bellini brothers and Giorgione, whom he helped with the frescoes of the Fondaco dei Tedeschi ▲ *284*. He became official state painter on the death of Gentile Bellini (1517). One of the greatest artists of the Renaissance, his principal strength was the power of his personality, which comes through in the innovative force of his altarpieces, portraits and mythological portraiture.

VERONESE
(1528–88)
Following the death of Titian, Veronese became the official state painter of the Republic. With his penchant for Palladian décors and architecture, he created some lavish stage sets for his figures. The dazzling quality of light and color in his compositions give them great power, as in this allegory of Venice in the Doge's Palace (below).

This *Last Supper* was renamed *The Feast at the House of Levi* after Veronese was prosecuted for introducing humble characters into the scene of the Holy Sacrament.

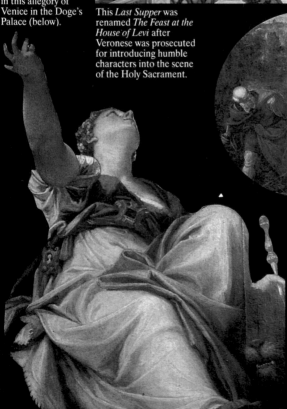

The Flight into Egypt (1583–7) is one of a series of paintings composed by Tintoretto for San Rocco ▲ *294*.

In the *Translation of the Body of Saint Mark* (1552–65), a stormy light bathes the scene, revealing the importance of light in the creation of dramatic tension. The construction in perspective (left) shows Tintoretto's close attention to architectural forms.

«A FINE EXCESS OF FANTASY AND SHEER MASTERY SEIZED THE ARTIST [VERONESE] AND DROVE HIM TO PUSH THE RESEMBLANCE OF BODIES AND OBJECTS TO THE BRINK OF TROMPE L'OEIL.»

PAUL VALÉRY

Jacopo Robusti, known as **TINTORETTO**, was born in Venice in 1518 and died there in 1594. He soon moved away from the Venetian tradition to concentrate on Mannerism. Restless by nature, he fashioned means of expression of new force, using light and chiaroscuro to heighten his dramatic effects.

PIETRO LONGHI
(Venice, 1702–85)
An attentive observer
of contemporary life,
Longhi was
principally a genre
painter.

In his
smaller
pictures,
which are
both vivid
and harmonious,
he sketched the
aristocrats and salons
of the 18th century, as
in *The Dancing
Lesson* (above), along
with the everyday life
of Venice. The spirit
of Longhi's work has
been justly compared
to Carlo Goldoni's
theater ▲ *290.*

ALESSANDRO LONGHI
(Venice, 1733–1813)
A disciple of his
father, Alessandro
enlarged his slender
figures and
transposed them into
portraits. His father's
sharp eye and
expressiveness are
equally evident in the
work of the son, as
demonstrated in
*The Family of
the Procurator
Pisani,*
(above).

ROSALBA CARRIERA
(1675–1757) was a portrait
painter who worked
particularly in pastels. She
achieved spectacular
success throughout
Europe.

GIAMBATTISTA TIEPOLO (1696–1770)
worked with prodigious speed, which
sometimes exposed him to the charge of
carelessness. An admirer of Veronese, he
broke free of academic precepts in about
1725 and began to investigate Rococo.

He introduced new
accents to painting,
with his penchant for
triumphal allegories,
both sacred and
profane. Tiepolo's
colors have silvery
nuances; his subject
matter has a sensual
overlay, and his light
is full of rich impasto.
Left, *The
Exaltation
of the Cross*.

In a move away from the traditional landscape in perspective,
Francesco Guardi evolved an "impressionist" vision in his
landscape work. His drawings are often handled with
quivering touches, the line rapid and sharp; his paintings
convey an emotional, vibrant atmosphere.
Below, *The Fire at San Marcuola*.

FRANCESCO GUARDI
(1712–93) was the
more famous of the
two Guardi brothers.
His views of the city
make him perhaps
the last painter-poet
of 18th-century
Venice. His work, in
which he shows an
acute sense of the
ephemeral and a
melancholy that
borders on the
romantic, is unusual
for a period in which
Neo-classicism was
very much the
fashion.

Antonio Canal, known as **CANALETTO** (1697–1768), began painting views of Venice after spending the years 1716–19 in Rome, where he was influenced by the landscape painters Gian Paolo Pannini and Gaspar van Wittel. Much admired by the English nobility, to whom he was introduced by Joseph Smith, a future British consul in Venice, Canaletto's name quickly became synonymous with the city. He honed his technique, his style of expression, his faultless sense of perspective and his photographic eye; at the same time his rendering of light was incomparably limpid, and his colors were as clear as his spatial sense was true. Following a long stay in London, he returned to Venice in 1756.

One of Canaletto's last paintings (above) is an academic study of a portico (1765), a trial piece which won him election as a member of the Academy. For this reason it is somewhat dry and technical. Strange as it may seem, there are very few views of Venice by Canaletto which are still on display in the city.

PLAN OF THE ACCADEMIA

I. Venetian painters: 14th century
II. Giovanni Bellini, Cima da Conegliano
III. Late 15th–early 16th century
IV. Italian painters: 15th century
V. Giovanni Bellini and Giorgione
VI. 16th century
VII. Lorenzo Lotto, GG Savoldo
VIII. Palma the Elder
IX. 16th-century schools of painting
X. Titian, Veronese and Tintoretto
XI. Veronese, Tintoretto and GB Tiepolo
XII. 18th-century landscape painters

XIII. Tintoretto, Bassano
XIV. Renovators of the 17th century
XV. Minor painters of the 18th century
XVI. Giambattista Piazzetta
XVII. Longhi, Canaletto, Carriera, Guardi
XVIII. 18th-century painters and engravers
XIX. 15th-century painters
XX. Gentile Bellini and Vittorio Carpaccio
XXI. Vittorio Carpaccio
XXII. Bookshop
XXIII. Venetian painters: 15th century
XXIV. Albergo Room, Titian

CAMPO S. VIO

PALAZZO CINI. At number 864 on La Piscina Forner stands the late 16th-century mansion of a great collector, Count Vittorio Cini, who died in 1977 ▲ *342*. In addition to quantities of furniture, ivories, enamel and porcelain, there are a number of remarkable paintings here, notably by Piero della Francesca, Sandro Botticelli and Pontormo.

CAMPO DI SAN VIO. This campo owes its name to the Church of San Vio (Venetian street slang for "Santi-Vito-e-

Modesto"), which stood here until the 19th century. San Vio was the scene of an annual celebration of the thwarting of Bajamonte Tiepolo's St Vitus' Day conspiracy on June 15, 1310 ▲ *214*; the Doge, with the Seignory, representatives of the scuole grandi and other Venetian institutions, would arrive along the Grand Canal to attend mass and a banquet at San Vio. To make it easier for them to disembark, the buildings which closed off the campo on the canal side were demolished; hence its peculiar look of a lengthy rectangle completely open to the water. The old church, probably founded in the 10th century, was rebuilt at the same time and enriched by items from Bajamonte Tiepolo's palace, which was dismantled after his plot was exposed. A cross and *patera* from the original building were inherited by the votive chapel which took its place in the 19th century. Also on the campo is the little CHURCH OF SAINT GEORGE THE EVANGELIST. (Take the Calle della Chiesa and the Fondamenta Venier.)

PALAZZO VENIER DEI LEONI (GUGGENHEIM FOUNDATION) ★. A wrought-iron gate marks the way in to the Peggy Guggenheim Foundation. Work on the original Palazzo

Venier, designed by Lorenzo Boschetti, was begun in 1749 but never got beyond the first floor – earning the palace the sobriquet of "nonfinito". The extent of the first floor, and (even better) a wooden

PALAZZO DARIO
The Palazzo Dario is said to bring ill-luck to its owners. This legend does not seem to have affected the French poet Henri de Régnier, who lived there from 1899 to 1901

JACKSON POLLOCK
Much influenced by his encounter with the European Surrealists during the war, the principal representative of American Abstract Expressionism worked on huge canvases, which he spread out on the floor and covered in paint from a dripping bucket.

maquette at the Correr Museum ▲ *246,* give an idea of what the palace would have looked like had it been completed. Finished or not, it was home to the illustrious Venier family, which had entered the ranks of the nobility in 1297 and over the centuries gave Venice no fewer than three Doges, including the great Sebastiano Venier, Supreme Commander of the Christian Fleet at Lepanto ● *36.* Yielding to the 18th-century penchant for the unusual, the Venier family surrounded themselves with exotic animals, even keeping a chained lion in the courtyard of the palace, hence its nickname, "Ca' Venier dei Leoni". In 1949 the American collector Peggy Guggenheim bought the property, made her home there and opened an art gallery. In 1976, a few years before her death, she donated the palace and contents to the Solomon R Guggenheim Foundation of New York, which has administered both the Guggenheim Museum in Venice and in Manhattan (assembled by Peggy Guggenheim's uncle) ever since. The Ca' Venier today contains one of the most important collections of modern art in the world. The entire avant-garde of the first half of the 20th century is represented here, especially the Surrealists. The gardens are filled with sculptures, and temporary exhibitions are regularly held at the museum.

PALAZZO DARIO ★. In 1490, Giovanni Dario, the ambassador to Constantinople, received a large cash reward for his part in convincing the Turks to ratify a treaty. The construction of a palace naturally followed, with the work directed by Pietro Lombardo and his team of stonemasons and carvers. Lombardo, always more concerned with the interaction of surfaces than with volumes, adopted a mainly pictorial approach to the façades. By covering them with medallions of colored marble, he transformed the exterior into an exercise in décor which gave no inkling of how the palace was organized inside. Sadly, extensive changes in the 19th century have perverted the Palazzo Dario almost beyond recognition. (Continue on along the Calle Barbaro.)

THE CHURCH AND CONVENT OF SAN GREGORIO. The old church here was rebuilt between 1445 and 1461, and is now the restoration center of the government's "Superintendance" of galleries and works of art in the Venice region. The monastery was rebuilt a hundred years earlier, and is now a private house.

PEGGY GUGGENHEIM
Born in New York in 1898, she became interested in avant-garde painting at an early age. She left the USA for Europe in 1921. In 1938 she opened the Guggenheim-Jeune Gallery in London. She travelled throughout Europe, unconcerned by the threat of war, but in the end the Nazi advance forced her to return to America, where she founded a new gallery, Art of this Century, in 1942. In the same year she began her short-lived marriage to Max Ernst. By 1949 she was back in Venice, where the Biennale gave her a special pavilion to show her collection. The exhibition was a huge success: Peggy Guggenheim fell in love with Venice and stayed there until her death in 1979, becoming an honorary citizen of the city.

THE BASILICA OF SANTA MARIA DELLA SALUTE. On October 22, 1630, the Senate decided to build a church in honor of the Madonna, in order to mark the end of a plague which had devastated the city. The site of the new sanctuary was one of the finest in Venice, adjoining St Mark's Basin. Its first stone was laid on April 1, 1631, before the Seignory had even chosen an architectural design from the various basilical and central models on offer. In the end, a central plan was decided upon, submitted by the thirty-two-year-old Baldassare Longhena, for whom this was to be the first major architectural commission. At that time, neither Bernini nor Borromini had yet undertaken any work of importance, so Longhena's project was entirely revolutionary, as he himself was the first to acknowledge. The effect was all the more striking in that his huge octagonal construction (which was covered in Istrian stone, crowned with two domes and flanked by a pair of campaniles) was made to rise out of such unassuming urban surroundings. On the outside of the building, half-columns resting on massive pedestals and a gigantic staircase distinguished the main Palladian façade from the seven other sides of the basic octagon. Inside, six chapels were clustered around the central space, which was crowned with a tall dome supported by eight enormous pillars. The second dome (over the choir) was built on a much smaller scale. At a later stage Longhena designed the high altar, which is brought to life with statues by Josse Le Court (1670). After the death of Longhena, his work was completed by Antonio Gaspari

THE "ORECCHIONI" OF LA SALUTE
The exterior and interior of this basilica are very different. The inside is austere, while the outside is exuberant with statues (no fewer than 125 of them) and ornaments. The great volutes of the façade serve as buttresses to the dome, and are affectionately referred to by the Venetians as *"orecchioni"* (big ears).

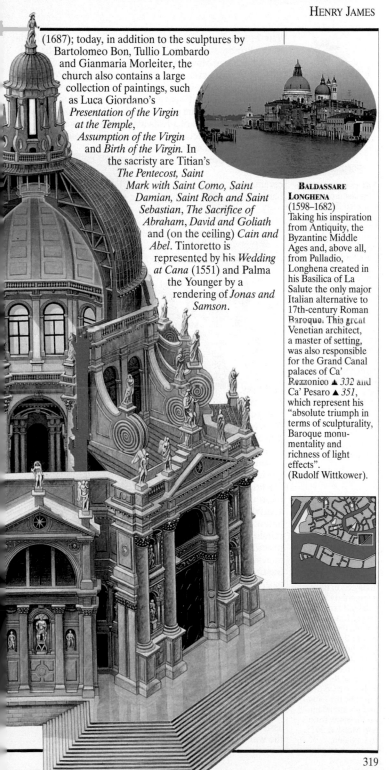

> «THE CLASSIC SALUTE WAITS LIKE SOME GREAT LADY ON THE THRESHOLD OF HER SALON [...] WITH HER DOMES AND SCROLLS, HER SCOLLOPED BUTTRESSES FORMING A POMPOUS CROWN.»
>
> HENRY JAMES

(1687); today, in addition to the sculptures by Bartolomeo Bon, Tullio Lombardo and Gianmaria Morleiter, the church also contains a large collection of paintings, such as Luca Giordano's *Presentation of the Virgin at the Temple*, *Assumption of the Virgin* and *Birth of the Virgin*. In the sacristy are Titian's *The Pentecost, Saint Mark with Saint Como, Saint Damian, Saint Roch and Saint Sebastian*, *The Sacrifice of Abraham*, *David and Goliath* and (on the ceiling) *Cain and Abel*. Tintoretto is represented by his *Wedding at Cana* (1551) and Palma the Younger by a rendering of *Jonas and Samson*.

BALDASSARE LONGHENA
(1598–1682)
Taking his inspiration from Antiquity, the Byzantine Middle Ages and, above all, from Palladio, Longhena created in his Basilica of La Salute the only major Italian alternative to 17th-century Roman Baroque. This great Venetian architect, a master of setting, was also responsible for the Grand Canal palaces of Ca' Rezzonico ▲ *332* and Ca' Pesaro ▲ *351*, which represent his "absolute triumph in terms of sculpturality, Baroque monumentality and richness of light effects".
(Rudolf Wittkower).

319

THE PLAGUE DOCTOR
This costume was invented in the 16th century by the French physician Charles de Lorme. The plague doctor, masked like a huge bird with spectacles and a beak filled with medicinal herbs and essences, visited the sick in the times of plague that so frequently afflicted Venice. He also wore gloves and a long linen or canvas coat soaked in wax, and he carried a stick with which he raised the bedcovers and clothing of the plague victims – expecting, somewhat naïvely, to be protected from contagion by all this paraphernalia.

THE WOODEN BRIDGE
Today, as in the past, a temporary bridge is still built across the Grand Canal at this point a few days before the Festival of La Salute takes place. Crossing at the level of Santa Maria del Giglio ▲ *264,* this walkway used to be taken by the Doge and his attendants on their way from San Moisè ▲ *261* to La Salute.

THE FESTIVAL OF LA SALUTE ● *49.* On November 21 (the day of the Presentation of the Virgin at the Temple) in the year 1687, the Doge Marcantonio Giustinian swore a solemn oath that henceforth, every year on the same date, the Venetians would repair to the Church of La Salute as a token of their devotion and their eternal gratitude to the Madonna for bringing an end to the plague which had ravaged the city. This oath forms the basis of a festival which, along with the Festival of the Redeemer ▲ *339,* is among Venice's most characteristic religious occasions. Still popular even today, this ceremony has been faithfully (and most sincerely) observed by many subsequent generations of Venetians; in it were united both their religious faith and the sentiment that they belonged to a community whose past glories were now reawakening after a dark interlude. Traditionally, on this day the gondoliers bring their oars to be blessed by a priest, who stands on the steps of the basilica.

CAMPO DELLA SALUTE. On the actual day of the Festival of La Salute, the campo is entirely occupied by stalls selling candles, religious images, toys and freshly cooked pastries. The promenade between the basilica and the Grand Canal quayside was built in 1681.

SEMINARIO PATRIARCHALE. This seminary stands beside the basilica, on a part of the site that was formerly occupied by the buildings of La Trinità (these were demolished so as to make way for La Salute). This ancient complex formerly included a Gothic scuola and a Venetian-Byzantine church dating from the 11th or 12th century and ceded to the Teutonic knights by the Republic in exchange for their assistance during the war against

> «THE STATUE OF FORTUNE, IN THE FORM OF A WEATHERVANE
> STANDING ATOP THE WORLD, GIVES A TRUE IDEA OF THE
> PERCEPTIONS OF THE TIME, AND OF THE HOPES AND IDEALS
> OF THE LAST DAYS OF VENICE.»
>
> JOHN RUSKIN

Genoa ● *31*. After the suppression of the Knights, Pope Clement VIII decided in 1596 to establish a seminary directed by monks and dedicated to the education of orphans. When La Salute was built, this seminary was reconstructed by Longhena. Abandoned when the monks were forced to leave the city by Napoleonic edict, the building was ultimately placed at the disposal of the Seminario Patriarcale by the Austrians in 1815. Today it contains a museum and the Manfrediniana picture gallery, created by Marchese Federico Manfredini (1743–1829). (Continue along the Fondamenta della Salute.)

THE CUSTOMS POINT
This is the small triangular area at the very tip of the Dorsoduro sestiere. It was also called La Trinità, as were the church and the scuola on the same site, and *Punta del sale*, after the many old salt depots of the Zattere.

THE CUSTOMS POINT

When the original customs post near San Biagio ▲ *181* became inadequate to handle the volume of goods entering Venice, the Republic decided to establish a *dogana di terrà* (land-based customs post) to check imports from the mainland on the Riva del Vin ▲ *287*, near the Rialto, and a *dogana di mare* (sea customs) at the end of the Dorsoduro sestiere. The latter was built in the 15th century; its role was to investigate the ships which entered the port of San Nicolò before they dropped anchor in St Mark's Basin in front of the Doge's Palace. Between 1677 and 1682, the customs buildings were reconstructed by Giuseppe Benoni, who won a contest for the project in 1677. For the warehouses, Benoni held to a strictly parallel distribution of buildings behind a continuous façade. Instead of the crenellated tower which stood at the point of the sestiere until the beginning of the 16th century, he erected a lower construction in the shape of an L, with a portico and a small white tower. The roof-ridge of the customs house is topped by bronze statues bearing a golden ball, on which stands a statue of *Fortune* which was sculpted by Bernardo Falcone.

THE ZATTERE

This broad quayside was built following a decree promulgated on February 8, 1516. In 1640, an order was given by Giovanni Valier and Giuseppe Barbarigo, the administrators of timber and forestry for the Republic that, from that time onwards, all cargoes of wood were to be unloaded at this point. Since lumber came from the Forests of the Cadore to Venice by flotation (*zattera*) on the current of the River Piave, the quay was named "Zattere". Beginning at the customs point and ending at Santa Marta, this area now constitutes a delightful promenade which was a favorite place of the American poet Ezra Pound ▲ *153*, who customarily spent six months of each year in the city. The second half of the walk is full of cafés with delightful terraces that extend over rafts over the water; these are particularly pleasant during warm weather because they face south. Here you can be sure of the best Gianduiotto ice-cream in Venice – a delicious blend of chocolate, honey, hazelnuts and whipped cream. (Take the Rio terrà ai Saloni.)

THE CHURCH AND HOSPICE OF THE CATECUMENI. The government of the Republic automatically gave asylum to all infidels who were prepared to renounce their faith. A large number of prisoners ready to do this were taken at the Battle of Lepanto ● *36* and installed in a group of houses in the vicinity of the old *dogana di mar*; nearby an oratory dedicated to John the Baptist was constructed. A century and a half later, in 1727, the architect Giorgio Massari was commissioned to design a new building for neophytes. On the rio terrà side, the wings of the hospice enfold the Corinthian pilasters and triangular pediment of the church façade; elsewhere it extends around a courtyard and an elegant little cloister with a portico. (Return to the Zattere.)

MAGAZZINI DEL SALE. This was where salt, Venice's only raw material, was stored. To judge by the acreage of saltpans, the industry must once have been a thriving one; certainly the levy raised on the mineral by the *proveditore* was one of the Republic's most important sources of revenue. The Biennale ▲ *184* at one time used these old warehouses as exhibition halls.

MAGAZZINI DEL SALE Built in the 14th century and restored during the Austrian occupation ● *34*, these depots stood on the Giudecca Canal. Nowadays, the Società Remiera Bucintoro puts up its boats there between regattas ● *55*.

THE CHURCH AND CONVENT OF SPIRITO SANTO. The Santo Spirito Church and Convent were founded in 1483 by Maria Caroldo, a Dominican nun belonging to the order of St Catherine of Siena. The convent quickly attracted rumors of scandal, its foundress being accused of having a priest as a lover and of squandering the funds of the community. The punishment imposed on her does not appear to have acted as a deterrent, however, because other scandals also broke out in the convent during the 16th century, and the Inquisition had to step in several times to restore order. At about the time that the Fondamenta delle Zattere was created, the religious complex was rebuilt, with a new rectangular cloister and portico in place of the former monastery and church. On a newly acquired site, another church was built to face the fondamenta, on which, in 1506, the neighboring Scuola dello Spirito Santo had already been installed. This scuola was suppressed in 1810 and its premises were then turned into a warehouse. The sanctuary contains Palma the Younger's *Marriage of the Virgin*.

The Churches of the Gesuati and Santa Maria della Visitazione.

OSPEDALE DEGLI INCURABILI. A charitable institution of the Venetian government, the Ospedale degli Incurabili was financed by the city's noble families and the rich bourgeoisie; one of the obligations of the dominant classes was to bear the cost of foundations such as these. It

« THE PALACES AND CHURCHES, IN THEIR GREAT MASSES, RISE
LIGHT AND MIRACULOUS LIKE THE HARMONIOUS DREAM
CREATIONS OF SOME YOUNG GOD.»

IVAN TURGENEV

would seem that, during the 16th century, the hospice was reserved for incurable syphilitics, but very soon after it was also taking in abandoned children. Like the Pietà ▲ *174*, the Derelitti ▲ *160* and the Mendicanti ▲ *159*, the Incurabili became a kind of music conservatory. In 1527 a program of restructuring was begun, which was not completed until 1591. The buildings were arranged around a broad rectangular courtyard containing a church which was destroyed in 1831. Transformed into a hospital (1807), and then into a barracks (1831), they were used until very recently as a center for the re-education of minors. (Take the Rio terrà dei Gesuati.)

THE CHURCH OF SANT'AGNESE. In contrast to many other Venetian churches, the 11th–12th century Sant'Agnese has only partially changed over the years. Although its structure has been modified and its interior décor destroyed, the organization of the inner space remains basically that of a Byzantine basilica. Closed in 1810, it was reopened for worship towards the middle of the 19th century and then became the oratory of the adjoining College of Cavanis. (Return to the Zattere.)

THE CHURCH OF THE GESUATI. The order of the Gesuati, dedicated to hospital service, was suppressed in 1668 on the grounds of immorality; as a result its headquarters on the Zattere (the Convent and Church of Santa Maria della Visitazione) reverted to the Dominicans. In 1724 the latter commissioned Giorgio Massari to build a new church and convent on an intermediate property, barely touching the original Renaissance ensemble. While the architect was working on his project, the monks managed to raise sufficient alms and donations to complete a church (1726–36). The interior of this building is made up of a single nave, or rather a long rectangle with rounded ends and three chapels on each side. The vault is pierced with large half-moon windows, while a dome with a lantern light in its center soars over the choir. Most of the statuary is by Gianmaria Morleiter, while the paintings are by Sebastiano Ricci, Giambattista Piazzetta and Giambattista Tiepolo, and deal mostly with subjects relevant to the Dominican tradition. Ricci created an altarpiece of *Pius V with Saint Thomas and Saint Peter the Martyr*; Piazzetta, in another altar painting, has depicted three Dominicans, Saint Vincenzo Ferrer, Giacinto and Luigi Beltran. Tiepolo's contribution included episodes in the life of St Dominic in the small side panels of the ceiling, as well as the *Institution of the Rosary* in the central panels. This shows the Virgin's

I GESUATI
Inspired by the classical Palladian manner, the Church of the Gesuati has a façade with four gigantic Corinthian half-columns, crowned by a cornice and a triangular pediment with an oval at its center.

Mist over the Zattere, beside the Incurabili.

PALAZZO CONTARINI CORFU
Where it stands on the junction of Rio di San Trovaso and the Grand Canal, the distinctive feature of this palace is its little corner tower. The Contarini family bore the surname of dagli Scrigni, a reference to the many jewel caskets said to be hidden in the walls of their villa near Padua.

apparition to Dominic with a rosary in her hand, followed by the saint's popularization of this convenient new way of praying. She proffers her rosary to Dominic, whose figure stands out starkly black and white against a background of vivid color; at the base of the composition, the faithful await the saint's transmission of the Virgin's gift. Also by Tiepolo is the altarpiece of three much-venerated Dominican saints – Catherine of Siena, Rose of Lima and Agnes of Montepulciano. Taken as a whole, this decorative ensemble confirms the Gesuati as one of the loveliest expressions of Rococo art in Venice.

THE CONVENT OF THE GESUATI. Due to a lack of funds, the convent here was not begun until 1751. Over the years the part of it directly behind the church was nearly completed; but the newer and much larger buildings planned for the area between this first edifice and Santa Maria della Visitazione have remained unfinished.

SANTA MARIA DELLA VISITAZIONE. This tiny church, which was reconstructed between 1494 and 1524, stands adjacent to the Church of the Gesuati. Its most notable features are a fine façade in the style of Lombardo, an early 16th-century cloister, and, near the entrance, the lion's mouth into which people dropped nasty notes denouncing one another to the authorities.

SAN TROVASO ★

"SQUERO" ● *69.* A curious sight awaits you as you round the corner of Rio Trovaso and Rio Ognissanti. Here you might think yourself not in a great and populous city, but in some corner of an Alpine village. There are three buildings, curiously built of wood; one even has a long balcony not unlike the ones on chalets in the Dolomites. The two taller buildings serve as living quarters, while the third is a

workshop fronting a small dock. It transpires that this is the oldest of the *squeri* (gondola boatyards) still in existence; it has been here since the 17th century. Though they are now very rare, the *squeri* ▲ *147* of Venice formerly numbered in the hundreds and could be found in every part of the city. Before the Arsenal ▲ *177*

Only two or three gondolas are built each year in each one of the *squeri*; but every vessel then requires some major maintenance. Every fourteen years, the axis of a gondola needs to be realigned.

monopolized the shipbuilding industry, these yards built and repaired boats of every size and description. Today the *squeri* are restricted to gondolas, and this one is the busiest of all. Despite the high cost of building a gondola (each costs about twenty million lire) the yard has enough advance orders to keep it working for ten years. The only difficulty it faces is a shortage of craftsmen.

RIO DI SAN TROVASO. As the link between Venice's two main arteries, the Grand Canal and the Giudecca Canal, this waterway has always carried heavy boat traffic. It was lined with splendid houses and some even finer gardens. Some of these gardens are no longer what they were, but nonetheless they count among the last of their size in Venice.

THE CHURCH OF SAN TROVASO. The word "Trovaso" is yet another baffling Venetian elision, in this case of the names of "Gervasio e Protasio". Founded in the 9th or 10th century, it was several times altered before being totally reconstructed at the end of the 16th century along Palladian lines. The main façade overlooking the Rio degli Ognissanti is divided into two registers. Two slender wings, defined by pilasters with Corinthian capitals, flank the central part of the building,

The Church of San Trovaso and its two entrances, one overlooking the campo, the other facing the river.

which has a broad half-moon window topped by a triangular tympanum. The rear façade is much the same. The floorplan takes the form of a Latin cross with a single nave and side-chapels. *Joachim Driven from the Temple* (in the choir), *The Temptation of Saint Anthony* (in the Milledonne Chapel), *The Last Supper* and *Christ Washing the Feet of the Leper* (in the Chapel of the Sacrament) are all by Tintoretto, with the possible exception of the last, which is merely attributed to him. Other treasures at San Trovaso are Palma the Younger's *Deposition from the Cross* and *Birth of the Virgin*, *Saint Chrysogonus Mounted on a Horse* by Giambono (15th century), and a magnificent Renaissance bas-relief of *Angels Bearing the Symbols of Christ's Passion*, surrounded by other angels with musical instruments, which is in the Clary Chapel.

CAMPO SAN TROVASO. As often happens in Venice, the Church of San Trovaso juts fairly extensively into its campo and effectively divides it into two parts. Each of these parts has its own well, the most interesting being the raised white-stone one in Campo San Trovaso proper. The Venetians, who were unable to reach the water table by digging, were obliged for many centuries to make do with rainwater supplemented by fresh supplies brought by ship from the mainland ● 81.

THE "SQUERAROLO"
The supply of timber for Venice's naval industry came from the mountains of the Cadore. After the close of the 16th century, the wood was sent exclusively to the Zattere. Naturally enough, the inhabitants of the Cadore region excelled in everything to do with wood and the working of wood. They became the first *squeraroli* (owners of *squeri*) and built vessels in their yards that looked not unlike the houses they lived in.

RIO DELL'ARZERE
Behind the Angelo Raffaele, a bridge spans this rio bearing the three escutcheons of the "Proveditore".

The area is an old one, traditionally occupied by fisherfolk who kept it busy and lively. In the early morning the fishermen would return here to sell their catch at the quayside.

THE CHURCH OF SAN SEBASTIANO
With their dazzling colors, daring effects of foreshortening and exuberant ornamentation, Veronese's decorations inside this church are uniquely beautiful.

THE CHURCH AND CONVENT OF THE OGNISSANTI

This part of Dorsoduro was virtually deserted when its religious occupation began. In the early 15th century, a group of Benedictine nuns abandoned their convent on Torcello as

the island had become unhealthy due to malaria ▲ *374* and their buildings were no longer inhabitable. So they established themselves at Dorsoduro. A new church had already been built when the nuns acquired a "miraculous" image of the Virgin in 1472. This stroke of fortune brought in much-needed cash to enable them to rebuild and enlarge the church and convent. But the order was not very wealthy, and work advanced so slowly that the second church was not consecrated until 1586. After the suppression of the order in the 19th century, the church and convent lay abandoned until GB Giustinian transformed them into a home for old men. It is now a hospital (the Ospedale Giustinian).

THE ANGELO RAFFAELE QUARTER

THE CHURCH OF SAN SEBASTIANO ★. This church, built in the 16th century by Lo Scarpagnino, has a modest exterior. Inside is one of the finest cycles of paintings by Veronese to be found in Venice. He began with the sacristy in 1555, decorating its ceiling with a scene of the *Crowning of the Virgin*, complete with images of the Four Evangelists. The following year he tackled the nave, completing the three major scenes from the life of Esther framed on the ceiling. The frescoes of the *Annunciation*, St Sibyl, and other saints were finished in 1558; the whole cycle was completed in 1565, with two great canvases for the main chapel: *San Marco e Marcellano esortati al martirio da San Sebastiano,* and *Il Martiro da San Sebastiano.* At his own request, Veronese is buried in this church. His tomb is marke‹

by a plaque, at the foot of the organ, which he decorated thirty years before his death ▲ 269.

THE CHURCH OF L'ANGELO RAFFAELE.

There was a place of worship on this spot as early as the 7th century; several times rebuilt, it was given its present dimensions in 1618 by the architect Francesco Contino, though the façade is somewhat later (1735). A group over the portal featuring the Angel Raphael and Prophet Tobias invites the visitor to enter. Above the entrance on the inside, five panels showing episodes from the life of Tobias extend to the organ loft. These were executed in about 1749 by one of the greatest proponents of Venetian Rococo, Gianantonio Guardi (1698–1760), brother of Francesco; they are considered his masterworks. The theme of the angel Raphael is echoed at the back of the choir in a work by Michelangelo Morleiter (1729–1806). A local story has it that two lacemakers living near the Church of l'Angelo Raffaele made a collar out of snow-white strands of hair, and it was worn by Louis XIV at his Coronation.

"I NICOLOTTI" ▲ 334
The Nicolotti were one of the city's two factions. The day they elected their leader, the *gastaldo*, was a holiday, and the mast used to fly their banner stands in the middle of the campo to this day.

I MENDICOLI

I Mendicoli is one of the outer districts of Dorsoduro, which today is mostly occupied by ordinary working people. It owes its name of Mendicoli (beggars) to the poverty of its original inhabitants, who were mainly artisans and fishermen.

SAN NICOLÒ DEI MENDICOLI.

The simplicity of this church is as charming as it is rare in Venice. Far from the political and economic hubs of the city, and thus deprived of the donations and benefits normally conferred by wealthy parishioners, it has changed little over the centuries. According to tradition, San Nicolò was founded in the 7th century by a group of Paduans displaced by the Lombard invasion; it was rebuilt in the 12th century, and the central part of the façade with its gemelled window dates from this era. The 15th-century portico is one of only two its kind in Venice (with that of San Giacometto ▲ 283) to have survived; apparently *pinzocchere* (zealots) were in the habit of spending long hours doing penance here. The central apse of the interior, with its Byzantine cornice, is the most ancient feature of the church.

San Nicolò in gloria, by Lorenzo Lotto (detail).

327

PALAZZO ZENOBIO
This building is unusual for Venice, since it has two wings on the side of its garden (one of the loveliest in the city). At the close of the 18th century, the building was further adorned with a pavilion designed by Temanza, which was used for its archives and library.

FONDAMENTA BRIATI

THE FONDAMENTA. This is named in honor of the glassmaker Giuseppe Briati (1686–1772). In the 18th century the Venetian glass industry was in deep crisis ▲ *366*, for while the craftsmen of Murano clung to traditional local methods, the rest of Europe had become infatuated with the robust cut-glass of Bohemia and Silesia. After a visit to Prague, Briati returned to Murano in 1730 and set up a works specializing in Bohemian-style glassware, obtaining from the Council of Ten a monopoly to produce it. But the other glassmakers resented Briati and attacked his workshop; Briati sought permission to move his business into Venice, finally alighting here.

PALAZZO ARIANI. The façade of this building offers one of the most attractive examples of Venetian Gothic to be seen in the

city. The rest is constructed in the L-shape which is so typical of 14th-century palaces, with a fine courtyard and an outside staircase. The Ariani family fortune lay in the increasing amount of traffic on the river passing through Fusina. At the time of the "closure" of the Grand Council ● *31*, the Arianis were invited to join the patricians of Venice, despite their bourgeois Istrian origins. A century later they were excluded, after an obscure squabble over a bad debt, and were never again reinstated.

PALAZZO ZENOBIO ★   ▲ 383

The Palazzo Zenobio was built at the close of the 17th century by the architect Antonio Gaspari. Today it is recognized as one of the most significant examples of Baroque architecture in the city. Its white façade, which is topped by a large curvilinear tympanum broken in the middle in the Romanesque manner, is something of a novelty for Venice. Though he himself had been a pupil and colleague of

Longhena, Gaspari seems to have preferred in this case to seek inspiration in the work of the great architect Francesco Borromini, whose style he sought to bring to the city. The interior has the special charm common to nearly all Venetian palaces built at that time. The landscapes of its *portego* were executed by one of the first artists to specialize in views of Venice, Luca Carlevaris, who was protected for many years by the patrician Zenobios. The trompe-l'oeil architectural perspectives enlarging the already enormous space of the ballroom, served three decades later as a model for the artists decorating a similar room at the Ca' Rezzonico. Over the entrance of this ballroom, adorned with undulating gold and white stucco, is the tribune where the orchestra sat. In the 19th century, Palazzo Zenobio was acquired by the Armenian brotherhood, founded by Méchitar, which converted it into a college for young people of Armenian origin ● *328*.

I CARMINI

SANTA MARIA DEL CARMELO (I CARMINI).
Though the Campo Santa Margherita was already a self-contained urban entity, the immediate environs of the future church were still deserted when work began on it. This may explain why two exits were planned, one towards Santa Margherita and the other towards the future Campo dei Carmini. Begun in 1286, the works were finished in 1348. In the early 16th century, the façade was rebuilt in Renaissance style, and between 1653 and 1674 wooden panelling was installed in the nave to cover Gothic features, some of which are still visible elsewhere in the church. Between the nave and choir are two choristers' galleries decorated with episodes from the life of Christ (Andrea Schiavone, 16th-century). Among other works, the church has a *Nativity* (c.1509) by Cima da Conegliano (right-hand nave, second altar) and *Saint Nicolas in Glory between Saint John the Baptist and Saint Lucy*, an altarpiece painted by Lorenzo Lotto c.1529 (left-hand nave, adjoining the side portal). There used to be a passage from the sacristy to the convent cloister. This elegant Renaissance building is now the seat of the Art Institute. (Entrance to the right of the church.)
SCUOLA GRANDE DEI CARMINI ★. From its beginnings in Palestine, the Order of Our Lady of Mount Carmel began to

spread to the West in 1235. Forty years later it was formed into a confraternity of women known as the *pinzocchere dei Carmini* (Carmelite zealots), who carried a scapular showing the image of the Virgin. The Virgin herself is said to have appeared to The Blessed Simon Stock to assure him of the perpetuity of the Carmelite order; as a consequence it was opened to males in 1595. The Counter Reformation was a time of great

splendour of its unique façade. At one time, the building was very richly decorated, but many of its paintings and tapestries were sold abroad. After their family's exclusion, several of the Ariani attempted to regain admittance to the Grand Council with results that were sometimes dramatic. One family member had counted on his military exploits during the Genoese war to bring him back into favor, and when this did not happen he abandoned his wife and children, took religious orders, and left Venice for ever.

Courtyard of Ca' Foscari.

expansion for the Carmelites because of the development of the cult of Mary as a counterweight to Protestantism, and by 1675 their order embraced no fewer than 75,000 members. The Carmelite church was their Venetian headquarters until 1625, at which time they purchased several other adjoining buildings and hired the architect Cantello to convert them. Following the acquisition of the corner building in 1667, Longhena was called in to unify the ensemble. In 1767 the order became a scuola grande ▲ 295, which was suppressed in 1806, then revived again in 1840. The fame of this scuola today lies in the decoration of its upper gallery, executed by Giambattista Tiepolo between 1739 and 1749; the middle of the ceiling is taken up by a rendering of *Our Lady of Mount Carmel Appearing to the Blessed Simon Stock*, with allegories of virtue and scenes from the life of the Virgin all around it. In the archive room there is a *Judith and Holophernes* by Giambattista Piazzetta (c.1743).

AROUND CAMPO SANTA MARGHERITA ★

CAMPO SANTA MARGHERITA During the warmer months of the year, it is a particular delight to sit in one of the many tree-shaded cafés around this broad campo. Plays and musical festivals are often held here.

CAMPO SANTA MARGHERITA. This is one of the liveliest squares in Venice. In place of the present Rio terrà Canal and Rio terrà della Scoazzera, there used to be a canal with a dumping ground beside it. This made the campo very much a working people's zone: the few patrician mansions here are all on the Rio di Santa Margherita side, and are all pre-15th century. They include two small Gothic palaces (one of which has an overhanging Tuscan roof, a rarity for Venice), and the lovely PALAZZO FOSCOLO-CORNER, which was worked on in the late 14th century by the Celegas, who were the architects of the Campanile of the Frari ▲ 293. Their contribution was probably no more than an adjustment, because most of the elements here (the gateway, for instance, with its Byzantine lunette) definitely date from the 13th century. The far side of the campo is closed off by the Church of Santa Margherita, which is now abandoned. The campanile to the side has at its foot some splendid Baroque sculptures in marble, notably a fearsome dragon. In the middle of the campo is the SCUOLA DEI VAROTERI, or Furriers' Guild, formed during the 13th century. The bas-relief (1501) over the door here was brought from the Furriers' previous headquarters in the Cannaregio district.

THE CHURCH OF SAN PANTALON. The first church on this site, dating from the 11th century, was demolished in the 17th century and rebuilt between 1668 and 1686 by Francesco Comino, an architect from Treviso. Comino reoriented its façade away from the canal and toward the campo, but it was never completed. The interior, which has a single vaulted nave and side chapels, is a perfect example of the Baroque ideal; in a stunning tour de force of perspective, the painted vault duplicates and prolongs the architecture of the nave, and abounds elsewhere in daring effects of foreshortening. The decoration of the choir by Gianantonio Fumiani

The picturesque Campo Santa Margherita, with its many shops, is also the scene of a daily fish and vegetable market.

(1650–1710) is in the same spirit, and the paintings include the *Miracle of Saint Pantalon* (1587) by Veronese, the *Crowning of the Virgin* (1444), an altarpiece by Antonio Vivarini and Giovanni d'Alemagna, and a triptych attributed to Paolo Veneziano (in the Sacro Chiodo chapel).

CA' FOSCARI. The building of the palace known as Ca' Foscari coincided with the start of the process of transforming the Grand Canal, which reached its height in the Renaissance and Baroque periods. Built by the Giustinian family at the turn of the 14th and 15th centuries, the original palace was flanked by two towers that were a characteristic of Venice's most ancient *fondachi*. It was purchased in 1428 by the Seignory, which presented it to one of the generals of the Republic, the Marchese di Mantua; it then seems to have passed to Francesco Sforza in 1439. In 1452 it was bought at auction by the Doge Francesco Foscari, who demolished it and raised the present building instead. According to Ruskin, Ca' Foscari is "the noblest example in Venice of the 15th-century Gothic style". The openwork décor of the windows counterbalances the massive size of the palace and its foursquare shape. On the landward side, the gateway is embellished with *putti* bearing the arms of Foscari. Francesco Foscari himself died in November 1457, aged 84, just a few days after he had been relieved of his office by the Council of Ten. Twice he had seen his only son banished from Venice for corruption, murder and treason, an episode which inspired Byron's historical drama *The Two Foscari*. His dogate was one of the longest in the city's history (1423–57) and, despite opposition, had successfully inaugurated the policy of expansion on the mainland ● *32*. By the 19th century Ca' Foscari was in a pitiful state of repair, so much so that it had to be bought and restored by the municipal authorities. Today it is the principal seat of the university, and adjoins the headquarters of the Venice Fire Department.

THE CEILINGS OF SAN PANTALON
This ceiling carries the largest painted decoration ever laid on canvas. It depicts the martyrdom of Pantalon, physician of the Emperor Diocletian, who was put to death for converting to Christianity. Fumiani worked on it from 1680 to 1704, filling forty panels mounted on wooden frames. Legend has it that the artist was killed in a fall from his scaffolding, and was buried in the church.

CA' REZZONICO

FROM LONGHENA TO MASSARI. Around 1667, the procurator Filippo Bon commissioned Baldassare Longhena to build a palace in place of two houses he owned at San Barnaba. Only the first floor and *piano nobile* were completed by the architect's death in 1682, after which the work ceased because the Bon family fell into serious financial straits. For over seventy years the palace remained covered with a temporary wooden roof, for its owners had been bled dry by the expense of building the first half. Finally, in 1751, they gave up and sold the unfinished building to the wealthy Rezzonico family. In his original design Longhena appears to have sought a classical balance of simplicity and formality; the ground floor was done in bossage stonework, and the first floor had windows with key arches embellished by masks (inspired by the Marciana ▲ *254*). Massari, who was engaged by the Rezzonicos to complete the second floor, replaced Longhena's half-columns with pilasters and tempered some of the original austerity with small oval windows. Inside, Massari's influence is more powerful. The traditional Venetian *portego* ● *88* was supposed to cross from one side of a palace to the other. Here it was reduced to leave room on the canal side for a ballroom two floors high. The fitting out of grandiose reception rooms on the *piano nobile* and the new use given to the mezzanine floor (changed from the original offices to winter living quarters) also reflect the development of a patrician way of life increasingly geared to luxury.

THE APOGEE OF THE REZZONICOS. The Rezzonico family originally came from Como; they joined the Venetian nobility in 1687 in exchange for the 100,000 ducats they contributed to pay for the war in Crete ● *34*. For Giambattista Rezzonico, the acquisition of the palace of San Barnaba was the confirmation of this new social position. And

PIETRO LONGHI ▲ *312*
The museum's collections contain paintings by 18th century Venetian masters such as Rosalba Carriera, Tiepolo and Guardi ... not forgetting Pietro Longhi. This "Molière among painters", as André Chastel has described him, contrived to record Venetian society at the height of its glory, portraying the city's inhabitants like so many actors in a play. In *La Cioccolata del mattino* (1775–80), (below) the figures

appear as if they are on stage, with the priest on the left, and the lady lounging in bed at the center with her *cavaliere* standing behind.

then, barely two years after the completion of the palace, his son Carlo, bishop of Padua, was elected Pope. The Venetians, scarcely able to contain their delight at the prospect of a Venetian reigning at the Vatican, awarded the title of Knights of St Mark to the Rezzonicos, an honor that had previously been strictly reserved to the three most ancient patrician families. The Pope responded by presenting the Republic with the order of the Golden Rose; and in 1769, the year of his death, Ca' Rezzonico was chosen as the venue for a reception

in honor of Emperor Joseph II. It was the scene of many similar balls and receptions before the collapse of the Republic, which was followed in 1810 by the death of the last Rezzonico and the dispersal of his goods and furniture. Ca' Rezzonico then went through a series of different owners before it was bought by the Italian state for conversion into a museum (1934).

THE MUSEUM OF 18TH-CENTURY DECORATIVE ARTS ★, ● 44.

Opened to the public in 1936, the collections at Ca' Rezzonico include paintings, pieces of furniture, faïence and porcelain from a number of different palaces. On the first floor, the ballroom and a smaller adjoining room (the "Brustolon" room) are devoted to work commissioned from the celebrated cabinet maker Andrea Brustolon by Pietro Venier. The most spectacular piece is an extravagant console table held up by a statue of Hercules set between Cerberus and the Hydra. A *Nuptial Allegory* painted by Giambattista Tiepolo on the ceiling of the Nuptial Room for the wedding of Ludovico Rezzonico and Faustina Savorgnan in 1758, is matched by another Tiepolo masterpiece, the *Allegory of Merit*, in the Throne Room. To get from one to the other, the visitor must pass through the Pastel Room (several works by Rosalba Carriera) and the Tapestry Room with its Flemish hangings. Here the *ciocche* (chandeliers in the shape of bouquets of flowers), the looking glasses and the mirrored wall-brackets constitute the glassmakers' contribution to the original 18th-century décor, the most extravagant *cioccha* of all being a 20-branched specimen (left) by Giuseppe Briati ▲ *328*. On the second floor, the rooms called "Villa Zianigo" are devoted to a cycle of frescoes painted by Giandomenico Tiepolo just after the fall of the Republic for his country house near Mirano; and farther on a blend of Rococo and chinoiserie characterizes the "Green Laquer Room", while the "Alcove Room" is a faithful reconstitution of an 18th-century bedroom, dressing-room and boudoir. Every element is here, down to a fifty-eight-piece silver *nécessaire*. Lastly, an 18th-century puppet theater and a reconstituted 18th-century pharmacy are displayed on the third floor.

The furniture of Andrea Brustolon (1662–1735) owes much to Baroque statuary, particularly in its combination of boxwood and ebony.

CARLO REZZONICO
Born in 1693 in a Grand Canal palazzo, ▲ *196*, he became the fifth Venetian Pope under the name of Clément XIII.

THE "FELZE"
A small wooden cabin used as a cover for gondolas ● *57*.

SAN BARNABA

CAMPO SAN BARNABA. The parish of San Barnaba was founded during the early 9th century, when the Doge was decamping from Malamocco in favor of Venice ● *30*. Its center grew from a group of houses on the southern side of the campo, which in fact shared the characteristics of the oldest campi – a simple rectangle bounded by a canal, with a church at one end. Today's Church of San Barnaba has a classic façade of half-columns and Corinthian capitals, built in the 18th century. By contrast the campanile has remained almost unaltered since its construction around the year 1000, with the exception of a conical spire that was added in the 14th century and which makes it one of Venice's more interesting silhouettes. It was from this parish of San Barnaba, where many of them lived, that the impoverished nobility of the city got their nickname of *barnabotti* ▲ *226*. The Casino dei Nobili was formerly in the sottoportico San Barnaba (on the right as you face the church) which was known as the *sottoportico del casin* in consequence. At the fall of the Republic, San Barnaba was still a refuge for ruined nobles, who were given free lodgings here. Nowadays one of its more singular features is a brightly colored barge that is tied up to the fondamenta, from which fruit and vegetables are sold.

In a scene from his sentimental comedy *Summertime* (1955), David Lean had Katharine Hepburn fall into the Rio di San Barnaba.

NICOLOTTI AND CASTELLANI
The caps and sashes of the Nicolotti ▲ *327* were black; those of their sworn enemies, the Castellani, were red.

PONTE DEI PUGNI. Although any bridge in Venice could become a battleground for brawling factions, some of them were specially favored: thus the Ponte della Guerra at San Zulian, the Ponte della Guerra at Santa Fosca, and the Ponte dei Pugni (literally, Bridge of Fists), where prints marking the dividing lines can still be seen. The district-by-district rivalries of Venice broadly separated the city into two clans: the Castellani, who lived in the sestieri of Castello, San Marco and part of Dorsoduro, and the Nicolotti, who hailed from Cannaregio, San Polo, Santa Croce and the parish of San Nicolò dei Mendicoli ▲ *327*. Tradition has it that this rivalry first came into existence before the city itself, when the two mainland towns of Heracleia and Jesolo migrated en bloc into the Lagoon bringing an old quarrel with them. Whether or not this is actually true, the factions of Venice liked nothing better than to engage in regular pitched battles, which the government was unable – or unwilling – to prevent. It should not be forgotten, of course, that it was in the Republic's interest to have seasoned fighting-men at the ready in case of war; moreover it was highly convenient that

Men who fell in the water during the struggle could return to their places in the ranks by passing over the boats of the spectators, or by clambering onto the nearest bridge. As the fight went on, the crowd grew progressively more excited, and since many of the spectators were perched on balconies and *altane*, it was not unusual to see stones, roottiles, chairs and boiling water showered down on the combatants below. As a rule the brawl tended to spread to the packed throngs along the canalsides and on the boats.

one side could be played off against the other to head off a united rebellion. Thus the government opted to feed the rivalry by imposing its own rules of engagement. The brawls usually took place on the bridges, they were permitted by law between September and Christmas, and they were precisely regulated. First of all, a challenge was issued, then "godfathers" were chosen as referees, and a bridge was selected for the encounter. On the appointed day, the factions turned out with their "godfathers" and formed ranks amid the din of castanets, trumpets and drums. Then, harking back to the days of chivalry, collective and individual challenges would be heralded; prior to a more general scrimmage, the best fighters of either faction were in the habit of duelling one to one, or in *mostre* (combats of two against two). After this the *guerra* commenced in earnest, with the two factions charging the bridge with the aim of taking possession and holding it. The subsequent mêlée might go on for several hours, after which a toll of a dozen men killed was considered nothing out of the ordinary. Until the 16th century, the two sides fought with their bare knuckles or else with rushes, double pointed, tipped with steel and then hardened by immersion in boiling water. In the latter case, they also wore breastplates, helmets and gauntlets. But the rushes eventually caused too many casualties, and so were banned in favor of fisticuffs – until 1705, when the Council of Ten promulgated its umpteenth decree that outlawed this factional brawling. For some obscure reason this decree appears to have had its effect, though all of those that had gone before it had been completely ignored.

PITCHED BATTLES
The last pitched battle where steel-tipped rushes were used was in 1574 during a visit by Henri III of France. Six hundred men were involved, and the carnage was so great that the king

335

MULINO STUCKY   SANTA LUCIA STATION   CHURCH OF SANT'EUFEMIA

| 🚤 | Two minutes |
| ⏲ | Two hours |

"There is only one street on the island of Spinalunga . . . with blind alleys running out of it like the teeth of a comb."

Frederick Rolfe,
*Desire and Pursuit
of the Whole*

THE GIUDECCA ★

THE HISTORY OF THE ISLAND. Originally called Vigano, after the early name of the Giudecca Canal, or else *Spinalunga* ("long spine") on account of its fishbone shape, this island owes its present sobriquet to the word *giudicato*, referring to a 9th-century judgement passed on dissident families, banishing them from Venice and assigning them certain parts of the "Giudecca" in which to live. The name has nothing to do with the presence of a Jewish community, as is commonly thought. In the 14th and 15th centuries, major palaces were built along the Giudecca Canal. On the other side of the island facing the Lagoon, the only buildings were monasteries hidden in the greenery (there were about seven of them, mostly now destroyed), and a few small palaces here and there, occupied by schools of philosophy and literature. At that time, and for several centuries, the Giudecca was a resort for wealthy patricians, who maintained villas and gardens there, which is why it was regularly visited by famous men like Michelangelo. Already the island possessed, in Sant'Eufemia, one of the oldest churches in Venice; in the 16th century it was further enriched by the Churches of Il Redentore and

CHURCH OF IL REDENTORE
BASILICA SANTA MARIA DELLA SALUTE
SAN MICHELE
MURANO
SAINT MARK'S SQUARE
CHURCH OF THE ZITELLE
CHURCH OF SAN GIORGIO MAGGIORE
BURANO

the Zitelle, both of which were designed by Palladio, the greatest architect of his time. In the 19th century, various industries were established on the Giudecca with a view to resuscitating the Venetian economy. Factories were set up, some moved into the surviving religious buildings. Little trace remains today of all this activity save gutted hulks like the highly visible Mulino Stucky. In the 20th century the Giudecca has remained on the fringes of Venice, to some extent ignored by the worlds of industry and commerce. Recently, it has drawn considerable profit from a program of decentralization.

FROM SANT'EUFEMIA TO MULINO STUCKY

THE CHURCH OF SANT'EUFEMIA.
Founded in the 9th century and dedicated (according to the 14th-century chronicles) to one of the four martyrs of Aquileia, Sant'Eufemia has been much altered over the years. The 18th century, in particular, has left its mark on the interior. The side portal (1596) came from the demolished Church of San Biagio e Cataldo on the island. The triple-naved basilica plan of Sant'Eufemia harks back to the 11th century, and some of its capitals are Venetian-Byzantine. On the first altar in the right-hand nave is *San Rocco and the Angel* by Bartolomeo Vivarini (1480); on the altar of the left-hand nave is a *Pietà* sculpture by Gianmaria Morleiter (18th century). After major restoration work in the 18th century by the Neo-classical architect Tommaso Temanza, the church was decorated in 1764 by Canaletto, then aged nineteen. For his frescoes, the young painter took the work of Giambattista Tiepolo at the Gesuati as his model, covering the ceiling of the naves with a *Santa Eufemia in Glory* (center), a *Baptism of the Saint* (left) and an *Episode from the Life of the Saint* (right). A short walk

The Giudecca has lost most of its old gardens, which can be seen here on De Barberi's magnificent map (c.1500). They have since made way for new buildings.

337

With the Mulino Stucky, Northern architecture made an incongruous entry into the Venetian skyline. But, not unlike the British House of Commons, it is now a familiar feature of the city.

along the Fondamenta del Rio di Sant'Eufemia leads to the charming presbytery garden, which is full of roses in the spring. (Take the Fondamenta San Biagio.) Note in passing PALAZZO FOSCARI (number 795), a flowered

Gothic building that dates from the 15th century, with two *piani nobili* each with a set of four windows (one set is three-cusped, the other topped with ornamental capitals).

MULINO STUCKY. In 1883, Giovanni Stucky established several mills at the western end of the Giudecca. His business was so successful that in 1895 he decided to enlarge it still further. The project submitted by a Hanoverian architect to satisfy Stucky's grandiose vision caused much bafflement, but Stucky found an infallible way to overcome the reservations of the municipality: he simply threatened to fire all his workers if he did not get his way. Around the huge new factory a number of lesser buildings used for subsidiary industries began to cluster; but the whole enterprise fell into decline after Stucky himself was murdered by one of his employees in 1910. The firm was finally closed down in 1954. The Mulino, whose condition today is nothing less than catastrophic, is to be transformed into a "multifunctional center". Returning by the same road, look out for the FORTUNY FABRIC FACTORY (number 804) ▲ *273*, founded in 1919 and enlarged in 1920, which today employs thirty people and exports its products all over the world. Number 801 is a former brewery; through its gates, one can see that the central building here apes the Neo-Gothic style of the Mulino Stucky. (Return to the Fondamenta del Rio di Sant'Eufemia and continue straight on.)

The Church of the Redeemer, Il Redentore, "is Palladio's most accomplished and beautiful work in Venice". (Terisio Pignatti)

FROM SANT'EUFEMIA TO ZITELLE

THE CHURCH OF IL REDENTORE. By the time the Senate voted in September 1576 to build a church dedicated to the Redeemer if Venice was freed from the plague, a quarter of the city's population had already perished. The death rate fell dramatically in the ensuing bitter winter. In February, Andrea Palladio was chosen as architect for the new church, and a green site was allocated on the north side of the Giudecca that was visible from every side of St Mark's Basin. Palladio had already left a strong impression on this panorama with his Church of San Giorgio. The works began in 1577 and were completed in 1592 by Antonio da Ponte after Palladio's death in 1580. The late 17th-century statues on the outside are by the school of Josse Le Court; inside, the single nave is lined with intercommunicating chapels. The altarpieces were commissioned by the Senate from the best available artists and conform to an agreed pattern: on the right, the *Nativity* (Francesco Bassano), the *Baptism of Christ* (School of Verona), *The Flagellation* (School of Tintoretto); on the left, *The Deposition* (Palma the Younger), *The Resurrection* (Francesco Bassano) and *The*

Ascension (probably by Domenico Tintoretto). The canvases on the reverse wall of the façade are later, while the Baroque high altar dates from the late 17th century. Behind the altar, beyond the five tall Doric columns, are the monks' stalls and there are sacristies at either side of the choir. The one on the right is open to visitors; it contains several Venetian masterworks, notably Veronese's *Baptism of Christ* and two very beautiful 18th-century reliquaries. In the monastery precinct is the Church of Santa Maria dei Angeli, the first Capucin sanctuary on the Giudecca (c.1560), along with the old monks' pharmacy, which is full of china and alchemical instruments from the 17th and 18th centuries.

CASA DEI TRE OCI. This odd Neo-Gothic house was built by a painter at the beginning of this century. It owes its name to its three round windows.

THE CHURCH OF THE ZITELLE. Designed by Palladio and completed in 1586, the Church of the Zitelle has a façade with a central tympanum flanked by two pinnacle turrets. Its interior is polygonal, with a large dome. Because it is currently being restored, the Zitelle is only open for Sunday mass. Its name alludes to the girls, who were poor but honest, and taken into the adjoining convent in the 18th century, where they produced the highly prized "Venice point" lace. Nearby is the 14th-century house of the family of Alvise da Mosto, the celebrated 15th-century navigator.

HOTEL CIPRIANI. The Cipriani stands on the south-eastern shore of the Giudecca, in its own park; it also boasts its own heated seawater swimming pool. There is no fondamenta along the south shore, but on the way back to Sant'Eufemia try cutting through the middle of the island, which turns out to be a busy working-class area. Head first for the old naval dockyard, near the Rio del Ponte Lungo; then for the Junghans watch factory, founded in 1878 and still in business, which until recently was the only firm in Venice that retained houses for its workers. From here, continue past the Corti Grandi, which were the headquarters of the Venetian coconut-fiber industry between 1878 and 1950.

FESTIVAL OF THE REDEEMER ● 49

After the first stone of the future church was laid on July 21, 1577, the Doge Alvise Mocenigo and the patriarch went to visit the building site. A bridge of boats was organized to enable people to join the ceremony, and so the Feast of the Redeemer began.

Every year after that, the Doge, high officials, clergy and population of Venice processed across the canal on a bridge of boats from the Zattere. In the time of the Republic, the ceremonies lasted three days. The lay festival was on the Saturday, the procession on Sunday, and on Monday the populace had a good time on the island. The Festival of the Redeemer is still held on the third Sunday in July, but a firework display has replaced the processions.

🚶 Two minutes
🕐 One hour

SAN GIORGIO MAGGIORE ★

HISTORY. The site of San Giorgio Maggiore appears to have been used in Roman times. In 982, the Benedictines established themselves there, and soon enough the island, known as the "Green Isle" or the "Isle of Cypresses" (a description shared by a cloister in the monastery), became one of the Republic's most favored locations for distinguished foreign visitors. Its position in St Mark's Basin opposite the Piazzetta ▲ *249* made it a strategic point controlling the traffic between the lagoon and the canals crisscrossing the city. After the fall of the Republic, it was turned into a free port; a new harbor was constructed in 1812, and subsequently the island became the headquarters of the artillery before

returning to its original cultural vocation thanks to the Cini Foundation. Administratively, it is a part of the San Marco sestiere ▲ *258*.

THE CHURCH OF SAN GIORGIO MAGGIORE. This church looks out over St Mark's Basin, of which it is one of the principal architectural components. Begun by Andrea Palladio in 1566, it was completed a quarter of a century later by Simone Sorella. For the façade Palladio borrowed a number of elements from classic pagan temples, such as a triangular pediment and a large *pronaos* (portico) with four columns, completed on the sides with half-pediments and pilasters. On the inside is a striking atmosphere of serenity and harmony, mostly due to the light flooding the building through broad window apertures inspired by Roman baths. The inner walls are covered with stucco and Istrian stone

CHURCH OF SAN GIORGIO MAGGIORE
Many of the architectural ideas reflected in this building are drawn from the late Roman Empire. For example its floorplan appears to have been dictated by the search for a balance between the centralized classical temple and the Latin cross shape of a Christian basilica – hence the unusual depth of the choir. Also, the great dome crowning the transept crossing is equidistant from the altar and the main entrance. The Cypress cloister (above) was rebuilt between 1579 and 1614.

of perfect smoothness; and at the rear of the building, four steps and a balustrade mark off the monks' stalls from the square choir, which has columns at each of its four corners. It was always the custom that on St Stephen's Day (December 26) the Doge came to hear Mass at San Giorgio, sung by a double choir of St Marks' choristers and the Benedictine monks of the adjacent monastery. Palladio

took this into account in his design for
the stalls, which were completed by
Gaspare Gatti in collaboration with
Albert van der Brulle, who also executed
the bas-reliefs of episodes from the life of
St Benedict (1594–8). The choir is
decorated with canvases by Tintoretto:
Manna from Heaven (left-hand wall) and
The Last Supper (right-hand wall). On the
high altar is a bronze group by Girolamo
Campagna (1591–3) who also sculpted
the marble of the second altar to the left.
A door to the right of the choir leads
through to the conclave room where Pius
VII was elected Pope in the last century.
Here there is an altar-piece by Carpaccio
(1516) of St George and the Dragon,
rather later than the one in San Giorgio
degli Schiavoni ▲ 162. On the way out,
note Sebastiano Ricci's *Madonna* (1708,
in the chapel to the right of the choir), a
15th-century crucifix in polychrome wood

(second altar to the left) and an *Adoration of the Shepherds* by
Jacopo Bassano (first chapel to the right). In the 17th century
four works by Giulio del Moro were added to the façade;
these were the statues of St George and St Stephen (to whom
the church is dedicated) and the funerary monuments of the
Doges Tribuno Memmo and Sebastiano Ziani. Anyone
wishing to contemplate the most beautiful view of the Lagoon
to be seen from any point in Venice should climb to the top of
the great campanile, erected by Scalfarotto in 1726.

THE MONASTERY OF SAN GIORGIO. In 829, Doge Partecipazio
could already refer in his will to a "Church of San Giorgio".
In 982, the Doge Tribuno Memmo gave the island to
Giovanni Morosini, a noble who had joined the Benedictine
order, with the proviso that the church should still depend on
St Mark's. In return, the monks undertook to drain the
surrounding marshes and repair a mill. The monastery was
reconstructed by order of Pietro Ziani, a former Doge, who
retired there. At the start of the 15th century, the
reorganization of the

The monumental
double-sided staircase
which leads from
Palladio's cloister to
the priest's
apartments was
designed by
Longhena. The
statue by the Paliari
brothers in the niche
on the landing
represents an
allegory of the
Serene Republic.

The Palladian façade of San Giorgio, directly opposite the Piazzetta ▲ *249*, has been reproduced by countless painters.

Benedictines into the congregation of St Justina prompted dissension, with some monks concerned at the consequences of a change in their relation to the Venetian government. This was resolved in 1430, when Doge Foscari decided the monastery should accept the congregation in exchange for a pledge of loyalty to the Republic. In cultural terms, the monastery retained close links with Florence and Padua: to such effect that Cosimo de' Medici, banished from Florence in 1433, took refuge at San Giorgio, bringing with him the architect Michelozzo. A library was built (demolished in 1614) on his orders and at his expense, which had a great influence on the Venetian masters. Towards the end of the 15th century, the architectural ensemble of San Giorgio Maggiore was radically altered. The Gothic church had overlooked the cypress cloister, facing the center of the island and the monastery. Its replacement faced the other way, toward St Mark's Basin. A new dormitory and "laurel" cloister designed by the Buoras, and a refectory by Palladio were added in 1561. Palladio continued to work at the monastery until his death.

THE LIBRARY
Today the library of San Giorgio boasts over a hundred thousand volumes, as well as two globes constructed in the early 18th century by a Franciscan cosmographer, Father Vincenzo Coronelli.

THE CINI FOUNDATION. In 1951, the art patron Count Vittorio Cini chose the Monastery of San Giorgio as headquarters for his foundation, which he named after his son Giorgio Cini, killed in a flying accident. Since then the rooms of the old building have been filled with permanent collections of paintings, furniture and other works; the foundation has also organized a range of temporary exhibitions.

THE TEATRO VERDE. Vittorio Cini was also behind the construction of this Greek-style open-air theater, called "green" because it is set in the middle of a large garden. The plays performed here used to be a major feature of the Biennale ▲ *184*; now it is unused, though kept in good repair.

Santa Croce

✱ Half a day

PIAZZALE ROMA

PAPADÓPOLI GARDENS

SANTA LUCIA STATION

CHURCH OF SAN NICOLÒ DA TOLENTINO

The creation of the tram line that runs between Venice and the mainland eventually meant that the Piazzale Roma had to be equipped with multi-storey garages. After this came the excavation of the Rio Nuovo (which was completed in 1938) to link the Piazzale with the station, the center of the city and the Lido ▲ 354. Since the garages were inadequate and expensive, another parking area was created just a few years ago in the Tronchetto area.

The sestiere of Santa Croce, in the northwest of Venice, covers ninety-four acres. It has two very distinct areas. The east side is very old and typically Venetian; to walk here is to be, to some extent, away from the crowds, in a minor area of Venice – but one which nevertheless can boast some of the loveliest palaces on the Grand Canal. The western part is completely different. During the last two centuries, industrial complexes have appeared in the old buildings, and in some cases have replaced them; at the same time, this part of the sestiere has grown in size with the filling-in of large expanses of water (notably the port area and the Tronchetto).

PIAZZALE ROMA. When one comes to Venice by car, one enters the city by way of Piazzale Roma. A remodeling of the Piazzale is now under way, which has so far entailed the demolition of several buildings and the modernization of the trolleybus terminus. All traffic will eventually be diverted to the Tronchetto, which is linked to the city by a public transport system; in future, only groups of tourists with hotel reservations will arrive in Venice through the Piazzale. (From the Fondamenta Cossetti, cross the elegant stone bridge that spans the Rio Nuovo.)

THE PAPADÓPOLI GARDENS. In 1810, a number of buildings were demolished to make way for these gardens; among them were the Church and Monastery of Santa Croce, which stood on the junction of the Grand Canal and the Rio dei Tolentini, and which had given the sestiere its name. (Cross the Ponte dei Tolentini.)

CHURCH OF SAN SIMEONE PICCOLO
CHURCH OF SAN SIMEONE GRANDE
CHURCH OF SANTA MARIA GLORIOSA DEI FRARI
SAN GIACOMO DELL'ORIO
CHURCH OF SAN ZAN DEGOLÀ
FONDACO DEI TURCHI
DEPOSITO DEL MEGIO
CHURCH OF SAN STAE
CHURCH OF SANTA MARIA MATER DOMINI
CÀ PESARO
PALAZZO MOCENIGO

THE TOLENTINI

THE CHURCH OF SAN NICOLÒ DA TOLENTINO. In 1527, when
Rome was sacked by the troops of Charles V, the Theatine
Order (founded just a few years earlier by St Gaetan de
Tiène and Jean-Pierre Carafa) sought and found asylum in
Venice. The following year, their congregation established
itself in an oratory which adjoined the Church of San
Pantalon ▲ *330*, and which was dedicated to San Nicolò da
Tolentino. Towards the end of the century, it was decided that
the ensemble should have rather different architectural
proportions, and so a new church and monastery were
planned. The project was initially entrusted to Scamozzi, but
after a disagreement with his employers, the Theatines
themselves decided to take control of the works. The new
church was duly consecrated in 1602. Its interior consists of a
single nave with three side-chapels. Until the 18th century
there was a dome above the transept; this was then
demolished and replaced with a flat ceiling decorated with
frescoes by Gerolamo Mengozzi Colonna and Gaetano
Zompini. On the outside, the roof was covered with tiles in
the usual way. Just like those in the side-chapels, the altars in
the two main chapels at the ends of the transept were paid for
by wealthy Venetian families. The high altar was

The Piazzale Roma
quarter.

"Shadows ripple on
the bridges, and on
the distant water
vessels move: you can
hear them puffing
and blowing, and
their wake churns the
water right up to our
canal.**"**

Jean Giono,
Voyage en Italie

The door of the Architecture Faculty.

commissioned from Longhena in 1661, who subcontracted it to the sculptor Josse Le Court. The interior of the church was finally completed in 1671. Thirty years later, the Theatine order set about constructing a façade, which was executed between 1706 and 1714 by Andrea Tirali and paid for by the patrician Alvise Da Mosto. Its principal features are an eight-columned Corinthian portico and a Palladian pediment.

THE MONASTERY. The monastery was begun at the same time as the church, but was not completed until the first decades of the 17th century. The cloister is broad and elegant, standing

to the left of the church almost back-to-back with its choir. The LIBRARY and REFECTORY were also built to the same impressive proportions. Today these premises are the seat of Venice's architectural faculty, which is one of the foremost institutions of its kind in Italy; it has a main entrance designed by Carlo Scarpa who, like many other great Italian architects, was once a teacher here.

SAN SIMEONE

THE CHURCH OF SANTI SIMEONE E GIUDA APOSTOLI. To distinguish it from its close neighbor, this church is still known as San Simeone Piccolo (the Lesser), despite the fact that it was much enlarged during the 18th century. Giovanni Scalfarotto designed and built it between 1718 and 1778 on a carefully integrated plan; its dome is immense and has much in common with the Neo-classical church of La Salute ▲ 318. The entrance portico consists of Corinthian columns with corner pillars which are crowned by a triangular tympanum in marble. At present, the church is not in use as a place of worship. (Continue to the Ponte dei Scalzi, then take the Calle Longa Chioverette, and then the Calle Bergama, and finally cross the little bridge.)

CARLO SCARPA (1906–78)
Carlo Scarpa taught architecture in Venice from 1926 onwards. His special interest was in museums and exhibitions: he was responsible for the Venezuelan pavilion at the Biennale ▲ 184, the Canova Museum in Possagno, the restoration of the Palazzo Querini-Stampalia ▲ 167, and the Castelveccio Museum in Verona.

SAN SIMEONE PROFETA (OR SAN SIMEONE GRANDE). Founded in 967, San Simeone Grande was rebuilt at the beginning of the 18th century by Domenico Margutti, and then again by Giorgio Massari in 1755. Massari added the Rosary altar and a façade, the stylistic unity of which was comprehensively wrecked by an 1861 restoration. San Simeone Grande is constructed along the lines of a basilica; it contains several paintings by Palma the Younger, as well as a fine monument to St Simon (1318) which reflects the influence of the school of Pisa. The second altar on the left belonged for a while to

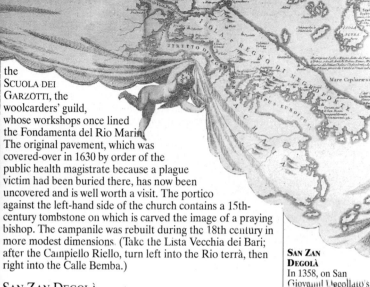

the
SCUOLA DEI
GARZOTTI, the
woolcarders' guild,
whose workshops once lined
the Fondamenta del Rio Marin.
The original pavement, which was
covered-over in 1630 by order of the
public health magistrate because a plague
victim had been buried there, has now been
uncovered and is well worth a visit. The portico
against the left-hand side of the church contains a 15th-
century tombstone on which is carved the image of a praying
bishop. The campanile was rebuilt during the 18th century in
more modest dimensions. (Take the Lista Vecchia dei Bari;
after the Campiello Riello, turn left into the Rio terrà, then
right into the Calle Bemba.)

SAN ZAN DEGOLÀ

CAMPO SAN ZAN DEGOLÀ. This campo, with its church in one
corner and the canal of the same name in front, has always
been a quiet place slightly apart from the bustle of Venice –
this was so even when the Fondaco dei Turchi attracted
hordes of merchants. The transformation of the adjoining
areas has had little effect on this atmosphere of calm.
THE CHURCH OF SAN ZAN DEGOLÀ. Dedicated to the
decapitated St John, the origins of this church are very
ancient. Starting as a simple oratory in the 7th and 8th
centuries, by 1007 it had become a parish church. The Venier
family is thought to have paid for the building, which was
restored by the Pesaros in the 13th century. Today its
proportions still offer a precise idea of Venetian-Byzantine
notions of architecture, despite changes
made to the apse and façade in the 18th
century. The triple-naved basilical
interior has a keel-vaulted ceiling, while
the simple volutes on the façade
accomplish a graceful marriage between
the two wings of the church and its taller
central body. San Zan Degolà was closed
during the Napoleonic occupation
because of fears it might collapse, then
reopened after restoration work in 1818.

FONDACO DEI TURCHI ★   ● 89, ▲ 193

THE RECONSTRUCTION OF A VENETIAN-BYZANTINE PALACE.
This building, which began as a palace, was so badly damaged
that it had to be completely rebuilt in the 1860's. The result was
a construction sumptuously coated in marble, with the same
expansive Venetian-Byzantine façade as its predecessor: a
long portico on the ground floor, arcades on the upper floors

**SAN ZAN
DEGOLÀ**
In 1358, on San
Giovanni Decollato's
day, the Venetians
defeated the Genoese
at Negroponte.

Inside, Venetian-
Byzantine capitals
crown the Greek
marble columns;
vestiges of Byzantine
frescoes have been
discovered in a side-
chapel.

347

THE TURKS' WAREHOUSE
Even when she was at war with the Ottomans, Venice maintained commercial links with

merchants. The Turks' fondaco had its doors and windows closed off, Muslim-style, and contained a mosque and a bath-house. At the same time, it served as a warehouse, trade center and a bazaar controlled by a special magistrature. There was one restriction (all imported goods had to be sold in Venice), one interdiction (no entry for Christian women and boys) and one special security measure (merchants had to deposit their money and weapons on arrival).

and two crenellated towers on either side. Materials from the old building were re-used and old documents and pictures referred to in this rebuilding, even though the project as a whole was not scientifically planned.

THE ORIGINAL BUILDING. The first palace was probably built in the early 13th century by Giacomo Palmieri, a former consul of Pesaro on the Adriatic coast, who took refuge in Venice and founded one of the city's greatest patrician and mercantile families, the Pesaros ▲ 195. On the canal side the original building had a long portico, where merchandise could be conveniently loaded and unloaded – a typical arrangement in Venice where great houses often doubled as warehouses ▲ 104. It was one of the largest establishments on the Grand Canal; indeed in 1381 the state purchased it as a gift for Nicolas d'Este, Marquis of Ferrara, as a reward for his loyalty during the Chioggia War ● 31. From that time, the palace was what might be called an occasional property of the d'Este; Venice would confiscate it when relations with Ferrara were bad, and give it back when they improved.

THE TURKS. In 1621 the Seignory rented the palace to Ottoman merchants as their main business locale, with a view to monitoring their activities. Major alterations were made to create twenty-four shops on the premises, to which were added fifty-two bedrooms along with quarters for servants. At this time the building became known as the Fondaco dei Turchi (the Turks' Warehouse). Later, as trade with the East began to decline, the palace was abandoned by its Ottoman occupants and fell into ruin.

THE MUSEUM. In 1880 the municipality purchased the Fondaco and restored it. In 1924, after a spell as the Correr Museum (1898–1922), this former palace became Venice's Museum of Natural History, and it has been ever since.

DEPOSITO DEL MEGIO

This austere brick building was one of the many depots in which the Republic stored its grain and flour during times of war and famine. Its date of construction remains unknown, but it is mentioned in an account of the 1346 famine. After being completely remodeled on the inside, it was recently turned over for use as a public school. (Take the Calle del Megio and the Calle Larga.)

CAMPO SAN GIACOMO DELL'ORIO ★

TEATRO ANATOMICO. From the 16th century onwards, this building, which is situated on the north side of the campo (number 1507), was a kind of medical center where many distinguished doctors from Bologna and elsewhere came in order to teach. Today it is a private residence.

THE CHURCH OF SAN GIACOMO DELL'ORIO. This church was built during the 9th and 10th centuries and reconstructed in 1225. It retains a number of its Byzantine traits, despite a series of modifications that have taken place over the years. Between the end of the 14th century and the beginning of the 15th, a broad transept was grafted on to the three-nave basilical plan of the old church. A number of elements (columns, capitals and arches) were also recast in the Gothic style. In 1549 the CHAPEL OF THE SACRAMENT was added to the right of the choir, and the apses were restored in the style of the Renaissance. The brick CAMPANILE dates from 1225. (Return to the Calle Larga and turn right after the bridge into the Calle del Tintor, then turn left into the Salizzada San Stae.)

CAMPO SAN GIACOMO DELL'ORIO
Different explanations have been given for this campo's strange name. The simplest is that it derives from a laurel tree (*lauro*) which once grew next to the church. Another, more fantastical, has it descending through a series of distortions from the word *lupo* (wolf), since packs of wolves used to overrun the area in the dim and distant past. According to yet another theory, the church was named San Giacomo dal Rio (St James of the River) to distinguish it from its namesakes on the Rialto ▲ *283* and the Giudecca. But the most likely derivation is that "Orio" comes from *luprio* (a piece of dry land emerging from a swamp). During the 18th century, the campo was roughly paved over.

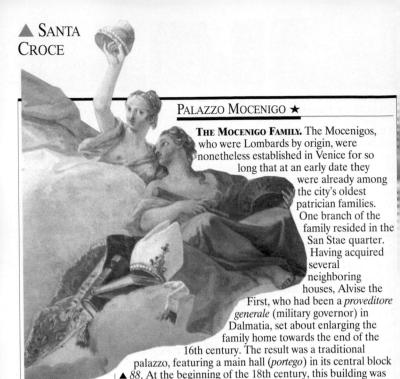

PALAZZO MOCENIGO ★

THE MOCENIGO FAMILY. The Mocenigos, who were Lombards by origin, were nonetheless established in Venice for so long that at an early date they were already among the city's oldest patrician families. One branch of the family resided in the San Stae quarter. Having acquired several neighboring houses, Alvise the First, who had been a *proveditore generale* (military governor) in Dalmatia, set about enlarging the family home towards the end of the 16th century. The result was a traditional palazzo, featuring a main hall (*portego*) in its central block ▲ 88. At the beginning of the 18th century, this building was once again enlarged on its right-hand side, where the *salizzada* is situated today.

THE CENTER FOR THE HISTORY OF COSTUME. When he bequeathed his palace to the city in 1954, Alvise Mocenigo presented the museums of Venice with a doubly remarkable asset. The interiors, for one thing, were completely intact; and for another the furniture and the interior still measured up to the standards of elegance that had prevailed in the great houses of the 18th century. A new library and museum have been installed since the legacy came into effect. The latter contains 5th–7th century Coptic textiles, Italian and French fabrics from the 14th–19th centuries, and 18th–19th century costumes. Palazzo Mocenigo also houses the Vittorio Cini collection of religious drapery and woven fabrics from many different sources. (Continue along the Salizzada San Stae.)

Palazzo Mocenigo was decorated with Rococo frescoes by Jacopo Guarana and Agostino Mengozzi Colonna in 1787; their theme was the apotheosis of the Mocenigo family.

THE "CARRO"
The Pesaros got their fortune and nickname "Pesaro del Carro" from the *carro*, a kind of chariot which they invented to transport boats between the river and the Lagoon. With the construction of locks, the family received dues from the vessels passing through. In 1613, this was appropriated by the State, but the Pesaros were well compensated.

SAN STAE

THE CHURCH OF SAN STAE. Following the destruction of the Venetian-Byzantine church, a replacement was built in 1678 overlooking the Grand Canal. In general, this church (designed by Giovanni Grassi) shows a strong Palladian influence. Its single nave is joined to a deep apse and six side-chapels, the ceiling is vaulted, and all along the walls a heavy coping is supported by stout columns. With its four pillars crowned by a triangular tympanum, Domenico Rossi's façade is likewise thoroughly Palladian. Inside are paintings by Piazzetta, Tiepolo and Ricci.

SCUOLA DEI TIRAORO E BATTILORO ● *87.*
To the left of the church stands an
elegant construction dating from 1711,
which was formerly the headquarters of
the goldsmiths' and silversmiths' guild.
An exhibition room was installed here in
1876 after the suppression of the scuola.
(Cross the bridge and turn left down the
Calle Pesaro.)

CA' PESARO ★   ● *91,* ▲ *195*

PALAZZO MOCENIGO
Antonio Corradini's
frame for a portrait of
the magistrate Giulio
Contarini da San
Beneto bears an
allegory of Justice,
symbolizing his office
within the Republic.

THE PATRICIAN PALACE. In 1628, after they had acquired three
contiguous palaces, the Pesaros began to unite them into a
single building. Leonardo Pesaro inherited the property and
set about completing this work, beginning in 1652. The idea of
his architect, Longhena, was to create a hall on the ground
floor giving on to the Grand Canal, with reception rooms
above. To reach the upper floors, he designed a majestic
staircase in the center of the building. The lavish wall-facing
of the façade was finished in 1679; with its play of chiaroscuro, exuberant sculptures and diamond-point bossage, this
represents a high point in the progress of Venetian
Baroque. The deaths of Leonardo Pesaro and
Longhena in 1682 brought work to a brief halt,
but shortly afterwards it was resumed and the
first floor was completed. Gaspari, who took
over from Longhena, finished the second floor in
1710, having displaced Longhena's central staircase to the
side of the hall, thereby releasing plenty of space.
THE MUSEUM OF MODERN ART. The Veronese Duke of La
Masa bought Ca' Pesaro in the 19th century. His widow
created a foundation with the aim of exhibiting the work of
Venetian artists who lacked the means to make themselves
known, before offering the building to the city in 1889. In
1902 the municipality installed a Modern Art Gallery;
between 1910 and 1920, exhibitions were organized there

PALAZZO AGNUSDIO
The landward door of
this palazzo is
surmounted by a
15th-century lunette,
which features two
angels holding the
family's coat of arms.
Among the symbols
of the Evangelists
that can be seen
above the windows
are the Bull of St
Luke and the Lion of
St Mark ▲ *250.*

which challenged the conformism of the
Biennale ▲ *184* and gave artists a chance
to express themselves. Today the gallery
possesses canvasses by many of the great
artists of the 19th and 20th centuries.
THE MUSEUM OF ORIENTAL ART. Partly
composed of the collections of Henri de
Bourbon-Parme, a great traveller and
ethnologist who lived for many years in
Venice, this museum has also found a
home in the Ca' Pesaro. (Continue along
the Fondamenta Ca' Pesaro.)

PALAZZO AGNUSDIO

This building stands at the foot of the
Ponte di Forner, number 2060. Three
elements of the original 14th-century
Gothic palace survive: the five ogival
windows, with sculpted representations of
the Annunciation and the symbols of the
Evangelists above; the landward door

with its angel in majesty, encircled by a 13th-century Romanesque frieze; and the waterside door, crowned by a *patera* featuring the mystical Lamb of God – after which the palace is named. (Take the Fondamenta Rimpetto Ca' Mocenigo as far as the Campiello Spezier, then follow the Calle della Chiesa.)

SANTA MARIA MATER DOMINI

CHURCH OF SANTA MARIA MATER DOMINI. According to tradition, the first church on this site was built in 960. It became a parish church in the 11th century, and adopted its present name, abandoning that of Santa Cristina. In the early 16th century the old Byzantine structure was demolished to make way for a Renaissance edifice with a Greek Cross floorplan, four corner chapels and a dome. Two classic volutes bind the lower register of the façade to its Corinthian columns and to the upper register, which consists of a triangular tympanum. (Cross the Ponte Santa Maria Mater Domini.)

PALAZZO GOZZI. At number 2269 on Ramo Calle della Regina stands the palace of the Gozzi brothers. The onslaught led by Carlo Gozzi against the playwright Goldoni was the central event in Venetian theater during the 18th century ▲ *291*. His brother Gasparo Gozzi was a talented moralist and humorist, who satirized many aspects of Venetian daily life in the press, particularly in the popular *Gazzetta Veneta*. (Continue along Calle della Regina and Calle di Ca' Corner.)

The north side of Campo Santa Maria Mater Domini is distinctive for the remains of buildings which date back to the Byzantine era.

THE QUEEN OF CYPRUS
In the 15th century, Venice – which had designs on Cyprus – took advantage of a quarrel over the succession between the two sons of the dead king, John II of Lusignan.

CA' CORNER DELLA REGINA ▲ *196*

A 14th-century Gothic palace on this site was the birthplace in 1454 of the celebrated Queen of Cyprus, Caterina Corner. At the beginning of the 17th century her descendants acquired some adjacent buildings, before purchasing Palazzo Grimani on the narrow Calle della Rosa in 1678. In 1700 the Corners commissioned the family architect, Domenico Rossi, to rebuild the palace. The old structure was duly demolished and the first stone of the new one laid in 1724. Rossi's plans envisaged a building on a scale that would rival the Ca' Pesaro ▲ *195, 351* but his project was only partially completed. The façade as it survives today is fascinating on account of its elongated form and extended balcony. After Rossi's death, Francesco Bagnolo enlarged the palace on the landward side between the Calle della Rosa and the Calle della Regina, and in the final quarter of the century the interior was decorated with a series of new frescoes. The last of the Corners died in the 19th century, and afterwards the palace passed through many hands before it was finally bought by the Biennale ▲ *184* in 1975 and turned into a depository for archives.

The old king's bastard, James II, appealed to Venice for help, and Caterina Corner was sent to marry him. Widowed within a year of her wedding in 1472, she usurped the Cypriot throne with the help of the Venetian Seignory. But, in 1489, she was recalled to Venice, and had to surrender the island. On June 1, she landed at St Mark's Basin and was received with the honours due to a great monarch.

CHIOGGIA

PELLESTRINA
ALBERONI
SACCA SESSOLA
POVEGLIA
MALAMOCCO
SAN CLEMENTE
LA GRAZIA
SAN SERVOLO

SAN LAZZARO
DEGLI ARMENI

HOTEL EXCELSIO

The Lido, a narrow bar of land seven and a half miles long and two and a half miles wide at its broadest point, lies between the Lagoon and the sea. Its long beaches of fine sand, so close to Venice, were "discovered" in the mid-19th century, when Byron, Shelley,

"After an hour, we arrive at the Lido, that long bank of sand which protects Venice from the open sea. At its center stands a church and a village, with vegetable gardens all around . . . on the left, an avenue of trees, old, but renewed by the coming of spring . . . we go forward and three hundred paces farther on we meet the open sea – no longer inert and lake-like as in Venice, but thundering with the perpetual rush and retreat of the ocean, the boil and foam of the waves. And all along the length of this strip of sand there is no-one to be seen . . .**"**
Hippolyte Taine,
Voyage en Italie

GRAND HOTEL DES BAINS

SANT'ERASMO

PUNTA SABBIONI

Musset and many of the other romantic writers raved about them. During the late 19th century, buildings began to appear on the Lido, which gradually became both a residential suburb of Venice and a fashionable resort. There are few traces of the past here now; apart from Malamocco ● *30* – with its fine campanile similar to that of San Marco ▲ *248* – only the remains of a church and convent, and of Fort San Nicolò, which controlled the entrance to the Lagoon, testify to an earlier occupation.

🚲 Half a day

THE LIDO PROMENADE. There is a car-ferry to the Lido from Tronchetto; otherwise most visitors tend to use public transport. Bicycles and tandems can be rented on the spot on the corner of the Gran Viale and Via Zara. The Lido's main avenue is lined with villas, gardens and elegant shops, and leads through to the open sea. From the Piazzale Bucintoro, you can either go left along the Lungomare Gabriele d'Annunzio and continue on to the military and civilian beaches of San Nicolò as far as the lighthouse, or else you can turn right

along the Lungomare Guglielmo Marconi. This route passes the splendid GRAND HOTEL DES BAINS, which was much frequented in the last century by rich European families. The hero of Thomas Mann's *Death in Venice* stayed in this hotel, which also features strongly in Luchino Visconti's film of the same title. After this you come to the CASINO, CINEMA FESTIVAL PALACE, and the GRAND HOTEL EXCELSIOR. Parallel to the Lungomare Marconi, the Via Sandro Gallo links Piazzale Santa Maria Elisabetta to Malamocco, between the sea and Lagoon. Beyond this is the small district of ALBERONI – one of the few places on the Lagoon where one can ride and play golf – which is so named on account of the trees (*alberi*) surrounding the fort. The Lido is very different from the city of Venice in aspect, because it consists almost entirely of Neo-Gothic, Neo-Byzantine or Liberty-style villas. Nonetheless, there are one or two interesting monuments to be found here: notably the CHURCH OF SANTA MARIA ELISABETTA (mid-16th century), the CHURCH AND CONVENT OF SAN NICOLÒ with its 16th-century cloister and adjoining planetarium, the church at NOTRE-DAME-DE-LA-VICTOIRE (1925) and the JEWISH CEMETERY, a forest of 16th- and 17th-century tombstones ▲ *143*.

THE GRAND HOTEL EXCELSIOR
At the southern end of the Lido stands the odd-looking, Neo-Moorish Grand Hotel Excelsior, side by side with the Grand Hotel des Bains. The residents of this legendary palace are the rich and famous (especially those who come for the Film Festival) and they are here to breathe the sea air and savour the hotel's atmosphere of turn-of-the-century grandeur. In such surroundings it is easy to imagine the aristocrats of the 1890's, sitting elegantly bored under their parasols while their sailor-suited offspring gambolled in the healthy fresh air.

LA MOSTRA : VENICE, CITY OF THE CINEMA

PALAZZO DELLA CINEMA
Designed by the architect Luigi Quagliata, the Palace of the Cinema was built in 1936. Today, it looks as though the Venice Film Festival will have to move to another building, designed by the Madrid architect Rafael Moneo.

CARDBOARD VENICE
The myth of Venice is so strong that film makers do not always take the trouble to go there on location. In Berlin, Vienna and Hollywood cardboard Venices have been built especially for films, and some people found them better than the original. One example is in the operetta *Top Hat* (1935), directed by Mark Sandrich, in which Fred Astaire and

Ginger Rogers tap dance in kitsch surroundings.

Many hundreds of movies and television films have been made about Venice, or with Venice providing the backdrop. Some would even say that the city has seen too many films and too few masterpieces – although among the latter have been works by Visconti, Antonioni, Fritz Lang, Ernst Lubitsch, Orson Welles and Joseph Losey. It is certainly true that international productions do tend to feature the same houses and public places over and over again, but how could a city as mythical as Venice escape such constant repetition of this kind? It is quite certain that St Mark's Square, the Rialto Bridge, the Bridge of Sighs, the Carnival, gondolas and the pigeons will always symbolize Venice, both in reality and on celluloid.

THE ORIGINS OF LA MOSTRA. The objective of the Festival of International Cinematographic Art, which was inaugurated on the Lido on August 6, 1932, was "to raise the new art of the cinema to a level with the other arts". The new festival was organized within the framework of the Biennale ▲ *184*, which already included world-ranking practitioners in music and the figurative arts. The success of the film festival, which was the first of its kind, was so great that the organizers quickly decided to make it a permanent feature of the Biennale's programme, with competing films. The following year, prizes were given, and three years after that the PALAZZO DELLA CINEMA, the present headquarters of the Festival, was built close to the Hotel Excelsior. At that time Italy was a Fascist state; nevertheless the cinema in Venice was relatively unconstrained, at least until 1939. Directors such as John Ford, Joseph von Sternberg, Frank Capra and Jean Renoir brought luster to the competition for best film, encouraging critics to give an intellectual basis to the new art – indeed the first history of the cinema in Italian was eventually written by a Venetian, Francesco Pasinetti. However during the period of Mussolini's dictatorship and the Second World War, the festival fell into neglect; between 1942 and 1945 nothing was achieved.

THE FESTIVAL AFTER THE WAR. During this period, La Mostra gave prominence to Neo-Realism in the cinema, with films like Rossellini's *Paisa*. A rival festival festival at Cannes was founded in 1946, but Venice for a while managed to hold its own by mounting retrospectives of the work of great directors.

FROM THE 1950'S TO THE PERIOD OF DISPUTE. All that glistened was not gold for the Mostra during the 1950's; commercial and political interference combined to penalize "controversial" film directors, even though the excellent health of the film industry in general contrived to obscure the defects of the Venice Film Festival. The high point in its history came with the revelation of the film cultures of Japan, India, the USSR and South America, along with the emergence and affirmation of new directions in international cinema. The reputation of the festival was particularly high between 1963 and 1968, under the enlightened guidance of Luigi Chiarini, when it regained all of its former weight and prestige as a showcase and a laboratory for the cinematographic arts. These were the years of the "Nouvelle Vague", when the most coveted film awards were won by such

Poster for the first Venice Film Festival (August 6, 1932).

COMPLICITY
In 1991, the director Federico Fellini presented the Golden Lion to Marcello Mastroianni, his favorite actor, in recognition of his career achievements. Among many films, the pair made *La Dolce Vita* (1960), *Eight and a half* (1963), *La Cité des Femmes* (1980) and *Ginger and Fred* (1985). Mastroianni (born in 1924) has also made films with other great Italian directors such as Antonioni, Visconti, Scola, the Taviani brothers, Marco Ferreri . . . and has had an international career with films directed by Boorman (*Leo the Last*, 1970), Demy (*L'Evénement le Plus Important*, 1972), Polanski

names as Resnais, Tarkowski, Godard, Antonioni, Pasolini, Bresson, Kluge, Buñuel, Bellochio and Visconti. Nevertheless some violent objections and disputes arose, with the result that many of the Festival's awards were spurned. The Biennale was forced into a long period of reform, remaining in a semi-paralyzed state until the late 1970's, when Carlo Lizzani took over and became its director.

THE VENICE FILM FESTIVAL TODAY. Today the Golden Lion awards have been re-established at the Venice Film Festival, although the Biennale and the city of Venice have both still had their difficulties. There are many more

competing festivals in existence today, and anyway the cinema is no longer the force that it was. Sixty years after its foundation, the Festival is once again attempting to move its locale and to change its habits, notably by a reduction in its bureaucratic procedures.

(*What?*, 1972), Mikhalkov (*Les Yeux Noirs*, 1987) and Chalonge (*Les Voleurs d'Enfants*, 1991).

🚲 Half a day

THE PELLESTRINA COAST
Along this long, narrow ribbon of land run the *murazzi*, giant embankments built in the 18th century to protect Venice and the Lagoon. The idea was first put forward by the geographer Vincenzo Coronelli in 1716, but it was not until April 24, 1744, that the Republic finally made its decision to go ahead. The work lasted from 1751 to 1782. The embankment was 46 feet thick at its base and 13 feet high; originally it was 12½ miles long, extending right up to the Lido.

CHIOGGIA   CATHEDRAL OF SANTA MARIA

Perhaps the most agreeable way to travel between Venice and Chioggia is by bicycle – you can rent one at the Lido and then follow the coastline. Your first stop will be the ALBERONI ▲ *355*, where there is a ferry to San Pietro in Volta. The countryside around here is typical of the area, and famous for its fishing; cross from San Pietro to the main road along the MURAZZI, continuing to Pellestrina, where there is a ferry to Chioggia.

HISTORY

FROM THE ORIGINS OF CHIOGGIA TO THE 14TH CENTURY. According to legend, the city of Chioggia (which was formerly one of the busiest fishing ports in the Adriatic) was founded by Clodius, a companion of Aeneas, hence its antique name of Clodia. This account is probably fairly close to the truth; in any case, the origins of Chioggia are extraordinarily ancient. The locality had been inhabited for many centuries prior to the era of Roman domination (first century BC). Pliny the Elder (23–79 AD) mentions it in his *Naturalis Historiae*. Under the Romans, Chioggia became an important port astride the sea and river routes to Padua; later its isolated position between the Adriatic and the Lagoon made it a safe haven for mainland refugees who were seeking shelter during the Barbarian invasions ● *30*. In the 9th century, the town was destroyed by the armies of Pepin, son of Charlemagne and King of Italy, then immediately rebuilt. The subsequent *Pactum*

SOTTOMARINA   PELLESTRINA   LIDO   VENICE

Fishing nets ■ *23*.

Clodiae defined the territory belonging to Chioggia and its relationship with the Realtine Islands, and for many years the town had its own government, laws and councils. In the 11th and 12th centuries, the exploitation of its salt pans brought about a period of economic expansion, during which the town was transformed into an urban conglomerate. In the 12th century, the salt pans numbered more than seventy, and the salt was exported to many regions of Italy and abroad. The city and the surrounding countryside became very wealthy as a result.

THE WAR WITH GENOA AND THE END OF CHIOGGIA'S AUTONOMY ● *31.* The salt boom lasted until the 14th century, when Chioggia was once again sacked during Venice's war with Genoa. Later it was to be the scene of a decisive battle which brought to an end a hundred years of conflict between these two great maritime powers over the monopoly of trade with the Levant. In 1378, Chioggia was taken by the Genoese, and the security of the Lagoon was seriously threatened; but in 1380 the Venetians recovered it again and defeated their commercial rivals once and for all. Thereafter the fate of Chioggia was bound to that of Venice, although it continued, as in the past, to claim autonomous status.

THE FISHMARKET
This was the earliest fishmarket in the Lagoon and still takes place every day except Mondays.

THE FISHING FLEET

CHIOGGIA'S FISHERMEN. The waters around Chioggia have always been rich fishing grounds, and after the decline of its salt industry the island reverted naturally to fishing as its principal resource. Some of the boats that were used by the Chioggiotti have since become famous; among them the

THE "BRAGOZZO"

This flat-bottomed boat is designed for fishing on the sea-bottom. Its length varies from 30 to 50 feet, and its width from 7 to 10 feet. Its decoration is very distinctive, for not an inch of the *bragozzo* is left unadorned. Its trapezoid sail is highly colored and its construction and embellishment are carried out with religious care. The central part tends to be yellow, orange or white, while the broader lower part may be white, blue or yellow. In the center of the sail are heraldic emblems, both religious and profane, and their variety is infinite. Some have religious themes – the Virgin, Christ on the cross, patron saints; others refer to nature (suns, moons, compass-cards) or bear monograms, symbols or designs related to the names, qualities or defects of the owner (the *paron*) or his family. On the beautiful black hull, the waterline is marked by a white or reddish-brown line. On the inside of the stern are inscribed various formulae invoking divine protection for the boat and those who sail in her. Almost without exception, the *bragozzi* seem to recall the splendid galleys which were once the pride and joy of the Venetian navy.

tartana (used for drag-netting), which was supplanted in the second half of the 18th century by the *bragozzo*. Since even today the Chioggiotti live mostly on the high seas, it is hardly surprising that their houses are small and modest affairs; their main interest is their boat, which is both their instrument of work and their families' most cherished possession. Here and there across the island one may still see the occasional palace, and there are plenty of churches as well. But still the most charming features of Chioggia are its attractive position, its air of vitality and its cheery disorderliness.

THE CHIOGGIOTTI OF THE PAST. During the course of the 19th century, Venetian painters such as Guglielmo Ciardi, Ettore Tito and Italico Brass came often to Chioggia in order to paint the island's fisherfolk, and their work exudes the relaxed and sunny atmosphere that was a feature of the island before the coming of the motor car. At that time the women of the island wore a nun-like traditional costume, a

feature of which was a white half-length apron that was tied in front, and which could be raised to head level and drawn tight around the face. Chioggia is also the setting for one of Goldoni's most famous plays, *Le Baruffe Chiozzotte* ▲ *291*, which was written in 1762, and in which the playwright casts an ironic eye over the island and its inhabitants. But Chioggia has done more than just inspire agreeable paintings and comedies: it is also the birthplace of such important figures as John Cabot ▲ *181*, who discovered Canada in the 15th century, and also Rosalba Carriera (1675–1757) ▲ *312*, a painter who was greatly honored by the French when she visited Paris in 1720–1.

▲ 291 ▲ 181 ▲ 312

THE FISHERMEN'S GUILD
Nobody knows exactly when the fishermen of Venice first organized themselves into a guild. But it would seem that the Venetian Republic quickly sought to assert control over the profession, which was of vital importance to Venice's economy. On the other hand, a decree of September 5, 1536, handed down by the Council of Sages, stipulated that the representatives of the fishermen's guild should take part in all sessions dealing with problems having to do with the Lagoon. Clearly, they knew the subject better than anyone else!

AROUND CHIOGGIA

THE GEOGRAPHY. Chioggia occupies two long, parallel islands, with the Canal della Vena passing in between them. A number of calli cross the canal and the main street (Corso del Popolo) at right angles, giving the town a distinctive aspect. Even though it has been destroyed and rebuilt several times, Chioggia has always clung to its regular chequerboard town plan, which may well reflect its Roman past. Moreover, from Roman times onward there was always a CHIOGGIA MAGGIORE and a CHIOGGIA MINORE. After the war of 1379–80, only the former was reconstructed. Today the site of Chioggia Minore is filled by the SOTTOMARINA resort, which is linked to Chioggia Maggiore by a bridge across the Lagoon.

PIAZZETTA VIGO. On this little piazza is a column surmounted

**THE LIONS OF THE
REPUBLIC**
The Venetians
customarily set up a
stone lion, symbol of
the Republic, in each
one of their territorial
possessions. Thus, at
the entrance to
Chioggia, as at the
entrance to Venice on

by a winged lion, symbolizing the island's bond with Venice.
CANAL DELLA VENA. The many bridges that cross the Canal
della Vena offer a fine view; also here is the 18th-century
PALAZZO GRASSI,
where Pope Pius VI
stayed when he
halted at Chioggia
on his journey to
Vienna.
CORSO DEL POPOLO.
This "avenue"
alongside the canal
has a succession of
arcades running

along one side of it. The most interesting building is the old
GRANAIO (grainstore, 1322). Modernized in the 19th century
in company with many of Chioggia's other monuments, the
Granaio has now been converted into a fishmarket; it does
still retain some of its original features (such as corbels,
pilasters and arches). See also the bas-relief *Virgin and Child*
by Sansovino (16th century).

THE CATHEDRAL OF SANTA MARIA.
Farther along the island is the
massive Cathedral of Santa Maria,
with its characteristic square
campanile (1347–50). Founded in
the 11th century and consecrated as
a cathedral in 1110, Santa Maria
was destroyed by fire in 1623 and
reconstructed by Longhena. Work
continued until 1647, and even by
then the façade had not been
completed. The building itself is
basilical in form featuring three
naves; it contains works by Palma
the Younger, Giambattista Piazzetta

the Piazzetta ▲ *249*,
we are greeted by
the statue of a
winged lion.

and Giambattista Tiepolo.
CAMPO DEL DUOMO. On this campo stands the little church of
SAN MARTINO (1392), one of the few 14th-century buildings in
Chioggia to have escaped destruction and alteration. It was
built of brick after the Chioggia war, as a memorial to the
churches of Chioggia Minore destroyed during that conflict;
its principal treasure is a 14th-century polyptych attributed to
one of the earliest painters of the Venetian School, Paolo
Veneziano. (Follow the Corso to the last bridge over the
Canal della Vena: cross to the Canal San Domenico. From
here the PONTELUNGO links Chioggia with the mainland.)

The canals of
Chioggia.

THE CHURCH OF SAN DOMENICO. This building stands on an
islet right at the end
of the Canal San
Domenico.
Founded in
the 13th century, it was
then restored
during the 19th
century. The church
contains a painting
of *St Paul* by
Carpaccio.

THE ISLANDS

CHURCH OF SANTA MARIA DEGLI ANGELI

CHURCH OF SAN PIETRO MARTIRE

🚤 Seven minutes
🕐 Half a day

A fragment of the magnificent floor of the Basilica Santa Maria e San Donato.

THE BARBARIGO ALTARPIECE (right)
This painting, which hangs in the Church of San Pietro Martire, was commissioned in the 15th century from Giovanni Bellini (who was then the official state painter of Venice ▲ *304*). The subject – the Doge Agostino Barbarigo presented to the Virgin of St Mark's and St Augustine – and the presence of the arms of the Barbarigo family indicate that this canvas originated in the Doge's private palace.

HISTORY

THE ORIGINS. The island of Murano, the largest of the islands in the Lagoon, is about a mile across the water from Venice and was already inhabited in Roman times. Refugees from Altino escaped here during the Barbarian invasions and gave the island the name of "Ammurianum", after one of the gates of the city they had left. Men and women from Oderzo later joined these settlers and, by the 7th and 8th centuries, the island's port of Sant'Erasmo was an important calling-place for merchant ships.

A PROSPEROUS ISLAND. Until the 10th century, Murano was a trading center in its own right, whose salt pans, water-mills and fishing fleet made it an economic force to be reckoned with. So densely was the island populated that, by the 11th century, the Doges were encouraging islanders to move to Venice (Dorsoduro). After the 13th century, Murano passed under the jurisdiction of a *podesta* chosen from the ranks of the Venetian patricians, but despite this it continued to have its own Grand Council (along with a smaller council which

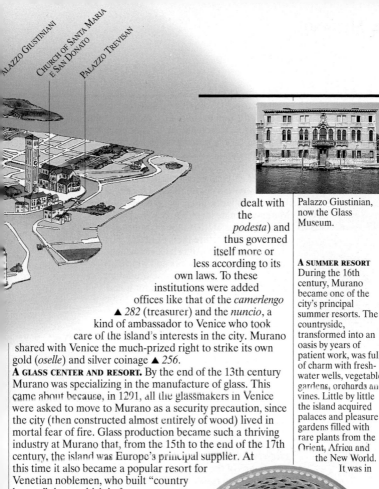

Palazzo Giustinian, now the Glass Museum.

dealt with the *podesta*) and thus governed itself more or less according to its own laws. To these institutions were added offices like that of the *camerlengo* ▲ 282 (treasurer) and the *nuncio*, a kind of ambassador to Venice who took care of the island's interests in the city. Murano shared with Venice the much-prized right to strike its own gold (*oselle*) and silver coinage ▲ 256.

A GLASS CENTER AND RESORT. By the end of the 13th century Murano was specializing in the manufacture of glass. This came about because, in 1291, all the glassmakers in Venice were asked to move to Murano as a security precaution, since the city (then constructed almost entirely of wood) lived in mortal fear of fire. Glass production became such a thriving industry at Murano that, from the 15th to the end of the 17th century, the island was Europe's principal supplier. At this time it also became a popular resort for Venetian noblemen, who built "country houses" there, which in fact were sumptuous palaces surrounded by beautiful gardens.

LANDSCAPE OF THE ISLAND. For many centuries the geography of Murano remained virtually unaltered and, at the close of the 18th century, its little town still contained more canals than streets and more pleasure gardens and vegetable plots than buildings. But, during the 19th century, all this began to change; the vegetable plots were built over, and two of the island's inlets were filled with earth in order to create new residential areas (Sacca Serenella and Sacca San Mattio).

A SUMMER RESORT
During the 16th century, Murano became one of the city's principal summer resorts. The countryside, transformed into an oasis by years of patient work, was full of charm with fresh-water wells, vegetable gardens, orchards and vines. Little by little the island acquired palaces and pleasure gardens filled with rare plants from the Orient, Africa and the New World. It was in surroundings like these that the poetess Gaspara Stampa fell in love with Count de Collalto, and Aretino read aloud his bawdy stories. But after a while the Venetians discovered the countryside of Treviso and the banks of the Brenta, and Murano was left to its green orchards.

MURANO GLASS ● 58

A TRADITION ROOTED IN ANTIQUITY. The origins of glassmaking are clearly very ancient in the Lagoon; excavations have yielded fragments of objects dating back as far as the Roman era. But it was not until the late 10th and early 11th centuries that glass production really took root in Venice itself, and the glassmakers quickly organized themselves into a guild; soon after, in 1291, they moved en bloc to Murano.

365

Contemporary objects from the Murano glassworks.

THE BAROVIER CUP
Now preserved in the glass museum, this is perhaps the most famous wedding cup in the world. Made of enameled blown glass, it is a perfect example of 15th-century art. The exterior was decorated by the daughter of Angelo Barovier, which explains its name.

The support, in dark blue, is embellished with effigies of the bride and groom, as well as with allegorical scenes showing young girls beside a fountain and gentlemen hunting.

EARLY GROWTH. From the mid-14th century onwards, the artisans of Murano started to sell their products abroad. They quickly gained a reputation for producing small pearls of glass, and for the mirrors which became a major Murano export during the course of the 15th century. Within fifty years the island's glasswork had lost much of its utilitarian character and had become a fully fledged art form.

NEW COMPONENTS FOR GLASS. During the 15th and 16th centuries, the glassmakers of Murano became increasingly preoccupied with the materials that they were using in order to manufacture their products. First of all they evolved ENAMELED GLASS, which came in mostly dark colors and which Murano continued to manufacture for export long after the Venetian fashion for it had faded. Then there was CRYSTALLINE GLASS, a kind of glass (not crystal) that had a remarkable degree of transparency; AVENTURINE GLASS (gold flux), which was invented at Murano; and other types of glass which resembled gemstones, such as CHALCEDONY GLASS. The workshops also resuscitated *milfiori*, a very ancient technique by which baguettes of colored glass were combined with transparent glass. Finally, there was also a considerable production of objects in *lattimo*, an opaque and milky type of glass, and *latticino*, a skillful blend of *lattimo* and clear glass.

THE STATUS OF THE GLASSMAKERS. Because of the growing importance of the glass industry, its artisans had to submit to severe political restrictions in order to balance their very considerable privileges. By contrast with the rest of Europe, Venice did not require a man to belong to a glassmaking family as a condition for learning the art. Any talented apprentice could rise, step by step, through the ranks, to become a master glassmaker. However, the glassmakers were forbidden to emigrate from Venice on pain of sequestration of all their goods. Nevertheless, it is known that in the 16th century several glassmakers did succeed in setting up factories in Northern Europe, where they also flourished.

NEW FORMS. During the 17th and 18th centuries, the search for new shapes in glass became paramount at Murano. Venetian mirrors and chandeliers had become so successful in Europe that Louis XIV was obliged to found a competitive glassworks in France in order to limit the huge expense of importing the Venetian product. At the same time, major innovations were being made in Northern Europe with the development of crystal production and techniques for glass-engraving. Soon Venice found itself imitating Bohemian crystal: in 1730 Giuseppe Briati founded a factory whose goal was to rival the products of the North. But the results were disappointing, because fine Venetian crystal was found to be unsuitable for cutting or facetting.

THE GLASS MUSEUM. The only institution of its type in Italy, the Glass Museum now occupies Palazzo Giustinian, one of the largest palaces in the Lagoon and the former seat of the bishopric. The museum is composed of three separate sections: the first houses the archeological collection and displays precious examples of Egyptian and Dalmatian glass; the second contains pieces manufactured between the 18th

THE "CORSO"
On Ascension Day, when the Doge "married" the sea
● *38,* a *corso* or regatta took place at Murano. At this time boats with oarsmen dressed in gold livery gathered in the island's grand canal, and an extravagantly dressed crowd assembled to watch the gorgeous procession. Today, a regatta is held at Murano on the first Sunday in July.

and 19th centuries; and the third (which is in another building nearby) offers examples of contemporary and industrial glass products. All three are well worth a visit, but the most interesting rooms are unquestionably those in the second section, because they give a clear idea of how tastes and techniques have evolved within the glass industry, how the various instruments on display were used, and how the different phases of glass manufacture, ● *58,* succeeded one another throughout the years.

EXPLORING THE ISLAND

A CLUSTER OF ISLANDS. The map shows that the organization of the urban center of Murano is almost identical to that of the city of Venice itself, consisting of ten separate islands grouped around a grand canal, which is proportionately much wider than the one in the city, and which is known by three different names at different stages along its course: the Canal San Giovanni, Canal Ponte Longo and Canal dei Angeli.

THE GLASSWORKS RESIDENCE. If Rio dei Vetrai is primarily medieval in its aspect, and notwithstanding the presence of a number of later structures, this is due to the survival of a specific type of building – the glassworks residence. These houses served as homes for the glassworks owners, and they also doubled up as workshops and warehouses for the storing of raw materials. Among the better examples of this type of construction are the CASA DEGLI OBIZZI E DEI SODECI and the PALAZZETTO CORNER, both with their series of columns and their three-cusped Gothic windows.

367

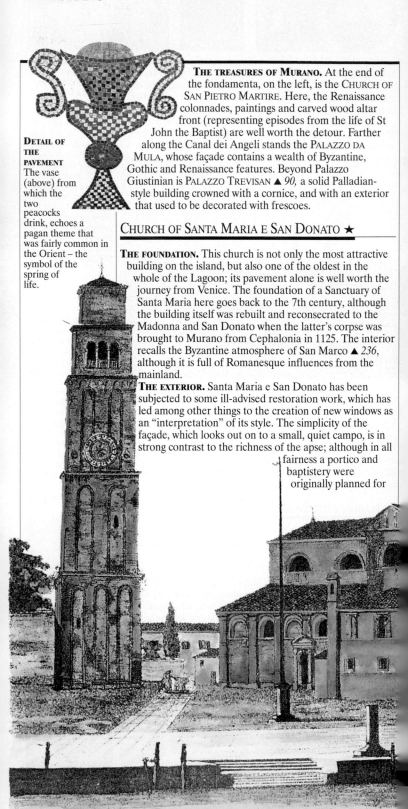

DETAIL OF THE PAVEMENT
The vase (above) from which the two peacocks drink, echoes a pagan theme that was fairly common in the Orient – the symbol of the spring of life.

THE TREASURES OF MURANO. At the end of the fondamenta, on the left, is the CHURCH OF SAN PIETRO MARTIRE. Here, the Renaissance colonnades, paintings and carved wood altar front (representing episodes from the life of St John the Baptist) are well worth the detour. Farther along the Canal dei Angeli stands the PALAZZO DA MULA, whose façade contains a wealth of Byzantine, Gothic and Renaissance features. Beyond Palazzo Giustinian is PALAZZO TREVISAN ▲ *90,* a solid Palladian-style building crowned with a cornice, and with an exterior that used to be decorated with frescoes.

CHURCH OF SANTA MARIA E SAN DONATO ★

THE FOUNDATION. This church is not only the most attractive building on the island, but also one of the oldest in the whole of the Lagoon; its pavement alone is well worth the journey from Venice. The foundation of a Sanctuary of Santa Maria here goes back to the 7th century, although the building itself was rebuilt and reconsecrated to the Madonna and San Donato when the latter's corpse was brought to Murano from Cephalonia in 1125. The interior recalls the Byzantine atmosphere of San Marco ▲ *236,* although it is full of Romanesque influences from the mainland.

THE EXTERIOR. Santa Maria e San Donato has been subjected to some ill-advised restoration work, which has led among other things to the creation of new windows as an "interpretation" of its style. The simplicity of the façade, which looks out on to a small, quiet campo, is in strong contrast to the richness of the apse; although in all fairness a portico and baptistery were originally planned for the church front but were never realized. The portal is crowned by a bas-relief of *San Donato and Votary* from the late 14th–early 15th century. In the buttresses supporting the church's central structure are fragments of pilasters from the ruins of Altino (2nd century).

THE REFLECTED APSE. With the customary Venetian awareness of the interplay between water and architecture, the church is so oriented in order to show its best point, a magnificent apse, to the people arriving from its seaward side. Atop the fine brick structure reflected in the water stands a line of blind arches, which are echoed by a gallery just above. Between these two levels runs a series of triangles, like the teeth of a saw: these are variously decorated with crosses, flowers and animals. This decoration, along with the rhythm of the columns and the Istrian stone parapets of the gallery above, lend the whole a kind of aerial grace.

THE INTERIOR. Inside, Santa Maria e San Donato is built on the lines of a basilica, with three naves separated by two rows of five columns in Greek marble. The keel vaulting, which was constructed at the beginning of the 15th century, is one of the most interesting features here. By the high altar are the RELICS OF SAN DONATO. Above the arcades of the main nave runs a BAS-RELIEF with, at one point, a winged lion separated from a wine cask by two escutcheons. According to the local legend, a cask like this at Burano used to fill up of its own accord with sacramental wine, but only while the cask was kept here beside the relics of St Alban. The prodigy ceased to occur in 1543 when the inhabitants of Murano insisted that the cask be brought to their island. As to the mosaics, note in the apse a large blue figure of THE VIRGIN AT PRAYER (called a *theotocos* by the Greeks) which stands out against a gold background: and, above all, the marble-mosaic pavement.

One of the two peacocks (below) and a chalice (far left) in the entrance to the main nave.

THE PAVEMENT OF SAN DONATO
This floor has the "softness of an oriental carpet", made of "... narrow bands of marble, finely knotted and woven into diamond shapes." (Pietro Toesca) It also reserves several surprises for anyone who cares to look at it closely. Both in its design and in its technique, it is similar to the pavement of St Mark's ▲ *240*. Among other features, it carries an inscription showing the date of its completion (1140), a vignette of two roosters carrying a dead fox (symbolizing the triumph of Christian vigilance over paganism and luxury) and a fragment of mosaic depicting a pair of crickets.

🚌 Forty-two minutes
🕐 Half a day

LACE AND THE SEA
The story goes that a sailor, leaving his fiancée at Burano, set out on a voyage and came to a place that was inhabited by mermaids. Bewitched, the rest of the ship's crew leaped into the water, but the lover resisted the lure of the mermaids' song. The queen of the mermaids, touched by his constancy, shook her tail and whipped up a crown of sea foam, which took solid form and became a bridal veil for the sailor's distant betrothed. Later the young girls of the island copied the veil with needle and thread. Although a fable, there is certainly some truth in the notion that Burano lace is connected with the sea, for its complex stitching and weaving derive from the techniques used for making fish nets.

Scuola Merletti Burano

HISTORY

Like the other islands in the Lagoon, Burano has probably been inhabited since Roman times, well before the Lombards established themselves in the mainland cities during the 6th century. When they did so, the inhabitants of Altino took refuge on the island, which they called Boreana, after one of the gates of their native city which had faced northwards and through which the *bora,* or north wind, blew. The island was already fully occupied in the year 1000, and has remained so ever since. For centuries it remained subordinate to Torcello (from which it was administered) and Mazzorbo nearby. Burano was referred to as a simple village, while its neighbors had the status of towns. However, the island began to gain importance in the 16th century when it became a center for lacemaking; moreover, its inhabitants were spared the ravages of malaria, which became a serious threat elsewhere as the marshes advanced further into the Lagoon. This was because Burano was providentially sited in the path of the wind and well away from stagnant waters. Anyway, the lace industry prospered, and the island had a period of glory which lasted until the end of the 18th century. With the collapse of the Republic, Burano joined the other island communities in decline. Named as capital of the islands in the northern part of the lagoon in the 19th century, it finally became an integral part of Venice in 1923.

THE ISLAND OF LACE ● 60

The streets of Burano are full of women doing embroidery, but there are practically none to be found who still know the true art of Burano – lacemaking. Apart from the fact that the profession is "deadly to the sight", it requires astonishing skill and patience to make lace, which was formerly one of Venice's most valued products.

TORCELLO

CHURCH OF SAN MARTINO

THE BEGINNINGS OF

LACEMAKING IN THE LAGOON. As early as the 15th century, women were making lace in the convents, charitable institutions and private houses of Venice, and also on the surrounding islands. But it was not until the mid-16th century and the invention of the *punto in aria* that the art of lacemaking with a needle was born, and immediately became the speciality of Burano.

THE VALUE OF LACE. As an accessory to fashion, fine lace symbolized the highest social status. The extreme refinement of Burano work was very popular among the princes, nobles and wealthy bourgeois of Europe; so popular, in fact, that a school of lacemaking had to be created to meet the growing demand. While Burano evolved lacemaking with needles alone, Chioggia ▲ *358* and Pellestrina developed a different product, which was made with lace bobbins. A number of manuals with illustrated designs for lace and embroidery were printed in Venice. So

FRENCH LACE
Louis XIV's minister Colbert employed lacemakers from Burano to launch the industry in France. This led to the invention of a new type of lace to rival that of Burano, known as that "noblest and most Italian variety."

THE PAINTED ISLAND
With its small, brightly colored houses bathed in sunlight, Burano has always attracted artists and painters. Before the First World War, the "Burano School" of painting evolved here; its members combined a grainy surface and strong use of color with a complete lack of respect for the academic rules of painting. Among them was the great Gino Rossi. Many paintings of the Burano School hang in one of Venice's more unusual galleries, namely the Restaurant Da Romano on Burano's via Galuppi. This celebrated trattoria first instigated the Burano art prize, which was inaugurated in 1947.

great was the enthusiasm for Burano lace that, in the mid-17th century, attempts were made to imitate it abroad; notably in France, with Louis XIV's creation in August 1665 of a "Manufacture Royale des Dentelles Françaises".

WHIMS OF THE 18TH CENTURY. Foreign competition eventually took its toll on Burano, along with the various difficulties brought about by the social, political and commercial decline of the Republic of Venice. By the 18th century Burano lace had lost much of its cachet and was perilously close to extinction.

THE REBIRTH OF THE LACE INDUSTRY. Towards the close of the 19th century an attempt was made to revive Burano lacemaking. In 1872, Contessa Marcello opened a lacemaking school at Burano under the aegis of Queen Margarita of Italy. Francesca Memo, known as La Scarpaiola, was at that time the only person left alive on the island who still knew the secret of *punto in aria*; she was brought in to teach the art to others, and before long the commercial production of lace had begun once again.

THE 20TH CENTURY. By the beginning of the 20th century Venice and the islands between them employed some five thousand lacemakers in seven major factories. The Burano school opened a shop on St Mark's Square, with branches at Chioggia and Jesolo. To survive, Burano was gradually obliged to produce more lace of inferior quality. The Fascist regime attempted to revive the old standards and restore the island's reputation for quality by offering financial aid and publishing advertisements in the press, but to no avail; the debts grew and standards continued to decline. Nowadays, real Burano lace is a phenomenally expensive luxury, since it takes three years for ten women to make a single tablecloth. The last of the lacemakers who still work in the great tradition of the island now firmly believe that "their art will die with them".

BURANO'S COLORS

Situated some six miles from Venice, Burano looks completely different from the other islands of the Lagoon. There are no imposing palaces here, but rather uniform ranks of houses that are all the same height and all painted in bright colors. They are small, one or two floors only, with façades and simple square windows all alike. There is no exterior ornament except bright color to distinguish one from the next. The job of repainting the houses in these deep reds, vivid yellows and intense blues was left to the women, since the men were usually away at sea. Tradition has it that these bright colors helped the sailors to recognize their homes from many miles off, as they sailed back toward the island. Today the boats still move up and down the canals and wait in lines, side by side, at their moorings along the bank. The nets hang drying in tiny backyards or in front of the houses. All of these images are a part of the island's landscape, as are the groups of women who sit gossiping or embroidering on their doorsteps, and whose voices represent the authentic sound of Burano.

A WALK ACROSS THE ISLAND

TO THE CENTER OF THE ISLAND. Walk along the Rio di Mezzo, then take the Via Galuppi to the square which is also dedicated to Burano's most famous son, the musician Baldassare Galuppi (1706–85), known as Il Buranello. The whole of this route is occupied by shops selling lace (most of it made in China). On the square are the only two large pieces of architecture on the island which have been spared demolition: these are the ORATORIO SANTA BARBARA (17th century) and the CHURCH OF SAN MARTINO (16th century), flanked by its 18th-century CAMPANILE, The façade of this church has, oddly, no door. Inside, among other things are a *Crucifixion* by Tiepolo (1725) and a *Miracle of Saint Alban* attributed to Zanchi. This picture was inspired by a legend which is very popular on Burano: apparently the sea threw up at this site a kind of casket made of stone, which the fishermen were unable to shift. To everyone's astonishment, however, some children succeeded where their elders had failed, and when the casket was opened it was found to contain relics of St Alban, St Dominic and St Orso, which were carried in procession across the island. On the square, the former Palace of the Podesta (14th century) contains the MUSEUM AND SCHOOL OF LACEMAKING. This museum commemorates three centuries of the art and has more than 68,000 pieces of lace on display. But only the 20th-century pieces come directly from Burano, since the older ones are all from Venetian public and private collections. The museum, which was created in order to promote the kind of quality lacemaking that has been all but eliminated by machine-made products, is now managed on a co-operative basis by ten lacemakers.

SECRET BURANO. If you leave the square and wander farther afield on the island, you will discover its quiet, secret places, shimmering with light and color. Look especially for Campo della Pescheria, Rio della Giudecca, or (in the north of Burano) Rio Mandracchio.

"On the thresholds of the small houses along the canal and in the narrow streets, one can see the lacemakers about their famous craft, using not a spindle but a simple needle and thread."
Maurice Barrès, *La Mort de Venise*

The vivid colors of the housefronts are all the more striking because their doors and windows are outlined in white. Perhaps in reaction to the unbroken greyness of the winter days, the Buranese sometimes cover their doors with strange geometrical motifs that bear an uncanny resemblance to modern works of art.

373

🚤 Forty minutes
🕐 Two hours

The visitor who comes to Torcello from Murano and Burano cannot fail to fall under its strange spell. For Torcello, lost in its solitude at the heart of the Lagoon, was once a thriving town in its own right, and is now no more than a ghost of its former self.

HISTORY

THE ORIGINS. The beginnings of Torcello are linked to the history of Altino and the Barbarian invasions of the 5th and 7th centuries. The word *torcello* comes from the name of a gate or tower at Altino, or perhaps from the ramparts and defensive towers by which that city was probably surrounded.

THE AUTONOMY OF TORCELLO. In the 7th century, the Bishop of Altino decamped, along with the entire population of the town, to Torcello – bringing with him the relics of Altino's first bishop, St Eliodorus, who thus became the patron saint of the island. Little by little Torcello acquired a degree of administrative autonomy to go with its growing political independence from Byzantium; as a result it prospered within the confederation of islands which were eventually to form the Venetian state. During the 10th century, Torcello had about ten thousand inhabitants, with no fewer than ten churches and several convents. At that time it was the richest and most powerful island in the Lagoon, and a trading outpost of considerable importance.

DECLINE. Thereafter Torcello fell into decline, and eventually had to submit to the jurisdiction of a Venetian *podesta* – though this dignitary was still nominated by the island's own Grand Council. Between the 14th and 16th century its decline was accelerated by the action of two rivers, the Sile and the Dese, which slowly transformed the water around Torcello into a malarial swamp. Their beds were not diverted until the 17th century.

> **"**An unearthly silence reigns over this place, where nature is so abundant that the works of man scarcely affect it.**"**
> Georges Sand,
> *Lettres d'un voyageur*

The Agnus Dei – detail of a mosaic in the right-hand apsidal chapel of Santa Maria Assunta.

THE CATHEDRAL
On the side of this cathedral, with its somewhat stark exterior, are curious stone shutters that move on stone hinges. Ruskin thought that the overall effect of this building was more like a storm refuge somewhere in the Alps rather than a cathedral in a populous area.

The inhabitants were forced by this scourge to move to Murano or Venice, and the former urban center was gradually dismantled. At the end of this long process Torcello was left almost deserted, and even today its population does not exceed sixty souls.

THE RELIGIOUS COMPLEX

There are no calles on Torcello, but merely a road which passes among fields and a few houses. After crossing the PONTE DEL DIAVOLO (built, according to tradition, in a single night), you arrive on the piazza where there is a marble seat known as the THRONE OF ATTILA, formerly used by the bishop or by the representative of the secular power. Here also is a large complex of religious buildings, comprising three separate edifices that are linked by a portico. This ensemble was designed to symbolize the progress of the Christian believer: the baptistry represents his birth and childhood, the cathedral the course of his life, and the church (where a canonized martyr lies entombed) symbolizes his death and transition into paradise.

THE BAPTISTRY. Only a few vestiges remain of the 7th-century building which once stood in front of the cathedral. Its circular ground-plan, punctuated by eight columns, was probably modeled on the architecture of Roman baths.

THE CATHEDRAL OF SANTA MARIA ASSUNTA ★. If one is to believe the inscription to the left of the choir, this cathedral is the oldest Venetian monument in existence. The first written record in the history of Venice is here, indicating the year 639 as its date of foundation. It was considerably modified in the 9th and 11th centuries; the church increased in length, the apses were reconstructed. The central apse was raised, as was the choir, and beneath these a crypt was dug. Today what remains of the ancient pavement can be viewed (through a pair of grilles) at a depth of some eight inches below the present one. In the 14th century the portico was linked to that of the adjoining Santa Fosca. Inside,

"THE LAST JUDGEMENT" ★
The two final registers show, on the left, the blessed entering paradise (detail below), and on the right the anguish of the damned, who writhe in a river of fire which flows from the feet of Christ. From top to base and from left to right, are the proud, the lustful, the gluttonous, the wrathful, the covetous, the miserly and the slothful.

375

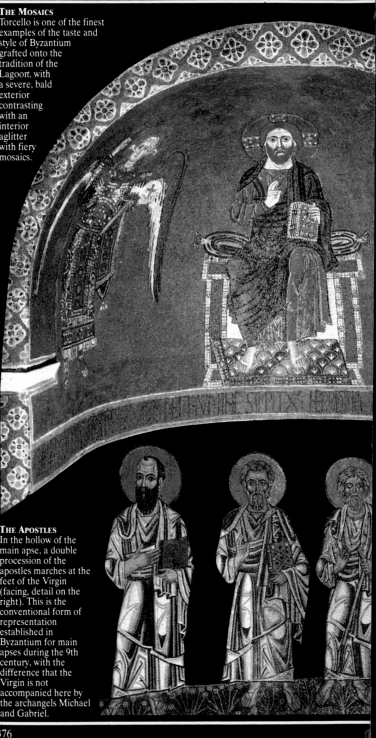

THE MOSAICS

Torcello is one of the finest examples of the taste and style of Byzantium grafted onto the tradition of the Lagoon, with a severe, bald exterior contrasting with an interior aglitter with fiery mosaics.

THE APOSTLES

In the hollow of the main apse, a double procession of the apostles marches at the feet of the Virgin (facing, detail on the right). This is the conventional form of representation established in Byzantium for main apses during the 9th century, with the difference that the Virgin is not accompanied here by the archangels Michael and Gabriel.

376

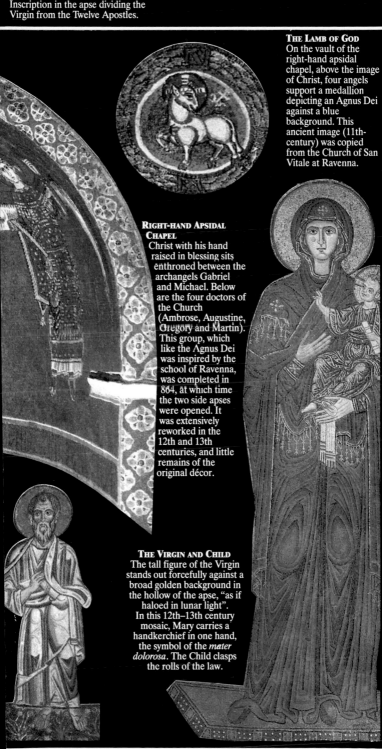

VIRTUTIS MARIS ASTRVM

Inscription in the apse dividing the
Virgin from the Twelve Apostles.

THE LAMB OF GOD
On the vault of the
right-hand apsidal
chapel, above the image
of Christ, four angels
support a medallion
depicting an Agnus Dei
against a blue
background. This
ancient image (11th-
century) was copied
from the Church of San
Vitale at Ravenna.

**RIGHT-HAND APSIDAL
CHAPEL**
Christ with his hand
raised in blessing sits
enthroned between the
archangels Gabriel
and Michael. Below
are the four doctors of
the Church
(Ambrose, Augustine,
Gregory and Martin).
This group, which
like the Agnus Dei
was inspired by the
school of Ravenna,
was completed in
864, at which time
the two side apses
were opened. It
was extensively
reworked in the
12th and 13th
centuries, and little
remains of the
original décor.

THE VIRGIN AND CHILD
The tall figure of the Virgin
stands out forcefully against a
broad golden background in
the hollow of the apse, "as if
haloed in lunar light".
In this 12th–13th century
mosaic, Mary carries a
handkerchief in one hand,
the symbol of the *mater
dolorosa*. The Child clasps
the rolls of the law.

THE UNFINISHED CHURCH
According to one interesting theory, related by the art historian Lauritzen, the dome which was to have crowned the Church of Santa Fosca was never finished because ". . . the Greek workers who began the building left the site halfway through, leaving its completion to local masons who were incapable of raising a dome . . ."

Two small 14th-century palaces stand opposite the churches. These are the PALAZZO DELL'ARCHIVIO, whose portico contains fragments from Altino, and the PALAZZO DEL CONSIGLIO, with its Gothic outside staircase leading to the first floor. These two palaces house the MUSEO DELL'ESTUARIO, which contains precious objects found in excavations here, as well as archeological evidence of Torcello's origins from Altino and two paintings by Veronese.

the three naves separated by two rows of nine columns stretch away toward their respective apses. The beautiful marble mosaics, the priceless iconostasis, and a ceremonial episcopal throne at the end of the choir combine to create an atmosphere that is quite extraordinary. With its marble panels separated by slender columns, the iconostasis of Santa Maria Assunta is undoubtedly among the loveliest traceries of stone ever produced by Byzantine art. Whether lions or peacocks, the animal shapes that inhabit it all strike heraldic poses; thus the peacocks are seen drinking at a fountain, the symbol of divine grace. At the foot of the altar is a marble Roman sarcophagus containing the relics of St Eliodorus. Apart from the mosaics in the apses, note the immense LAST JUDGEMENT (11th–12th century) on the reverse of the façade. This picture-narrative extends over six registers and should be viewed in order from top to bottom. First comes the crucifixion, followed by the descent into Limbo; Jesus in triumph towers over the conquered Lucifer, hurls down the Gates of Hell and seizes Adam by the arm. Eve stands in the background, and on either side of the panel are the archangels Michael and Gabriel. At the third level Jesus is seen in glory in his mandorla of light, flanked by the Virgin and John the Baptist. Next is a scene of the throne prepared for the Last Judgement; two angels, to the left and right, call upon the dead, who are yielded up from the bowels of the earth and the stomach of wild animals and sea monsters. Finally, in the last two registers, the elect are sorted from the damned after their souls have been placed in the balance.

SANTA FOSCA. This church, constructed in the form of a Greek cross, was erected between the 11th and 12th centuries. It probably began as a *martyrium*, or sanctuary for the relics of martyrs. Today it is shaped as an octagon surrounded by a portico, whose raised arches rest on columns with Venetian-Byzantine capitals. With its double row of blind arcades and saw-tooth motif, the apse and its two accompanying chapels are strongly reminiscent of San Donato on Murano ▲ 368. So movingly simple is Santa Fosca that it borders on the abstract; in fact it is the perfect expression of the Byzantine idea of space emerging from structural coherence and unity. To crown it all, the church is bathed in a light of unearthly clarity.

THE LAGOON

SACCA SESSOLA
POVEGLIA
SANTO SPIRITO
SAN CLEMENTE
LA GRAZIA
SAN GIORGIO MAGGIORE
MURANO
LAZZARETTO VECCHIO
SAN SERVOLO
SAN LAZZARO DEGLI ARMENI

HUNTING IN THE LAGOON
The wooded edges and marshlands of the Lagoon used to be a sporting paradise, swarming with pheasants, partridges, deer, wild boar and foxes. They were used by the nobility, for whom hunting and shooting were favorite pastimes, as Longhi's painting shows. Hunting was viewed by the Venetians as a useful, healthy occupation and with time it became the excuse for excursions to the *casoni*, the thatched hunting lodges on wooden pilings that were so characteristic of the Lagoon foreshore. Later, much of the countryside was stripped of woodland and cultivated, but the *valli* (reserves) and the *barene* (mudflats) ■ *18* continued to attract both hunters and game.

The smaller islands around Venice can be split between the northern and southern parts of the Lagoon. Some can be reached by public transport and others not. If you have money and time, you can rent a boat from one of the *fitabarche*, as the boat rental sites are called, and tour around those islands within rowing distance – or motor distance – of the city. It is essential to buy a chart to look out for the markers, and to follow the *bricole* (mooring posts) ■ *24* and buoys indicating the navigable channels. The visitor confined to the vaporetto must use his imagination and perhaps an old map like the one drawn by Bordoni in the 16th century ("Venezia e le isole") to identify the places he will not put into. Then he will see how the scope of Venice itself expands in his mind's eye, how the islands rise, like pearls on a necklace, around the city, and how Venice is the rational focus of a far larger Lagoon. Everything had a place in the web that vanished in the 19th century with the linking of the city to the mainland by railway bridge, and the dredging of a canal between the city and Lido. This created a direct route from Mestre (and subsequently Marghera) by way of San Marco to the open sea. All the little

LA CERTOSA
LIDO
SAN GIACOMO IN PALUDE
LE VIGNOLE
MADONNA DEL MONTE
MAZZORBO
BURANO
TORCELLO
SAN FRANCESCO
DEL DESERTO
SANT'ERASMO
CAVALLINO

islands not directly
linked to the historic center
were abruptly excluded from the
economic life of Venice, and then
abandoned by their inhabitants. Today, of the
thirty-four islands in the Lagoon (which belong to
the Italian state, the city of Venice or private individuals)
at least a score are totally abandoned. There is a sense in
which all once enjoyed equal importance since none could be
reached except by boat, although each had specific functions
according to its position. The most densely populated islands
lay along the main arteries between the sea and *terra firma*;
the convents and monasteries clustered around Venice; near
the Lido and port entrances stood the defensive and military
installations and the quarantine stations.

THE NORTHERN LAGOON

MAZZORBO. Today, Mazzorbo is made up of vines, orchards,
fruit gardens and a handful of houses, though it was once a
place of commercial importance. Its name has connotations
of grandeur, since *maiurbium* in Latin means "greater city". It
is linked to Burano by a long wooden bridge ▲ *370* and now
has just a few hundred residents. Its monasteries, churches
and palaces have all been destroyed, but a few Gothic houses
still stand along the canal (which is served by a vaporetto).

TIMBER FOR VENICE
In the 11th–12th
century, wood
became indispensable
to the urban and
economic
development of
Venice. As an entirely
artificial town, the
city required an
enormous quantity of
wood for building
purposes, and in the
13th century virtually
everything there was
made of it, including
houses (hence the
frequent fires),
bollards, pilings
indicating navigable
channels and mooring
posts. The lumber
trade grew apace,
augmented by the
needs of a powerful
fleet. Once the
woodland on the
islands had
succumbed to
uninterrupted
logging, the Venetians
turned instead to the
huge forests along the
Istrian Coast,
shipping lumber from
the Cadore and
Belluno regions in
Northern Italy.

381

Sarcophagus of the Egyptian Prince Nehmekhet (c.1000 BC) in the library of the museum at San Lazzaro degli Armeni.

Likewise, Mazzorbo still has its 14th-century CHURCH OF SANTA CATERINA, a blend of Gothic and Romanesque, with a picturesque campanile covered in greenery and the oldest bell in the Lagoon (1318).

SAN FRANCESCO DEL DESERTO. South of Burano is one of the Lagoon's loveliest and quietest spots, San Francesco del Deserto, the "monastery-island". According to legend, St Francis of Assisi passed through here on his way back from the Middle East, where he had been to preach the Gospel. As the saint approached the island a storm that was raging suddenly dropped and the birds began to sing. Whatever the reason, a group of Franciscans established themselves here in the 13th century. Two hundred years later they abandoned the monastery, only to return in the mid-19th century. Thus San Francesco del Deserto has maintained its original function and to this day is run by the same religious community, which admits visitors to admire the serene beauty of its cloisters, trees and cultivated land. Above all, San Francesco del Deserto is a haven of greenery and tranquility.

LE VIGNOLE AND SANT'ERASMO. These two islands are the market gardens of the estuary; they face the port of the Lido, and for centuries have supplied Venice with delicious fresh vegetables, notably *spareselle* and *castradure* (slender green asparagus and baby artichokes, obtainable at the Erberia ▲ *284*). For centuries Le Vignole and Sant' Erasmo were used as summer resorts; today the Venetians still like to go on excursions to them by boat, and maybe take a meal in one of the taverns. Of the two, only SANT' ERASMO is open to visitors; it is also larger than its neighbor. These huge market gardening centers used to be surrounded with fortifications, the size of which can be gauged by the ruins of the so-called TOWER OF MAXIMILIAN. The islands played their part in the general defensive plan of Venice, as did the FORT OF SANT'ANDREA, built in the 16th century by the brilliant state architect Sanmicheli. His stout Renaissance bastions, designed to impede a sea-borne attack, are now in a woeful state of repair and in some places have completely collapsed. Also worthy of mention are the islands of MADONNA DEL MONTE and SAN GIACOMO IN PALUDO (visible from the Murano–Burano vaporetto), which little by little have sunk into the Lagoon. No trace remains of the monasteries that once stood on them – the ruins you see are of a gunpowder magazine and a military barracks dating from the 18th and 19th centuries.

Lazzaretto Nuovo.

" The Lagoon and the mist swallowed up all shapes and all colors. Only the groups of worshippers stood out against the grey monotony of the scene: they looked like monks moving along a way covered in ashes. **"**
Gabriele d'Annunzio, *Fire*

San Lazzaro
degli Armeni.

LAZZARETTO NUOVO. Hermits were the first permanent inhabitants of this island, before 1486 when it became a *lazzaretto* (quarantine station) where goods that might carry infection from their country of origin were stored. In 1576, about ten thousand people were isolated here, and those who developed the plague were transferred to the Lazzaretto Vecchio. Next the island was completely evacuated until the 19th century, when it became a military site with a fortress. Since then, it has been overwhelmed by wild vegetation and today the buildings on it are steadily falling into ruin.

THE SOUTHERN LAGOON

SAN LAZZARO DEGLI ARMENI. A monastery has survived on this island (left), which was much loved by Lord Byron. Indeed it is one of the few places in or around Venice that has not been altered from its original function over the years. Monks first arrived here during the 12th century and built a leper colony. After that, the island was more or less abandoned until 1717, when the Venetian Republic gave it to the Armenian monk Manug de Pierre, known as Mechitar the Consoler ▲ *329*, who had escaped from the Turks. Mechitar founded a new community on the site, using and adapting the existing buildings. Today, about thirty fathers and seminarists live permanently in the monastery, whose goal is to preserve Armenian culture. There is a museum in the monastery, a picture gallery, a late 18th-century printing press which is the only one of its kind in the world and a rich library containing more than 150,000 volumes and also a precious collection of illuminated manuscripts. All around it is a huge garden, where peacocks wander among the rare flowers and plants.

SAN CLEMENTE AND SAN SERVOLO. These two islands, whose history is linked to religious orders, are among those which were, until recently, used for hospital and quarantine purposes. SAN CLEMENTE (above) was once the site of a charity hospital and a stopping place for pilgrims to the Holy Land; later it was changed into a hermitage. A number of distinguished guests of the Republic have stayed here, most

"We slipped along a narrow canal, past half-drowned land and rotted greenery, from which great birds rose and flapped away. All around us were poles standing in the water to direct the boatmen: they looked like marks left on a sublime painting, to guide some inept copyist."
Maurice Barrès,
La Mort de Venise

LORD BYRON
A complete room in the museum of San Lazzaro degli Armeni is devoted to Lord Byron, who regularly visited the convent in order to study the Armenian language.

SAN CLEMENTE
This aerial photograph clearly shows the walls built along the edge of the island against the sea. The buildings were all erected after 1834.

Isla della Grazia.

notably the Duke of Mantua who brought the plague with him in 1630. After this, the island was used as a powder magazine, until, in 1834, the Austrian government had the idea of turning it into a lunatic asylum, which was nevertheless closed down a few years afterwards. A Benedictine monastery was established on SAN SERVOLO during the 8th century, but in the first half of the 18th century this was turned into a psychiatric institution. Today its buildings are empty; they stand within a large park planted with trees and flowers which has been left in a state of complete abandon. Since 1977 the island has housed a center for training craftsmen in the restoration of historic monuments.

SANTA MARIA DELLA GRAZIA OR DELLA CAVANA. Santa Maria is linked to San Zaccaria by a vaporetto service. Formerly it too offered shelter to pilgrims on their way to or from the Holy Land. Later, churches and monasteries were built here, but after their abolition by Napoleon a powder magazine and then a hospital were built in their place. Today, the hospital of Santa Maria della Grazia still specializes in the treatment of infectious diseases.

LAZZARETTO VECCHIO. Lazzaretto Vecchio used to have its own church dedicated to St Mary of Nazareth (whose name was distorted first into *nazaretum*, then into *lazzaretto*). It was a quarantine station for plague victims during the first great epidemic of the 14th century. Later it was used as a military depot, before being abandoned in the early 19th century. Today it is a center for stray dogs, which is financed and run by volunteers.

The islands of the Lazzaretto Vecchio, facing the Lido, were once a haven for pilgrims en route to the Holy Land.

SANTO SPIRITO AND POVEGLIA. These two islands, which lie opposite the Lido behind San Clemente and La Grazia, once possessed some great art treasures. SANTO SPIRITO, today little more than a wasteland, had a church designed by Sansovino which was decorated with works by Palma the Elder and Titian, masterpieces that are now, for the most part, to be seen in the church of La Salute ▲ *318*. Like Poveglia, it was variously used during the last two centuries as a barracks and munitions depot, and today it is dismally run-down.

POVEGLIA, a former residence of the Doge's entourage which was abandoned in the 14th century, looks altogether better, with well-maintained gardens and vineyards. At the tip of the island stands a curious octagonal construction, formerly a part of the defensive system installed throughout the Lagoon by the Venetian government.

PRACTICAL INFORMATION

Marco Polo Airport
Santa Lucia Station
Piazzale Roma
(left to right)

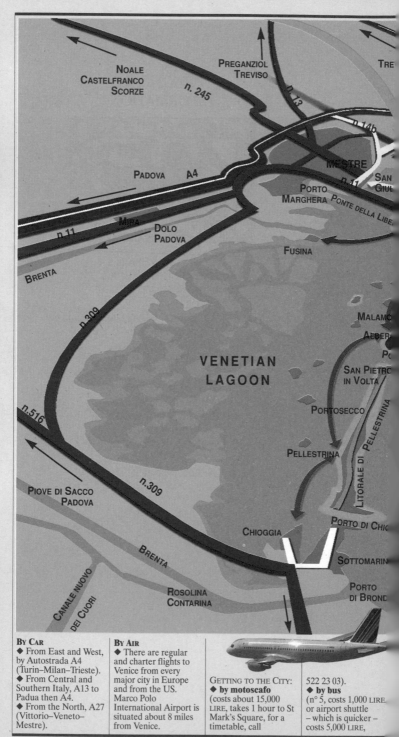

NOALE
CASTELFRANCO
SCORZE

PREGANZIOL
TREVISO

TRE

n. 245

n. 13

n. 14b

MESTRE

PADOVA   A4

SAN
GIU

PORTO
MARGHERA

n. 11

PONTE DELLA LIBE

MIRA

n 11

DOLO
PADOVA

FUSINA

BRENTA

n. 309

MALAMO

ALBER

P

SAN PIETRO
IN VOLTA

VENETIAN
LAGOON

PORTOSECCO

LITORALE DI PELLESTRINA

n.516

PELLESTRINA

PIOVE DI SACCO
PADOVA

n.309

PORTO DI CHIO

CHIOGGIA

SOTTOMARIN

BRENTA

PORTO
DI BROND

CANALE NUOVO
DEI CUORI

ROSOLINA
CONTARINA

BY CAR
◆ From East and West, by Autostrada A4 (Turin–Milan–Trieste).
◆ From Central and Southern Italy, A13 to Padua then A4.
◆ From the North, A27 (Vittorio–Veneto–Mestre).

BY AIR
◆ There are regular and charter flights to Venice from every major city in Europe and from the US. Marco Polo International Airport is situated about 8 miles from Venice.

GETTING TO THE CITY:
◆ **by motoscafo** (costs about 15,000 LIRE, takes 1 hour to St Mark's Square, for a timetable, call

522 23 03).
◆ **by bus** (n° 5, costs 1,000 LIRE. or airport shuttle – which is quicker – costs 5,000 LIRE,

TRIESTE A27 A4

SAN DONA DI PIAVE

SAN DONA DI PIAVE

SILE

n.14

JESOLO

LIDO DI JESOLO

MARCO POLO AIRPORT

TORCELLO

CAVALLINO

MURANO

BURANO

TREPORTI

LITORALE DI CAVALLINO

SAN ERASMO

CA SAVIO

VENICE

LIDO

PORTO DI LIDO

LITORALE DI LIDO

ALAMOCCO

Crossing	Line	Embark	Time in mins
Venice–Murano	52	P.le Roma	71
	52	Fond. Nuove	7
Venice–Burano	12	Fond. Nuove	42
Venice–Torcello	12/14	Fond. Nuove	47
Murano–Burano	12		35
Burano–Torcello	14		5
Venice–Lido	1	P.le Roma	60
	1	San Marco	20
Venice–Lido	52	P.le Roma	35
	52	San Marco	15
Venice–Lido	6	Schiavoni	15
Venice–Lido (Ferry)	17	Tronchetto	35
Venice–Lido	34	San Marco	20
Venice–San Giorgio Maggiore	82	San Zaccaria	3
Venice–Giudecca	82	San Zaccaria	11
	82	Zattere	2
San Giorgio Maggiore–Giudecca	82		3
Venice–Sant'Erasmo	13	Fond. Nuove	29
Venice–San Lazzaro degli Armeni	10	Schiavoni	15

TRAVEL INFORMATION
INFORMATION OFFICE :
Piazzale Roma
Tel. 528 78 86
Open 8am to 4pm
Monday to Friday
Closed 2.30pm
Saturday and Sunday

RAIL INFORMATION :
Santa Lucia Station
and Mestre
Tel. 71 55 55
Open 7.10am to
9.30pm

FLIGHT INFORMATION :
Marco Polo Airport
Tel. 66 12 62
Airline: Italtravel, San
Marco 72/b
Tel. 522 91 11
Tel. 523 65 11
Tel. 523 64 24

TAXIS :
Radio taxi
Tel. 523 23 26

BICYCLE RENTALS :
– Bruno Lazzari,
Gran Viale Santa
Maria Elisabetta,
Lido 21/b
Tel. 526 80 19
Open 9am to 7.30pm
Closed Monday
– Giorgio Barbieri,
Via Zara, Lido 5
Tel. 526 14 90
Open 8.30am to 8pm
daily
Closed in winter

departs every hour to Piazzale Roma).
◆ **by water-taxi** (to the centre of Venice, costs about 83,000 LIRE)

BY TRAIN
(takes 24 hours from London, costs

from £160 for second class and £229 for first class; a sleeping berth costs from £41.20).
There is also the Orient Express, which departs from London (takes 22 hours), and travels via Switzerland

and Austria.
All trains arrive at Santa Lucia Station, which is situated in the heart of Venice.
◆ From the station, take either the vaporetto n° 1 or the motoscafo n° 2 to St Mark's Square.

A

B

ACCADEMIA (C4) : *1-34*
ARSENALE (E4) : *1*
BURANO (H1) : *12 - 14*
CASINÒ (G6) : *11*
CA' D'ORO (D3) : *1*
CA' REZZONICO (C4) : *1*
CIMITERO (D2) : *52 Rossa-52 Verde*
CELESTIA (E3) : *52 Rossa*
COLONNA (D2) : *52 Rossa-52 Verde*
FARO (D2) : *52 Rossa - 52 Verde -12-13*
FERROVIA (B3) : *1 - 34 - 2*
52 Blu - 52 Rossa - 52 Verde
82 Blu - 82 Rossa
FONDAMENTA NUOVE (D2) : *24 -*
13 - 12 - 52 Rossa - 52 Verde
GIARDINI (E4) : *1*
G. BIENNALE (F5) : *34*

C

GUGLIE (C3) : *52 Rossa - 52 Verde*
MADONNA DELL'ORTO (D2) :
52 Rossa - 52 Verde
MAZZORBO (H2) : *12*
MUSEO (D2) : *52 Rossa - 52 Verde*
NAVAGERO (E2) : *52 Rossa - 52 Verde*
OSPEDALE (D3) : *52 Rossa*
PIAZZALE ROMA (B2) :
52 Blu - 52 Rossa - 52 Verde
82 Blu - 82 Rossa - 1 - 34 - 2
PALANCA (C5) : *82 Verde - 82 Rossa*
PUNTA SABBIONI (H3) : *14 - 17*
REDENTORE (D5) : *34*
82 Verde - 82 Rossa

D

RIALTO (D3) : *82 Verde*
82 Rossa
RIVA DI BIASIO (C3) :
SACCA FISOLA (B5)
82 Verde - 82 Rossa
SALUTE (D4) : *1*
SERENELLA (D2) :
52 Verde - 52 Rossa
S. ALVISE (C2) :
52 Verde - 52 Rossa

Vaporetto
The most used lines are numbers 1, 82, 52 and 12.
The term vaporetto covers three types of vessel.

◆ **The vaporetto** is slow and stops all along the Grand Canal.

◆ **The motoscafo** is lower in the water and slightly faster than the vaporetto. It stops less frequently – for example, one route travels from Piazzale Roma to the Lido, stopping at San Marco.

◆ **The motonave** is much larger and more imposing. It resembles a small passenger steamer and is used for longer crossings – to the Lido or Punta Sabbioni, for example.

FARES :
◆ The ordinary fare is between 2,500 LIRE and 3,500 LIRE per trip.
◆ *Giornaliero* (day) tickets are valid for 24

hours after first use on all lines except 52.
They cost 14,000 LIRE.
◆ Three-day passes are valid for 72 hours after first use on all lines except the 52. They cost 20,000 LIRE.

E	**F**	**G**	**H**

S. ANGELO (C4) : 1
S. BASILIO (B4) : 82 Verde - 82 Rossa
S. CLEMENTE (D5) : 10
S. ELENA (F5) : 2 - 1
52 Blu - 52 Verde - 52 Rossa - 14
S. ERASMO (H2) : 13
S. GIORGIO (D4) : 82 Verde - 82 Rossa
S. GIULIANO : 24
S. LAZZARO (F6) : 20
S. MARCO (D4) : 82 Rossa - 1
S. MARCUOLA (C3) : 82 Rossa - 1 - 34
S. MARIA DEL GIGLIO (D4) : 1
S. MARIA ELISABETTA (G5) : 1 - 2 - 6 - 11 - 34
52 Blu - 52 Verde - 52 Rossa - 14
S. MARTA (A4) :
52 Verde - 52 Rossa - 82 Verde
S. NICOLÓ (G5) : 17
S. SAMUELE (C4) : 82 Rossa - 2 - 34

S. SERVOLO (E5) : 20
S. SILVESTRO (C3) : 1
S. TOMÀ (C4) : 82 Rossa - 1 - 34
S. STAE (C3) : 1
S. ZACCARIA (D4) : 1 - 2 - 6 - 10 - 14 - 20
52 Verde - 52 Rossa - 82 Rossa - 82 Verde
TANA (E4) : 52 Rossa
TRAGHETTO (C4) : 9 - 16
82 Rossa - 82 Verde
TRONCHETTO A (B3) : 82 Rossa - 1 - 34
TRONCHETTO B (A3) : 17
TORCELLO (H2) : 14
TRE ARCHI (B2) : 52 Verde - 52 Rossa
TREPORTI (H3) : 14
VENIER (D2) : 52 Verde - 52 Rossa
VIGNOLE (G3) : 13
ZATTERE (C4) : 52 Verde - 52 Rossa
ZITELLE (D5) : 82 Rossa - 82 Verde

◆ Three-day youth passes (*Tre Giorni Giovane*) may only be obtained from an office on the Piazzale Roma and are reserved for the holders of youth cards (Municipal or Rolling/Venice ◆ 395). They are valid for 72 hours from first use on all lines except 2 and 28. They cost 16,000 LIRE.

◆ The *Tessera Convegnisti*, card (valid for 8 days) is reserved for conference participants and offers reductions on all lines except 2.

◆ The *Carta Venezia* (valid for 3 years) offers reductions of 50 or 60 percent on vaporetti and other forms of transportation on Venice's canals. Photographs and identity papers are required to obtain this card. Tickets and cards are available from the A.C.T.V. offices on Piazza San Marco (number 38880), the Fondamente Nuove, and the Lido.

Venice is the regional capital of the Veneto. With Mestre, Marghera and the islands of the Lagoon, it covers 178 square miles, of which 100 are water and 78 are dry land. Its population is 312,000 (40 percent of the total population of the Veneto) and includes 76,000 residents of Venice proper, 45,000 on the islands of the Lagoon and 191,000 on the mainland. For the last 30 years, younger people have been steadily moving out of Venice to the mainland because they simply cannot afford the city's high rents. As a result, the average age of Venetians is now about 46. By the year 2000, it is thought that the population will have fallen to about 50,000 people. Venice's official language is Italian, but a Venetian dialect is also spoken.

THE VENETIAN ECONOMY

Local AGRICULTURE is concentrated on cereals and market gardening, with livestock rearing very much a secondary occupation. The FISHING INDUSTRY, once one of the area's most characteristic features, is currently in steep decline. The principal INDUSTRIAL SECTORS are chemicals, metallurgy, engineering and shipbuilding. Building and glass manufacture remain small-scale, while PORT ACTIVITY has suffered from a decline in traffic. Venice's TOURIST INDUSTRY plays a major part in the economy, but has fallen off a great deal in recent years.

GONDOLAS

A GONDOLA RIDE lasts between 30 and 50 minutes, with a maximum of 5 passengers. The PRICE is calculated as a flat fee and is not based on the number of passengers – so it is definitely open to negotiation. In principle, gondola fares are regulated as follows: 70,000 lire for 45 minutes, 40,000 lire for each extra 30 minutes, 80,000 lire at night (between 8pm and 8am). Points at which gondolas may be hired, and their telephone numbers if you wish to reserve are:
Bacino Orseolo Tel. 528 93 16; Calle Valaresso Tel. 520 61 20; San Marco Tel. 520 06 85; Hotel Danieli Tel. 522 22 54; Ferrovia Tel. 71 85 43; Santa Maria del Giglio Tel. 522 20 73; San Tomà Tel. 520 52 75; Campo San Moisè Tel. 523 18 37; Rialto Riva del Carbon Tel. 522 49 04.

TRAGHETTO S. SOFIA

TRAGHETTO

The traghetto is a gondola-ferry used by Venetians to cross the Grand Canal. There are 7 traghetto embarkation points, indicated by yellow signs in the streets beside the Grand Canal. Traghetti link Santa Maria del Giglio and La Salute, San Samuele and Ca' Rezzonico, Sant'Angelo and San Toma, Riva del Carbon and San Silvestro, Santa Sofia (Ca' d'Oro) and Pescheria (Rialto), San Marcuola and Fondaco dei Turchi, and the railway station and Fondamenta San Simeon Piccolo.

WATER TAXI FARES

In the center of Venice, the first 7 minutes in a water taxi cost 27,000 lire, after which the meter adds 450 lire every 15 seconds. These fares do not include the various supplements which are charged.

WATER TAXIS
Central tel: 522 23 03
TAXI STATIONS:
◆ Piazzale Roma
Tel. 71 69 22

◆ Ferrovia
Tel. 71 61 24
◆ Rialto
Tel. 523 05 75
◆ San Marco

Tel. 522 97 50
◆ Lido
Tel. 526 00 49
◆ Airport
Tel. 54 15 084

1030

STREET NUMBERS

In Venice, the numbering of houses in streets is organized in a most original fashion. Each sestiere has its own numbers, and there can be anything up to 5,000 or 6,000 of them. Hence it is advisable to take in as much information as possible in advance about the place to which you are going.

1029

SESTIERE DI S. MARCO

The term *sestiere* is applied to the six sections of Venice. This administrative division of the city dates from 1170.

PAROCHIA S. CANZIAN

The *parochia* (*parrocchia* in Italian) is a parish. During the time of the Republic, Venice had seventy *parrochie* .

CAMPO S. BARTOLOMEO

The open squares of Venice are known as *campi* (fields). The term *piazza* is exclusive to San Marco.

CAMPIELLO DEL MAGAZEN

A *campiello* is a small square (*piazzetta* elsewhere in Italy).

SALIZADA S. ANTONIN

A *salizada* (*salizzada* in Italian) is a main thoroughfare paved from the outset, in contrast to the *calli*, which were not.

CALLE LARGA XXII MARZO

Calle means "street" in Venetian (*via* or *strada* in Italian). Thus a *calletta* is a narrow street.

RIVA DEGLI SCHIAVONI

The *riva* is a quayside. It is broader than a *fondamenta*, and was formerly a place where big ships could berth.

RAMO LICINI

A *ramo* is a very short *calle*, usually leading to a dead end.

FONDAMENTA DELLO SQUERO

A *fondamenta* is a quay running alongside a canal.

PISCINA DE FREZZARIA

A *piscina* is an arm of the Lagoon, first surrounded with buildings and then filled in, where children once came to bathe.

RIO DE S. VIDAL

The term *rio* applies to all Venice's lesser canals.

RIO TERRÀ ANTONIO FOSCARINI

A *rio terrà* is a canal that has been filled in and turned into a street.

CORTE MUAZZO

The *corte* is a public courtyard, shared by several houses; a *cortile*, on the other hand, is the inner courtyard of a palace.

SOTOPORTEGO DE LA SCRIMIA

A *sotoportego* (*sottoportego* in Italian) is a covered public passage.

The Venetian is a vanishing species, in contrast to the tourist, who is on the increase. While the tourist spends his time ferreting out the picturesque and is not averse to meeting the Venetian – when he does not actively seek his company – the Venetian will take secret, timesaving shortcuts around his town (known as *sconte*) which may not be beautiful but are certainly effective. An ambivalent relationship exists between Venetians and tourists, each side having something to gain and something to lose from the association. One need only think of pedestrian traffic blocks in the city's narrow calli, the vaporetti stuffed with passengers and the overcrowded restaurants to appreciate the frustration of the locals in high season.

IF YOU DO NOT WANT TO LOOK LIKE A TOURIST IN VENICE:
– Never wear a light, transparent nylon raincoat.
– Do not go about in bathing suits and beachwear. Venice is not a holiday resort.
– Do not allow yourself to be fleeced in the bars and restaurants of the Rialto or St Mark's Square.
– Do not under any circumstances allow yourself to be seen in one of the shops that purport to sell blown glass and genuine Venetian masks.
– Do not linger by the souvenir stalls on the Piazzale Roma.

– If you must buy a silver gondola with a music box inside it, do so discreetly.
– Do not sit down anywhere you please on the steps of churches and bridges.
– Avoid drinking your can of Coke leaning against a Renaissance well.
– Make sure that your enthusiasm for picturesque details or studying your map of Venice does not hold up the traffic.

IF YOU WANT TO EMULATE THE VENETIAN:
– Do your shopping at the Rialto, or in the supermarket at Mestre.
– When you go to a bar with your friends, order an *ombra*.
– At times of *acqua alta*, wrap your feet in black garbage bags and carry your shoes in your hands.
– Walk in zig-zag fashion, with one eye

on the ground (dogs, rubbish) and the other on the sky (pigeons).

evenings (either watch television or read a book in your hotel).
– Go fishing along the

– Be at the Campo Santa Lucia punctually at 11am for the ritual of the Venetian civil service coffee break.
– Stay home in the

Zattere and the quays of the Giudecca, under the admiring eyes of the tourists; better still, go fishing in the far from tempting *seragia*.

Products for the Venetian markets arrive by boat.

KIOSKS

The main local papers are the *Gazzettino*, Venice's highest circulation daily, the *Nuova Venezia*, another daily, and *Marco Polo*, a monthly review devoted to the city and carrying a theater and cinema section.

MARKETS

Most of Venice's markets are concentrated around the Rialto. They include the Erberia, where herbs, fruit and flowers are sold wholesale and retail, and where prices are lower than elsewhere, and the fishmarket on the Campo della Pescheria. Markets are also held on other campi in the mornings, while a barge anchored at San Barnaba offers fruit and vegetables daily.

(left) The traditional way of transporting goods through the Venetian streets.

(right) The Pescheria fish market.

1,200 Lire — Coffee

1,200 to 1,600 Lire — Cappuccino

500 to 1,500 Lire — Ombra (glass of wine)

1,500 Lire — Tramezzino (sandwich)

3,000 to 10,000 Lire — Museum

25,000 to 100,000 lire — An evening out at La Fenice

30,000 to 80,000 lire or more — Evening meal

70,000 to 200,000 lire or more — Double room in a hotel

Prices in Venice vary widely quarter by quarter, reflecting the tourists' relative affluence. Restaurants range from the very reasonable to the super expensive – an average "menu turistico" should work out between 20,000 and 30,000 lire per head. For a night in a double room with breakfast included, the price should be between 100,000 and 150,000 lire near Santa Lucia Station, but will be between 600,000 and 700,000 lire a night at the Hotel Danieli, with its view across the Lagoon.

POST OFFICE

Venice's central post office is at 80100 Fondaco dei Tedeschi, near the Rialto.

A postcard will cost about 700 lire to send, a letter 750 (850 lire for countries outside the EC). It costs 3,950 lire to send a registered letter and 3,750 lire for an express letter.

CURRENCY AND CHANGE

There are denominations of 100,000 lire, 50,000 lire, 2,000 lire and 1,000 lire. The banks open from Monday to Friday between 8.30am and 1.20pm. Exchange bureaux (*cambio*) observe the same opening hours as the shops – queues are not so long as at the banks and exchange rates are roughly the same.

CASHPOINTS

Beware, there is only one automatic cash dispenser in Venice, located on Calle Larga XXII Marzo. Money can be changed at the American Express offices (San Marco 1471). Hotels will accept traveler's checks but always extract a high commission on them.

50 LIRE
Smaller coins are rare.

100 LIRE

It is worth remembering that 200 lire telephone tokens are also accepted as change, and that some coins of very small value are no longer in circulation.

TELEPHONES

Phone booths can be found in the center of town, but in general it is more convenient to place international calls from a public telephone center, where payment is made at the cash desk when the call is completed. These centers are located beside the main post office on Fondaco dei Tedeschi (open daily from 8am to 7.45pm), near the Rialto (Ruga Vecchia San Giovanni), in the Santa Lucia railway station, and at the SIP (telephone company) building on Piazzale Roma.

THE PRICE OF A TELEPHONE CALL

VENICE	3 MIN	+3 MIN
ROME (06)	1235 LIRE	735 LIRE
VENICE	2 SEC	+1 MIN
FRANCE (00 33)	508 LIRE	1 378 LIRE
GERMANY (00 49)	508 LIRE	1 378 LIRE
GREAT BRITIAN (00 44)	508 LIRE	1 524 LIRE
UNITED STATES (00 01)	508 LIRE	3 110 LIRE
JAPAN (00 81)	508 LIRE	4 010 LIRE

TO MAKE A CALL:

◆ From the UK to Venice: dial 010 + 39 + 41 + the number you require.
◆ From Venice to the UK: dial 00 + 44 + the number you require.
◆ From the USA to Venice: dial 011 + 39 + 41 + the number you require.
◆ From Venice to the USA: dial 00 + 01 + the number you require.
◆ For collect calls from Venice: dial 15 or 170.
For Directory Enquiries, dial 12.

Phone booths work with 200 lire pieces, phone tokens and telephone cards.

200 LIRE

TELEPHONE CARDS

These can be purchased in post offices, bars, tobacconists, some newsagents' kiosks, at the station and at the SIP (telephone company) building.

YOUTH CARD

Distributed free of charge and strictly non-transferable, the *carta giovani* offers visitors aged 14 to 29 reductions in cinemas, museums, and some shops and restaurants. The *carta giovani* is issued by tourist offices in the city.

YOUTH CARD/ROLLING VENICE

A card for those aged 14–29 which costs between 5,000 and 10,000 lire and offers a number of advantages, notably price reductions for hotels and other facilities.
500 LIRE For further information call 270 76 50.

FESTIVALS & EVENTS

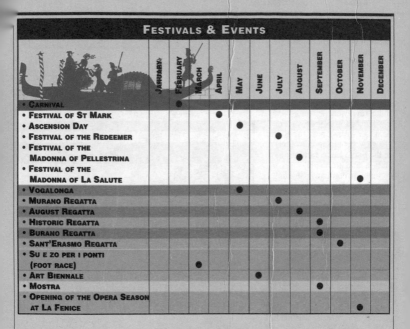

	JANUARY	FEBRUARY	MARCH	APRIL	MAY	JUNE	JULY	AUGUST	SEPTEMBER	OCTOBER	NOVEMBER	DECEMBER
• CARNIVAL		●										
• FESTIVAL OF ST MARK				●								
• ASCENSION DAY					●							
• FESTIVAL OF THE REDEEMER							●					
• FESTIVAL OF THE MADONNA OF PELLESTRINA								●				
• FESTIVAL OF THE MADONNA OF LA SALUTE											●	
• VOGALONGA					●							
• MURANO REGATTA							●					
• AUGUST REGATTA								●				
• HISTORIC REGATTA									●			
• BURANO REGATTA									●			
• SANT'ERASMO REGATTA										●		
• SU E ZO PER I PONTI (FOOT RACE)			●									
• ART BIENNALE						●						
• MOSTRA									●			
• OPENING OF THE OPERA SEASON AT LA FENICE											●	

HOLIDAYS
January 1, January 6 (*La Befana*), Easter Monday, April 25 (Feast of St Mark)
May 1, August 15 (*Ferragosto*), November 1, December 8, December 25, December 26.

HUMIDITY AND RAINFALL

60%												10 days
40%												8 days
												6 days
												4 days
												2 days
30%												0 days
J	F	M	A	M	J	J	A	S	O	N	D	

It is best to visit Venice in the fall or in the spring, thus avoiding the summer heat – and the summer crowds. The *acqua alta* occurs in summer and winter, and when it does everybody gets their feet wet.

MAXIMUM AND MINIMUM TEMPERATURES

30°C												30°C
25°												25°
20°												20°
15°												15°
10°												10°
5°												5°
0°												
-5°												
J	F	M	A	M	J	J	A	S	O	N	D	

The lunar calendar for 1994 should help choose the ideal night for a cruise along the Grand Canal, when the moon is shining at its brightest.

SAVING VENICE
After the catastrophic *acqua alta* of 1966, a group of international associations took part in an effort to preserve Venice, notably by financing the restoration of monuments and artworks. Among these associations were:

ARBEITSKREIS VENEDIG DER DEUTSCHEN UNESCO KOMMISION

ASSOCIAZIONE AMICI DEI MUSEI E MONUMENTI VENEZIANI

ASSOCIAZIONE VENEZIA NOSTRA

PRO VENEZIA SWEDEN

SAVE VENICE INC. N.Y.

STICHTING NEDERLANDS VENETIE COMITE

SAUVONS VENISE, COMITÉ FRANÇAIS POUR LA SAUVEGARDE DE VENISE

THE VENICE IN PERIL FUND

Gondolas and water taxis at the Rialto, ready for a tour of the Grand Canal.

8AM. After leaving your train or car, go to the center of town either by gondola, by water taxi (very expensive) or by the more prosaic vaporetto (line 82). This itinerary will take you past two and a half miles of palaces ▲ *187*, and under the arch of the Rialto Bridge to the landing-stage of St Mark's Square at the foot of the Doge's Palace.

10AM. Visit the galleries of the Accademia, where the collections offer the most complete panorama of Venetian painting in existence ▲ *301*. In particular, look out for the work of Giovanni Bellini, Carpaccio (15th-century), Titian, Veronese (16th-century), all of whom are fully represented – among many others.

12PM. Stop to have a drink and listen to the street music while sitting on the terrace of the Florian, the famous café which was once a favorite haunt of both Balzac and Byron.

A single day spent in Venice will be long enough to leave an unforgettable impression, provided you conform to the city's special pace.

2PM. Facing St Mark's Square – "the World's most beautiful drawing room" – is the magnificent Gothic façade of the Doge's Palace ▲ *224*. Inside, the successive galleries recount the story of the Serene Republic of Venice. The adjoining Basilica of St Mark's ▲ *234*, Gabriele D'Annunzio's "deep golden cave", awaits you with its 43,057 square feet of exquisite mosaics.

5PM. A walk along the Zattere ▲ *321* will allow you the chance to sample the ice creams of the *gianduiotto*, at Nico Gelati ◆ *442*.

8PM. Complete the day with dinner at La Caravella ◆ *424* (the *risotta alle seppie* is highly recommended) or at Trattoria alla Colomba ◆ *422* (rather more expensive, but full of paintings by Chagall, de Chirico and Picasso).

10PM. Walk out to the Punta della Dogana (Customs House Point) beyond Longhena's architectural masterpiece, La Salute ▲ *214, 318*, for a final and magnificent view of St Mark's Square.

FIRST DAY. Try and stay in the Hotel Danieli, situated right beside the Doge's Palace, the reputation (and extremely high prices) of which are certainly justified by the spectacular view of St Mark's Basin that it offers from its windows. We suggest that you have breakfast at Harry's Bar, which was Ernest Hemingway's favorite Venetian watering hole. If you decide to visit the monuments of St Mark's Square on your first day ▲ *220*, make sure that you do not miss the Correr Museum ▲ *246* (open from 9am to 2pm), where the collections of Venetian paintings and Renaissance porcelain are uniquely beautiful.

12PM. Stop off for an aperitif in one of the typical Venetian *bacari*. These friendly wine bars are mostly to be found in the San Polo sestiere ◆ *409*. Order an *ombra* and some *cicchetti*.

8PM. Attend a performance at La Fenice ▲ *262*, Venice's fabled opera house. Afterwards, have dinner at the Al Teatro restaurant ◆ *422* which is located nearby. If you have sufficient energy after all of this, you may wish to go dancing at Martini's ◆ *425*, a nightclub which stays open until 4am.

If you only have two days to spend in Venice, this itinerary should suffice to lure you back on another occasion.

SECOND DAY. Leaving St Mark's Square by way of Riva degli Schiavoni, walk down to the magnificent gateway of the Arsenal ▲ *177* (Note that the Arsenal is a restricted military zone, and so entry is prohibited). The landing stage for vaporetto line 52 is nearby. From here, take the boat across the basin called "Rio delle Galleazze" and then you will get some idea of the scale of Venice's naval installations.

12PM. Leave the vaporetto at the next halt and have lunch at La Corte Sconta ◆ *417*, a restaurant which owes its reputation to the wide variety of its Venetian specialities. If you then take vaporetto line 82 in the opposite direction, you will eventually arrive at the Giudecca, from which the view of St Mark's Basilica and the rest of the city is quite spectacular. On your walk around the island, make sure you do not miss Palladio's masterpiece, the Church of Il Redentore ▲ *338*, which was built in gratitude to Christ for bringing an end to the plague of 1576 (an epidemic which wiped out twenty-five percent of the Venetian population). The church contains a number of remarkable paintings, among them Veronese's *Baptism of Christ*. Continuing to walk in the same direction, stop at the Church of Sant'Eufemia ▲ *337*, before relaxing at Harry's Dolci.

8PM. By the time that you get back to the San Zaccaria landing-stage on the Riva degli Schiavoni, you will certainly have earned dinner at the piano bar of the Londra Palace hotel ◆ *419*.

THE ARSENAL
The power of the Venetian Republic lay in its mastery of shipbuilding and of the use of naval and commercial vessels. When the Republic finally collapsed, the Arsenal effectively ceased to exist as a working entity.

VENICE SEEN FROM ABOVE
When you arrive on St Mark's Square, climb to the top of the great campanile. The view of St Mark's Basin and the city is incomparable. The view of the Lagoon and the gardens of the Giudecca from the campanile of San Giorgio Maggiore is equally spectacular.

MONDAY. If you want to avoid spending too much money on accommodation, opt for one of the smaller, centrally located pensiones, such as La Fiorita. From the station, go down the Grand Canal ▲ *187* by vaporetto. Venice's main throughfare is bordered on either side by the city's principal palaces. Disembark at the Doge's Palace, and explore the only official piazza in Venice, Piazza San Marco (St Mark's Square). Do not miss the basilica ▲ *234*, with its 43,000 square feet of mosaics and the sensational Pala d'Oro. Next, do the conventional round of the Doge's Palace, which offers an insight into Venetian government through the ages ▲ *224*, or better, do the "secret" tour which goes up to the Leads prison ▲ *252*. Even if you have not read Casanova's account of his escape from here, this is still a unique experience. Afterwards, drop in at the Florian or the Quadri ▲ *245, 246* for a restorative drink, remembering that these venerable but expensive 18th-century cafés are seldom visited by the natives nowadays. From here walk through the Merceria to the Rialto ▲ *279*, Venice's principal commercial center and one of the liveliest quarters.

TUESDAY. Set aside the whole morning for the galleries of the Accademia, with its stunning selection of Venetian masterpieces ▲ *301*. Lunch nearby at the Antica Locanda Montin ◆ *429*, then walk on to Santa Maria della Salute, a basilica built after the great plague ▲ *318*, the city's most beautiful Baroque church and well worth the detour. You may wish to inspect one of the oldest *squeri* (gondola construction yards) still active in Venice ▲ *324*, which you will find on the corner of Rio San Trovaso and Rio Ognissanti after a walk past the bars and restaurants of the Zattere. An alternative would be a walk to one of the peripheral quarters of Dorsoduro, the Mendicoli. Here, the charming Church of San Nicolò gave its name to one of the two factions of old Venice, the Nicolotti ▲ *327*, who were always brawling in the streets with their rivals, the Castellani ▲ *334*.

WEDNESDAY. Begin with a tour of the Ghetto ▲ *140*, which is remarkable for the unusual tallness of its buildings (some are nine stories high). On your way through Castello, do not miss the Church of Santi Giovanni e Paolo ▲ *157*, a veritable pantheon of Venice's past glories. San Giorgio degli Schiavoni, originally the scuola of Venice's Dalmatian inhabitants, contains Carpaccio's wonderful St Ursula series ▲ *162*; this is a must. From here, continue on foot to the Arsenal ▲ *177*, the symbol of Venice's maritime power. The Arsenal is off-limits to the public, but may be viewed from the no. 52 vaporetto which crosses it. The Naval Museum here offers an excellent resumé of the history of the Venetian and Italian navies, with more than 25,000 items on display ▲ 180. After Via Garibaldi, cross the small bridge to the island of San Pietro, where you should visit the church (once the seat of Venice's bishops) and the public gardens containing the pavilions of the Biennale.

THURSDAY. A visit to the basilica of the Frari, another shrine to Venice's past glory, is essential ▲ 292. The Frari contains two major features – Titian's majestic *Assumption* ▲ 293, ◆ 406, and the monks' stalls which are the only ones of their kind in Venice. No one should visit Venice without seeing paintings by Tintoretto – and there are no fewer than fifty works by this painter at the Scuola Grande di San Rocco ▲ 294. After this make your way to Campo Santa Margherita ▲ 330 – one of the liveliest spots in Venice – and have a coffee before moving on to the Church of San Pantalon, where the ceiling is covered by the largest picture ever painted on canvas ▲ 331. When you finally reach the Zattere, take the motoscafo to the Giudecca, which was formerly a resort of the Venetian nobility. Do not miss the Church of Il Redentore, Palladio's masterwork ▲ 338. And after this, if you still have the energy, press on to the "Green Island" of San Giorgio Maggiore, with its monastery and church ▲ 340.

FRIDAY. Set aside the whole day for a tour of the Lagoon islands, starting with TORCELLO (ideally, spend Thursday night at the Locanda Cipriani on Torcello ▲ 441). In the morning, tour the Cathedral of Santa Maria Assunta, with its mural mosaics and *Last Judgement* ▲ 375. On BURANO, note the brightly colored houses along the canals. This is a perfect place to wander in the sunshine, with no particular objective ▲ 370. When you reach MURANO ▲ 364, by all means visit a glassblowing factory, but be sure not to miss the island's most beautiful building, the Church of Santa Maria e San Donato. The apse and pavement alone are worth the trip.

SATURDAY. Between May and October, take a *burchiello* along the Brenta (embark from St Mark's). This charming boat trip takes you past some of the great Palladian villas which the rich patricians built from the 16th century onwards, when this portion of the mainland became a favored resort. The return journey from Padua to Venice is by bus. Another time you may wish to visit the smaller islands of the Lagoon, notably San Lazzaro degli Armeni, with its fabulous library ▲ 383.

BICYCLING TO CHIOGGIA

If the weather is fine, why not visit Chioggia – by bike ▲ 358. Set out from the Lido, where bicycles can be rented on the corner of Via Zara and the Gran Viale, and then pedal the length of the coastline. At the Alberoni, take the ferry to San Pietro in Volta, then cross the fishing grounds to the main road along the *murazzi*, huge sea

walls built during the 18th century, to Pellestrina. From Pellestrina, take the ferry across to Chioggia, a fishing port which has retained all of its original charm. Note that, if you start out early from the Lido, you will arrive in time for the spectacular fish market, which is held in Chioggia's 14th-century grain depot. In any case, you are bound to see some *bragozzi*, flat-bottomed boats with hulls and sails embellished with emblems and designs, religious or otherwise.

The calli, the canals and the bridges of Venice constitute a world of magic that is sure to awaken the curiosity and imagination of the very young. Anyone who has taken a child to Venice, or seen the city through his own child's eyes, will know exactly how thrilling the experience can be, provided that the programme of discovery is carefully planned for the purpose.

ON FOOT TO SAINT MARK'S SQUARE

At San Samuele, window shopping is very much in order, given the number of interesting craftsmen's shops in the area. For example, in the marbled paper shops one can find remarkable figurines made of papier mâché, such as this character from the Commedia dell'Arte (below).

SAN GIACOMO DELL'ORIO. From Santa Lucia Station, take the Ponte dei Scalzi and Rio Marin. Then follow a narrow alleyway to the broad Campo San Giacomo dell'Orio. After a pause in order to view the church, with its magnificent wooden roof like the hull of a ship (built by the shipwrights of the Arsenal ▲ *177*), drop in on the Da Carlo Pistacchi ice-cream shop on Rio terrà dei Nomboli. Nearby is the Natural History Museum in the Fondaco dei Turchi, which contains many fantastic treasures.

THE RIALTO. The Rialto during the morning, with its market stalls and boats filled with produce, is a place full of life and color.

SAINT MARK'S SQUARE. Take the Calle Vallaresso from the Rialto through to San Marco. The great mosaics in the basilica are bound to fascinate a child. Likewise the Doge's Palace, with its fairytale pinnacles and arcades, pink and white façade, wells of bronze, Giant's staircase, Scala d'Oro and armory. Inside, the "secret" tour is best, heading as it does to the Leads prison cells, the former top-floor kitchens and the colossal beams under the roof, through a series of secret passages (telephone the palace for further information). Back on the piazza, the clocktower with its Moorish figurines hammering out the hours gives an opportunity to explain the importance of the sun and the phases of the moon to Venetian mariners. Also take care to find and point out a bizarre ammonite fossil set into the marble steps on the angle of the Procuratie Vecchie and the Napoleon Wing. In the alley that leads off the Ponte della Paglia, round the corner from the prison, is the Bonifacio pastryshop – very conveniently located.

THE ARSENAL AND SAN PIETRO DI CASTELLO

THE NAVAL MUSEUM. Take the Riva degli Schiavoni, from which you can see the Bridge of Sighs. With its pieces of ships, astrolabes, compasses, portolans, sextants, plans of fortresses and culverins, and models of different vessels (notably the Bucintoro) ● *38*, this museum contains treasures that will mesmerize any child.

SAN PIETRO DI CASTELLO. Continue along the Via Garibaldi to San Pietro di Castello, an island which has been largely unaffected by the passing of time; the cathedral here contains the mysterious "Throne of St Mark" inscribed with verses from the Koran. After this it's only a short walk to the Castello public gardens, where old and young can relax as they will.

TOUR OF THE ARSENAL BY VAPORETTO. Anyone deterred by the idea of the long walk described above may prefer to pick up vaporetto no. 52 at the Tana landing stage near the Naval Museum. This offers a view of the Arsenal, because the vaporetto passes through the oldest area of the shipyard, a dock surrounded by workshops, slipways and boathouses. Since the same vaporetto also serves Murano, it would be a pity not to extend the trip to include a visit to the master glassblowers.

SANTA MARGHERITA TO THE ZATTERE

CAMPO SANTA MARGHERITA. Set children to find the representations of St Margaret killing the dragon (just beside the church), or to count the various monsters and dragons on the truncated campanile. Afterwards, sample the ice-creams at Cansin or Il Doge. If you arrive early enough on the campo, take a walk around the fish, fruit and vegetable markets.

CA' REZZONICO. On the way to La Salute, stop at Ca' Rezzonico, the museum of 18th-century Venice. Some of the objects here, notably the chinoiseries and the sedan chair, may amuse children; likewise the reconstruction of a contemporary pharmacy. Younger children will be intrigued by the small puppet theater.

THE ZATTERE. Continue to the Zattere and walk along the Giudecca Canal, stopping for the celebrated *gianduiotto* at the Da Nico gelateria (ice-cream shop). A short walk farther on is the *squero* San Trovaso, a unique gondola boatyard.

SANTA MARGHERITA TO THE MERCERIA

SAN SAMUELE BY GONDOLA. Just behind the Church of San Pantalon, in Calle Crocera, is a children's bookshop. At San Tomà you can take the traghetto across the Grand Canal, thus discovering what it is like to ride in a gondola for the nominal price of 500 lire. By way of San Samuele, continue on to Campo Morosini-Santo Stefano. The statue of Nicolò Tommaseo here is bound to make your child laugh, especially when you volunteer the information that the pile of books beneath him has earned poor Nicolò the nickname of "Cagalibri" (book-shitter).

CAMPO MOROSINI TO THE MERCERIA. This quarter of Venice is full of places in which to eat and drink, but we strongly advise you to sample the toasted sandwiches and *tramezzini* of the semi-vegetarian resturant Da Zorzi, in Calle dei Fuseri. For a tour of La Fenice theater, which includes backstage and the various pulleys and contraptions used for the scenery, telephone 521 01 61. In the Merceria, the little Casino Venier (with its indispensable secret passage leading from a concealed door) offers a vivid glimpse of what life was like for 18th-century Venetian nobles (open during the afternoon, Monday to Friday).

OTHER PLACES OF INTEREST FOR CHILDREN. San Giorgio degli Schiavoni ▲ *162*, a small scuola noted for its fabulous series of paintings by Carpaccio, is well worth a visit for a child. So, too, is San Zanipolo, which contains the funeral urn of Bagradin, who was flayed alive by the Turks at the Siege of Famagusta.

**"And up and down the long canals they go,
And under the Rialto shoot along,
By night and day, all paces, swift and slow"**

Byron, *Beppo* (1819)

STAIRCASE AT THE PALAZZO CONTARINI DEL BOVOLO
From Campo Manin, by way of the Ramo della Salizzada, one can reach this famous palace, which was named for its spiral staircase. *Bovolo* means "snail". Like the loggias of which it is the connecting feature, this staircase built by Giovanni Candi was attached to the palace's façade at the start of the 15th century to satisfy the owner's desire for more space.

The crafts that made Venice rich (lacemaking, fine textiles, weaving, glass and mirror manufacturing, gold and silver work) all went into steep decline at the end of the 18th century. Although the guilds created in the 14th century were abolished by Napoleon in 1805–6, a few workshops managed to revive the old traditions in the 1860's, perpetuating ancestral crafts which survive to this day.

LEGATORIA PIAZZESI
San Marco 2511
This, the oldest papershop and bookbinder in Venice, uses marbled paper and paper stencilled in the traditional *carta varese* manner, to make cards, envelopes, boxes and papier mâché figurines. Everything is handmade in limited quantities.

JESURUM
Piazza San Marco (shop) and Ponte della Canonica 4310 (showroom)
A lace manufacturer, established since 1869 in the desanctified 13th-century Church of Sant'Apollonia. The women who work here still make lace by hand. Some of their patterns require several years of careful labor. Beautiful examples of the lacemaker's craft are displayed in the firm's showroom, while the shop sells handkerchiefs, tablecloths, blouses, bedcovers and many other articles, all of which are quite exquisite, but also extremely expensive.

LACEMAKING

SCUOLA DEI MERLETTI, Piazza Galuppi, Burano 183
The work of local lacemakers, organized as a cooperative, is on sale in Burano. There is a museum devoted to the craft.

GILDING AND FURNITURE RESTORATION

CANESTRELLI, Campiello Barbaro, Dorsoduro 364
One of the last gilders in Venice. Restoration of picture frames, furniture and fine mirrors.
CICOGNA, Campo San Tomà, San Polo 2867
Michel Cigogna has restored much of the furniture displayed at the Ca' Rezzonico Museum of 18th-century decorative arts.
GIANNI CAVALIER, Campo Santo Stefano, San Marco 2863
An artisan who has been painting and restoring furniture and objects since 1943. Among the last great Venetian specialists in gilding and lacquer work.
PEGGY STUFFI, Calle Fiubera, San Marco 815
One of the finest lacquer restorers in the world, with a special interest in old fans.

MASKS

LABORATORIO ARTIGIANO MASCHERE, Barbaria delle Tole 6656
Giorgio Clanetti makes superb masks in cardboard or leather.
MONDO NUOVO, Dorsoduro 3063
Over three hundred cardboard masks are on sale in this shop. Giano Lavato's customers include many theater companies.

MOSAICS

ORSONI, Sotoportego dei Vedei, Cannaregio 1045
The architect Gaudi commissioned the Orsoni to decorate his Cathedral of the Sagrada Familia in Barcelona. Mosaic techniques have changed little since the workshop first opened in 1888.
SANTAGOSTINO, Fondamenta della Sensa, Cannaregio 3272
Since 1952, Olivo Santagostino has been using enamel and semi-precious stones to construct his remarkable mosaics. Among other things, he has restored the San Marco Clocktower and the ground floor paving of the Ca' d'Oro.

JEWELRY, GOLD AND SILVERWORK

ATTILIO CODOGNATO, San Marco 1295
This antique dealer and jeweler finds gems for discerning collectors the world over.
HERRIZ, Calle XXII Marzo, San Marco 2380
Jewelry 1900–50, particularly 1920–30 (Cartier, Van Cleef,

Mauboussin, Webb and Mellerio).
MISSIAGLIA, Piazza San Marco 125
This jewelry shop, which has been open since 1836, is famous all over Italy for its silver and gems.

MARBLED PAPER

PAOLO OLBI, Calle della Mandola 3653
Sketchbooks, agendas, gifts in paper or leather. Reasonable prices.

FABRICS

ARS NOVA/VENETIA STUDIUM, Calle XXII Marzo, San Marco
Taking its inspiration from the Fortuny "plissé" technique, this little shop offers a wide choice of scarves, shawls, pocket handkerchiefs and cushions.
BEVILACQUA, Campiello della Comare, Santa Croce 1320
Since 1875, this firm has been making sumptuous fabrics (brocades, damasks and raised velvets) on hand looms.
NORELENE, Campo San Maurizio, San Marco 2606
Helena and Nora Ferruzzi dye and stamp silks, velvets and cottons, using time-honored techniques but resolutely modern motifs.
RUBELLI, Campo San Gallo, San Marco 1089
Since 1858, a manufacturer of handwoven damasks, brocades and raised silks. When the last two workers here retire, the shop will be turned into a museum.
V TROIS, Campo San Maurizio, San Marco 2666
A dealer in old fabrics with exclusive rights on certain very precious Fortuny fabrics (average price $200 per square yard).

GLASSBLOWERS

BAROVIER E TOSO, Fondamenta Vetrai 28, Murano
The vases, glasses, chandeliers and other objects produced in this workshop are inspired by the 26,000 pieces in the historic collection of Ercole Barovier and Giusto Toso. There are also contemporary pieces made in collaboration with famous designers.
ARCHIMEDE SEGUSO, Fondamenta Serenella 18, Murano/Piazza San Marco 143
Archimede Seguso has been known since 1946 as a master of filigree glass and *latticino*. Lampstands, decorative plates and contemporary vases.
SALVIATI, Fondamenta Radi 16, Murano/San Gregorio, Dorsoduro 195
This glassblowing concern was founded in 1866 by Antonio Salviati. The original splendid collection of vases which made his reputation is now on display here behind glass. Today the Salviati firm produces lampstands, glasses and decorative plates.
VENINI, Piazzetta dei Leoncini 314.
Since the 1930's, this has been the temple of Venetian glassblowing design. Over the years major artists like Scarpa, Tapio, Bianconi and Santilliana have reinforced Venini's solid reputation.

The tradition of the Venetian mask and its manufacture have undergone a revival since 1980, thanks to renewed interest in the Carnival. Mask-makers today mostly reproduce characters from the Commedia dell'arte, but are also inspired by old paintings and engravings and portraits of contemporary personalities.

CA' MACANA, Dorsoduro 3172
This workshop was opened in the 1980's and specializes in craquelé and cloth masks.

ALBERTO VALESE-EBRU
Salizzada San Samuele 3135/Santo Stefano 3471/Calle della Fenice 1920
A papershop and bookbindery which produces handmade marbled paper fashioned into cards, notebooks and agendas, as well as marbled plaster sculptures.

Venice's extraordinary stock of masterworks by Titian (c.1490–1570) ranges from the dazzling altarpieces of his early years (such as *Saint Mark Enthroned*, at La Salute), to the muted colors and less distinct outlines of his maturity (*La Pietà*, at the Accademia).

FROM SAN MARCO TO SAN ROCCO

The DOGE'S PALACE ▲ 229 contains several fine examples of Titian's work, among them a fresco of *Saint Christopher* (1523) and a huge commemorative painting *Doge Grimani* (1555, mostly painted by the master's pupils). The LIBRERIA MARCIANA ▲ 254 possesses a single work by Titian (*Wisdom*, 1530). From here, make your way through the Merceria to the CHURCH OF SAN SALVADOR ▲ 274, where there is a dramatic *Transfiguration* (1560–5), which has sadly been damaged, and an *Annunciation* (1564–5) which is full of vibrant yellows, reds and golds. Nearby at SAN LIO ▲ 171 there is a Mannerist portrait of St James the Greater (1545–50). Just over the Rialto Bridge, stop at SAN GIOVANNI ELEMOSINARIO ▲ 286 to view another portrait of the saint; then on to the CHURCH OF THE FRARI ▲ 292, which contains Titian's grandiose altarpiece *The Assumption* (1516). At the SCUOLA DI SAN ROCCO ▲ 294 farther on is another *Annunciation* (1540), and a *Bearing of the Cross* (1519) which for centuries was thought to be the work of Giorgione – or at least Giorgione in collaboration with Titian.

At the Doge's Palace, Titian painted his *Saint Christopher* over a door of the Philosophers' Chamber ▲ 229.

FROM SAN SEBASTIANO TO SAN MARZIALE

The second Titian itinerary through Venice should take up at least half a day. Begin at the CHURCH OF SAN SEBASTIANO ▲ 326, which contains an admirable *Saint Nicolas of Bari* (1563). From here, go to the ACCADEMIA ▲ 301, with its forcefully executed *Saint John the Baptist* (1550), light-filled *Presentation of Mary at the Temple* (1539) ▲ 308, and the great *Pietà* (1576), which Titian painted for his own tomb and which had to be completed after his death by Palma the Younger. From here the trail leads you to LA SALUTE ▲ 318, and the magnificent *Saint Mark Enthroned* (1511–12) in the sacristy; there is also a series of paintings from the Church of Santo Spirito, most notably *Cain and Abel*, *David and Goliath* and the *Sacrifice of Isaac* (1524–44). All of these works are intensely dramatic and Mannerist in their style. From La Salute, take the vaporetto to the CA' D'ORO ▲ 148, where you will see Titian's rendering of *Venus* (1555). After this, visit the JESUIT CHURCH ▲ 153, which contains the *Martyrdom of Saint Lawrence* (1559), a remarkable exercise in chiaroscuro. Finally, make sure that you save enough time to call in at the CHURCH OF SAN MARZIALE ▲ 145, where there hangs a little-known painting by Titian entitled *Tobias and the Angel Raphael* (c.1530).

As a variation on a theme well-known to the artist, *Venus at her Looking Glass* in the Ca'd'Oro (room 7, 2nd floor) dates from Titian's mature years and was probably executed with the help of several painters working under the master.

For much of her history, Venice was a passionately musical city and a breeding ground for musicians, becoming in the 15th century a major European center for the art. Though the old fervor has long since abated, efforts have recently been made to revive the great musical traditions of the Lagoon.

CENTERS OF MUSIC IN VENICE

THE OSPEDALI, ANCIENT AND MODERN ▲ 160, 174, 322. The four Ospedali of Venice began as institutions that took in orphans and abandoned children; by the 18th century they had become music conservatories which gave highly popular concerts on a regular basis. Nowadays, musical events are still held in the auditorium of the Ospedaletto and in the Church of La Pietà. Throughout the year, La Pietà offers a widely varied programme encompassing soloists, musical ensembles and small chamber orchestras.

SAINT MARK'S BASILICA. The two great choirstalls of St Mark's remind us that it was here that a Flemish master of music invented the double choir ▲ 174. Human voices and musical instruments combine admirably in the ideal acoustic conditions of the basilica; apart from the many concerts held here, organ recitals are also staged annually at St Mark's, and feature some of the world's greatest virtuosos.

LA FENICE ▲ 262. Built in the 18th century according to plans by the architect Giantonio Selva, this theater remains the mecca of Venetian opera. Its auditorium is decorated with stuccos and can seat 1,500 spectators. Another very fine auditorium is the Apollinea, which is used for concerts and musical conferences.

Music is seldom absent from the streets and squares of the city. In spring and summer choirs sing and orchestras play in St Mark's Square. These open-air concerts are part of a tradition going back to the 18th century, when concerts were held in the gardens of the Giudecca and in the parks of the great palaces.

CHURCHES AND FOUNDATIONS

During the season, musical events are put on alternately in the CHURCH OF SANTO STEFANO ▲ 267 and the CHURCH OF SAN STAE ▲ 350. The latter offers a programme of symphonies during the winter. Close to Santo Stefano is the LEVI FOUNDATION MUSIC CENTRE, which occupies the former Palazzo Giustinian-Lolin ▲ 208 and which organizes regular musical evenings. This foundation also possesses a rich specialist library, offers lodgings to musicologists who are passing through Venice, and supports musical research projects. The CINI FOUNDATION ▲ 342 on the island of San Giorgio Maggiore is somewhat different in that its main interest lies with contemporary composers. In the sestiere of San Polo, on the other side of the Grand Canal, is the Gothic CHURCH OF THE FRARI ▲ 292 which, in addition to exhibiting some of the greatest masterpieces of Venetian art, also mounts concerts of all kinds, and particularly organ recitals. Finally, the varied concerts staged at the nearby SCUOLA GRANDE DI SAN GIOVANNI EVANGELISTA ▲ 295 are always well worth attending.

In 17th-century Venice the opera emerged from the courts of the aristocrats to enter the public world of the theater. The 18th century saw the Venetian passion for theatrical and musical spectacles reach its height, and the city's complement of theaters grew in proportion. It is worth noting that the same appetite for theater had been evident in the high masses at St Mark's from time immemorial.

Venice has always been a favorite setting for film directors, ever since the first-ever exterior shots in real surroundings were filmed there in the spring of 1896 by the Lumière brothers' camera operator, Albert Promio. During the 20th century the city has served as a backdrop for many hundreds of feature films.

THE LAGOON, THE GRAND CANAL AND "IDENTIFICATION OF A WOMAN". A director looking for an actress meets a young aristocrat who intrigues him. She disappears and he sets out to find her. At the end of the film the two protagonists are seen in a boat on the Lagoon; they go into the Hotel Gritti on the Grand Canal.

PIAZZA SAN MARCO AND "MOONRAKER". After a mad gondola chase around the canals, 007 (Roger Moore) discovers SPECTRE's hideout in the San Marco Clocktower, where a laboratory is concealed behind a false glassworks.

THE PIAZZETTA AND "EVA". A writer (Stanley Baker) meets a courtesan named Eva (Jeanne Moreau) in Venice, and falls in love with her – but she rejects him. One remarkable sequence shows Jeanne Moreau on the terrace of the Caffé Lavena on the Piazzetta.

THE DANIELI AND "THE GUIGNOLO". On his release from prison, Alexandre Baroni (Jean-Paul Belmondo) is given a briefcase containing a microfilm which he must smuggle into Italy. After a number of adventures, the hero succeeds in returning the microfilm to the French government. In one memorable stunt, Belmondo rides a motorboat into the Hotel Danieli.

LA FENICE AND "SENSO". Venice is under the Austrian yoke; Countess Serpieri (Alida Valli) has a doomed love affair with Mahler, an Austrian lieutenant. Their first meeting takes place at La Fenice during a performance of Verdi's *Il Trovatore*, which is interrupted by Italian patriots bursting into the theater.

SAN BARNABA AND "SUMMERTIME". An American spinster (Katharine Hepburn) spends her first holiday abroad in Venice. She explores the city guided by a mischievous boy and has a love affair with a handsome antique dealer – at one point falling spectacularly into the San Barnaba canal. But David Lean's Pensione Fiorini is pure fabrication – its windows somehow open on to every famous view in Venice.

In *Senso*, adapted by Visconti from the novel by Carlo Boito, Countess Serpieri meets her Austrian lover on the Campo del Ghetto and declares her love for him by the well. Later, they walk together as far as the Fondamenta di Cannaregio.

SAN BARNABA AND "INDIANA JONES AND THE LAST CRUSADE". It is 1938, and Indiana Jones and his father arrive in Venice in search of the Holy Grail. After his father's sudden disappearance, Jones discovers a crypt full of crusader knights under the paving in the Church of San Barnaba.

THE LIDO AND "DEATH IN VENICE". This film recreates the majestic Hotel des Bains and the Lido as they were at the close of the 19th century. The composer Gustav von Aschenbach (Dirk Bogarde) falls in love with Tadzio, a young adolescent, on the Alberoni beach.

It is a long-established Venetian habit to take a break at intervals during the day – particularly towards noon and before the evening meal. At these times people go out to drink an *ombra*, which is simply a glass of wine – usually white – accompanied by delicious snacks. These snacks are the celebrated *cichetti*, of which there are an immense variety, notably meatballs, small portions of fried fish or vegetables and hard-boiled eggs. In any event, the ritual visit to the *bacaro* (wine-bar) is an important part of the rhythm of life in Venice, and the Venetian way of keeping up with one's friends. *Bacaros* exist all over Venice, but are especially numerous in San Polo.

AI DO MORI, San Polo 429, Tel: 522 54 01. Closed Sunday and Wednesday pm. This *bacaro* has two entrances and is one of the most famous institutions around the Rialto Market. With its copper pots hanging from the ceiling, it has considerable charm. Wine is drunk by the glass, standing up, as in most *bacari*. There is a range of delicious *cichetti* and *tramezzini* variously made with crab, shrimp or aubergines, and cut into small bite-sized pieces.

ALL'ARCO, San Polo 436, Tel: 520 56 66. Closed Saturday pm and Sunday.
A wine bar founded fairly recently. Specialities include *crostini* (toast rubbed with garlic and sprinkled with olive oil, or otherwise garnished) and an excellent selection of wines and beers. In summer, tables are set up outside.

ANTICO DOLO, San Polo, Tel: 522 65 46. Closed Sunday.
For years this was the *bacaro* of the boatmen delivering produce to the Rialto Market. The atmosphere remains authentic and unchanged. Traditional Venetian dishes are made with seasonal ingredients fresh from the market.

CANTINA DO SPADE, San Polo 860, Tel: 521 05 74. Closed Sunday.
Big wooden tables and a wide choice of sausages and hams – especially *coppa de toro*, a Venetian speciality.

OSTERIA AL PONTE, San Polo 2742, Tel: 523 72 38. Closed Saturday pm and Sunday.
A lunchtime meeting-place for gondoliers, workmen and students. This little establishment at one end of the San Polo bridge specializes in deep-fried or sautéed potatoes, served on brochettes with a wide choice of wines.

VINI DA PINTO, San Polo, Campo della Pescheria 367, Tel: 522 45 99. Closed Monday.
Established in 1890, this *bacaro* is frequented by the people who work at the Pescheria and Erberia markets. There is a wide choice of wine, and delicious creamy fish paste on toast is also served.

SOME ADDRESSES IN OTHER PARTS OF VENICE

CANNAREGIO
OSTERIA CA' D'ORO
Cannaregio 3912, Tel: 528 53 24.
Closed Thursday.
A simple, charming bar with the atmosphere of another age. The choice of wines is excellent, as are the *cichetti* and other food. The *pasta ai fagioli* is particularly good.

CASTELLO
OSTERIA AL MACCARON
Calle Larga Santa Maria Formosa, Castello 5225
Tel: 522 59 95.
Closed Sunday.
An excellent bar where you can drink either standing up or sitting at a table.

DORSODURO
CODROMA
Dorsoduro 2540, Tel: 70 41 71.
Closed Thursday.
This very old wine bar is furnished with antique wooden tables and has retained all of its original charm. It serves very good sandwiches and *cichetti*. Backgammon and other games are popular here.

◆ 5000 lire to 40,000 lire
◆◆ 40 000 lire to 80 000 lire
◆◆◆ 80 000 lire and more

	PRICE/QUALITY	FURNITURE-DECOR.	VIEW	PRIVATE DINING-ROOMS	TERRACE/GARDEN	SPECIALITIES	REGULAR CU...
CANNAREGIO							
Al Milion	◆◆	●				L	
Antica Mola	◆◆	●			●	L	LV
Arca di Noe	◆					V	
Fiaschetteria Toscana	◆◆				●	LN	
L'Iguana	◆				●	V	
Pizzeria Trattoria «La Perla»	◆				●	P	LN
Trattoria Enoteca «Alla Bomba»	◆	●			●	W	VLT
CASTELLO							
Al Covo	◆◆	●				L	
Al Mascaron	◆	●				L	LT
Cip Ciap	◆	●				P	
Corte Sconta	◆	●			●	L	
Da Franz	◆◆	●			●	L	
Danieli Terrazza (Hôtel Danieli)	◆◆◆	●	●		●	LI	
Da Remigio	◆◆					L	L
Do Leoni (Londra Palace)	◆◆◆	●	●			LI	
Il Golosone	◆					L	
La Grande Muraglia	◆					V	
Pizzeria al Vecio Canton	◆					PL	L
Trattoria Acciughetta	◆				●	LW	LT
Trattoria alla Rivetta	◆					L	LT
SAN MARCO							
Al Bacaretto	◆◆				●	L	VY
Al Graspo de Ua	◆◆					L	TV
Alfredo Alfredo	◆					NIR	
Alla Colomba	◆◆◆					L	LTV
Antico Martini	◆◆◆	●	●		●	LI	
Caravella (Hôtel Saturnia e International)	◆◆◆					LI	LT
Chat qui rit	◆				●	PR	LT
Da Arturo	◆◆					L	L
Da Mario alla Fava	◆◆	●			●	L	
Da Ivo	◆◆◆					LN	T
Da Raffaele	◆◆	●			●	L	T
Devil's Forest	◆					R	Y
Do Forni	◆◆	●		●	●	L	
Harry's Bar	◆◆◆					L	
La Mansarde et Al Teatro	◆◆		●	●	●		
Latteria Zorzi	◆					V	L
Pizzeria Bora Bora	◆	●				PR	LY
Rosticceria Al Teatro Goldoni	◆					LPR	
Rosticceria San Bartolomeo	◆					LR	
Snack-Bar Borsa	◆					PR	
Terrazza Tiepolo (Hôtel Europa e Regina)	◆◆◆	●	●		●	NI	T
Club del Doge (Gritti Palace)	◆◆◆		●			LNI	T
Vino Vino	◆					L	
SAN POLO							
Al Giardinetto	◆				●	LP	
Al Peoceto Risorto	◆◆	●				L	
Antiche Carampane	◆◆					L	
Caffè Orientale	◆◆	—			●	L	
Da Fiore	◆◆◆	●				L	

	PRICE/QUALITY	FURNITURE-DECOR	VIEW	PRIVATE DINING ROOMS	TERRACE/GARDEN	SPECIALITIES	REGULAR CLIENTELE
DA IGNAZIO	◆◆	●			●	L	
PIZZERIA DA MARCO	◆	●				P	
TRIPPERIA ANTICO DOLO	◆	●				L	
DORSODURO							
AGLI ALBORETTI	◆◆				●	LNI	T
AI GONDOLIERI	◆	●				NR	TL
AL PROFETA	◆				●	LP	Y
AL SOLE DI NAPOLI	◆		●		●	LP	L
ANTICA LOCANDA MONTIN	◆◆				●	L	
ANTICO CAPON	◆◆				●	L	T
CREPIZZA	◆					V	Y
DA BRUNO	◆					L	LT
DA GIANNI	◆		●	●	●	LI	T
INCONTRO	◆				●	V	L
LA DOLCE VITA	◆				●	LR	LY
LA FURATOLA	◆◆					L	
TAVERNA SAN TROVASO	◆					LP	T
TRATTORIA ANZOLO RAFFAELE	◆					L	L
GIUDECCA							
CIPRIANI	◆◆◆◆	●	●	●	●	LI	V
HARRY'S DOLCI	◆◆		●		●	LD	
L'ALTANELLA	◆◆		●		●	L	
SANTA CROCE							
AE OCHE	◆				●	PR	TY
ANTICA BESSETA	◆◆					L	LT
NONO RISORTO	◆				●	LP	
TRATTORIA AL PONTE	◆					L	L
LA ZUCCA	◆◆					V	
LIDO							
BELVEDERE	◆◆		●		●	LI	T
DA ANDRI	◆◆				●	L	
DA CICIO	◆◆				●	L	
DA NANE	◆◆		●		●	L	
DA VALENTINO	◆◆				●	L	
FAVORITA	◆◆				●	L	
PIZZERIA RESTAURANT VENEZIA 2000	◆		●		●	PI	
SELF SERVICE GRAN VIALE	◆					IR	
CHIOGGIA							
AL BERSAGLIERE	◆◆	●				L	
IL GARIBALDI	◆◆				●	L	
IL GATTO	◆◆	●				L	
LA BELLA VENEZIA	◆◆	●			●	L	
VAL D'OSTRICA	◆◆	●			●	L	
MURANO							
TRATTORIA AL CORALLO	◆◆	●			●	L	
TRATTORIA BUSA ALLA TORRE	◆◆	●			●	L	
TRATTORIA VALMARANA	◆				●	L	
BURANO							
DA ROMANO («TRE STELLE DA ROMANO»)	◆◆◆	●			●	L	
GATTO NERO-DA RUGGERO	◆◆				●	L	
TORCELLO							
LOCANDA CIPRIANI	◆◆◆	●			●	LV	

Legend:

C celebrities
D desserts
I international
L local
N national
P pizza
R rapid service
T tourists
V various
W wine
Y young people

up to 150 000 lire
150 000 lire to 250 000 lire
250 000 lire and over

	PRICE	GARDEN/TERRACE	TV IN BEDROOM	DECOR/ARCHITECTURE	QUIET	VIEW	CONFERENCES/SEMINARS	RESTAURANT	24 HOUR ROOM SERVICE	NO. OF ROOMS
CANNAREGIO										
ADRIATICO **	◆									15
ALBERGO BERNARDI SEMENZATO *	◆	●			●					18
ALBERGO SANTA LUCIA *	◆	●			●					15
ALLOGGI SILVA	◆	●								9
AMADEUS ****	◆◆◆	●	●	●		●		●	●	63
ARCHIE'S HOUSE	◆									7
CORSO ***	◆◆	●			●					26
FLORIDA **	◆	●	●		●					29
GIORGIONE ***	◆◆	●	●		●					56
HESPERIA **	◆◆		●		●	●		●		20
LA FORCOLA **	◆				●					22
HÔTEL MARTE ***	◆◆		●							35
LEONARDO VENEZIA **	◆				●					18
STELLA ALPINA **	◆	●			●					38
VILLA ROSA	◆	●								32
CASTELLO										
ALBERGO CORONA *	◆					●				10
AL PIAVE DA MARIO *	◆									12
ATLANTICO **	◆									36
BISANZIO ***	◆◆		●		●					39
CASA VERARDO *	◆◆									9
DA BRUNO **	◆	●			●			●		26
DANIELI *****	◆◆◆	●	●	●	●	●	●	●	●	221
FORESTERIA VALDESE	◆				●					100
LA RESIDENZA **	◆◆		●	●						15
LOCANDA CANAL *	◆									7
LONDRA PALACE ****	◆◆◆	●	●	●	●	●	●	●	●	68
METROPOLE ****	◆◆◆	●	●	●	●	●	●	●		74
PAGANELLI **	◆◆	●			●					22
PELLEGRINO E COMMERCIO **	◆◆				●					24
RIO *	◆		●		●					
SAVOIA E JOLANDA ***	◆◆	●	●		●	●		●		80
TROVATORE **	◆◆	●								34
SAN MARCO										
AI DO MORI *	◆					●				12
ALA ***	◆◆	●	●		●			●		85
AL GAMBERO *	◆	●						●		30
ALL'ANGELO ***	◆◆	●					●	●		60
ATENEO ***	◆◆		●		●					20
BAUER GRUNWALD *****	◆◆◆	●	●	●	●	●	●	●	●	215
BONVECCHIATI ***	◆◆	●			●			●		86
BUDAPEST *	◆				●					12
CASA PETRARCA *	◆				●					7
CAVALLETTO E DOGE ORSEOLO ****	◆◆◆		●	●	●		●	●	●	80
CENTAURO **	◆◆									32
CITTÀ DI MILANO **	◆				●	●		●		24
CONCORDIA ****	◆◆◆		●		●		●	●		55
DIANA **	◆◆		●							30
EUROPA E REGINA *****	◆◆◆	●	●	●	●	●	●	●	●	192
FLORA ***	◆◆	●	●	●	●					44
GORIZIA ALLA VALIGIA **	◆		●					●		45
GRITTI PALACE HÔTEL *****	◆◆◆	●	●	●	●	●	●	●		96
ISTITUTO CILIOTA	◆				●					
LA FENICE ET DES ARTISTES ***	◆◆	●	●		●					69
LISBONA **	◆		●		●					15
LOCANDA FIORITA *	◆	●								10
LUNA HÔTEL BAGLIONI ****	◆◆◆		●	●	●		●	●		118
MERCURIO **	◆◆				●			●		18
MONACO E GRAN CANAL ****	◆◆◆	●	●		●	●		●		70
ORION **	◆◆		●							18
SAN GALLO **	◆				●	●				14
SAN GIORGIO **	◆		●		●					16
SAN MARCO ***	◆◆◆		●					●		55
SAN SAMUELE *	◆				●					10
SAN ZULIAN **	◆◆		●		●					22

	PRICE	GARDEN/TERRACE	TV IN BEDROOM	DECOR/ARCHITECTURE	QUIET	VIEW	CONFERENCES/SEMINARS	RESTAURANT	24 HOUR ROOM SERVICE	NO. OF ROOMS
SATURNIA E INTERNATIONAL ★★★★	♦♦♦	●	●	●			●	●		95
SAN POLO										
ALBERGO GUERRATO ★	♦			●		●				14
ALEX ★	♦				●					11
CASA DELLO STUDENTE-DOMUS CIVICA	♦									71
CARPACCIÒ ★★★	♦♦	●				●				17
HÔTEL IRIS ★★	♦	●			●					31
LOCANDA STURION ★★★	♦♦		●		●	●	●			26
MARCONI ★★★	♦♦♦		●	●		●		●		11
RIALTO ★★	♦♦♦	●	●			●		●		71
DORSODURO										
ACCADEMIA-VILLA MARAVEGE ★★★	♦♦	●			●					27
AGLI ALBORETTI ★★	♦♦	●			●			●		20
ALLA SALUTE DA CICI ★★	♦	●			●					50
AMERICAN ★★★	♦♦	●	●		●			●		29
DA PINO ★	♦									16
FORESTERIA DOMUS CAVANIS	♦									100
LA CALCINA	♦	●		●	●	●				37
LA GALLERIA ★	♦			●	●	●				9
LOCANDA MONTIN ★	♦	●		●	●			●		7
MESSNER ★★	♦	●			●					35
PAUSANIA ★★★	♦♦	●			●					25
SEGUSO ★★	♦♦	●	●		●	●		●		30
TIVOLI ★★	♦	●			●					23
GIUDECCA										
CIPRIANI ★★★★★	♦♦♦	●	●	●	●	●	●	●	●	104
ISTITUTO SUORE CANOSSIANE	♦				●	●				
OSTELLO DELLA GIOVENTÙ	♦				●		●			254
SANTA CROCE										
AI DUE FANALI ★★	♦									18
AIRONE ★★	♦									13
AL GALLO ★	♦							●		7
AL SOLE ★★★	♦♦	●			●			●		79
CANAL E WALTER ★★	♦♦	●								30
CASA PERON ★	♦									18
GARDENA ★★★	♦♦		●							22
MARIN ★	♦		●		●					19
PULLMAN PARK HÔTEL ★★★★	♦♦♦		●				●	●		100
SAN CASSIANO ★★★	♦♦♦	●				●		●		36
LIDO										
ATLANTA AUGUSTUS ★	♦♦									
AZIENDA AGRITURISMO O. RENZA	♦	●			●	●		●		5
CRISTALLO ★★	♦	●			●					24
GRAND HÔTEL DES BAINS ★★★★	♦♦♦	●	●	●	●	●	●	●	●	191
EXCELSIOR ★★★★★	♦♦♦	●	●	●	●	●	●	●	●	197
LA PERGOLA ★	♦	●			●					16
REITER ★★	♦	●						●		27
RIGEL ★★★	♦♦	●			●					42
STELLA ★★	♦	●								12
VIANELLO ★★	♦	●			●			●		22
VILLA AURORA ★★	♦	●			●	●		●		17
VILLA CIPRO ★★	♦	●								18
VILLA DELLE PALME ★	♦	●			●					12
VILLA PANNONIA ★★	♦	●						●		32
VILLA TIZIANA ★★	♦	●			●					19
CHIOGGIA										
BELLEVUE ★★★	♦	●			●			●		27
BRISTOL ★★★★	♦♦	●	●		●	●		●		70
CAPINERA ★★★	♦	●			●			●		47
GAMBERO D'ORO ★★	♦	●	●							20
GRAND'ITALIA ★★★	♦				●					20
TOURING ★★★	♦		●		●			●		62
MURANO-BURANO-TORCELLO										
PENSIONE AL SOFFIADOR	♦				●			●		5
LOCANDA-RISTORANTE RASPO DE UA	★ ♦				●			●		6
LOCANDA CIPRIANI ★★★	♦♦♦	●			●	●		●		4

413

STELLA ALPINA FLORIDA VILLA ROSA ALBERGO SANTA LUCIA CORSO HESPERIA ADRIATICO AMADEUS HOTEL MARTE ALLOGGI SILVA ANTICA MOLA LA FORCOLA

CANNAREGIO

EMERGENCIES

PRIVATE HOSPITAL
Fate Bene Fratelli
Madonna dell'Orto 3458
Tel: 78 31 11
*Free emergency
service.*
AMBULANCES
Tel: 523 00 00
*See also Useful
Telephone Numbers.*

BASIC INFORMATION

POSTAL CODE
30 121
POST OFFICE
Lista di Spagna 233
Tel: 71 65 94
EXCHANGE BUREAU
Santa Lucia 122/a
PUBLIC TOILETS
– Santa Lucia Station
Open 7am–9pm
Showers available.
– Campo Santi Apostoli
Open day and night

CULTURE

**LIBRARY ARCHIVIO
RENATO MAESTRO**
Ghetto Vecchio 1189
Tel: 71 88 33
Open 2–6pm (Tue,
Thur), 9am–1pm (Wed)
*Library of the Jewish
community.*

CA' D'ORO
GALLERIA FRANCHETTI
Tel: 523 87 90
Open 9am–2pm
(9am–1pm Sat, Sun and
holidays), ticket office
closes half an hour
earlier
This superb Gothic

*palace contains the art
collection of Baron
Franchetti (13th–15th
century paintings and
14th–15th century
sculptures).*

**CHURCH OF LA
MADONNA DELL'ORTO**
Campo Madonna
dell'Orto
Tel: 71 99 33
Open in season
9.30am–12 noon,
4–7pm
Open out of season
9.30am–12 noon,
3.30–5pm
*This church contains
the tomb of Tintoretto,
in addition to 10 of his
paintings. Ceremonies
to mark the 400th
anniversary of the
artist's death are
scheduled from May 31,
1993 to May 31, 1994.*

**CHURCH OF THE
GESUITI (SANTA
MARIA ASSUNTA)**
Campo dei Gesuiti
Tel: 528 65 79
Open in season
10am–12 noon, 5–7pm
Open out of season
10am–12 noon, 4–6pm
Closed Sun after 12
noon

**CHURCH OF THE
SCALZI (SANTA MARIA
DI NAZARETH)**
Fondamenta Scalzi,
near the station, in front
of the Scalzi bridge
Tel: 71 51 15
Open 7am–12 noon,
3.30–7pm

**CHURCH OF
SAN GEREMIA**
Campo San Geremia
Tel: 71 61 81

Open 7am–12 noon,
3–7pm.

**CHURCH OF SAN
GIOBBE**
Campo San Giobbe,
Open 8.30am–12 noon,
3.30–6pm

**CHURCH OF SAN
GIOVANNI
CRISOSTOMO**
Campo San Giovanni
Crisostomo
Tel: 522 71 55
Open 7am–12.30pm,
3–7.15pm

**CHURCH OF SAN
MARZIALE**
Campo San Marziale
Tel: 71 99 33
Open for mass only
6–7pm
Open out of season
10–11am (Sun)

**CHURCH OF SANTA
FOSCA**
Campo Santa Fosca

**CHURCH OF SAN
MARCUOLA**
Campo Santa Marcuola
Tel: 71 38 72
Open 8.30 am–12 noon,
4.30–7pm

**CHURCH OF SANTA
MARIA DEI MIRACOLI**
Campo dei Miracoli
Open 10am–12 noon,
3–6pm

**CHURCH OF SANTA
SOFIA**
Strada Nuova, Campo
Santa Sofia
Open for mass at
11.15am (Sun and
holidays)

**CHURCH OF SANTI
APOSTOLI**
Campo Santi Apostoli

HEBREW MUSEUM
Campo Ghetto Nuovo

2902/b
Tel: 71 53 59
Open in season
10am–7pm
Open out of season
10am–4pm
Closed Sun and on
Jewish feastdays
*Exhibition of Jewish
religious objects,
furniture and collection
of embroidered fabrics.*

**PALAZZO LABIA
SALONE DEL TIEPOLO**
Campo San Geremia
Tel: 78 11 11
Open 3–4pm
*Visit by prior
arrangement.*

RESTAURANTS

AL MILION
Corte Al Milion; San
Giovanni Grisostomo
5841
Tel: 522 93 02
Open 11am–2pm,
6–10pm
Closed Wed
*Venetian specialities at
the bar or at one of the
small wooden tables in
this charming tavern.
Specialities include
fegato alla veneziana,
seppie alla veneziana.
50,000–60,000 lire.*

ANTICA MOLA
Fondamenta degli
Ormesini 2800
Tel: 71 74 92
Open 8am–12pm
Closed Sat
*Charming and
hospitable, off the
tourist circuit, and
serving typical Venetian
cuisine. Specialities
include baccala and
risotti.
45,000 lire.*
◑ ▭

ARCA DI NOE
Calle Larga G Gallina
5401
Tel: 523 81 53

Map labels: L'IGUANA — TRATTORIA ENOTECA "ALLA BOMBA" — ALBERGO BERNARDI SEMENZATO — GIORGIONE — PIZZERIA TRATTORIA "LA PERLA" — FIASCHETTERIA TOSCANA — AL MILION — ARCA DI NOÈ

Open 12 noon–3pm,
5pm–11pm
Closed Thurs and in
Aug
*Vegetarian and Indian
cooking – small
helpings.*
20,000–25,000 lire.
◐ ○ 🎫

FIASCHETTERIA
TOSCANA
San Giovanni
Crisostomo 5719
Tel: 528 52 81
Open 12.30–2.30pm,
7.30–10.30pm
Closed Tue
*Close to the Rialto, in a
lively working
neighborhood; a much-
praised fish restaurant
serving Venetian and
Italian specialities.*
40,000–55,000 lire.
◐ 🎫 🐾

L'IGUANA
Fondamenta della
Misericordia 2515
Tel: 71 67 22
Open 12 noon–2.30pm,
7–10.30pm
Closed Tues and Jan
*A brand new Mexican
restaurant – but only
room for 35 people out
of season. In summer,
there are tables in the
garden.*
25,000 lire.
○ 🎫

PIZZERIA TRATTORIA
"LA PERLA"
Barba Fruttariol 4615
Tel: 528 51 75
Open 12 noon–2.30pm,
7–11pm
Closed Mon and

Christmas
*Superb pizzas – more
than 60 different kinds.*
5,000–12,000 lire.
○

TRATTORIA ENOTECA
"ALLA BOMBA"
Calle dell'Oca
Tel: 523 74 52
Open 10am–2pm,
4.30–11pm
Closed Mon and Aug
*Big tables and excellent
wines. Seafood
specialities.*
30,000 lire.
○

HOTELS

ADRIATICO **
Lista di Spagna 224
Tel: 71 51 76
*Near the station. Rooms
clean and reasonable.
Breakfast included.*
70,000–110,000 lire.
🏛 ⌂ 🎫 🐾

ALBERGO BERNARDI
SEMENZATO *
Santi Apostoli
4363–4366
Tel: 522 72 57
Closed Nov 15–Dec 15
*Unpretentious reception
area, but the bedrooms
are charming, with
exposed beams; the
padrone is delightful.*
42,000–62,000 lire.
⌂ 🏚 🐾 🎫

ALBERGO SANTA
LUCIA *
Lista di Spagna, Calle
Misericordia 358
Tel: 71 51 80
Closed Dec

---

*Hidden in a small, quiet
alley, this is a charming
15-room pensione
where you can count on
a kindly reception.
Excellent value, with
pretty, sunny bedrooms.
Breakfast included.*
70,000–95,000 lire.
⌂ 🏚 ⌂ 🐾

ALLOGGI SILVA
Calle della Masena
1391/a
Tel: 72 03 26
Closed Nov
*Good value for money.
Nine small but
comfortable rooms. For
preference, choose one
on an upper floor, for
maximum light and air.*
70,000–90,000 lire.
⌂ 🏛 🏚 🐾 🎫

AMADEUS ****
Lista di Spagna 227
Tel: 71 53 00
Fax: 524 08 41
*Near the station,
overlooking a lively
street. A luxury hotel.*
210,000–350,000 lire.
🏛 📺 🐾 🐾

ARCHIE'S HOUSE
San Leonardo 1814/b
Tel: 72 08 84.
*Unquestionably the
cheapest hotel in this
lively quarter. Fairly
rudimentary, and you
must appear in person
to reserve a room. Two
nights minimum.*
30,000–40,000 lire.
⌂ 🐾

CORSO ***
Lista di Spagna 119

Tel: 71 64 22
Fax: 524 24 32
*Gardens – but still
overpriced at*
160,000–235,000 lire.
⌂ 🐾 ✸ 🐾

FLORIDA **
Calle Priuli
Tel: 71 52 53
Closed Nov 15–Dec 15
*A quiet hotel, facing the
Scalzi bridge.*
100,000 lire.
⌂ 🏚 📺 🐾

GIORGIONE ***
Santi Apostoli 4587
Tel: 522 58 10
Fax: 523 90 92
*A comfortable, tastefully
decorated hotel, with a
pretty garden.
Reception somewhat
icy. Shower and
breakfast included.*
140,000–220,000 lire.
🏛 🏚 📺 🐾 ✸

HESPERIA **
Cannaregio 459
Tel: 71 60 01
Fax: 71 51 12
Closed Dec, except
Christmas
*View over the
Cannaregio Canal:
delightful padrone.*
100,000–150,000 lire.
⌂ 📺 ✸ 🐾

LA FORCOLA **
Ponte dell'Anconetta
2356
Tel: 72 02 77
Fax: 72 03 20
*Five minutes from the
station. A fine hotel in a
former palace, by a
canal. Breakfast
included.*
81,000–110,000 lire.
⌂ 🏚 🎫 🐾

HOTEL MARTE ***
Cannaregio 338
Tel: 71 78 38
Near the station. A recently renovated palace with large, sunny rooms. View across the canal and the Ponte delle Guglie.
80,000–130,000 lire.
⌂ ▭ ☐ ⌷··

LEONARDO VENEZIA **
Calle della Masena 1385
Tel: 71 86 66
Typical Venetian pensione, run by a charming old lady. Cosy bedrooms and kindly reception. This is an excellent address, in a quarter of Venice that has all too many characterless hotels. Breakfast included.
120,000 lire.
⌂ ⌂ ⌷·· ▭

STELLA ALPINA**
Calle Priuli 99/d
Tel: 71 51 79
Fax: 72 09 16
Near the station. A family-style hotel overlooking a calle, with a garden behind. Classic Venetian décor.
60,000–125,000 lire.
⌂ ⌂ ⚲ ⚲

VILLA ROSA
Lista di Spagna,
Calle Misericordia 389
Tel: 71 65 89
Closed Nov to mid–Dec and Jan
When you see this pink-painted pensione at the end of its alley, you think you are in a different quarter of Venice, far from the station bustle. Charming and very good value. Breakfast included.
60,000–100,000 lire.
Reduction for guests displaying this Guide.
⌂ ⌂ ⌷·· ▭ ⚲

BARS AND NIGHT LIFE

AL MILION
Corte del Milion 5841
Tel: 522 93 02
Open 11am–2pm, 6–10pm
Closed Wed
Small, authentic bar close to Marco Polo's house. Good wines and typically Venetian

◆ HOTEL BELLINI ◆
Close to the station in the Lista di Spagna. From the top floor, yaou can see the entrance to the Grand Canal.

snacks (see Restaurant section).
◐

BAGATELA
Cannaregio 2924
Tel: 71 78 88
Open 9pm–2am
Closed Mon
Music, videos and occasional minor concerts take place. Risotto and pasta available on request after midnight.
☐ ♫ ⇥

BAR CICCHETTO
Calle Misericordia 367/a
Tel: 71 60 37
Open 7.30am–8.30pm, (7.30am–4pm Sat)
Closed Sun
Tramezzini and cicchetti.

BAR GELATERIA DA NINI
Ponte delle Guglie 1306
Tel: 71 78 94
Open in season
5am–midnight
Open out of season
5am–10pm
Closed Thur
A lively bar, much favored by younger Venetians. Delicious hot chocolate.
♫ ☐

BAR "GIALLO"
Cannaregio 5548
Tel: 520 62 66
Open 7am–9pm
Closed Sun
Giallo (yellow) is the name of this excellent

sandwich bar. Friendly atmosphere.
♫

CANOTTIERI
San Giobbe 690
Tel: 71 54 08
Open 4pm–2am
Closed Sun
Live concerts on Thur and Sat
⇥

CIRCOLO AI MIRACOLI
Cannaregio 6075
Tel: 523 06 16
Open 5pm–midnight
Closed Tue, and July–Aug
A club for lovers of classical music and art. Art and photography exhibitions, occasional book signings, poetry and prose readings.
♫

ENOTECA BOLDRIN
San Canciano 5550
Tel: 523 78 59
Open 9am–9pm
Closed Sun
Good wines. Self-service at lunch. Friendly atmosphere.

IL PARADISO PERDUTO
Fondamenta Misericordia 2540
Tel: 72 05 81
Open 7pm–1am
Closed Wed
A restaurant-bar much favored by Venetians – a bit expensive, but splendid atmosphere of jazz and poetry.
◐ ⇥

OSTERIA LA BOTTEGHE
Calle delle Botteghe
Tel: 522 81 81
Open 8am–10pm
Closed Sun
Spritz and cicchetti.

TIZIANO
Salizzada San Giovanni Grisostomo 5747
Open 7.30am–10pm.
Closed on Sat out of season
A quiet, friendly bar, serving fresh panini and hot meals. Refreshing fruit cocktails.
5,000–10,000 lire.
◯ ▭

CASTELLO

EMERGENCIES

HOSPITAL
San Giovani e Paolo
Tel: 529 45 17
Tel: 529 45 16
See also Useful Telephone Numbers

BASIC INFORMATION

POSTAL CODE
30 122
POST OFFICE
Campiello del Vin 4666
Tel: 520 00 73
TOURIST OFFICE
Calle del Rimedio 4421
Tel: 529 87 11
Fax: 523 03 99
PUBLIC TOILETS
– Campo Bandiera e Moro
Open 8am–2pm
Showers available.
– Sant'Elena Pineta
Open 10am–6pm

CULTURE

SCUOLA SAN GIORGIO DEGLI SCHIAVONI
Calle Furlani
Tel: 522 88 28
Open 10am–12.30pm, 3.30–6pm
(11am–12.30pm Sun and holidays)
Closed Mon
Don't miss Carpaccio's St Ursula series here.

CHURCH OF LA PIETÀ
Riva degli Schiavoni
Tel: 520 44 31
Open for mass at 5.30pm, and for concerts
For permission to visit outside these hours, refer to the Istituto S Maria della Pietà.

CHURCH OF SAN FRANCESCO DELLA VIGNA
Campo San Francesco della Vigna
Tel: 520 61 02
Open 8am–12 noon, 4.30–7pm

CHURCH OF SAN GIORGIO DEI GRECI
Calle dei Greci 3412
Tel: 523 95 74
Orthodox church, liturgy at 10.30am.

CHURCH OF SAN GIOVANI E PAOLO (SAN ZANIPOLO)
Campo San Zanipolo
Tel: 523 75 10
Open 7.30am–12.30pm, 3.30–7pm
Free entry.

CHURCH OF SAN GIOVANNI IN BRAGORA
Campo Bandiera e Moro
Tel: 520 59 06
Open 8–11am, 5–7pm

CHURCH OF SAN LIO
Campo San Lio
Seldom open, except for mass at 9.30am.

CHURCH OF SANTA MARIA DEI DERELITTI (OSPEDALETTO)
Salizzada Santi Giovanni e Paolo
Open 7am–3pm

CHURCH OF SANTA MARIA DELLA FAVA
Campo della Fava 5501
Tel: 522 46 01
Open 8am–12 noon, 4.40–7.30pm

CHURCH OF SANTA MARIA FORMOSA
Campo Santa Maria Formosa
Tel: 523 46 45
Open 8.30am–12.30pm, 5–7pm

CHURCH OF SAN ZACCARIA
Campo San Zaccaria
Tel: 522 12 57
Open 10am–12 noon, 4–6pm

QUERINI-STAMPALIA FOUNDATION
PICTURE GALLERY
Campo Querini 4778
Tel: 522 52 35
Open 10am–12.30pm
Closed Mon
The 2nd-floor gallery contains a large

◆ HOTEL GABRIELLI SANDWIRTH ◆

Riva degli Schiavoni in the Castello sestiere. The rooms of this luxurious hotel overlook St Mark's Square on one side and the Biennale gardens on the other.

collection of superb 16th–18th century paintings.
LIBRARY
Tel: 520 34 33
Open 2.30–11.30pm (3–7pm Sun and holidays)
Access to card holders only.

MUSEUM OF THE GREEK INSTITUTE FOR BYZANTINE AND POST-BYZANTINE STUDIES
Castello 3412
Tel: 522 65 81
Open 9am–1pm, 2pm–5pm
Closed Sun and holidays

GUIDI MUSEUM
Campo San Giovanni Nuovo
Open 10am–12 noon, 3–7pm
Closed Mon

NAVAL MUSEUM
Campo San Biagio, Arsenale 2148
Tel: 520 02 76
Open 9am–1pm
Closed holidays
Interesting collection of models of Venetian vessels.

RESTAURANTS

AL COVO
Campiello della Pescaria 3968
Tel: 522 38 12
Open 12.30–2.15pm, 7.30–10.15pm
Closed Wed, Thur, January and 15 days in Aug
This is a restaurant with plenty of cachet – wooden bar and Murano glass bottles. The cooking is all done here, with fresh ingredients. More than 140 different wines.
40,000–60,000 lire.
◐ ▭

AL MASCARON
Calle Lunga Santa Maria Formosa 5225
Tel: 522 59 95
Open 12 noon–3pm, 7–10pm
Closed Sun, Dec and Jan
Furnished in 19th-century Venetian tavern style. Good local cuisine, with neighborhood clientèle mingling with tourists. Youthful, relaxed atmosphere. Low prices.
35,000 lire.
◐ ○

AL MONDO NUOVO
Salizzada San Lio 5409
Open 8–11pm
Closed Thur and 10 days in Nov
A brand-new restaurant which doubles as a piano bar from 10pm–2am. Relaxed, softly lit atmosphere. Fish and seafood specialities.
22,000–30,000 lire.
○ ◐ ▣ ▭ ⚙

CIP CIAP
Ponte del Mondo Nuovo 5799
Tel: 523 66 21
Closed Tue
Also called La Bottega della Pizza, this celebrated establishment offers a wide choice of pizzas by the slice. Try the famous Disco Volante which the padrone will tailor to your tastes, simply by looking at your face. This costs about 9,000 lire.
○ ◐ ▣

CORTE SCONTA
Calle del Pestrin 3886
Tel: 522 70 24
Open 12.30–2pm, 7.30–10pm,
Closed Sun, Mon and from July 20 to Aug 20.
This old and beautiful osteria has become very fashionable – you will have to reserve. Good fish cuisine, but expensive, parsimonious servings. Specialities include crostini, San Pietro alle erbe and cuttlefish eggs.
37,000–50,000 lire.
◐ ▭

DA FRANZ
Fondamenta Sant'Iseppo 754
Tel: 522 08 61
Open 12 noon–2.30pm, 6.30–10pm
Closed Tue
Typical Venetian cooking. A friendly restaurant in an ordinary working neighborhood (quiet terrace on the Rio San Giuseppe). Specialities include fish and seafood.
35,000–60,000 lire.
◐ ▭

DANIELI TERRAZZA (HOTEL DANIELI)
Riva degli Schiavoni 4196
Tel: 522 64 80
Open 12 noon–3pm, 7–10.30pm
Closed Tue
The most luxurious, if not the most beautiful restaurant in Venice. The cooking has a very good reputation and the service is excellent. On the top floor of the hotel there is a magnificent view across the Lagoon.

Specialities include gamberetti, granzeole con polenta, branzino al forno.
133,000–158,000 lire.
◑ ▱ ⌇ �

DA REMIGIO
Salizzada dei Greci 3416
Tel: 523 00 89
Open 12.30–2.30pm
Closed Mon and Tue evenings
Unfrequented by tourists, this popular trattoria serves simple, reasonably priced food to inhabitants of the Castello quarter. Service friendly but a little slow.
24,000–50,000 lire.
○ ◐ ▱

IL GOLOSONE
Salizzada San Lio 5689
Open 9.30am–7.30pm.
A typical Venetian café serving local food. Fresh panini and other specialities.
8,000–10,000 lire.
◐ ○

LA GRANDE MURAGLIA
Calle Morosini 3958
Open in season 12 noon–3pm, 7pm–midnight
Closed Mon out of season
A Chinese restaurant, very reasonably priced.
15,000–18,000 lire.
○ ▱

LES DEUX LIONS (LONDRA PALACE)
Riva degli Schiavoni 4171
Tel: 520 05 33
Open 12 noon–3pm, 7.30–11pm,
Closed Tue and from Nov 15 to Dec 15
Overlooking the Grand Canal, this high-class restaurant will receive

you simply and courteously. Venetian and French nouvelle cuisine. Karaoke after 11 pm.
40,000–60,000 lire.
◑ ▱ ▱ ⌇

PIZZERIA AL VECIO CANTON
4738/a (near the Calle della Corona)
Tel: 528 51 76
Open 12 noon–3pm, 7–10.30pm
Closed Tue, Aug and Christmas
One of Venice's best pizzerias, but some way from the city center. Pizzas 12,000–15,000 lire. Meals alla Veneziana 25,000 lire.
○ ▱• ▱ ✎

TRATTORIA ACCIUGHETTA
Campo San Filippo e Giacomo
Tel: 522 42 92
Open 8am–11pm
Closed Tue

Restaurant and wine bar. Lively atmosphere, brasserie-type establishment where Venetians and tourists mingle in the evenings. Good cooking and reasonable prices.
15,000–20,000 lire.
○ ▱ ✎

TRATTORIA ALLA RIVETTA
Salizzada San Provolo 4625
Tel: 528 73 02
Open 11.30am–10pm
Closed Mon and July 15 to Aug 15
Typical fish restaurant. In season, Venetians tend to abandon this place to the tourists; staff somewhat sluggish in consequence. Check your bill carefully. Specialities include fried calamari, grilled sole, spaghetti alle vongole.
20,000–26,000 lire.
○ ◐ ▱ ✎

◆ HOTEL DANIELI ◆

The rooms overlook St Mark's Basin. This grand hotel, unrivalled for its comfort and hospitality, stands as a testimony to Venice's former glory. Dickens, Wagner, Proust, Fred Astaire, Sofia Loren and David Bowie have all stayed here.

HOTELS

ALBERGO CORONA *
San Filippo e Giacomo, Calle Corona 4464
Tel: 522 91 74
Closed for 1 month in spring
A charming little hotel with pretty bedrooms, breakfast and a view across the rooftops, for a very reasonable price. This hotel is equipped for handicapped guests.
48,0000 lire.
⌂ ▣ ⌂ ⌇

AL PIAVE DA MARIO *
Ruga Giuffa 4838–4840
Tel: 528 51 74
Closed for part of Jan and Feb
A family hotel. The reception is a trifle cantankerous. In a lively part of the sestiere. Breakfast is included.
71,000 lire.
⌂ ⌂ ▣ ▱ ⚲

ATLANTICO **
Calle dei Rimedio 4416
Tel: 520 93 71
Open all year round
Impersonal reception, but the rooms are pleasant enough, with exposed beams and fireplaces. Unfortunately the partitions are very thin and the ceilings too low. Popular with students.
60,000–140,000 lire.
⌂ ▣ ⌇ ⚲ ▱

BISANZIO **
Calle della Pietà 3651
Tel: 520 31 00
Fax: 520 41 14
Open all year round
Very quiet hotel. The rooms are attractive, with attached terraces. Breakfast included.
150,000–220,000 lire.
▦ ⌂ ▱ ▱ ⚲

418

DA FRANZ

CASA VERARDO *
Campo San Provolo
4765
Tel: 528 61 27
Fax: 523 27 65
Open all year round
*Cavernous vestibule
filled with bibelots and
photos. A real family
pensione. Rooms are of
varying sizes, mostly
spacious, and overlook
courtyard, canal or
calle. Comfortable and
good value.
77,000–87,000 lire.*
⌂ ⌂ ⌂ 夫 ⌂

DA BRUNO **
San Lio 5726/a
Tel: 523 53 24
Fax: 522 11 57
Closed Dec 10–25
*Reasonable hotel with a
small terrace area.
Breakfast included.
110,000–140,000 lire.*
⌂ ⌂

DANIELI *****
Riva degli Schiavoni
4196
Tel: 522 64 80
Fax: 520 02 08
*A world-famous palace
of breathtaking beauty
and comfort. The
service is still simple,
obliging and friendly.
Breakfast not included.
375,000–619,000 lire.*
⌂ C 夫 ⌂ 夫

FORESTERIA VALDESE
Calle Lunga Santa
Maria Formosa 5170
Tel and Fax: 528 67 97
Open 11am–1pm,
6–8.30pm
Closed Nov 1 to Nov 15
*Reservation is
advisable here. The
hotel is mostly occupied
by young people and*

groups from
Switzerland. Bedrooms,
dormitories and
apartments for 4–5
people. Modestly
equipped. Breakfast
included.
20,000–80,000 lire.*
⌂ ⌂ C 夫

LA RESIDENZA **
Campo Bandiera e
Moro 3608
Tel: 528 53 15
Fax: 523 88 59
Closed Nov 6–Feb 20
*Extraordinary. A superb
15th-century palace
with an authentic
interior. Because of the
fragility of the décor,
children are not allowed
in this hotel.
130,000 lire.*
⌂ ⌂ ⌂ ⌂
⌂ 夫

LOCANDA CANAL *
Fondamenta del
Rimedio 4422/c (near
Piazza San Marco)
Tel: 523 45 38
Closed Dec 23–Jan 31
*Two nights minimum are
required in this small,
unpretentious, quiet and
comfortable pensione.
Breakfast included.
66,000–100,000 lire.*
⌂ C ⌂ 夫

LONDRA PALACE ****
Riva degli Schiavoni
4171
Tel: 520 05 33
Fax: 522 50 32
*Superb setting; friendly,
attentive service. This is
a big hotel which offers
a number of extras,*

such as free entry to the
casino, and use of a car
for the day. Breakfast
included. 20 percent
reduction for children
under 7.
(See Restaurant Les
Deux Lions, above).
126,000–435,000 lire.*
⌂ C ⌂ 夫 ⌂
⌂ 夫

METROPOLE ****
Riva degli Schiavoni
4149
Tel: 520 50 44
Fax: 522 36 79
*A beautiful hotel, very
comfortable and full of
charm. Splendid views
across the Lagoon and
inner courtyards. Two
small conference
rooms. All bedrooms
have marble baths.
250,000–400,000 lire.*
⌂ C ⌂ 夫 ⌂ 夫

PAGANELLI **
Riva degli Schiavoni
4182 and Campo San
Zaccaria 4687
Tel: 522 43 24
Fax: 523 92 67
*The modest entrance
conceals a small,
gracious hotel with
beautiful, spacious
rooms reasonably
priced. Shower and
breakfast included. Ask
for rooms in the annexe,
which is quieter.
Reductions for children.
90,000–121,000 lire.*
⌂ ⌂ ⌂ C 夫 ⌂ 夫

PELLEGRINO E
COMMERCIO **
Calle delle Rasse
4551/a
Tel: 520 79 22
Fax: 522 50 16
*Modern, unpretentious
hotel, 5 minutes from St
Mark's Square. Free for
children under 2. 50
percent reduction on
third bed for children
3–7 years old.
105,000–165,000 lire.*
⌂ C 夫

RIO *
Campo San Filippo e
Giacomo 4536
Tel: 523 48 10
*Modern, recently
decorated, quiet, with a
view across the campo.
All bedrooms have
bathrooms. Free
accommodation for
children under 5.
About 110,000 lire.*
⌂ ⌂ C ⌂ ⌂ 夫

SAVOIA E
JOLANDA ▲▲▲
Riva degli Schiavoni,
Castello 4187
Tel: 520 66 44
Fax: 520 74 94
*A well-located hotel,
comfortable but
impersonal. Free
accommodation for
children under 4, and
reductions for children
under 12.
Maximum 220,000 lire.*
⌂ 夫 C ⌂ ⌂ 夫

TROVATORE **
Calle delle Rasse 4534
Tel: 522 46 11
Fax: 522 78 70
*Modern, elegant hotel
with terrace and good
views from the top-floor
bedrooms. Breakfast
included.
100,000–145,000 lire.*
⌂ C ⌂ 夫 ⌂

BARS AND
NIGHT LIFE

BAR CLODIA
Calle delle Rasse 4590
Tel: 522 93 24
Open 6am–9.30pm
Closed Tue and in Jan
*An unpretentious little
bar serving good
sandwiches.*

BIRRERIA FORST DA
ERNESTO E RICCARDO
Calle delle Rasse 4540,
Tel: 523 05 57
Open 10am–midnight
Closed Sat out of

SAN SAMUELE
ISTITUTO CILIOTA
AL BACARETTO
LA FENICE E DES ARTISTES
SAN GIORGIO
DA ARTURO
DA RAFFAELE
ANTICO MARTINI
SATURNIA E INTERNATIONAL

FLORA

PALAZZO GRI

season
Frequented by tourists and Venetians alike. Sandwiches made with whole grain and rye bread. Specialities include the toasted sandwiches.

SAN MARCO

EMERGENCIES

POLICE STATION
San Marco 996
Tel: 522 54 34
EMERGENCY ASSISTANCE
Tel: 522 58 26

BASIC INFORMATION

POSTAL CODE
30 124
POST OFFICE
Calle Larga dell'Ascensione
Tel: 528 59 49
AUTOMATIC CASH DISPENSERS
BANCA D'AMERICA E D'ITALIA
Calle Larga XXII Marzo 2216/2217
Tel: 520 07 66
BANCO SAN MARCO
Santa Lucia 1112/a
Tel: 71 53 11
TOURIST OFFICE
Calle dell'Ascensione 71
Tel: 522 63 56
Fax: 529 87 30
PUBLIC TOILETS

– Calle della Bissa

Open 9am–8pm
– Giardini Ex reali
Open 8am–8pm
– Calle Ascensione
Open 8am–9pm
Showers available.

CULTURE

ST MARK'S BASILICA, PALA D'ORO AND THE TREASURE OF ST MARK'S
Piazza San Marco
BASILICA OF ST MARK'S SACRISTY
Tel: 522 56 97
Procuratoria di San Marco
Tel: 522 52 05
Open in summer 9.45am–5.30pm
Open in winter 9.45am–4pm, 2–5.30pm Sun
In addition to the golden altarpiece, the basilica possesses a beautiful collection of objects in wrought gold and silver. High Mass is celebrated in the basilica at 10am.

LIBRERIA MARCIANA
Piazzetta San Marco 7
Tel: 520 87 88
Visit by prior arrangement Mon–Sat. Access to reading rooms on presentation of ID and letter of

introduction. The building was designed by Sansovino. Rooms with frescoes by Titian, Veronese and Tintoretto.

CAMPANILE DI SAN MARCO
Piazza San Marco
Tel: 522 40 64
Open in summer 9am–9pm or 10pm
Open in winter 9.30am–4pm.

COLLEZIONE CA' DEL DUCA
San Marco 3052
Tel: 528 79 03
Scheduled to reopen in 1994.
Visits by prior arrangement. Oriental art, 18th-century Venetian and German porcelain.

CHURCH OF SAN BARTOLOMEO
Campo San Bartolomeo
Now converted into an art gallery, used for temporary exhibitions.

CHURCH OF SAN BENEDETTO
Campo San Benedetto
Closed.

CHURCH OF SAN FANTIN
Campo San Fantin
Tel: 523 52 36
Open 7.15am–12 noon, 4–7pm

CHURCH OF SAN MOISÈ
Campo San Moisè
Tel: 528 58 40
Open 3.30–7pm

CHURCH OF SAN SALVADOR
Merceria San Salvador
Tel: 523 67 17
Open 9.30am–5.30pm
Sat, Sun and holidays

CHURCH OF SAN SAMUELE
Campo San Samuele
This church is used as a display and sale room for items produced by the Foundation based in the Palazzo Grassi.

CHURCH OF SANTO STEFANO
Campo Santo Stefano 3825
Tel: 522 23 62
Open 4–11pm
Concerts and recitals.

CHURCH OF SAN VIDAL
Campo Santo Stefano

BONVECCHIATI · CASA PETRARCA · EUROPA E REGINA · **GRITTI PALACE HOTEL** · BAUER GRÜNWALD AND GRAND HOTEL · CAVALLETTO E DOGE ORSEOLO · LUNA HOTEL BAGLIONI · **DA MARIO ALLA FAVA** · CITTA DI MILANO · **HARRY'S BAR** · AL DO MORI · **DE FORNI** · **ALFREDO ALFREDO**

Open 10.30am–4pm in March and Oct
The annexe is used as an art gallery.

CHURCH OF SANTA MARIA DEL GIGLIO
Campo Santa Maria Zobenigo
Tel: 522 57 39
Open 9am–12 noon, 3–6pm (11.30am–6pm Sun)

FONDACO DEI TEDESCHI (CENTRAL POST OFFICE)
Via Rialto
Tel: 528 62 12
Open 8am–7pm
Closed Sun
To visit this building, write to the Direzione Provinciale for an authorization. The central post office of Venice occupies this magnificent 16th-century palace.

ARCHEOLOGICAL MUSEUM
Piazza San Marco 52
Tel: 522 59 78
Open 9am–2pm (Sat, Sun and holidays 9am–1pm)
Roman copies of Greek statues, Greek and Egyptian art.

CORRER MUSEUM AND LIBRARY
Piazza San Marco 52
Tel: 522 56 25
Library open to the public in the morning
Museum open out of season 9am–4pm
In season 9am–7pm
Closed Tue
Historical collections on the 1st floor (history of the Venetian Republic), picture gallery on 2nd floor containing masterpieces of the Italian Renaissance by Carpaccio, Bellini, A da Messina and Lorenzo Lotto. Also temporary exhibitions.

DOGE'S PALACE
Piazzetta San Marco
Tel: 522 49 51
Open Nov–March 9am–4pm, April–Oct 9am–7pm (ticket office closes an hour earlier)
Closed Jan 1, May 1 and Christmas holidays.
For guided tours, reserve by telephone. Beautiful Gothic building, former residence of the Doges of Venice and seat of Venetian government.

PALAZZO FORTUNY (PESARO DEGLI ORFEI)
Campo San Benedetto

3780
Tel: 520 09 95
Open 9am–6.30pm
Closed Mon
Exhibition of Fortuny dresses and fabrics.

PALAZZO GRASSI
Campo San Samuele 3231
Tel: 523 16 80
Hours vary according to current exhibitions
A private foundation organizes displays of modern, contemporary and antique art in this palace.

THE PRISONS
and the Bridge of Sighs.
Information at entrance to the Doge's Palace
Tel: 522 49 51
Open 9am–4pm (ticket office closes 3pm)
Tour of the main chambers (Senate, Grand Council) and the Prisons, including the Bridge of Sighs. Guided tours of the Leads, in Italian, twice daily (10am and 12 noon).

CLOCKTOWER
Mercería, Piazza San Marco
Tel: 523 18 79
Currently under restoration.

RESTAURANTS

AL BACARETTO
Salizzada San Samuele

3447
Tel: 528 93 36
Open 7am–11pm
Closed Sat evening, Sun and during Aug
Regular clientèle of artists and students. An old Venetian house simply decorated and pleasantly located (Calle Larga). The terrace, open in summer, can hold up to 20 people. Typical Venetian cooking, also breakfasts and cichetti. 35,000–60,000 lire.
◑ ⊡ ✕

AL GRASPO DE UA
Calle dei Bombaseri 5094
Tel: 522 36 47
Open 12 noon–3pm, 7–11pm
Closed Mon and Tue
Venerable Venetian tavern, now a fashionable fish restaurant. Located near the Rialto. Reservations essential. 60,000 lire.
◑ ⊡

ALFREDO ALFREDO
Campo San Filippo e Giacomo 4294
Tel: 522 53 31
Open 11am–midnight.
Closed Wed
Recently opened bar and restaurant, a favorite with well-bred young Venetians. Often full. Food good and promptly served. The other Alfredo Alfredo at Santa Croce is less appealing. Specialities:

ravioli al gorgonzola, polenta bianca, ice-cream.
17,000–21,000 lire.
○ 🅲 ⊡

ALLA COLOMBA
Piscina della Frezzeria 1665
Tel: 522 11 75
Open 12 noon–3pm, 7–11pm
Closed Wed and Sept–Nov
Near La Fenice theater, a luxury restaurant frequented by artists. Priceless collection of paintings (de Chirico, Chagall, Picasso and many others paid for their meals here with pictures). Specialities include fish, carpaccio, cartoccio, pasta con fagioli.
70,000–200,000 lire.
🕕 🅲 ⊡

ANTICO MARTINI
Campo San Fantin 1983
Tel: 522 41 21
Fax: 528 98 57
Open 12 noon–3pm, 7.30–10.30pm
Closed Tue and Wed lunchtime
A traditional restaurant, founded in 1720; highly praised, open after the opera. Terrace meals include risotto and fegato alla Veneziana.
70,000–100,000 lire.
🌓 🅲 ⊡

CARAVELLA
(HOTEL SATURNIA E INTERNATIONAL)
Calle Larga XXII Marzo 2397
Tel: 520 89 01
Open 12 noon–3pm, 7pm–midnight
Cozy, intimate restaurant, international and Venetian food of exceptional quality. Nautical varnished wood décor. Specialities: risotto alle seppie, bigoli in salsa.
70,000–120,000 lire.
🕕 🌓 🅲 ⊡ ✗

CHAT QUI RIT
Calle del Salvadego, 1131 Angolo Frezzeria
Tel: 522 90 86
Open out of season 11am–9.30pm
Closed Sat and from Nov 1–May 30
A self–service pizzeria near St Mark's Square.

◆ HOTEL GRITTI PALACE ◆

Rooms with views over the Grand Canal. This hotel, named after the great Doge Andrea Gritti, is one of the most famous in Venice. Ruskin, Hemingway and countless other famous visitors have stayed here.

Crowded at midday with Venetians and tourists. Garden open in summer. Specialities include the pizzas.
10,000–28,000 lire.
○ 🅲

DA ARTURO
Calle degli Assassini 3656
Tel: 528 69 74
Open 12 noon–2.30pm, 7–11pm
Closed Sun, Aug and during Carnival.
Ernesto, the charming padrone, has a loyal Venetian clientèle. Specialities include the meat and misto di verdure.
60,000–80,000 lire.
🌓 🅲

DA MARIO ALLA FAVA
Calle Stagneri 5242
Tel: 528 51 47
Closed Wed
Gastronomic cuisine. Reductions for anyone displaying this guide.
40,000–60,000 lire.
○ 🅲

DA IVO
Ramo dei Fuseri 1809
Tel: 528 50 04
Open 12 noon–2.30pm
Closed Sun and during Jan.
Small, friendly, luxurious restaurant close to La Fenice, patronized by guests staying at the larger hotels. Rustic décor and some private dining rooms, with

windows overlooking the canal. Tuscan, Florentine and Venetian specialities. Reservations essential.
70,000+ lire.
🕕 🅲 ⊡

DA RAFFAELE
Fondamenta delle Ostreghe 2347
Tel: 523 23 17
Open 9am–4pm, 6pm–midnight
Closed Thur
A high-class restaurant with a magnificent dining room, collection of arms and armor. Terrace open in summer. Specialities: risotto and rombo alla Raffaele.
About 60,000 lire.
🌓 🅲 ⊡ ⤢

DEVIL'S FOREST
Calle dei Stagnieri 5181
Tel: 520 06 23
Open 8am–midnight
Closed Mon
Near the Rialto. A modern, pub-style establishment. Original salads, delicious and inventive tramezzini, youthful clientèle. Extensive choice of wines and beers.
5,000–10,000 lire.
○ 🅲

DO FORNI
Calle dei Specchieri 468
Tel: 523 21 48
Open 12 noon–3.30pm, 7pm–midnight

Closed Thur
Thirties décor bar, not unlike the one in the Orient Express. Although located in a tourist-infested area, this restaurant is favored by well-off Venetians and Italians. Specialities include maccheroni alla Pezzuto, spaghetti alla Silvestri, tortellini San Erasmo.
50,000–70,000 lire.
🕕 🌓 🅲 ⊡

HARRY'S BAR
Calle Vallaresso 1323
Tel: 528 53 31
Open 10am–11pm
Closed Mon
Harry's Bar is one of the few places on earth that remains resolutely authentic, despite the assaults of time and publicity. Chic, simple, wildly expensive and always packed. Venetian specialities, non-fattening dishes and grilled fish.
80,000–90,000 lire.
🕕 ⊡ ⤢ 🅲

LA MANSARDE ET AL TEATRO
Ramo Feretta Campo San Fantin 1912/18
Tel: 522 10 52
Fax: 523 72 14
– Al Teatro (bar) open 8am–midnight
– La Mansarde (restaurant) open 11am–4pm, 7pm–midnight
Reservations obligatory
This more or less private club (apply to Al Teatro for membership) is on the 4th floor, with a terrace and a magnificent view across Venice. Open after the theater. Clientèle largely artists.
40,000–60,000 lire.
🌓 🅲 ⊡ ⤢

LATTERIA ZORZI
Calle dei Fuseri 4359
Tel: 522 53 50
Open 12 noon–3pm, 7.30–8.30pm
Closed Sun
Close to the Teatro Goldoni, a vegetarian restaurant in a former dairy products shop (exposed beams and ceramic tiles). The dining rooms on the 1st floor, decorated in 1900s bistro style, are

charming. The cooking is good and the atmosphere friendly. A clientèle of younger Venetians. Specialities: whipped homemade chocolate and cream.
30,000 lire.
🔵 ⭕ 🅖 ⬚

PIZZERIA BORA BORA
Calle dei Stagneri 5251
Tel: 523 65 83
Open 11.45–3.30pm,
6.45–11pm
Closed Wed
Good value, youthful restaurant, often packed. Varied menus, reasonable cooking, uneven service. A favorite meeting place for young Venetians.
5,000–25,000 lire.
⭕ 🅖 ⬚

ROSTICCERIA AL TEATRO GOLDONI
San Marco 47–47
Tel: 522 24 46
Open 8am–10pm
Closed Wed out of season
Self-service canteen on the ground floor, restaurant on 1st floor.
From 20,000 lire.
⭕ 🅖

ROSTICCERIA SAN BARTOLOMEO
Calle della Bissa 5424
Tel: 522 35 69
Open 9am–2.30pm,
5–9pm
Closed Mon
Self-service canteen and restaurant. Venetian clientèle. Fast and cheap; simple food but good value.
8,000–12,000 lire.
⭕ 🅖 ⬚

SNACK–BAR BORSA
Calle Larga XXII Marzo 2033
Tel: 522 50 17
Open in season
8am–midnight
Open out of season
8am–11pm
Closed Sun and 20 days in Dec
Quick service bar and restaurant. Hot meals, sandwiches and panini at reasonable prices. Terrace open in summer.
7,500–12,000 lire.
⭕ 🅖 ⬚

TERRAZZA TIEPOLO (HOTEL EUROPA E REGINA)

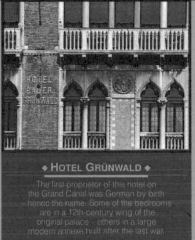

◆ HOTEL GRÜNWALD ◆

The first proprietor of this hotel on the Grand Canal was German by birth hence the name. Some of the bedrooms are in a 12th-century wing of the original palace – others in a large modern annexe built after the last war.

Calle Larga XXII Marzo 2159
Tel: 520 04 77
Open 7–10.30am,
12 noon–2.30pm,
7–10pm
The restaurant of the luxury Hotel Europa e Regina, with terrace overlooking the Grand Canal. International clientèle; remarkable view of the basilica of Santa Maria della Salute. Terrace open in summer. Italian and international cuisine.
120,000 lire.
🔵 🅖 ⬚ ⤳

CLUB DEL DOGE (GRITTI PALACE HOTEL)
Campo Santa Maria del Giglio 2467
Tel: 79 46 11
Open 8–10.30am,
12.30–3pm,
7.30–10.30pm
Five minutes from St Mark's Square, a gastronomic restaurant in a superb setting. Magnificent terrace overlooking the Grand Canal and the basilica of Santa Maria della Salute. Refined cuisine.
80,000–170,000 lire.
🔵 🔵 🅖 ⬚ ⤳

VINO VINO
Ponte delle Veste 2007
Tel: 522 41 21
Open 10am–11.30pm
Closed Tue
Close to La Fenice; a wide choice of wines

are on offer in this friendly bar, along with typically Venetian dishes (before 9pm). Relaxed atmosphere, youthful clientèle. From 30,000 lire.
⭕ 🅖 ⬚

HOTELS

AI DO MORI *
Calle Larga San Marco 658
Tel: 520 48 17
Close to St Mark's; quiet and comfortable. View of the campanile and basilica. One room with a view across the rooftops is reserved for painters. Friendly reception, free accommodation for young children.
75,000–89,000 lire.
⌂ ⌂ 🅖 ⤳ ⬚ ⚘

ALA *
Campo Santa Maria del Giglio, San Marco 2494
Tel: 520 83 33
Fax: 520 63 90
Near the church of Santa Maria del Giglio. Some of the rooms here are very beautiful, with old furniture and décor. Breakfast included. Reductions for children under 12.
150,000–212,000 lire.
⌂ 🅖 ⌂ 🔲 ⬚ ⚘

AL GAMBERO *
Calle dei Fabbri 4687–4689
Tel: 522 43 84

An impersonal hotel between the Rialto and San Marco. Good value for its location and low prices, but the accommodation is spartan and the service scant.
38,000–80,000 lire.
⌂ 🅖 ⬚

ALL'ANGELO *
Calle Larga San Marco 403
Tel: 520 92 99
Fax: 523 19 43
Fine stone staircase and majestic hallway; rooms clean but unremarkable. Reduction for children.
130,000–218,000 lire.
⌂ 🅖 ⬚ ⚘

ATENEO *
Campo San Fantin 1876
Tel: 520 07 77
Fax: 522 85 50
This recently restored hotel is comfortable but a trifle impersonal Accessible by gondola.
140,000–212,000 lire.
⌂ 🅖 🔲 ⬚

BAUER GRÜNWALD AND GRAND HOTEL ***
Campo San Moisè 1459
Tel: 520 70 22
Fax: 520 75 57
Very close to St Mark's and accessible by gondola. Most of the hotel is post-war and ponderous, but its 230 rooms of all different styles have a certain class. The old part of the hotel dates from the 12th century. There is also a view across the Grand Canal. Free of charge for children under 3.
214,000–500,000 lire.
🏛 🅖 ⌂ ⤳ 🔲 ⬚ ⚘

BONVECCHIATI *
Calle Goldoni 4488
Tel: 528 50 17
Fax: 528 52 30
A charming hotel full of paintings, most of which were given to the former owner (who also ran the La Colomba restaurant) in lieu of payment (modern art 1940–50). Cosmopolitan clientèle, reduction for children under 12. Breakfast included.
130,000–240,000 lire.
⌂ 🅖 ⌂ 🔲 ⬚ ⚘

BUDAPEST *
Calle Larga XXII Marzo 2143
Tel: 522 05 14
Near St Mark's, well located in the antique dealers' quarter. The entrance is unprepossessing, but this turns out to be a friendly if rudimentary family pensione. Breakfast included. Reductions for children.
75,000–110,000 lire.
⌂ ⌂ 🄲 ⌂ ♀

CASA PETRARCA *
Calle delle Schiavine 4336
Tel: 520 04 30
Charming little pensione – a home from home with a very kind padrone. An excellent address for students in the heart of Venice. Breakfast included.
40,000–75,000 lire.
⌂ 🄲 ⌂

CAVALLETTO E DOGE ORSEOLO ****
Calle Cavaletto 1007
Tel: 520 09 55
Fax: 523 81 84
Discreetly luxurious hotel, typically Venetian setting overlooking a gondola mooring. Expensive rooms, but charming and spacious.
250,000–350,000 lire.
⌂ ⌂ 🄲 ⌂ 🔆 ☐ ⌂ ♀

CENTAURO **
Campo Manin 4297/a
Tel: 522 58 32
Fax: 523 91 51
In the center of Venice, but quiet and protected. Views of the canal, or across the rooftops.
110,000–150,000 lire.
⌂ ⌂ ⌂ 🄲 ⌂

CITTÀ DI MILANO **
Campiello San Zulian 590
Tel: 522 70 02
Fax: 522 78 34
Between the Rialto and St Mark's Square, on the quiet, delightful Campo San Zulian.
94,000–131,000 lire.
🄲 ⌂ ⌂ ⌂

CONCORDIA ****
Calle Larga San Marco 367
Tel: 520 68 66
Fax: 520 67 75
Modern, centrally located hotel, pseudo-

◆ HOTEL EUROPA E REGINA ◆
This spendid palace, close to St Mark's Square, has a terrace overlooking the Grand Canal.

Venetian décor, comfortable but charmless. This is the only lodging house of which a part looks directly on to St Mark's Square. Free accommodation for children under 10. Breakfast included.
250,000–300,000 lire.
⌂ 🄲 🔆 ☐ ⌂ ♀

DIANA **
Calle Specchieri 449
Tel: 522 15 61
Fax: 523 87 63
Breakfast included.
160,000 lire.
🄲 ☐

EUROPA E REGINA *****
Via XXII Marzo 2159 Tel: 520 04 77
Fax: 523 15 33
Superbly sumptuous palace, beautiful terrace overlooking the Grand Canal, attentive service. Out of season, this hotel seems dark and deserted, no doubt haunted by ghosts from the past.
291,000–476,000 lire.
⌂ 🄲 ⌂ 🔆 ☐ ⌂

FLORA ***
Calle Bergamaschi 2283/a,
Tel: 520 58 44
Fax: 522 82 17
Closed Dec–Jan
Charming, slightly run-down hotel, with magnificent Liberty-style staircase and inner

courtyard and garden. In summer, breakfast is served on a delightful patio.
123,000–215,000 lire.
⌂ 🄲 ⌂ 🔆 ⌂

GORIZIA ALLA VALIGIA **
Calle dei Fabbri 4696/a
Tel and Fax: 522 37 37
Closed Jan 7–Feb 13.
Some of the rooms here are very small indeed. The collection of pictures is not very good, but suffices to lend this rather pleasant hotel a note of kitsch. Breakfast included. Reduction for children under 6.
42,300–130,000 lire.
⌂ 🄲 ⌂ ☐ ♀

GRITTI PALACE HOTEL *****
Campo Santa Maria del Giglio 2467
Tel: 79 46 11
Fax: 520 09 42
Luxurious palace built in the 15th century for Count Gritti. Today's hotel has Ciga Hotel service, including a garage on the Piazzale Roma and an airport shuttle. Free for children under 6.
400,000–560,000 lire.
⌂ ⌂ 🔆 ☐ ⌂ ♀

ISTITUTO CILIOTA
Calle Muneghe 2976
Tel: 520 48 88.
Religious establishment admitting women only.

Open to female students all year round (until 10.30pm) and to tourists from mid-June to mid-Sept (until 11pm). Telephone for further information.
⌂ ⌂ 🄲

LA FENICE E DES ARTISTES ***
Campiello della Fenice 1936
Tel: 523 23 33
Fax: 520 37 21
Close to La Fenice theater, this old-fashioned hotel is centrally located and quiet. Breakfast is served in the garden behind.
135,000–230,000 lire.
⌂ 🄲 ⌂ ☐ ⌂

LISBONA **
Calle Larga XXII Marzo 2153
Tel: 528 67 74
Fax: 520 70 61
High prices for small, rather melancholy bedrooms – if possible, go to the Flora instead (just round the corner). Breakfast included.
100,000–150,000 lire.
⌂ ⌂ 🄲 ⌂ ☐

LOCANDA FIORITA *
San Marco 3457/a
Tel: 523 47 54
Small, pleasant hotel behind Campo Santo Stefano. Friendly reception.
60,000–70,000 lire.
⌂ 🄲

LUNA HOTEL BAGLIONI ****
Calle Valaresso 1243
Tel: 528 98 40
Fax: 528 71 60
Open all year round
This building began in the 12th century as a Templars' hospice and was later turned into a convent. Magnificent marble inner courtyard, completely renovated luxury hotel restaurant. Splendid salon decorated with school of Tiepolo frescoes.
310,000–510,000 lire.
⌂ 🄲 ⌂ 🔆 ☐ ⌂

MERCURIO **
Calle del Fruttariol 1848
Tel: 522 09 47
Fax: 528 52 70
Small, unpretentious hotel where you can

count on a kindly reception. The bedrooms with showers are pretty and most comfortable. Breakfast included.
90,000–160,000 lire.
⌂ ⌂ Ⓒ ☐ ▭ ☥

MONACO E GRAN CANAL ★★★★
Calle Vallaresso 1325
Tel: 520 02 11
Fax: 520 05 01
Terrace overlooking the Grand Canal; garden. Superb, but slightly soulless.
300,000–450,000 lire.
🏛 Ⓒ ⌂ ☀ ☐ ▭ ☥

ORION ★★
Spada Ria 700/a
Tel: 522 30 53
Fax: 523 88 66
130,000–160,000 lire.
⌂ Ⓒ ☐

SAN GALLO ★★
Campo San Gallo 1093/a
Tel: 522 73 11
Fax: 522 57 02
Venetian-style décor, pleasant rooms if slightly small. The terrace is ravishing. Breakfast included.
130,000 lire.
⌂ 🏛 Ⓒ ⌂ ☀ ▭

SAN GIORGIO ★★
Calle della Mandola 3781
Tel: 523 58 35
Closed Dec–Jan
Excellent pensione, efficiently run by a young couple. Tasteful décor, with replicas of 17th-century furniture.
140,000 lire.
🏛 Ⓒ ⌂ ▭

SAN MARCO ★★★
Piazza San Marco 877, Ponte dei Dai
Tel: 520 42 77
Fax: 523 84 47
A characterless but superbly located hotel on the edge of the Piazza. Many bedrooms. Breakfast included.
130,000–240,000 lire.
Ⓒ ☐ ▭

SAN SAMUELE ★
Salizzada San Samuele 3358
Tel: 522 80 45
This hotel is in an ideal situation, 3 minutes from the Accademia.

◆ HOTEL MONACO E GRAN CANAL ◆
Features at this late 18th-century building include a terrace that overlooks the Grand Canal, and a garden behind.

The décor is slightly run-down in this family hotel, though the bedrooms are large, simply furnished and clean.
52,000–83,000 lire.
⌂ Ⓒ ⌂

SAN ZULIAN ★★
534/535
Tel: 522 58 72
Fax: 523 22 65
Quiet, comfortable rooms; unprepossessing entrance, décor pseudo-Venetian and a little over the top. Shower and breakfast included.
120,000 lire.
⌂ ⌂ Ⓒ ☐ ▭

SATURNIA E INTERNATIONAL ★★★★
Calle Larga XXII Marzo 2398
Tel: 520 83 77
Fax: 520 71 31
A palace which used to belong to the family of Doge Pisani. The foyer is a trifle strident, though decorated with splendid 14th-century bas-reliefs. Inner courtyard.
175,000–380,000 lire.
🏛 Ⓒ ☐ ▭ ☥

SAN SALVADOR
Calle Galleazza
Tel: 528 91 47
Family pensione, youthful clientèle.
38,000–90,000 lire.
⌂ ⌂ Ⓒ

NIGHT LIFE

ALFREDO ALFREDO
Campo San Bartolomeo 5546
Tel: 528 52 49
Open 11am–midnight
Closed Mon in winter
A fast-food establishment that stays open late.

BAR TORINO
Campo San Luca
Tel: 522 39 14
Open 7.30am–8.30pm
Closed Sun
Snack bar serving tramezzini and hors d'oeuvres.
3,000–5,600 lire.

DEVIL'S FOREST
Calle dei Stagnieri 5181
Tel: 520 06 23
Open 10am–midnight
Closed Mon
A lively pub near Campo San Bartolomeo. In the evenings, this is a popular meeting place for young Venetians. Food available.

ENOTECA AL VOLTO
Calle Cavalli-San Luca
Tel: 522 89 45
Open 9am–1pm, 5–9pm
Closed Sat mornings.
A typical bacaro with an excellent choice of wines and cichetti. Young clientèle.
From 1,500 lire.

FLORIAN
Piazza San Marco 56

Tel: 528 53 38
Open 9am–midnight.
Closed Wed
One of the most celebrated cafés in Italy, and probably among the oldest – founded in 1720. Marble guéridon tables, 18th-century paintings, irreproachable service, astronomical prices.
⑪ Ⓞ Ⓒ

HAIG'S
Campo Santa Maria del Giglio 2478
Tel: 523 23 68
Open 12 noon–11pm except Wed
One of Venice's choicest and most expensive bars.
🏛 Ⓒ

HARRY'S BAR
Calle Vallaresso 1323
Tel: 523 53 31
Bar open 10.30am–11pm
Closed Mon
Founded by Giuseppe Cipriani and frequented in its early days by Hemingway, Harry's has become a Venetian institution, along with its trademark Bellini cocktail (champagne and fresh white peach juice). See Restaurants.
⑪ Ⓒ ☀

ITALY ITALY
Campo San Luca
Tel: 523 24 22
Open 11am–10pm (11pm Sat)
Closed Tue in winter
Fast food: hamburgers, spaghetti, grills.
7,000–13,000 lire.
Ⓞ Ⓒ

LAVENA
Piazza San Marco 133–134
Tel: 522 40 70
Open 9am–midnight
Closed Tue in winter
This establishment was founded in 1750. Wagner was an habitué between 1879 and 1883. Luxury tearoom, 18th-century décor, Venetian glass chandelier, mirrors, marble.
⑪ Ⓒ ☛

MARTINI SCALA CLUB
Campiello San Gaetano
Tel: 522 41 21
Open in season 10pm–3.30am

Open out of season
9pm–3.30am
Closed Tue
*Piano bar decorated
with oriental rugs. A
very convenient place to
round off an evening at
La Fenice.
12,000–80,000 lire.*
◫ ⓒ ⌁

QUADRI
Piazza San Marco 120
Tel: 522 21 05
Open 8am–midnight
Closed Mon
*Historic café, founded in
1638. Like Florian,
Quadri has seen many
celebrated guests,
Stendhal, Byron,
Dumas and Proust
among them. Concerts
on the terrace in
summer.*
◫ ⓒ ⌁

VINO VINO
Calle del Cafetier 2007
Tel: 523 70 27
Open 10am–11.30pm
Closed Tue
*Pleasant spot for a
quiet drink or a bite to
eat. See Restaurants.*
○ ⓒ

SAN POLO

EMERGENCIES

MEDICAL TREATMENT
Tel: 523 00 00
*See list of Useful
Telephone Numbers.*

BASIC INFORMATION

POSTAL CODE
30 125
POST OFFICE
Campo San Polo 2022
Tel: 520 03 15
PUBLIC TOILETS
– Ramo Parangon-
Mercato Rialto
Open at all hours
– Campo San Polo
Open at all hours
– Rialto Erberia-Mercato
Open at all hours
– Campo Rialto Nuovo
Rialto
Open 6am–6pm

CULTURE

STATE ARCHIVES
Campo dei Frari 3002
Tel: 522 22 81
Open 8.30am–2pm
(Mon, Fri, Sat),
8.30am–6pm (Tue,
Wed, Thur)
Closed Sun and

holidays
*Open to students and
university academics
only. When temporary
exhibitions are on, the
cloisters here are open
to the public. A
thousand years of
Venetian history is
displayed here.*

PALAZZO CENTANI CASA GOLDONI
Campo San Tomà
2792794
Tel: 523 63 53
Open 8.30am–1.30pm
Closed holidays
*Center for theatrical
studies and museum of
the Goldoni theater.*

◆ HARRY'S BAR ◆

When he was staying in Venice, Ernest
Hemingway was an appreciative patron of
Giuseppe Cipriani's celebrated bar near
St Mark's Square.

CHURCH OF THE FRARI (SANTA MARIA GLORIOSA DEI FRARI)
Campo dei Frari
Tel: 522 26 37
Open 9–11.45am,
2.30–6pm (3–6pm Sun
and holidays)
*Concerts are held on Fri
evenings in June and
Sept.*

CHURCH OF SAN CASSIANO
Campo San Cassiano
Tel: 72 14 08
Open 9am–12noon,
5.30–7pm

Closed afternoons, Sun
and holidays

CHURCH OF SAN GIACOMETTO
Campo San Giacometto
Open 9am–12 noon
Closed Sat, Sun and
holidays 10.30am–6pm

CHURCH OF SAN GIOVANNI EVANGELISTA
Campiello della Scuola
(near the Frari)
Tel: 523 39 97
Open 7–10am Closed
Sat, Sun and holidays
Open for mass at 11am
and 6.45pm

CHURCH OF SAN POLO
Campo San Polo
Tel: 523 76 31
Open 8am–12 noon,
4–6pm
Closed afternoons, Sun
and holidays

CHURCH OF SAN SILVESTRO
Rio terrà San Silvestro
Tel: 523 80 90
Open 7.30–11.30am,
3.30–7pm (Sun
7.30am–12.30pm)
Closed afternoons, Sun
and holidays.

CHURCH OF SAN TOMÀ
Campo San Tomà.
Closed for restoration

DA IGNAZIO CARPACCIO **DA FIORE** **ANTICHE CARAMPANE** **PIZZERIA DA MARCO** LOCANDA STURION **AL PEOCETO RISORTO** ALBERGO GUERRATO

SCUOLA GRANDE SAN ROCCO
Campo San Rocco
Tel: 523 48 64
Open Nov–March
from Mon to Fri
10am–1pm, Sat and
Sun 10am–4pm
Open from Christmas to
Epiphany 10am–4pm
Open April–Oct
9am–5.30pm
*Collection of 50 works
by Tintoretto.*

RESTAURANTS

AL GIARDINETTO
San Tomà 2908 (near
the church of the Frari)
Tel: 522 41 00
Open 12 noon–3pm,
7–11pm
Closed Mon
*A quiet, reasonably
priced restaurant beside
the Rio de la Frescara.
Specialities: pizza, fish.
20,000–35,000 lire.*
○ **C** ▭

AL PEOCETO RISORTO
Calle Donzella 249
Tel: 522 59 53
Open 12 noon–3pm,
7–10pm (except Thur
afternoon and Aug)
*Formerly a fishermen's
tavern, this venerable
restaurant has had its
moments of glory –
Cocteau, Josephine
Baker, Eisenhower and
Elizabeth II have all
dined here. Specialities*

*include the seafood.
45,000–60,000 lire.*
◑ ▭

ANTICHE CARAMPANE
Rio terrà delle
Carampane 1911
Tel: 524 01 65
Open 12 noon–3.30pm,
7.30–10pm
Closed Sun evenings,
Mon and Aug
*A small fish restaurant,
but full of charm. Often
busy, so it is best to
reserve.
Minimum 45,000 lire.*
◑ ▭

CAFFÈ ORIENTALE
San Polo 2426
Tel: 71 98 04
Open 12 noon–3pm,
7–10.30pm
Closed Mon
*Elegant restaurant,
refined cooking.
Servings less than
generous. Terrace.
Minimum 60,000 lire.*

DA FIORE
Calle del Scaleter 2202
(near Campo San Polo)
Tel: 72 13 08
Open 12.30–2.30pm,
7.30–10pm
Closed Sun and Mon, at

◆ THE RIALTO BRIDGE ◆

Until the 19th century, this bridge was the only
fixed connection between the two banks
of the Grand Canal. Under its portico are a
number of luxury shops, which are mostly
patronized by tourists.

Christmas and for 3
weeks in Aug
*Better reserve if you
want to try this excellent
restaurant, which is
much appreciated by
Venetians and tourists
alike. Specialities:
risotto con scampi or
seppie.
50,000–90,000 lire.*
◑ ▭

DA IGNAZIO
Calle dei Saoneri 2749
Tel: 523 48 52
Open 12 noon–3pm,
7–10pm
Closed Sat and 15 days
at end of July and at
beginning of March
*Small trattoria near the
Rialto. Friendly service,
excellent, unpretentious
cooking. In summer,
terrace and arbor.
50,000–60,000 lire.*
◑ ▭

PIZZERIA DA MARCO
Campiello del Sansoni
900
Tel: 522 65 65
Open 12 noon–2.30pm,
7.30–10pm
Closed Mon and 15
days in Jan
*Mediocre pizzas.
20,000–25,000 lire.*
○ ♫

TRIPPERIA ANTICO DOLO
Calle Ruga Vecchia 778
Tel: 522 65 46
Fax: 522 71 31
Open 10.30am–3pm,
6–10.30pm
Closed Sun, 1st week
in Jan, 2 weeks in
June–July

◆ SAN POLO

This 130-year-old bacaro offers a wide choice of wines and cicchetti. Specialities are the tripparissa and Venetian cuisine. 25,000–40,000 lire.
◐ ○

HOTELS

ALBERGO GUERRATO *
Calle drio la Scimia 240/a
Tel and Fax: 522 71 31
Closed Dec
Fifty yards from the Rialto, a hotel kept by a delightful couple with friendly reception, sunny, large rooms, copious breakfast. An excellent choice. Breakfast included. 65,000–95,000 lire.
⌂ ⊬ ▭

ALEX *
Rio terrà Frari 2606
Tel: 523 13 41
Closed midnight–7am and Jan
A small hotel, with pleasant rooms. Breakfast included. 40,000–72,000 lire.
⌂ ⌂

CASA DELLO STUDENTE-DOMUS CIVICA
San Rocco 3082
Tel: 522 71 39
Open 7.30am–11.30pm.
Closed Oct–May and Aug
Cheap, spacious rooms for students in the university area. Reductions for holders of youth cards. 22,000–25,000 lire.
⌂ ⌂

CARPACCIO
San Polo 2765
Tel: 523 59 46
Fax: 524 21 34
Closed end of Nov to mid-March.
A small hotel near San Tomà, quiet and well run. Breakfast included. 110,000–195,000 lire.
⌂ ⊬ ▣ ♀ ▭

HOTEL IRIS **
San Tomà 2912 (near the Frari)
Tel and Fax: 522 28 82
Some rooms overlook a small canal, others the garden-restaurant. Breakfast included. 60,000–120,000 lire.
⌂ ▭

◆ DO SPADE ◆

A typical *bacaro* ▲409. The tradition of these winebars goes back as far as the 15th century, when their first patrons were Venetian merchants. In his memoirs, Casanova recalls taking a young married woman whom he had seduced to a *bacaro*.

LOCANDA STURION **
Calle dello Sturion 679
Tel: 523 62 43
Fax: 522 83 78
One of the oldest locandas in Venice. Centrally located near the Rialto and Grand Canal. Reductions for children. Breakfast included. 130,000–160,000 lire.
⌂ ⌂ ⌂ ▭ ▢ ♀

MARCONI **
Fondamenta del vin 729
Tel: 522 20 68
Fax: 522 97 00
Fifteenth-century palace, completely restored. Small rooms, pleasant service. Free for children under 10. 175,000–252,000 lire.
▣ ⌂ ▣ ▢ ▭ ♀

RIALTO **
Riva del Ferro 5149
Tel: 520 91 66
Fax: 522 89 58
Near the Rialto Bridge. Well located but a trifle noisy and impersonal. Comfortable rooms. 240,000–280,000 lire.
▣ ▣ ⊬ ▢ ▭

BARS AND NIGHT LIFE

CAFFÈ BLUE MUSIC BAR
Calle della Crosera 3778
Tel: 523 72 27
Open 7am–midnight.

Closed Sun
Lively, full of students. Sandwiches served.
♫

CAFFÈ DEI FRARI – TOPPO
Ponte dei Frari 2564
Tel: 524 18 77
Open 7am–midnight (8am–8.30pm Sat)
Closed Sun
Opposite the Church of the Frari, a bar on two levels patronized by a youngish clientèle.

CANTINA DO MORI
San Polo 401/403
Tel: 522 54 01
Open 8.30am–1.30pm, 5–8.30pm
Closed Sun
Much favored by Venetians. Excellent wines and a wide selection of cicchetti.
◐

CANTINA DO SPADE
Calle do Spade 860
Tel: 521 05 74
Open 9am–2pm, 5–9pm.
Closed Sun and Aug
Typical bacaro, since 1475. Wide choice of wines, excellent cicchetti made with game of all kinds – varied and original.
◐

◆ DORSODURO

EMERGENCIES

MEDICAL TREATMENT
Tel: 523 00 00

See also the list of Useful Telephone Numbers.

BASIC INFORMATION

POSTAL CODE
30 123
POST OFFICE
– Fondamenta Gaffaro 3510
Tel: 520 05 70
– Zattere 1508
Tel: 520 05 65
EXCHANGE BUREAUX
– Campo Santa Marguerita 2934
– Zattere ai Gesuati 928 (near the Accademia)

CULTURE

BASILICA SANTA MARIA DELLA SALUTE
Campo della Salute
Tel: 523 55 58
Open 8.30am–12 noon, 3–5.30pm (except Sun)
Masses take place at 9am and 11am

CA' REZZONICO
Calle San Barnaba
Tel: 522 45 43
Open 9am–7pm from May 15 to August 15
Open 9am–3.30pm for the rest of the year
This is a quite magnificent palace containing a superb collection of paintings and some lacquered furniture dating from the 18th century. There is also a reconstitution of an 18th-century pharmacy.

CHURCH OF ANGELO RAFFAELE (ANZOLO RAFFAELE)
Campo Angelo Raffaele
Open Mon to Fri 7.30am–12 noon, 4.30–7.30pm
Also open during hours of mass (on Sun) 10am, 11.30am and 6.30pm; 6.30pm on Sat and holidays

CHURCH OF THE CARMINI (SANTA MARIA DEL CARMELO)
Campo dei Carmini
Tel: 522 65 53
Open Mon–Fri 7.30am–12 noon, 4–5pm
Open Sat 8.30–9.15am
Open Sun 8.30–11.30am, 6.30pm
Open holidays at 6.30pm

CHURCH OF THE GESUATI (SANTA MARIA DEL ROSARIO)
Fondamenta Zattere dei
Gesuati
Tel: 523 06 25
Open 8am–12 noon,
5–7pm

CHURCH OF OGNISSANTI
Fondamenta degli
Ognissanti
Open for mass at
6.30pm
*Now part of the
Giustinian Hospital.*

CHURCH OF SAN BARNABA
Campo San Barnaba
Open 7.30am–12 noon
except Sun 9am–3pm

CHURCH OF SAN GREGORIO
Campo San Gregorio
(near La Salute)
*Closed. Now a
restoration workshop for
museum paintings.*

CHURCH OF SAN NICOLÒ DEI MENDICOLI
Campo San Nicolò
Tel: 528 59 52
Open 10am–12 noon,
4–6pm
Sunday mass at 8.30am
and 10am
*This church, which is in
one of the poorer
quarters of Venice, has
a 15th-century portico
like the one at the
Church of San Giacomo
di Rialto.*

CHURCH OF SAN PANTALON
Campo San Pantalon
Open 7.45–11.30am,
4.15–7pm

CHURCH OF SAN SEBASTIANO
Campo San Sebastiano
Tel: 528 24 87
*Currently closed for
restoration.*

CHURCH OF SAN TROVASO
Campo San Trovaso
Tel: 522 21 33
Open 8–11am,
4pm–6pm
Open Sat 8–11am,
4.30–7pm
Open Sun and holidays
8.30am–1pm

CHURCH OF SPIRITO SANTO
Fondamento Zattere del

◆ GUGGENHEIM FOUNDATION ◆

This institution is in the Dorsoduro sestiere,
close to the Accademia. The great collector Peggy
Guggenheim bought the Palazzo Venier dei Leoni
in 1949 and filled it with the world's finest private
collection of modern art.

Spirito Santo
Open 8am–12 noon,
3–6pm (Sun only)

PEGGY GUGGENHEIM FOUNDATION
San Gregorio 701
Tel: 520 62 88
Open 11am–6pm
Open Sat 11am–6pm
(free entrance
6pm–9pm)
Closed Tue
*One of the world's most
notable private
collections of modern
art.*

GALLERY OF THE ACCADEMIA
Ponte dell'Accademia,
Tel: 522 22 47
Open 9am–2pm,
(9am–1pm Sun and
holidays)
*Remarkable,
comprehensive
collection of Venetian
paintings, including
Giorgione's magnificent
"Tempest".*

GALLERY OF PALAZZO CINI
San Vio 864
Tel: 521 07 55
Open 2pm–6pm
Closed Mon and late
Aug–early Nov

TOTEM IL CANALE GALLERY
Accademia 878
Tel: 522 36 41
Open 10am–1pm,
3pm–7pm
*Gallery of contemporary
and African art.*

PALAZZO ZENOBIO – COLLEGIO ARMENO
Fondamenta del
Soccorso 2596
Tel: 522 87 70
*Seventeenth-century
palace. Visit by prior
arrangement.*

PINACOTECA MANFREDIANA
Campo della Salute 1
Tel: 522 55 58
*Closed to the public
By arrangement only.
Ask for Monsignor
Giuliano Bertoli.*

SCUOLA GRANDE DEI CARMINI
Campo dei Carmini
2617
Tel: 528 94 20
Open 9am–12 noon,
3pm–5pm
Closed Sun
*Collection of paintings
by Tiepolo.*

RESTAURANTS

AGLI ALBORETTI
Accademia 882–884
Tel: 523 00 58
Fax: 521 01 58
Open 7.30pm–midnight
Closed Wed and 3
weeks in Jan and Aug
*Very well located
gastronomic restaurant
beside the Accademia
and close to the Grand
Canal. Plush
atmosphere. Expensive.
Specialities: hot
avocado and shrimps.
50,000–70,000 lire.*
🄲 ⬚

AI GONDOLIERI
Fondamenta
dell'Ospedaletto 366
Tel: 528 63 96
Restaurant open
12–3pm, 7.30–10pm
Fast food 9am–10pm
Closed Tue
*Huge, succulent panini;
relaxed, friendly
atmosphere. A very
good choice.
20,000–40,000 lire.*
◑ ○

AL PROFETA
Calle Lunga Santa
Barnaba 2671
Tel: 523 74 66
Open 11.30am–3pm,
6.30–11pm
Closed Mon
*Pleasant restaurant with
a pretty garden.
Young, unpretentious
atmosphere.
25,000–35,000 lire.*
○ ⬚

AL SOLE DI NAPOLI
Campo Santa
Margherita 3023
Tel: 528 56 86
Open 12 noon–2.30pm,
6.30–10.30pm
Closed Thur
*Simple restaurant,
cheap pizzas,
undistinguished décor.
18,000–30,000 lire.*
○ ⬚ ☀

ANTICA LOCANDA MONTIN
Fondamenta di Borgo
1147
Tel: 522 71 51
Open 12.30–2.30pm,
7–10pm.
Closed Tue evenings,
Wed and Jan 7–20
*Immortalized by
d'Annunzio. Still
magical and nostalgic,
though slightly marred
now by group tours.
Specialities: grigliata
dell'Adriatico, coda di
raspo ai ferri.
About 40,000 lire.*
◑ ⬚ ☀

ANTICO CAPON
Campo Santa
Margherita 3004
(bordering San Polo)
Tel: 528 52 52
Open 10am–3pm,
6.30–11pm
Closed Wed
*Overlooking one of the
biggest campi in the city,
the terrace of this
gastronomic restaurant
is flooded with sunshine
in summer – unusual for*

shady Venice.
36,000–42,000 lire.
🌓 ⚪ ▭ ▱

CREPIZZA
San Pantalon 3757
Tel: 522 91 89
Open 9.30am–2.30pm,
7–10.30pm
Closed Tue
*Large, paneled,
country-style dining
room. One of Venice's
few creperies.*
25,000–35,000 lire.
⚪ ▭

DA BRUNO
Calle Lunga Santa
Barnaba 2754
Tel: 520 69 78
Open 10–11.30am,
6–10.30pm
Closed Sat and Sun
*Fish restaurant,
patronized by locals at
midday. Speciality:
deep-fried fish.*
16,500–35,000 lire.
⚪

DA GIANNI
Zattere 918
Tel: 523 72 10
Open 7.30am–11pm
Closed Wed and Jan
*Overpriced restaurant
facing the Giudecca.
Beautiful view. Clientèle
mostly tourist groups,
hence somewhat curt
service. Specialities
include carpaccio e
parmigiano, seppie alla
Veneziana.*
33,000–40,000 lire.
🌓 ⚪ ▭ ✕

INCONTRO
Dorsoduro 3062
Tel: 522 24 04
Open 12 noon–3pm,
7.30–10.30pm
Closed Mon and July
*Youthful, friendly
atmosphere.*

*Specialities include
bonito, ravioli with goat's
cheese, grated orange
peel and saffron.*
35,000 lire.
🌓 ⚪ ▭

L'ISOLA MISTERIOSA
Rio terrà della
Scoarsera 2894
Tel: 523 83 66
Open 12 noon–3.30pm,
8–11.30pm
Closed Sat noon and
Sun
*A small restaurant/bar,
modern décor,
patronized by students.
Mainly vegetarian
cuisine.*
20,000–25,000 lire.
⚪

LA FURATOLA
Calle Lunga Santa
Barnaba 2870/a
Tel: 520 85 95
Open 12 noon–3pm,
7–9.30pm
Closed Wed evenings
and Thur
*The fish is guaranteed
to be extra fresh.
Specialities are the fish
and shellfish.*
70,000 lire.
▭

LA SOSTA
Campo Santa
Margherita 3019
Tel: 528 52 55
Open 7am–8.30pm
Closed Sun
Snack bar.

RIVIERA
Dorsoduro 1473
Tel: 522 76 21
Open for lunch only
Open for dinner Fri and
Sat evenings
Closed Sun evening
and Mon

Closed May 15–Sept 30
*Delightful simple
restaurant with tables
on the quay at the end
of the Zattere. Much
frequented by
Venetians.*
40,000–50,000 lire.

**TAVERNA SAN
TROVASO**
Fondamenta Priuli 1016
Tel: 520 37 03
Open 12 noon–3pm,
7–10pm
Closed Mon
*An authentic restaurant
with good cooking and
impeccable service.
Specialities are the fish
and pizzas.*
17,000–26,000 lire.
⚪ 🌓 ▭

**TRATTORIA ANZOLO
RAFFAELE**
Campo San Raffaele
1722
Tel: 523 74 56
Open 12.30–2pm,
7.30–9pm
Closed Mon, Tue
and Aug
*Off the beaten track;
excellent fish-based
cuisine. Best to reserve
in advance.*
30,000 lire.
🌓 ⚪

HOTELS

**ACCADEMIA-VILLA
MARAVEGE ★★★**
Fondamenta Maravegie
1058
Tel: 523 78 46
Fax: 523 91 52
*A pretty 17th-century
villa well known to
guidebook writers – so
reserve well in advance.
Charming gardens, but
don't let them put you in*

their noisy annexe.
150,000–198,000 lire.
🛏 🏠 ✕ ▭

AGLI ALBORETTI ★★
Accademia 884
Tel: 523 00 58
Fax: 521 01 58
Closed for repairs in
Jan 1993
*A cosy, panelled hotel
with simple bedrooms –
come here for peace
and quiet, or if the Hotel
Galleria is full. Breakfast
included.*
120,000–160,000 lire.
🅒 🏠 ▭ ✻

**ALLA SALUTE
DA CICI ★★**
Fondamenta Ca' Bala
Salute 222
Tel: 523 54 04
Fax: 522 22 71
Closed Nov to
Christmas
*Quiet pensione with
garden, in a pretty
palazzo round the
corner from Ca' Salute.
View across to St
Mark's. Good value for
money. Breakfast
included.*
95,000–130,000 lire.
🏠 🏠 📠 ▭ 🍴 ✕

AMERICAN ★★★
San Vio 628,
Accademia
Tel: 520 47 33
Fax: 520 40 48
*Rooms good value but
banal. Some overlook
the canal. Breakfast
included.*
150,000–200,000 lire.
🅒 ▢ ▭ 🍴 ✻

DA PINO ★
Ca' Foscari 3941–3942
Tel: 522 36 46

AMERICAN
Ai GONDOLIERI
ALLA SALUTE DA CICI
MESSNER

Good value rooms, in a students' quarter which is full of people during the day. Breakfast included. Extra bed for a child – 10,000 lire.
33,000–66,000 lire.
⌂ ▭ 🄲 ♀ ⌘

FORESTERIA DOMUS CAVANIS
Rio terrà Antonio Foscarini 912/a
Tel and Fax: 528 73 74
Closed Oct 1–June 9
A religious foyer, reserved for students under 25. Plenty of cheap, rudimentary bedrooms, with shower on the landing. Breakfast included.
20,000 lire.
⌂ 🄲 ⌂

LA CALCINA **
Zattere 780
Tel: 520 64 66
Fax: 522 70 45
Attractive pensione with magnificent view across to the Giudecca. Spacious, sunny bedrooms.
118,000–130,000 lire.
🏠 ⌂ ⌂ 🄳·· ⌇ ▭

LA GALLERIA *
Accademia 878/a
Tel: 520 41 72
Ravishing pensione in an 18th-century palace. Superb view of the Grand Canal and Accademia – excellent value, though somewhat noisy. Breakfast included.
75,000–105,000 lire.
🏠 ⌂ 🄲 ⌇ ♀

LOCANDA MONTIN *
Fondamenta di Borgo 1147
Tel: 522 71 51
Fax: 520 02 55
The dream pensione, on the banks of a beautiful canal. Garden. Reserve many months in advance.
65,000 lire.
🏠 ⌂ ⌂ 🄳··

MESSNER **
Dorsoduro 216
Tel and Fax: 522 74 43
Closed Nov 15–Dec 28
Hotel with garden in a pleasant, tranquil quarter.
76,000–111,000 lire.
⌂ ⌂ ▭

PAUSANIA ***
Fondamenta Gherardini

◆ THE ZATTERE ◆

In the Dorsoduro sestiere. This long wharf, built in the 16th century to receive timber floated across the Lagoon from the mainland, links the Punta della Dogana with Santa Marta. The length of the Zattere was a favorite walk for Ezra Pound, among many others. The Hotel Calcina, where Ruskin stayed, is on the waterfront here.

28824
Tel: 522 20 83
Telex: 42 01 78
Fourteenth-century palace; graceful and full of sunshine, but all too familiar with tour operators. Prices much too high. Shower and breakfast included.
220,000 lire.
🏛 ⌂ ▭ ▭ ♀

SEGUSO **
Zattere 779
Tel and Fax: 522 23 40
Closed end Nov–early March
A Venetian institution, with the faded charm of an authentic turn-of-the-century pensione. Fine view across to the Giudecca. Half board obligatory. Reduction for children under 3.
170,00–220,000 lire.
🏛 ⌂ ⌇ ▭ ♀ 🄳··

TIVOLI **
Ca' Foscari 3838
Tel: 523 77 52
Fax: 522 26 56
Impersonal hotel with only the most basic comforts, but close to monuments, vaporetto and universities. Breakfast included.
94,000–120,000 lire.
⌂ 🄲 ▭

BARS AND NIGHT LIFE

AI DO DRAGHI
Campo Santa Margherita 3665
Tel: 528 97 31
Open 8am–9pm
Closed Sun and 15 days in Aug
Small but busy, with live music and a terrace outside in summer.
🎵 ▭

ANTICA OSTERIA VENEZIANA
Calle Lunga San Barnaba 2753/a
Tel: 522 19 51
Open 7.30am–8.30pm
Closed Sat
Tramezzini and cichetti.

BAR SALUS
Rio terrà Ponte dei Pugni 3112
Tel: 528 52 79
Open 7–2am
Closed Sun
Very popular in summer. Terrace stays open late

CODROMA
Ponte del Soccorso 2540
Tel: 270 31 31
Open until 1.30am
Closed Thur
Pleasant osteria, always full of chess, backgammon and card players. Lively jazz ambiance.
⌇ 🎵 🍴 ▭

EL SOUK
Calle Contarini Corfu 1056/a
Tel: 520 03 71
Open 10pm–4am
Closed Tue
Small, slightly passé discotheque. These days young Venetians tend to head for Mestre. Worn-out red armchairs and passable music.
🎵

GREEN PUB
Campo Santa Margherita 3053/a

Tel: 523 73 45
Open 8pm–1am
Closed Wed
Brand new, agreeable bar, opened Aug 1992. Lively, youthful atmosphere.

IL CAFFÈ
Campo Santa Margherita
Tel: 528 79 38
Open 8am–midnight
Closed Sun
Small bar with terrace.

LINEA D'OMBRA
Zattere 19 (close to the Punta della Dogana)
Tel: 528 52 59
Open 8–1am
Closed Wed
Hip piano bar, prices very steep. Food available at mealtimes only.
🍴

ROUND MIDNIGHT (INSTITUTE FOR RESEARCH, CULTURE AND LEISURE)
Fondamenta dei Pugni 3102
Tel: 523 10 78
Open 10pm–3am
Closed Sun.
Jazz concerts take place on Mon. Open to members only. Very fashionable, high-spirited club.
🍴 ▢

SOTTOSOPRA
Calle San Pantalon 3740
Tel: 528 53 20
Open 8pm–12.30am
Closed Sun
Modern bar, high-tech décor.

GIUDECCA

EMERGENCIES

MEDICAL TREATMENT
Tel: 523 00 00
See also the list of Useful Telephone Numbers.

POLICE STATION
Giudecca 543
Tel: 522 55 90

BASIC INFORMATION

POSTAL CODE
30 133
POST OFFICE
Giudecca 430
Tel: 528 90 46

CULTURE

CHURCH OF THE REDEEMER (IL REDENTORE)
Campo Redentore
Tel: 523 14 15
Open 8am–12 noon, 4–7.15pm

CHURCH OF SANT'EUFEMIA
Fondamenta Sant'Eufemia 680
Tel: 522 58 48
Open 9.30–11.30am, 6–7.15pm

CHURCH OF THE ZITELLE (SANTA MARIA DELLA PREZENTAZIONE)
Fondamenta della Zittelle
This church is currently closed for restoration work

◆ THE GIUDECCA ◆

For many years this island was used as a resort by the patrician families of Venice. Some of the gardens and orchards of their villas can still be seen. Overlooking one of its canals is the "Casa dei Tre Oci", a neo-Gothic building with three odd-shaped windows (above). This was built by a painter at the beginning of the 20th century.

RESTAURANTS

CIPRIANI
Zitelle 10, Giudecca
Tel: 520 77 44
Open 12.30pm–2.30pm, 8pm–10.30pm
Closed Nov 15–March 15
Restaurant in the quiet, refined hotel of the same name. Superb location, terrace open in summer; succulent antipasti. Venetian and international specialities.
About 110,000 lire.
⑪ ⊠ ▨ ▣⋯

HARRY'S DOLCI
Fondamenta Sant'Eufemia 773
Tel: 522 48 44 and 520 83 37
Open 10.30am–3pm, 7.30–10.30pm
Closed Tue, from Nov to March, and one week before Carnival
Less expensive than Harry's Bar; beautiful terrace overlooking the canal, delicious patisseries served outside lunch and dinner hours. All Cipriani products available.
About 60,000 lire.
⑪ ⊠ ▨ ▣⋯

L'ALTANELLA
Calle dell'Erbe 268
Tel: 522 77 80
Open 12.30–2.30pm, 7.30–9pm
Closed Mon, Tue and 1st fortnight of Aug and Jan
An authentic Venetian restaurant. In summer, the terrace by the canal is covered in flowers. Specialities: cuttlefish à la Venitienne and grilled monkfish.
About 50,000 lire.
◐ ⊠ ▨ ▣⋯

HOTELS

CASA FROLLO ★★★
Fondamenta delle Zitelle 50
Tel: 522 27 23
Fax: 620 62 03
Highly individual establishment, a former convent which recently mobilized its clientèle in a petition to stay open.
⌂ ⌂ ▣⋯ ▨

CIPRIANI ★★★★★
Zitelle 10
Tel: 520 77 44
Fax: 520 39 30
Open 12.30–2.30pm, 8–10.30pm
Closed Nov 15–March 15

Luxury complex, with private tennis court, Olympic seawater swimming pool, sumptuous bedrooms, private moorings. The restaurant has an excellent reputation (see list of restaurants). *410,000–740,000 lire*

ISTITUTO SUORE CANOSSIANE
Ponte Piccolo 428
Tel: 522 21 57
Open 4–10pm
A religious institution close to Sant'Eufemia, with two dormitories for women only.
14,000 lire.

OSTELLO DELLA GIOVENTÙ ·
Fondamenta delle Zitelle 86
Tel: 523 82 11
Fax: 523 56 89
Open 7.30–9am, 5–11pm
Office opens at 6pm – deposit your card in the morning. Groups must reserve by fax
Youth card obligatory for this pearl among youth hostels. View to the Doge's Palace. Breakfast included.
19,000 lire.

SAN GIORGIO MAGGIORE

CULTUR

CHURCH OF SAN GIORGIO MAGGIORE
Island of San Giorgio Maggiore

Tel: 528 99 00
Open 9am–5.30pm
Open until 7pm during the season
There is also a monastery on the island of San Giorgio Maggiore. A mass takes place with Gregorian chants each Sun at 11am.

CINI FOUNDATION LIBRARY
Tel: 528 99 00
Open 9am–12.30pm
Closed Sat, Sun and holidays
The library is open to students only.

CINI FOUNDATION
Tel: 528 99 00
Visit by special request only.

◆ SAN GIORGIO MAGGIORE ◆

The Church of San Giorgio Maggiore is one of Andrea Palladio's greatest masterpieces. It faces St Mark's Basin, and the view of Venice, the Lagoon and the Giudecca from the top of its campanile is incomparable.

SANTA CROCE

EMERGENCIES

MEDICAL TREATMENT
Tel: 523 00 00
See also the list of Useful Telephone Numbers

BASIC INFORMATION

POSTAL CODE
30 135
EXCHANGE BUREAUX
Fondamenta San Simeon Piccolo 714
PUBLIC TOILETS
– Piazzale Roma – Giardini Papadopoli
Open 9am–3pm
–Piazzale Roma – Calle Cassetti
Open 8am–8pm

CULTURE

CA' PESARO (MUSEUM OF MODERN ART)
Fondamenta Mocenigo, San Stae 2076
Tel: 72 11 27
Open 10am–4pm (sometimes until 6pm when exhibitions are under way)
Closed Mon
Permanent exhibition of Modern Art on the ground floor. Temporary exhibitions are held on the 1st floor.

CA' PESARO (ORIENTAL MUSEUM)
Fondamenta Mocenigo, San Stae
Tel: 524 11 73
Open 9am–2pm, (9am–1pm holidays)
Ticket office closes 30 minutes earlier
Closed Mon
On the 3rd floor of the Pesaro Palace. Largest collection of oriental art in Europe.

CHURCH OF SAN ZAN DEGOLÀ (SAN GIOVANNI DECOLLATO)
Campo San Zan Degolà
Currently closed for restoration.

CHURCH OF SAN GIACOMO DELL'ORIO
Campo San Giacomo dell'Orio
Tel: 524 16 72
Open 8am–12 noon, 4.30–6.30pm

CHURCH OF SAN SIMEON GRANDO (SAN SIMEON PROFETA)
Campo San Simeon Grande
Open Sun and holidays at 11am for Mass.

LOCANDA STEFANIA
CANAL E WALTER
AIRONE
AL SOLE
AL GALLO

CHURCH OF SAN SIMEON PICCOLO
Campo Nuova San Simeon
Open for mass at 6.30pm

CHURCH OF SAN STAE
Campo San Stae
Open 9am–12 noon, 3pm–5.45pm
Sat and Sun, classical music concerts.

CHURCH OF SANTA MARIA MATER DOMINI
Campo Santa Maria Mater Domini
Mass at 5.30pm daily

CHURCH OF SAN NICOLÒ DA TOLENTINO
Campo dei Tolentini 265
Tel: 522 58 06
Open 9.30–11.30am, 5–6.30pm

FONDACO DEI TURCHI (NATURAL HISTORY MUSEUM)
Fondaco dei Turchi 730
Tel: 524 08 85
Open 9am–1.30pm (9am–1pm Sun)
Closed holidays
On the ground floor and 2nd floor of the former Turkish merchants' warehouse.

FABRIC AND COSTUME MUSEUM
Palazzo Mocenigo, Santa Croce 992
Tel: 72 17 98
Open 8.30am–1.30pm
Closed Sun and holidays
This former palace of the Mocenigo family houses a collection of Coptic fabrics (5th–7th century), Italian and French fabrics (14th–19th century) and costumes from the 18th and 19th centuries.

RESTAURANTS

ALLE OCHE
Calle Tintor 1552 a/b (near San Giacomo dell'Orio)
Tel: 524 11 61
Open 12 noon–3pm, 7–11pm
Closed Mon
Excellent address. Lively, youthful clientèle, friendly service. Reserve at weekends. Menu includes 70 pizzas. Delicious and very good value
(5,000–9,500 lire). Meals around 20,000 lire.
○ ◻·· ◻

ANTICA BESSETTA
Salizzada Zusto 1395
Tel: 72 16 87
Open 12.30–2.30pm, 7–9.30pm
Closed Tue and Wed
A restaurant which is somewhat isolated but still a favorite with the locals. Traditional cuisine. Reserve in advance. Specialities include the risi e bisi and fish.
20,000–42,000 lire.
◐ ○ ◻·· ◻

CORONA
Calle Regina 2262
Open 12 noon–2.30pm, 7–10pm
Closed Sun and Mon at noon.
Gastronomic cooking in a small back street restaurant.

◆ FONDACO DEI TURCHI ◆

A very ancient Venetian-Byzantine construction used in the 17th century as a warehouse by Venice's community of Turkish merchants. The Fondaco was restored earlier this century and now houses the city's Natural History Museum.

45,000–65,000; special menu 55,000 lire.
⓪ ◻ ◻··

NONO RISORTO
Santa Croce 2237
Tel: 524 11 69
Open 12 noon–2.30pm, 7pm–1am
(Orders taken until 11.30pm)
Closed Wed
Pleasant garden. The speciality is fish.
About 40,000 lire.

REGINA CORNARO
Calle della Regina 2330
Tel: 524 14 02
Closed Mon

TRATTORIA AL PONTE
Ponte di Lazzarin Giuliano e Giovanni 1666, San Giacomo dell'Orio
Tel: 71 97 77
Open 8am–midnight
Closed Sun and Aug
A small, lively brasserie, patronized by working people and generally packed at noon. The ambiance here is the real thing.
16,000–25,000 lire.
○ ◻ ◻··

LA ZUCCA
San Giacomo dell'Orio 1762
Tel: 524 15 70
Open 12.30–2.30pm, 7–10.30pm

Labels on image (top): AI DUE FANALI, MARIN, ANTICA BESSETA, ALLE OCHE, TRATTORIA AL PONTE, LA ZUCCA, REGINA CORNARO, CORONA, NONO RISORTO, SAN CASSIANO

Closed Sun
Plenty of people want to eat at La Zucca, but very few get to do so – there are only 25 places. One or two vegetarian dishes, but mainly delicious pasta and pumpkin soup. About 40,000 lire.

HOTELS

AI DUE FANALI **
Campo San Simeon Grande 946
Tel: 71 84 90
Fax: 71 83 44
Closed Dec–Jan but open for the Christmas holidays
*Alas, the tour operators have discovered this hotel. Decent rooms on a quiet square beside the church. Some of them overlook the Grand Canal. Breakfast included. Reductions out of season and for students.
80,000–120,000 lire.*
⌂ ⌂ ⊡·· ▭

AIRONE **
Santa Croce 557
Tel and Fax: 520 48 00.
Closed Nov–mid Feb
*Opposite the station, on the Grand Canal. Breakfast included. Free for those under 6.
70,000–121,000 lire.*
⌂ ▭ ☆

AL GALLO *
Calle Amai 197/g
Tel: 523 67 61.
Closed Nov 15–Dec 15
*Tiny pensione with 7 rooms and rudimentary conveniences. Pleasant reception and prices that fluctuate according to the owner's whim. Free for children under 10 years old.
40,000–70,000 lire.*
⌂ ⊡·· ☆

AL SOLE ***
Santa Croce 136
Tel: 523 21 44
Fax: 71 90 61
Closed Nov–end March.
*Beautifully decorated rooms, with view over a small canal. Free for children under 2.
140,000–205,000 lire.*
⌂ ▭ ⊡·· ☆

CANAL E WALTER **
San Simeon Piccolo 553
Tel: 523 84 80
Fax: 523 91 06
*Situated near the station. Two renovated hotels which belong to the same owner. Decent rooms and an interior garden. Breakfast included.
100,000–160,000 lire.*
♠ ⌂ ▯ ▭ ⊡··

CASA PERON *
Salizzada San Pantalon 84–85
Tel: 528 60 38.
Closed Jan after Epiphany
*For small groups and students, this entirely charmless hotel may prove a lifesaver. Located in the lively university quarter, near interesting monuments. Breakfast included.
47,000–92,000 lire. The hotel's annexe is vey cheap for Venice, at 25,000–50,000 lire, but there are no showers and breakfast is extra.*
⌂ ▭ ⊡··

GARDENA ***
Fondamenta dei Tolentini 239
Tel: 523 55 49
Fax: 522 07 82
*A well positioned hotel with fairly comfortable rooms, but the prices are high for this area, which is noisy and crowded. Breakfast included.
105,000–195,000 lire.*
♠ ▯ ▭ ⊡··

LOCANDA STEFANIA *
Fondamenta dei Tolentini 181/a
Tel: 520 37 57
Hotel mainly occupied by Venetian students throughout the school year.
⌂ ⊡··

MARIN *
San Simeone Piccolo/ Santa Croce 670/b
Tel and Fax: 71 80 22
Closed Jan
*Charming owners. Located in a quiet, residential area. Family atmosphere, and 16th-century fresco in the dining room.
Breakfast included.
43,000–94,000 lire.*
⌂ ♠ ⌂ ⊡·· ▯

PULLMAN PARK HOTEL ****
Santa Croce 245
Giardini Papadopoli
Tel: 528 53 94
Fax: 523 00 43
*A hotel belonging to Accor, a French chain of hotels. Located close to the station, with comfortable modern rooms. Breakfast included. Free for children under 12.
160,000–320,000 lire.*
♠ ▯ ⊡·· ▭ ☆

SAN CASSIANO***
Calle Rosa 2232
Tel: 524 17 68
Telex: 420 810
An elegant palazzo dating from the 14th-century, with good

435

DA NANE AL CANTON

AZIENDA AGRITURISMO O. RENZA

DA CICIO STELLA

period furniture. Very comfortable. Polite service and international clientèle. Breakfast included.
212,000–252,000 lire

BARS AND NIGHT LIFE

AI POSTALI
Rio Marin 821
Tel: 71 51 56
Open 10am–3pm, 6pm–1am
Closed Tue out of season
A small wine bar serving sandwiches and crêpes. Lively clientèle of Venetian and foreign students. Highly original décor.

EMERGENCIES

HOSPITAL
AL MAR HOSPITAL
Tel: 526 17 50

BASIC INFORMATION

POST CODE
30 126
TOURIST OFFICE
Gran Viale Santa Maria Elisabetta 6/a
Tel: 526 57 21
Fax: 529 87 20

POST OFFICE
Via Doge D. Michiel 1/e
Tel: 526 50 32

CULTURE

JEWISH CEMETERY
Via Cipro 70
Tel: 526 01 42
Open 9.30am–2.30pm
Closed Sat and during Jewish festivals.
16th–17th century tombs.

CHURCH AND CONVENT OF SAN NICOLÒ
Riviera San Nicolò 26
Tel: 526 02 41
Open 8am–12 noon, 3–7pm

CHURCH OF SANTA MARIA ELISABETTA
Piazzale Santa Maria Elisabetta
Tel: 526 00 72
Open 6.30am–12.30pm, 3.30–5.30pm

RESTAURANTS

BELVEDERE
Piazzale Santa Maria Elisabetta 4
Tel: 526 01 42
Open 12 noon–2.30pm, 7–10pm
Closed Mon and Oct 15–March 31
This little family restaurant is not much to look at and is

relatively expensive. Still, it appears popular with Venetians.
35,000–80,000 lire.

DA ANDRI
Via Lepanto 21
Tel: 526 54 82
Open 12.30–4.00pm
Closed Mon, Tue and Jan 1–Feb 28
Beside the canal in a busy spot, especially in summer. The speciality is fresh fish.
45,000 lire.

DA CICIO
Via Sandro Gallo 241
Tel: 526 00 49
Open 6am–11pm
Closed Tue
Small, typically Venetian restaurant accessible by vaporetto and bus. Known for simple, fresh food. The speciality is fish.
About 40,000 lire.

DA NANE AL CANTON
San Pietro in Volta, Pellestrina 282
Tel: 527 91 10
Open 12 noon–2pm, 7–9pm
Closed Mon and Feb
A restaurant with an excellent reputation in the middle of a fishing village. Plenty of authentic charm.

Terrace in summer. Specialities: pasticcio di pesce, risotto di seppioline, fresh fish.
50,000–60,000 lire.

DA VALENTINO
Via Sandro Gallo 81
Tel: 526 01 28
Open 12.30–11pm
Closed Mon from April 1 to Oct 30
Closed Mon, Tue, Wed from Nov 1 to March 31
Good fish restaurant; the menu features fresh, locally caught fish. In winter, ducks from the Lagoon are served here. Specialities are the grilled fish and risotto.
45,000–50,000 lire.

FAVORITA
Via F. Duodo 33
Tel: 526 16 26
Open 12.30–3pm, 7.30pm–midnight
Closed Mon and Jan
Excellent fish restaurant. Exclusively Venetian cooking. Terrace and piano bar open in summer.
50,000–60,000 lire.

PIZZERIA RESTAURANT VENEZIA 2000
Lungomare d'Annunzio 2
Tel: 526 81 21
Open 7–11pm
Closed Mon and Dec 15–Jan 15
Terrace with view on the Adriatic. International cuisine and pizzas.
Minimum 20,000 lire.

SELF SERVICE GRAN VIALE
Gran Viale Santa Maria

Elisabetta 10/b
Tel: 526 03 22
Open 9am–1am.
Closed Wed
*Restaurant-cafeteria.
International cooking.
Minimum 14,000 lire.*
○

HOTELS

ATLANTA AUGUSTUS *
Via Lepanto 15
Tel: 526 05 69
Closed Nov 1–Feb 28
*Simple, clean rooms. A
small, well kept 1930's
style hotel. Shower and
breakfast included.
140,000–222,000 lire.*

**AZIENDA
AGRITURISMO O.
RENZA**
Lungomare Alberoni 32,
Tel: 73 10 78.
*Near the sea and the
golf club, an authentic
farmhouse with a
fabulous view of the
Adriatic and the Lagoon.
Five double bedrooms
with baths. Possibility of
demi-pénsion. Family
style cooking, fresh
vegetables from the
garden, fish. Best to
reserve. Breakfast
included.
70,000 lire.*
🏨 ⌂ ☆

CRISTALLO *
Gran Viale Santa Maria
Elisabetta 51
Tel: 526 52 93
Fax: 526 56 15
Closed in winter, except
during Christmas
holidays
*On the Lido's liveliest
boulevards .
Convenient garden and
bathing cabins reserved
in summer for clients.
Reductions for children.
Breakfast included.
130,000 lire.*
⌂ ⌂ ▭ ☆

**GRAND HOTEL DES
BAINS ****
Lungomare Marconi 17
Tel: 526 59 21

Fax: 526 01 13
Closed Nov 1–April 15
*Internationally famous
hotel, immortalized by
Thomas Mann (and
Luchino Visconti) as the
setting for "Death in
Venice". Park,
swimming pool, private
beach, various sports.
Free for children under
6 years old.
240,000–475,000 lire.*
🏨 ⌂ ☼ ▭ ▱ ▭
☆ ⌘ 🅿

EXCELSIOR ***
Lungomare Marconi 41
Tel: 526 02 01
Fax: 526 72 76
Closed Nov 1–March 31
*Built at the beginning of
the century, this great
hotel is a mixture of
Moorish, Byzantine and
Gothic styles. It is the
HQ of the jury of La
Mostra del Cinema, and
close to the casino and
the beach.
390,000–470,000 lire.*
🏨 ⌂ ▭ ▱ ▭

LA PERGOLA *
Via Cipro 15
Tel: 526 07 84
*This is a delightful
family-run pensione with
modern décor and
rooms overlooking the*

*garden. Breakfast
included.
75,000–98,000 lire.*
⌂ ☆

REITER **
Gran Viale 57
Tel: 526 01 07
*Completely renovated
hotel-restaurant. Double
rooms with view on
garden. Breakfast
included.
130,000 lire.*
⌂ ☆

RIGEL***
Via Dandolo 13
Tel: 526 88 10
Fax: 520 40 83
Closed Nov 1–Feb 28
*A very quiet hotel with
its own garden. Meals
are available for groups
only. Situated 5 minutes
away from the landing
stage. Breakfast
included.
130,000–249,000 lire.*
⌂ ▭

STELLA **
Via Sandro Gallo 111
Tel: 526 07 45
Fax: 526 93 97
Closed Nov 1–March 31
*With car park and
garden. Five minutes
from the casino.
Breakfast included
60,000–130,000 lire.*
⌂ ▭ ☆ 🅿

VIANELLO **
Via Casa Rosa 10
Tel: 73 10 72
Closed Nov 1–March 31
*Hotel with garden.
Possibility of demi-
pension.
30,000–80,000 lire.*
⌂

VILLA AURORA **
Riviera San Nicolò 11/a
Tel: 526 05 19
Closed Jan 1–Feb 15
*Quiet hotel-restaurant,
with terrific view over
the canal and Lagoon.
Double rooms.
Breakfast included.
70,000–130,000 lire.*
⌂ ⌂ ☆ ☼

VILLA CIPRO **
Via Zara 2
Tel: 526 14 08
Fax: 276 01 76
*Modern hotel with small
garden. Breakfast
included.
107,000–140,000 lire.*
⌂

VILLA DELLE PALME *
Via Dandolo 12
Tel: 526 13 12
*Fine "Liberty"-style villa.
Some of the bedrooms
have balconies
overlooking the garden.
Quiet, but close to the
beach and San Marco.
45,000–90,000 lire.*
⌂ ⌂ 🅿

VILLA PANNONIA **
Via Doge Michiel 48
Tel: 526 52 77
Closed for Christmas
holidays
*1900's hotel-restaurant
with garden. Breakfast
included. Reductions for
children.
85,000–120,000 lire.*
⌂ ☆

VILLA TIZIANA**
Via A Gritti 3
Tel: 526 11 93
Fax: 526 89 03
Closed Nov1–March 1,
except Christmas
holidays and Carnival.
*Quiet villa with garden,
50 yards from the sea.
Private beach.
Breakfast included.
60,000–124,0000 lire.*
⌂ ⌂

BARS AND
NIGHT LIFE

BAR TRENTO
Via Sandro Gallo 82
Tel: 526 59 60

AL BERSAGLIERE — LA BELLA VENEZIA — IL GATTO — GRAND' ITALIA — VAL D'OSTRICA

Open 7am–9pm
Restaurant open at
midday only.
Closed Sun.
*Traditional Venetian
cooking and wine
served by the jug.*

BOUNTY BAR
Gran Viale 6/b
Tel: 276 00 83
Open 7am–midnight
Closed Mon
*An elegant snack-bar,
with nautical décor. Tea
room, specializing in
Venetian pastries,
cantuccini alla
mandorle, assorted
home-made tarts.*

ACROPOLIS
Lungomare Marconi 22
Tel: 526 04 66
Open 10pm–3am
Closed Mon
Open weekends only
out of season
*Small discotheque, a
popular meeting place
for young Venetians.*
♫

**ROUGE ET NOIRE
DISCOTECA
(MAYA DESNUDA)**
Lungomare
Marconi–Casino
Tel: 526 85 08
Open 10pm–2am,
except in winter.
Small and rather fun.
♫

CHIOGGIA

EMERGENCIES

POLICE STATION
Corso del Popolo
Tel: 40 02 85
Tel: 40 17 00
HOSPITAL
Via Madonna Marina 500
Tel: 553 41 11

BASIC INFORMATION

POST CODE
30 015
TOURIST OFFICE
Lungomare Adriatico 101
Tel: 554 04 66
POST OFFICE
Corso del Popolo 1200
Tel: 40 08 83
BANKS
BANCA CASSA DI
RISPARMIO
Via Granatieri di
Sardegna
Borgo San Giovanni
Tel: 496 72 58
BANCO AMBROSIANO
VENETO
Rione Duomo 966
Tel: 40 35 22
BANCO SAN MARCO
Viale Veneto 17
Sottomarina
Tel: 40 30 85

TRANSPORTATION

RAILWAY STATION
STAZIONE FS
Viale Stazione
Borgo San Giovanni
Tel: 40 04 62
BUS
ACTV – Piazza Europa
Sottomarina
Tel: 49 22 55
Public transport service.
SHIP
PORT AUTHORITY
Campo Santa Croce 1290
Tel: 40 02 42
PORT
Campo Marconi 92
Tel: 40 16 00
CAR RENTALS
DEGRASSI
Via Saloni
Tel: 40 54 93
SANTINATO
Valli 118/e
Tel: 49 97 87

CULTURE

**CATHEDRAL OF SANTA
MARIA**
Calle Duomo 77
Tel: 40 04 96
Open Sat 3–6.30pm
Open Sun 7.30am–
12 noon, 3–6.30pm

**CHURCH OF SAN
DOMENICO**
Canal San Domenico
Tel: 40 35 26.
Open out of season
7.30am–12 noon,
3–6pm
Open in season
7.30am–12 noon,
4–8pm
*Church founded in the
13th century and
restored in the 19th
century, with a painting
of St Paul by Carpaccio.*

**CHURCH OF SAN
MARTINO**
Sottomarina
Tel: 40 00 54
Open 6.30am–12.30pm,
2.30–8pm
Closes at 10pm in
season

PALAZZO GRASSI
Riva Vena
Now a hospital.

RESTAURANTS

AL BERSAGLIERE
Via C Battisti 293
Tel: 40 10 44
Open 12 noon–3pm,
7–10pm
Closed Tue
*Very good fish
restaurant.*
50,000 lire.
◑ ▭

IL GARIBALDI
Via San Marco 1924
Sottomarina
Tel: 554 00 42
Open 12 noon–2pm,

Pittore degli Angeli

GAMBERO D'ORO BELLEVUE CAPINERA BRISTOL

IL GARIBALDI

7–10.30pm
Closed Mon
Large dining room, with rustic décor and friendly atmosphere. Reserve in advance. Terrace. Fresh fish specialities. Menus based on what's available in the market.
45,000–50,000 lire.
〇

IL GATTO
Corso del Popolo-
Campo Sant'Andrea
653
Tel: 40 18 06
Open 12 noon–2.30pm,
7–10.30pm
Closed Mon, Sun evenings out of season and Jan
Highly praised fish restaurant, fine arcaded dining room and pleasant ambiance. Specialities include lumachine di mare, polenta, spaghetti with mussels.
Minimum 50,000 lire.
〇 🖵

LA BELLA VENEZIA
Calle Corona 51,
Tel: 40 05 00.
Open 10am–3pm,
7–10pm.
Closed Thur and January.
Known for its fish specialities. With garden and spacious reception room.
40,000–50,000 lire.
〇 🖵

VAL D'OSTRICA
Calle Sant'Andrea 763
Tel: 40 05 27.
Open 8am–3pm,
6pm–midnight.
Closed Wed and January.
Piano bar on Fri, Sat

and Sun. Very friendly atmosphere. Hotel-restaurant with garden.
50,000–60,000 lire.
〇 🖙 🖵

HOTELS

BELLEVUE ★★★
Lungomare Adriatico 22
Sottomarina,
Tel and Fax: 40 19 05
In a very lively quarter; modern, comfortable rooms with view on the sea. Restaurant, salle de jeux, billiard room. Breakfast included.
60,000–80,000 lire.
🏠 ☀ 🖵

BRISTOL ★★★★
Lungomare Adriatico 46, Sottomarina
Tel: 554 03 89
Fax: 554 18 13

Bragozzo

Closed Nov–Feb
The best hotel in Chioggia, with garden, pool and private beach. Taverna for dancing in the evenings. Full pension possible.
85,000–150,000 lire.
☀ 🖵 ⚓ 🖵 🅿

CAPINERA ★★★
Lungomare Adriatico 12
Sottomarina
Tel: 40 09 61
Closed Nov to May.
Very quiet hotel-restaurant. Rooms overlooking a garden on one side and the sea on the other. Private beach. Reductions for children, full board possible.
🏠 🏠 ☀ ⚓ 🅿

GAMBERO D'ORO ★★
Viale Venezia 1,
Sottomarina
Tel and Fax: 40 30 54
Small hotel-restaurant in the center of town, close to the sea. Pleasant and quiet with terrace.
45,000–65,000 lire.
🏠 🏠 🖵 🖵 🚐

GRAND'ITALIA ★★★
Piazzetta Vigo
Tel: 40 01 85.
Pretty hotel in the historic center of Chioggia, close to the landing-stage.
38,000–65,000 lire.
🏠 🏠 🅿

TOURING ★★★
Lungomare Adriatico

44, Sottomarina
Tel: 554 05 04
Closed Nov to Feb, except during Carnival
By the sea. Decent, good value rooms. Private beach.
55,000–75,000 lire.
🏠 🖵 ☀ 🅿

BARS AND NIGHT LIFE

CIAK VOSTOK
Via C. Colombo 166
Sottomarina
Tel: 406 06 01
Open Sat 10pm–4am,
Open Sun 6.30–11pm
Closed weekdays in winter
Fashionable night-club with American style snackbar.
♫

HIJACK
Viale Padova 18
Sottomarina
Tel: 554 01 70
Open 10pm–4am
Closed weekdays in winter
Disco with garden, bar, restaurant and snack bar.
♫

SHAKER
Lungomare Adriatico 28
Sottomarina
Tel: 40 18 09
Open in season
10.30pm–4am
Open in winter
10.30pm–4am (Sat),
4pm–10.30pm (Sun)
Very popular with the locals. Packed with tourists in the summer.
♫

MURANO

EMERGENCIES

MEDICAL TREATMENT
Tel: 523 00 00

BASIC INFORMATION

POST CODE
30 141
POST OFFICE
Fondamenta Navagero
48
Tel: 527 44 99
PUBLIC TOILETS
Piazza Colonna
Open 8 am–6 pm

CULTURE

CHURCH OF SANTA MARIA SAN DONATO
Campo San Donato

439

TRATTORIA AL CORALLO

TRATTORIA BUSA ALLA TORRE

TRATTORIA VALMARANA

Tel: 73 09 56
Open 8am–12 noon,
4–7pm
Open at hours of mass:
Sun 7.30am, 9.30am
11am, 6.30pm;
Weekdays 8.30am; Fri
and Sat 6pm (6.30pm in
summer)

MUSEO VETRARIO ANTICO

Fondamenta Giustinian
Tel: 73 95 86
Open in season
9am–7pm.
Open out of season
10am–4pm
Closed Wed

MUSEO VETRARIO MODERNO

Fondamenta Mani 1/c
Tel: 73 94 07
Open in season
9am–7pm
Open out of season
10am–4pm
Closed Wed
*This museum is shortly
to be reopened.*

RESTAURANTS

TRATTORIA AL CORALLO

Fondamenta Vetrai 73
Tel: 73 95 36
Open 12 noon–3pm,
7–8pm
*There is friendly service
at this trattoria, which is
open all year round.
Meals at tables or at the
bar. Pleasant
atmosphere. The
speciality is fish.
Excellent value for
money.
30,000–35,000 lire.*
◑ ○ ▭

TRATTORIA BUSA ALLA TORRE

Campo Santo Stefano 3
Tel: 73 96 62
Open 11.45–3pm
Closed Mon and Jan
*The oldest private
mansion in Murano
(11th century), close to
the Church of San
Pietro. Fish restaurant
specializing in spaghetti
agli scampi e alle
rucole.
About 50,000 lire.*
◑ ▭

TRATTORIA VALMARANA

Fondamenta Navagero
31
Tel: 73 93 13 .
Open 11.30am–3pm

Open evenings by
reservation only
Closed Wed and Jan
*In season, meals are
served in the garden.
delicious "rombo".
Grilled meat and fresh
fish specialities.
60,000–70,000 lire.*
◑ ▭

HOTELS

PENSIONE AL SOFFIADOR

Viale Bressagio 10
Tel: 73 94 30
Closed Dec 15–Jan 15.
*Double rooms with bath.
Fish restaurant open at
midday. Excellent value.
70,000 lire.*
⌂ ⌂ ▭

BURANO

EMERGENCIES

MEDICAL TREATMENT

Tel: 523 00 00
*See list of Useful
Telephone Numbers*

BASIC INFORMATION

POST CODE

30 012

POST OFFICE

San Martino Destro 863
Tel: 73 00 43

CULTURE

SCUOLA DI MERLETTI DI BURANO

Piazza Galuppi
Tel: 73 00 34
Open Tue to Sat
9am–6pm
Open Sun 10am–4pm
Closed Mon
*Lace Museum and
cooperative, where
lacemakers can be
seen at work.*

RESTAURANTS

DA ROMANO ("TRE STELLE DA ROMANO")

Via Baldassare Galuppi
221
Tel: 73 00 30
Open 12 noon–2.30pm
and 6.30–9pm
Closed Tue, Sun
evenings
*In the center of Burano,
one of Venice's finest
fish restaurants. The
walls are hung with
paintings by artists who
have passed through at
one time or another.*

Reserve at weekends.
Specialities are the
fresh fish and fish risotti.
50,000–80,000 lire.
◑ ▭

RISTORANTE GATTO NERO

Via Giudecca 88
Tel: 73 01 20
Open 9am–10pm
Closed Mon and
end Oct–mid Nov
*A typical local
restaurant, included in
all the guides. The
picture collection is the
chef's pride and joy.
Clients of all types.
Specializes in fish only
(risotto alla buranella).
40,000–80,000 lire.*
◑ ▭

HOTELS

LOCANDA-RISTORANTE RASPO DE UA *

Piazza Galuppi 560
Tel: 73 00 95
Closed mid Nov–mid
Dec
*In a very old palazzo, a
small 6-bedroom hotel
with plenty of charm.
A favorite with painters.
40,000–70,000 lire.*
⌂

TORCELLO

EMERGENCIES

MEDICAL TREATMENT

Tel: 523 00 00

◆ THE LAST BURANO LACEMAKERS ◆

At the school of lacemaking in Burano, women
dressed in traditional white aprons work for
hours on end at their lacemakers' cushions.
Today, true Burano lace is rare
and very precious.

See Useful Telephone
Numbers

BASIC INFORMATION

POST CODE

30 012

CULTURE

CATHEDRAL OF TORCELLO

Open 10am–12.30pm,
2–5pm
*Concerts are frequently
organized here.*

HOTELS

LOCANDA CIPRIANI ***

Island of Torcello
Tel and Fax: 73 01 50
Closed Nov–mid March
*A small, 6-bedroom
hotel in the middle of
this tiny island. Half
board obligatory.
Excellent cuisine.
260,000–350,000 lire.*
🏛 ⌂

RESTAURANTS

LOCANDA CIPRIANI

Island of Torcello
Tel and Fax: 73 01 50
Open 12 noon–3pm
Closed Tue and
Nov–mid March
*This restaurant is
frequently packed with
tourists in summer.
View over gardens;
excellent cuisine, restful
surroundings. Speciality.
risotto alla torcellana.
About 110,000 lire.*
🍴

LOCANDA CIPRIANI   GATTO NERO   LOCANDA RASPO DE UA   DA ROMANO

DEPARTMENT STORES

COIN
Cannaregio 5787.
Open 9.30am–1pm,
3.30–7.30pm
Closed Sun, Mon
morning

STANDA
Cannaregio 3659
Open 8.30am–7.20pm
Closed Sun except from
March 15–Nov 1

CASINOS AND THEATERS

CASINO MUNICIPAL
Lungomare G Marconi,
Lido 4
Tel: 526 06 26
From Oct to March, the
casino occupies
Palazzo Vendramin-
Calergi, Cannaregio
2040
Tel: 72 04 44

TEATRO GOLDONI
San Marco 4650/b
Tel: 520 52 41

TEATRO LA FENICE
San Marco 2549
Tel: 521 01 61
Ticket office open
9.30–10.30am, 4–8pm

SHOPS

CIPOLATO SIGIFREDO
San Lio, Castello 5336
Tel: 522 84 37
Open 11am–7.30pm
Closed Sun
*Gold and silver
ware*

COLUSSI IL FORNAIO
San Marco 4579
Tel: 522 26 59
Open 8am–1.30pm,
4.30–8pm
Closed Sun
*Bakery and
pastryshop.*

EX LIBRIS
San Polo 1462
Tel: 522 40 04
Open 10am–7pm
Closed Sun
Marbled paper.

LELE NASON
Calle del Fumo,
Cannaregio 5306/b
Tel: 522 81 13
Open 8am–12 noon,
3–7pm
Closed Sun
*Mirrors, masks.
Reductions for clients
displaying this guide.*

MARCHINI
Calle del Spezier 2769
Tel: 522 91 09
Open 8.30am–8.30pm
Closed Tue
Venetian pastries.

**MASCARI LA
DROGHERIA**
San Polo 381
Tel: 522 97 62
Open 8am–1pm,
4.30pm–7pm
Closed Wed
Venetian food.

PAOLO OLBI
Calle della Mandola,
San Marco 3653
Tel: 528 50 25
Open 9.30am–12.30pm,
3.30–7.30pm
Closed Mon morning
Marbled paper.

VALESE FONDITORI
Calle Fiubera,
San Marco 793
Tel: 522 72 82
Open in season
10.30am–7.30pm
Open out of season
10.30am–12.30pm,
3–7.30pm
Closed Sun
*Foundry which casts
"Lions of St. Mark".*

VENEZIARTIGIANA
Calle Larga, San Marco
412
Tel: 523 50 32
Open 9.30am–11pm
March to Nov
Closed Mon morning
out of season
Craftwork.

BOOKSHOPS

**SANTI GIOVANNI E
PAOLO**
Barbaria de la Tole,
Castello 6358

LUCIANO FILIPPI
Calle della Bissa, San
Marco 5458
Tel: 523 69 16
Open 8.30am–12.30pm,
3–7.30pm
*Reproductions of old
Venetian texts.*

LUMINA
Castello 5785/b
Tel: 520 01 64.
Open 10am–1pm,
3.30–8pm
Closed Mon

TOLETTA
Sacca Toletta,
Dorsoduro 1214
Tel: 523 20 34
Open 9am–12.45pm,
1.30–7.30pm
Closed Sun and
15–31 Aug
*New and second-hand
books at half price.*

ICE-CREAM SHOPS

CAUSIN CAFFÉ GELATI
Campo Santa
Margherita, Dorsoduro
2996
Tel: 523 60 91
Open 8am–9pm
Closed Sat and Aug

NICO GELATI
Zattere, Dorsoduro 922
Tel: 522 52 93
Open 7am–10pm
Closed Thur and Dec
20–Jan 20
*One of Venice's best-
known ice-cream
shops. Don't miss the
"gianduiotto" and the
"Coppa Cardinale".*

PAOLIN
Campo Santo Stefano,
San Marco
Tel: 522 55 76
Open in season
7.30am–midnight
Open out of season
7am–8.30pm.
Closed Dec and Jan

ART GALLERIES

ARTE CONTINI
San Marco 2765
Tel: 520 49 42
Open 10am–1pm,
3.30–7.30pm
Closed Sun
*Conceptual art,
abstract art and 20th
century masters.*

BAC ART STUDIO
San Marco 2663
Tel: 522 81 71
Open 10am–1pm,
3pm–7pm
Closed Sun
*Drawings; original and
editions.*

FENICE ART
San Marco 1895
Tel: 523 88 55
Open 10.30am–
12.30pm, 3.30pm–
7.30pm
Closed Sun and Mon

GRAZIUSSI
San Marco 1998
Tel: 528 50 81
Open 10.30am–
12.30pm, 4–7.30pm
Closed Sun and Mon
morning
*Lithographs, silk-screens
by contemporary artists.*

PROVA D'ARTISTA
San Marco 1994/b
Tel: 522 48 12
Open 11am–1pm,
4.30–7.30pm
Closed Sun and Mon
morning
*Prints by international
artists.*

SANTO STEFANO
Campo Santo Stefano
San Marco 2953
Tel: 523 45 18
Open 10.30am–
12.30pm, 4–7pm
Closed Sun
*Contemporary figurative
art.*

**GALERIE VENICE
DESIGN 2**
Calle Valaresso
Tel: 523 90 82
Open 10am–1pm,
3–7.30pm
Closed Tue
*Modern and
contemporary paintings
and sculptures.*

LIVIO DE MARCHI
San Samuele, San
Marco 3157
Tel: 528 56 94
Open 8am–6.30pm
Closed Sun
*Sculptures in wood
inspired by everyday
objects.*

CAMPING SITES

CAMPING
Riviera San Nicolo,
Lido 65
Tel: 526 74 15
Closed Oct 15–May.15

**CAMPING ALBA
D'ORO** ★★★★
Via Triestina 214/b, Ca'
Noghera, Mestre
Tel: 541 51 02
Closed Oct–March
*Luxury camping ground
with bungalows and
caravans, located
about an hour from the
station.*

**CAMPING MARINA
DI VENEZIA**★★★★
Punta Sabbioni, Via
Montello 6, Treporti
Tel: 96 61 46
Closed Oct 31–April 1
*Well-equipped luxury
camping site with
private beach. Shops,
bars, restaurants,
pizzeria.
4,000–8,000 lire.
Bungalows and
caravans.
30,000–145,000 lire.*

APPENDICES

◆ BIBLIOGRAPHY

◆ ESSENTIAL ◆

◆ BLUE GUIDE: *Venice*, 1980
◆ GRUNDY (M.): *Venice, An Anthology Guide*, London, 1976
◆ HONOUR (H.): The Companion Guide to Venice, London, 1965
◆ LINKS (J.G.): *Venice for Pleasure*, London, 1966
◆ LORENZETTI (G.): *Venice and Its Lagoon*, Rome, 1961
◆ McCARTHY (M.): *Venice Observed*, Penguin Books, New York, 1982
◆ MORRIS (J.): *Venice*, London, 1960; also *The Venetian Empire*, London 1980
◆ NORWICH (J. J.): *The History of Venice*, London 1988
◆ PIGNATTI (T.): *Venice*, London, 1960
◆ SHAW-KENNEDY (R.): *Art and Architecture in Venice. The Venice in Peril Guide*, London, 1972

◆ GENERAL ◆

◆ BERTUZZI (F.): *Couleur de Venise*, Mengès, Paris, 1986
◆ BELLAVITIS (G.), ROMANELLI (G.): *Venezia*, Laterza, Bari, 1985
◆ BRILLI (A.): *Le Voyage d'Italie*, Flammarion, Paris, 1989
◆ CANESI, (M.): *Venise*, De Vecchi, 1986
◆ FRANZOI (U.), DI Stefano (D.): *Le Chiese di Venezia*, Azienda Autonoma Soggiorno e Turismo, Venice, 1976
◆ MASIERO (F.): *Venise vue du ciel*, Gallimard, Paris, 1991
◆ PEROCCO (G.), SALVADORI (A.): *Civiltà di Venezia*, 3 vol., La Stamperia di Venezia, 1979
◆ PIGNATTI (T.): *Venezia, Mille Anni d'Arte*, Arsenale Editrice, Venice, 1989
◆ *Storia della cultura veneta*, col., Neri Pozza, Vicenza, 1976-86, 6 vol.
◆ *Venezia, città industriale*, col., Marsilio, Venice, 1980

◆ NATURE ◆

◆ BERENGO (G.G.), MOLDI-RAVENNA (C.), SAMMARTINI (T.): *Giardini segreti a Venezia*, Arsenale Editrice, Venice, 1988
◆ *Laguna, Conservazione di un Ecosistema*, Arsenale Editrice, Venice, s. d.
◆ *Laguna tra fiumi e mare*, Filippi Editore, Venice, 1982
◆ *La Salvaguardia fisica della Laguna* (catalogue of the exhibition), Comune di Venezia, 1983

◆ HISTORY ◆

◆ BENZONI (G.): *I dogi*, Electa, Milan, 1982
◆ BERENGO (M.): *La società veneta alla fine del '700*, Firenze, 1970
◆ BERNARDELLO (A.), BRUNELLO (P.), GINSBERG (P.): *Venezia 1848-1849, La rivoluzione e la difesa*, Comune di Venezia, Stamperia di Venezia, 1980
◆ BETTINI (S.): *Venezia. Dalla prima crociata alla conquista di Costantinopoli del 1204*, Firenze, 1966
◆ BETTINI (S.): *Venezia. Nascita di una città*, Milan, 1978
◆ BRAUDEL (F.), QUILICI (F.): *Venise*, Arthaud, Paris, 1984
◆ BRAUDEL (F.): *La Méditerranée et Le Monde Méditerranéen à l'Epoque de Philippe II*, Tr. Sian Reynolds, 2 vols, London and New York, 1973
◆ BRAUNSTEIN (P.), DELORT (R.): *Venise: portrait historique d'une cité*, Seuil, Paris, 1971
◆ BROWN (H.): *Studies in the History of Venice*, 2 vols, London 1907
◆ CAMBRIDGE MEDIEVAL HISTORY *Vol V, Venice section* by R. Cessi
◆ CALIMANI (R.): *Histoire du ghetto de Venise*, Stock, Paris, 1988
◆ CARILE (C.), FEDALTO (G.): *Le origini di Venezia*, Patron, Bologna, 1978
◆ CESSI (R.): *Storia della Repubblica di Venezia*, Giunti-Martello, Firenze, 2 vol., 1991
◆ CESSI (R.), ALBERTI (A.): *Rialto. L'Isola, il ponte, il mercato*, Zanichelli, Bologna, 1934
◆ CHAMBERS (D.S.): *The Imperial Age of Venice, 1380-1580*, London 1970
◆ COLIN (R.-P.): *Les Privilèges du Chaos: la Mort à Venise et l'esprit décadent*, Le Lérot, Aigre, 1991
◆ COMISSO (G.): *Les Agents secrets de Venise: 1705-1797*, Le Promeneur, Paris, 1990
◆ COMISSO (G.): *Les Ambassadeurs vénitiens*, Le Promeneur, Paris, 1989
◆ CONCINA (E.): *Venezia nell'età moderna*, Venice, 1989
◆ COZZI (G.), KNAPTON (M.): *La repubblica di Venezia nell'età moderna-Dalla querra di Chioggia al recupero della Terraferma*, UTET, Turin, 1986
◆ COZZI (G.): *Repubblica di Venezia e Stati Italiani. Politica e Giustizia dal secolo XVI al secolo XVIII*, Einaudi, Turin, 1982
◆ CURIEL (R.), COOPERMAN (B.): *Le Ghetto de Venise*, Herscher, Paris, 1990
◆ DA MOSTO (A.): *I Dogi di Venezia*, Martello, Milan, 1960
◆ DAVID (J.C.): *The Decline of the Venetian Nobility as a Ruling Class*, Baltimore 1962
◆ DIEHL (C.): *La République de Venise*, Flammarion, Paris, 1985
◆ DREGE (J.-P.): *Marco Polo et la route de la soie*, Découvertes, Gallimard, Paris, 1989
◆ DUBY (G.), LOBRICHON (G.): *L'Histoire de Venise par la peinture*, Belfond, Paris, 1991
◆ FINLAY (R.): *Politics in Renaissance Venice*, New Brunswick, 1980
◆ FORTIS (U.): *Ebrei e Sinagoghe*, Storti, Venice, 1973
◆ GEORGELIN (J.): *Venise au siècle des lumières: 1669-1797*, EHESS, Paris, 1978
◆ HALE (J.R.): *Ed., Renaissance Venice*, London 1973
◆ HAZLITT (W.C.): *History of the Origin and Rise of the Venetian Republic*, 2 vols, London 1900
◆ HOCQUET (J.-C.): *Le Sel et la fortune de Venise*, Presses Universitaires de Lille, 1982
◆ JONARD (N.): *La vie quotidienne à Venise au XVIIIᵉ siècle*, Hachette, Paris, 1965
◆ KNEZEVICH (M.): *Il magnifico principe di Venezia. Norme e tradizioni legate al dogado*, Storti, Venice, 1986
◆ KOFMAN (S.): *Conversions: le marchand de Venise sous le signe de Saturne*, Galilée, Paris, 1987
◆ LANE (F.C.): *Venice, a Maritime Republic*, Baltimore, 1966
◆ LANE (F.C.): *Venice and History*, Baltimore 1966
◆ LANE (F.C.): *Venetian Ships and Shipbuilders of the Renaissance*, Baltimore 1934
◆ LAURITZEN (P.L.): *The Palaces of Venice*, London,1978
◆ LAURITZEN (P.L.): *Venice*, London, 1978
◆ LONGWORTH (P.): *The Rise and Fall of Venice*, London, 1974
◆ LOWRY (M.): *Le Monde d'Alde Manuce: imprimeurs, hommes d'affaires et intellectuels dans la Venise de la Renaissance*, Promodis, Cercle de la Librairie, Paris, 1989
◆ McNEIL (W.H.): *Venice, the Hinge of Europe 1081-1797*, University of Chicago, 1974
◆ MONNIER (P.): *Venise au XVIIIᵉ siècle*, Complexe, Brussels, 1982
◆ PULLAN (B.): *Rich and Poor in Renaissance Venice*, Oxford, 1971
◆ *Rinascimento Europeo e Rinascimento Veneziano* (a cura di V. Branca), col., Venice, 1977
◆ TENENTI (A.): *Naufrages, corsaires et assurances maritimes à Venise d'après les notaires Catti et Spinelli: 1592-1609*, EHESS, Paris, 1959
◆ THIRIET (F.): *Registres des délibérations du Sénat de Venise concernant la Romanie*, EHESS, Paris, vol.1: 1958, vol. 2: 1959, vol.3: 1961
◆ THIRIET (F.): *Histoire de Venise*, PUF, Paris, 1985
◆ TUCCI (U.): *Mercanti, Navi e Monete nel Cinquecento Veneziano*, Bologna, 1981
◆ VALENSI (L.): *Venise et la Sublime Porte: la naissance du despote*, Hachette, Paris, 1987
◆ *Venezia e la peste*, col., Venice, 1979
◆ WOWTHORNE (S.T.): *Venetian Opera in the 17th. Century*, Oxford University Press, 1954
◆ ZORZI (A.): *La République du lion: histoire de Venise*, Perrin, Paris, 1988
◆ ZORZI (A.): *Une cité, une république, un empire*, Nathan, Paris, 1980
◆ ZYSBERG (A.), BURLET (R.): *Gloire et misère des galères*,

Découvertes, Gallimard, Paris, 1987

◆ TRADITIONS ◆

◆ ALBERICI (C.): Il Mobile Veneto, Electa, Milan, 1980
◆ ARTHUS-BERTRAND (Y.): Safari vénitien: carnaval de Venise, Laffont, Paris, 1985
◆ BAROVIER MENTASTI (R.): Il vetro veneziano, Electa, Milan, 1982
◆ BAROVIER MENTASTI (R.), DORIQATO (A.), GASPARETTO (A.), TONINATO (T.): Mille anni di arte del vetro a Venezia — catalogo della Mostra, Albrizzi, Venice, 1982
◆ BRAZOLO (U. del): La Gondola, Canova, Treviso, 1979
◆ BRUNELLO (F.): Arti e mestieri a Venezia nel Medioevo e nel Rinascimento, Neri Pozza, Vicenza, 1981
◆ BUSETTO (G.): Cronaca veneziana – Feste e vita quotidiana nella Venezia del Settecento, Fondazione Scientifica Querini-Stampalia, Venice, 1991
◆ BUIAZZI (G.), MONTI (P.): Venezia e la sua gondola, Görlich, Milan, 1974
◆ CERVIN (R. de): Batoaux et batellerie de Venise, Vilo, Paris, 1970
◆ CLAUSEL (J.): Venise exquise: propos de tables et de recettes, Laffont, Paris, 1990
◆ DOIZY (M.-A.), IPERT (S.): Le papier marbré, Technorama, Paris, 1985
◆ FABRE (D.): Carnaval ou la fête à l'envers, Découvertes, Gallimard, Paris, 1992
◆ FIORIN, (A., a cura di): Fanti e Denari, Arsenale Editrice, Venice, 1989
◆ FRAIGNEAU (A.): Les Enfants de Venise, Arléa, Paris, 1988
◆ GHIRARDINI (G.): El parlar figurato, Venice, 1980
◆ LAROCHE (R. de), LABAT (J.-M.): Chats de Venise, Casterman, Paris,1991
◆ La voga alla veneta, col., Comune di Venezia, Assessorato Turismo e Sport, 1983
◆ LEVI-PISETZKY (R.): Il Costume e la Moda nella Società Italiana, Einaudi, Turin, 1978
◆ MAFFIOLI (G.): La Cucina Veneziana, Padua, 1962
◆ MARIACHER (G.), VALERI (D.): Il Settecento

veneziano a Ca' Rezzonico, Sadea/ Sansoni, Firenze, 1966
◆ MENEN (A.): Vivre Venise, Mengès, Paris, 1978
◆ MORAZZONI (G.): Mobili veneziani laccati, Milan, 1954
◆ REATO (D.): Histoire du Carnaval de Venise, Oréa-Marco-Polo, Bordeaux, 1991
◆ ROMANELLI (S.), PEDROCCO (S.): Bissone, Peote e gallegianti, Alfieri, Venice, 1980
◆ SALVAGGION (N.), SAVELLA (A.), GRANZOTTO (G.): Le Carnaval de Venise, Amilcare Pizzi, 1986
◆ TAMASSIA-MAZZAROTTO (B.): Le Feste Veneziane, Sansoni, Firenze, 1961
◆ TASSINI (G.): Curiosità veneziane, Filippi Editore, Venice, new ed. 1990
◆ VEDRENNE (E.): Demeures secrètes de Venise, Albin Michel, Paris, 1990
◆ VITOUX (F.), DARBLAY (J.): L'Art de vivre à Venise, Flammarion, Paris, 1990
◆ ZANELLI (G., a cura di): Squeraroli e squeri, Ente per la conservazione della Gondola e la tutela del Gondoliere, Venice, 1986
◆ ZUHZI (A.): Venetia Felix, Gabriel Bella cronista della Serenissima, Franco Maria Ricci, Milan, 1989

◆ ART/ARCHITECTURE ◆

◆ ACKERMANN (J.S.): Palladio, Turin, 1972
◆ ARSLAN (E.): Venezia Gotica, Venice, 1970
◆ BALISTRERI (C.): Case Veneziane a loggia, Cluva universitaria, Venice, 1986
◆ BARRAL I ALTET (X.): Les Mosaïques de pavement médiévales de Venise, Murano, Torcello, Picard, Paris, 1985
◆ BASSI (E.): Architettura del Sei e Settecento a Venezia, Filippi Editore, Venice, s.d.
◆ BASSI (E.): Palazzi di Venezia, Stamperia di Venezia, Venice, 1976
◆ BRUSATIN (M.): Venezia nel Settecento. Stato, Architettura, Territorio, Einaudi, Turin, 1980
◆ BRUYERE (J.), STAINER (M.): Sols: Saint-Marc, Venise, Imprimerie Nationale, Paris, 1989
◆ CHASTEL (A.): Italie.

Renaissance mériodionale, 1460-1500, L'Univers des Formes, Gallimard, Paris, 1965
◆ CONCINA (E.): Structure urbaine et fonctions des bâtiments du xiᵉ au xvᵉ siècle, UNESCO-Save Venice Inc., 1981
◆ CONSTANT (C.):Guida a Palladio, Lidiarte, Berlin, 1889
◆ CRISTINELLI (G.): Baldassare Longhena... Architetto del Seicento a Venezia, Venice, 1978
◆ FAURE (E.): Histoire de l'art, 1909, 3 vol., Folio, Gallimard, Paris, 1988
◆ FONTANA (G.J.): Cento palazzi tra i più colobri di Venezia, Venice, 1865
◆ GIANIGHIAN (N., a cura di): Dietro i Palazzi, Tre secoli di architetturo minore a Venezia, 1492-1803, Arsenale Editrice, Venice
◆ GRANDESSO (E.): I Portali Medievali di Venezia, Helvetia, Venice, 1988
◆ HELLENKEMPER (G.): La Création du monde: les mulli ulyuub de Saint-Marc à Venise, Le Cerf, Paris, 1986
◆ HEYNDENREICH (L.H.): Italie: éclosion de la Renaissance, 1400-1460, L'Univers des Formes, Gallimard, Paris, 1972
◆ LECLERC (H.): Venise baroque et l'opéra, Armand Colin, Paris, 1987
◆ Le Trésor de Saint-Marc de Venise, Musées Nationaux, col., Paris, 1984
◆ LEVI (C.A.): I Campanili di Venezia, Venice, 1980
◆ LIEBERMAN (R.): L'Architettura del Rinascimento a Venezia, Becocci, Firenze, 1982
◆ L'Immagine e il mito di Venezia nel cinema, col., Comune di Venice, 1983
◆ MARETTO (P.): La Casa Veneziana nella storia della città, dalle origini all'Ottocento, Marsilio, Venice, 1986
◆ MARETTO (P.): L'Edilizia Gotica Veneziana, Venice,1978
◆ MARIACHER (G.): Il Sansovino, Milan, 1962
◆ McANDREW (J.): Venetian Architecture of the Early Renaissance, M.I.T., Cambridge, Mass., 1980
◆ MURARO (M.): La vita

nelle pietre, Arsenale Editrice, Verona, 1985
◆ MURARO (M.), GRABAR (A.): Les Trésors de Venise, Skira, 1987
◆ MURATORI (S.): Studi per un'operante storia urbana di Venezia, Rome, 1960
◆ MURRAY (P.): Architettura del Rinascimento, Electa, Milan
◆ NORBERG-SCHULZ (C.): Architettura Occidentale, Milan, 1981
◆ PIGNATTI (T.): Le Scuole di Venezia, Milan, 1981
◆ PIZZARRELLO (U.), CAPITANIO (E.): Guida alla città di Venezia, L'Altra Riva, Venice, 4 vol., 1986-1990
◆ PUPPI (L.): A. Palladio, Milan, 1973
◆ RIZZI (A.): Vere da pozzo di Venezia, La stamperia di Venezia, Venice, 1981
◆ RIZZO (T.): I Ponti di Venezia, Newton Compton, Rome, 1983
◆ RUSKIN (J.): The Stones of Venice, 3 Vols., London, 1851-3
◆ RUSKIN (J.): St. Mark's Rest, London, 1877
◆ SALVADORI (A.): Architect's Guide to Venice, Canal Libri, Venice, 1990
◆ SCARABELLO (G.), MORACHIELLO (P.): Venise: Guide historique et culturel, Larousse, Paris, 1988
◆ TAFURI (M.): Venezia e il Rinascimento, Einaudi, Turin, 1985
◆ TRINCANATO (E.R.), FRANZOI (U.): Venise au fil du temps, Joël Cluenot, Boulogne-Billancourt, 1971
◆ WITTKOWER (R.): Art et architecture en Italie 1600-1750 – L'âge du baroque, Hazan, Paris, 1991
◆ ZORZI (A.):Venezia Scomparsa, Electa, Milan, 1984

◆ PAINTERS ◆

◆ BURCKHARDT (J.): Pale d'Altare del Rinascimento, Cantini, Firenze, 1988
◆ DE VACCHI (P.), BERNARI (C.): Tintoretto, Rizzoli, Milan, 1970
◆ FIOCCO (G.): La Pittura Veneziana del '600 e '700, Verona, 1929
◆ HOCHMANN (M.): Peintres et commanditaires à Venise (1540-1628), Ecole Française de Rome, 1992

◆ HONOUR (H.), Fleming (J.): *The Venetian Hours of Henry James, Whistler and Sargent*, Walter Books Ltd, London, 1991

◆ HUSE (N.), WOLTERS (W.): *Venezia. L'Arte del Rinascimento*, Venice, 1989

◆ *La Pittura nel Veneto: il Quattrocento*, Electa, Milan, 1987

◆ LEVEY (M.): *Painting in 18th Century Venice*, University of London, 1959

◆ LOGAN (O.): *Culture and Society in Venice 1470-1790*, Batsford, London, 1972

◆ LONGHI (R.): *Viatico per cinque secoli di Pittura Veneziana*, Firenze, 1946

◆ NEPI-SCIRÉ (G.): *I Capolavori dell'Arte Veneziana, Le Gallerie dell'Accademia*, Arsenale Editrice, Venice, 1991

◆ OLIVARI (M.), *Giovanni Bellini*, Scala, Firenze, 1990

◆ OLIVATO (L.), PUPPI (L.): *Mauro Codussi*, Rome, 1971

◆ PALLUCCHINI (R.): *L'Opera Completa di Giambattista Tiepolo*, Milan, 1968

◆ PALLUCCHINI (R.): *La Pittura Veneziana del '700*, Instituto per la collaborazione culturale, Venice-Rome, 1960

◆ PALLUCCHINI (R.): *La Pittura Veneziana del Trecento*, Venice, 1964

◆ PALLUCCHINI (R.), ROSSI (P.): *Tintoretto, le Opere Sacré e Profane*, Alfieri Electa, Milan, 1982

◆ PIGNATTI (T.): *Giovanni Bellini, l'opera completa*, Rizzoli, Milan, 1969

◆ PIGNATTI (T.): *L'Opera completa di Pietro Longhi*, Venice, 1974

◆ PIGNATTI (T.): *Origini della Pittura Veneziana*, Istituto Italiano di Arti Grafiche, Bergamo, 1961

◆ PIGNATTI (T.): *Paolo Veronese, l'opera completa*, Alfieri, Venice, 1978

◆ PIGNATTI (T.): *Carpaccio*, Skira, Geneva, 1958

◆ PIGUET (P.): *Monet et Venise*, Herscher, 1989

◆ SCHULTZ (J.): *Venetian Painted Ceilings of the Renaissance*, University of California, Berkeley

◆ STAINTON (L.): *Turner in Venice*, British Museum 1985

◆ *The Genius of Venice (1500-1600)*, (catalogue of the exhibition), Royal Academy of Arts, London, 1983

◆ *Tiziano* (catalogue of the exhibition), Marsilio, Venice, 1990

◆ VASARI (G.): *Le Vite de Più Eccelenti Architetti, Pittori et Scultori Italiani, Firenze, 1550*, Einaudi, Turin, new ed. 1986 (Lives of the most eminent Italian architects, painters and sculptors)

◆ ZAMPETTI (P., a cura di): *Guardi*, Venice, 1965

◆ ZERI (F., a cura di): *La Pittura del Quattrocento*, Milan, 1987

◆ ZORZI (L.): *Carpaccio et la représentation de sainte Ursule*, Hazan, Paris, 1991

◆ ZUFFI (S.): *Giorgione*, Arnoldo Mondadori Arte, Milan, 1991

◆ LITERATURE ◆

◆ ARAGON (L.): *Les Voyageurs de l'impériale*, Folio, Gallimard, Paris, 1972

◆ BALZAC (H. de): *Massimilla Doni*, José Corti, Paris, 1964

◆ BARRÈS (M.): *La Mort de Venise*, Christian Pirot, Saint-Cyr-sur-Loire, 1990

◆ BOITO (C.): *Senso*, Actes Sud, Arles, 1983

◆ BROSSES (C. de): *Lettres familières d'Italie*, Mercure de France, Paris, 1986

◆ BUTOR (M.): *Description de Saint Marc*, Gallimard, Paris, 1963

◆ BYRON (Lord): *Beppo, A Venetian Story*

◆ BYRON (Lord): *Childe Harold's Pilgrimage*

◆ CALVINO (I.): *Contes populaires italiens*, Denoël, Paris, 1984

◆ CARPENTIER (A.): *Concert baroque*, Folio, Gallimard, Paris, 1978

◆ CASANOVA (G.J.): *Memoirs*

◆ CHASE (J.H.): *See Venice and Die*

◆ CHATEAUBRIAND (F.-R. de): *Voyages en Italie*, la Pléiade, Gallimard, Paris, 1969

◆ CHATEAUBRIAND (F.-R. de): *Mémoires d'outre-tombe*, la Pléiade, Gallimard, Paris, 1950

◆ COMISSO (G.): *Les Agents secrets de Venise*, Le Promeneur, Paris, 1990

◆ COMISSO (G.): *Les Ambassadeurs vénitiens*, Le Promeneur, Paris, 1989

◆ D'ANNUNZIO (G.): *Il Fuoco*, 1900

◆ D'ANNUNZIO (G.): *Notturno*, Mondadori, Milan, 1975

◆ DICKENS (C.): *Pictures from Italy*, Baudry's European Library, London, 1846

◆ DRODSKIJ (J.): *Fondamenta degli Incurabili*, Adelphi, Milan, 1991

◆ DU BELLAY (J.): *Les regrets*, Poésie Gallimard, Paris, 1975

◆ FRUTTERO (C.) et LUCENTINI (F.): *L'Amant sans domicile fixe*, Seuil, Paris, 1989

◆ GAUTIER (T.): *Voyage en Italie*, Fasquelle, Paris, 1930

◆ GIONO (J.): *Voyage en Italie*, Folio, Gallimard, 1953

◆ GOETHE (J. W. von): *Voyage en Italie*, Slatkine Reprints, 1990

◆ GOLDONI (C.): *Dramatic Works and Memoirs*

◆ GUILLOUX (L.): *Parpagnacco ou la conjuration*, Gallimard, Paris, 1954

◆ HEMINGWAY (E.): *Across the River and into the Trees*, Cape, London, 1952

◆ HOFMANNSTHAL (H. von): *Andreas*, L'Imaginaire, Gallimard, Paris, 1970

◆ JAMES (H.): *The Wings of the Dove*

◆ JAMES (H.): *The Difference*

◆ JAMES (H.):*The Aspern Papers*

◆ LAWRENCE (D.H.): *Lady Chatterley's Lover*

◆ MALRAUX (A.): *L'irréel*, Livres d'Art, Gallimard, Paris, 1974

◆ MANN (T.): *Death in Venice*

◆ MAURIAC (F.): *Le Mal*, la Pléiade, Gallimard, Paris, 1978

◆ MONTAIGNE (M. de): *Journal de voyage*, Folio, Gallimard, Paris, 1983

◆ MONTESQUIEU (C. de): *Lettres persanes*, Folio, Gallimard, Paris, 1973

◆ MORAND (P.): *Venises*, L'Imaginaire, Gallimard, Paris, 1971

◆ MUSSET (A. de): *Oeuvres complètes*, la Pléiade, Gallimard, Paris, 1938

◆ PASINETTI (P.-M.): *De Venise à Venise*, Liana Levi, Paris, 1984

◆ PASINETTI (P.-M.): *Le Pont de l'Accademia*, Calmann-Levy, Paris, 1970

◆ PASINETTI (P.-M.): *Rouge vénitien*, Albin Michel, Paris, 1963

◆ POUND (E.): *Cantos*

◆ PRATT (H.): *Fable de Venise*, Casterman, Paris, 1984

◆ PROUST (M.): *Albertine disparue*, Folio, Gallimard, Paris, 1989

◆ RÉGNIER (H. de): *Esquisses vénitiennes*, Complexe, Brussels, 1991

◆ RILKE (R.-M.): *Les Cahiers de Malte Laurids Brigge*, Gallimard, Paris, 1991

◆ ROMAIN (J.) et ZWEIG (S.): *Volpone*, Gallimard, Paris, 1950

◆ ROUSSEAU (J.-J.): *Les Confessions*, Folio, Gallimard, Paris, 1973

◆ SAND (G.): *Consuelo*, Glénat, Paris, 1991

◆ SAND (G.): *Lettre d'un voyageur*, la Pléiade, Gallimard, Paris, 1971

◆ SARTRE (J.-P.): *Situations IV*, Gallimard, Paris, 1964

◆ SHAKESPEARE (W.): *The Merchant of Venice*

◆ SHAKESPEARE (W.): *Othello*

◆ SHELLEY (P. B.): *Collected Works*

◆ SOLLERS (P.): *La Fête à Venise*, Gallimard, Paris, 1990

◆ STAEL (Mme. de): *Corinne ou l'Italie*, Folio, Gallimard, Paris, 1985

◆ STENDHAL: *Chroniques italiennes*, Folio, Gallimard, Paris, 1986

◆ STENDHAL: *Œuvres intimes*, la Pléiade, Gallimard, Paris, 1982

◆ STENDHAL: *Voyages en Italie*, la Pléiade, Gallimard, Paris, 1973

◆ SUARÈS (A.): *Le Voyage du condottiere*, Granit, 1985

◆ WAGNER (R.): *My Life*

◆ EXPLORING VENICE ◆

◆ ARTHUS-BERTRAND (Y.), LE GUELBOUT (P.): *Venise vue du ciel*, Chêne, Paris, 1988

◆ BELLAVITIS (G.): *L'Arsenale di Venezia. Storia di una grande struttura urbana*, Marsilio, Venice, 1983

◆ BERGAMO (S.): *La Basilica dei Frari*, Venice, 1983

◆ BERTOLI (B.), NIERO (A.): *I Mosaici di San Marco*, Electa, Milan, 1987

◆ BONECHI (E.): *Un jour à Venise*, Bonechi-Edizioni Il turismo, 1988

◆ BROCCATO (C.): *L'Antico Cimitero Ebraico di San Nicolò del Lido a Venezia*, Venice, 1992

◆ Brunetti (M.): *Santa Maria del Giglio, vulgo Zobenigo, nell'arte e nella storia*, Venice, 1952

◆ Concina (E.): *Chioggia*, Canova, Treviso, 1977

◆ *Dal Museo alla Città*, a cura della Soprintendenza ai Beni Artistici e Storici di Venice 1980-1990

◆ Damerini (G.): *L'Isola e il Cenobio di San Giorgio Maggiore*, Firenze, 1968

◆ Dazzi (M.), Merkel (E.): *Catalogo della Pinacoteca della Fondazione Scientifica Querini Stampalia*, Neri Pozza, Vicenza, 1979

◆ De Coster (L.), Vranckx (G.): *16 promenades dans Venise*, Editions Universitaires, Begedis, 1987

◆ Dolcetta (M.), Orlandi (F.): *Di Isola in Isola*, Brentani, Dolo, 1983

◆ Dorigato (A.): *Il Museo Vetrario di Murano*, Electa, Milan, 1986

◆ Flint (L.), Chils (E.): *Collezione Peggy Guggenheim*, Mondadori/Solomon R. Guggenheim Foundation, 1986

◆ Fontana (P.): *Les jours et les nuits de Venise*, Nathan, Paris, 1991

◆ *Fortuny nella Belle Epoque*, col., Electa, Milan, 1984

◆ Franzoi (U.): *L'Armeria del Palazzo Ducale a Venezia*, Canova, Treviso, 1990

◆ Franzoi (U.), Pignatti (T.), Wolters (W.): *Il Palazzo Ducale di Venezia*, Canova, Treviso, 1990

◆ Franzoi (U.): *Itinerari segreti nel Palazzo Ducale a Venezia*, Canova, Treviso, 1983

◆ Franzoi (U.): *Le Palais ducal de Venise*, Storti, Venice, 1978

◆ Frosini (P.), Nordio (M.): *Venise porte a porte*, FMR, Paris, 1981

◆ Gascar (P.): *Saint-Marc*, Delpire, Zurich,

1964

◆ Gramigna (S.), Perissa (A.): *Scuole di Arti, Mestiere e Devozione a Venezia*, Arsenale Editrice, Venice, 1981

◆ *Itinerari Veneziani*, col., Comune di Venezia, 1983-1992

◆ Jouffroy (A.): *Libre Venise*, Bordas, Paris, 1980

◆ Mangini (N.): *I Teatri di Venezia*, Mursia, Milan, 1974

◆ Marabini (J.): *Venise*, Seuil, Paris, 1988

◆ Masiero (F.): *Le Isole delle Lagune Venete*, Mursia, Milan, 1981-85

◆ Maupas (C.): *A Venise*, Hachette, Paris, 1989

◆ Niero (A.): *La Chiesa dei Carmini*, Venice, 1965

◆ Niero (A.): *La Chiesa di San Giacomo dell'Orio*, Venezia Sacra, 1990

◆ Niero (A.): *La Basilique de Torcello et Santa Fosca*, Ardo Editori d'Arte, Venise, s.d.

◆ Perry (M.): *La Basilica dei SS. Maria e Donato di Murano*, Parrocchia della Basilica, 1984, 2nd edit.

◆ *Piazza San Marco. l'Architettura, la storia, le funzioni*, Marsilio, Venice, 1970

◆ Pignatti (T. a cura di): *Gran teatro La Fenice*, Marsilio, Venice, 1981

◆ Pignatti (T.): *Le Scuole di Venezia*, Electa, Milan, 1981

◆ Pizzarello (U.), Fontana (V.): *Pietre e Legni dell'Arsenale di Venezia*, L'Altra Riva, Venice, 1983

◆ Polacco (R.): *La Cattedrale di Torcello*, L'Altra Riva – Canova, Venice-Treviso, 1961

◆ Polacco (R.): *La Cattedrale di Torcello*, Treviso-Venice, 1981

◆ Ramos (M.-J.): *Venise*, Marcus, Paris, 1989

◆ Reinish Sullam (G.): *Il Ghetto di Venezia*, Carucci, Roma, 1985

◆ Rezvani (S.): *Venise: avec Rezvani*, Autrement, Paris, 1985

◆ Ribadeau-Dumas (F.):

Les Mystères de Venise ou les secrets de la Sérénissime, Albin Michel, Paris, 1978

◆ Rizzi (P), Martino (E. di): *Storia della Biennale, 1895-1982*, Electa, Milan, 1902

◆ Romanelli (G.): *Le Musée Correr*, Electa, Milan, 1984

◆ Romanelli (G.): Pedrocco (F.): *Ca' Rezzonico*, Electa, Milan, 1991

◆ Romanelli (G.): *Venezia Ottocento*, Officina, Rome, 1977

◆ Roiter (F.): *Venise, guide photographique*, Co-Grof, 1984

◆ Rosa Salva (P.), Semenzato (M.): *Laguna di Venezia – Itinerari*, Cassa di Risparmio di Venezia, Fondo Mondiale per la Natura (W.W.F.), sezione di Venezia (s.d.)

◆ Salzano (E.): *Venise, portrait d'une ville: atlas aérien, portrait d'une ville à l'échelle 1/1000e*, Gallimard, Paris, 1990

◆ Tricanato (E.R.): *Il Palazzo Ducale di Venezia*, Florence, 1966

◆ Tricanato (E.R.): *Venezia Minore*, Milano, 1948

◆ Valcanover (F.): *Ca' d'Oro – La Galerie Giorgio Franchetti*, Electa, Milan, 1991

◆ Vahotto (A.): *Venise 360°*, Glénat, Paris, 1987

◆ *Venezia una guida per la città – Tre itinerari inconsueti*, col., Comune di Venezia, Assessorato al Turismo, Venice, 1985

◆ Vianello (R.): *La Giudecca*, Venice, 1966

◆ Wolters (W.): *Storia e politica nei dipinti di Palazzo Ducale*, Arsenale Editrice, Venice, 1987

◆ Zander Rudenstine (A.): *Peggy Guggenheim Collection*, Venice, Harry N. Abrams, Inc., Publishers, New York and the Solomon R. Guggenheim Foundation, N.Y., 1985

◆ Zorzi (A.): *Canal Grande*, Rizzoli, Milan,

1991

◆ Zorzi (A.), Marton (P.): *Les palais vénitiens*, Mengès, Paris, 1989

◆ REVUES ◆

◆ *Dentelles et broderies*, Antiquités et Objets d'art, Fabbri, Paris, 1991

◆ *Isole di Venezia*, Bell'Italia, Giorgio Mondadori, numéro spécial, septembre 1990

◆ *Italie*: Monuments Historiques, Paris, n°149, janvier-février 1987

◆ *La Marine de Venise*, Time-Life, 1981

◆ I ambert (E.), Matthieussent (E.): *Venise et les Vénitiens*, Autrement, hors-série n°4, 1985

◆ *Le mobilier italien*, Antiquités et Objets d'art, Fabbri, Paris, 1991

◆ *Le verre*, Antiquités et Objets d'art, Fabbri, Paris, 1991

◆ *Lustres, lampes, lampadaires*, Antiquités et Objets d'art, Fabbri, Paris, 1991

◆ Menen (A.): *Venise*, Time-Life, 1976.

◆ *Venise, un voyage intime*, Autrement, hors-série n° 14, octobre 1985, Paris

◆ *Venezia*, Meridiani, Domus, n. 1, 1986

◆ CHILDREN ◆

◆ Calvino (I.): *Le palais du sieur mort*, Folio Junior, Gallimard, Paris, 1982

◆ Del Torre (C. et G.), Battiston (M.-B.): *La Cité des doges au XVe siècle*, Venise, Albin Michel Jeunesse, Paris, 1989

◆ Scutari (A.), Pezzetta (E.): *Scolta che te conto, Storia di Venezia*, Filippi Editore, Venice, 1982

◆ Ventura (P.): *Venise: naissance d'une cité*, Nathan, Paris, 1988

◆ TABLE OF ILLUSTRATIONS

◆ TABLE OF ILLUSTRATIONS

1780, colored sketch © Correr Museum.
380 Duck hunting in the Lagoon, Longhi, oil on canvas © Querini-Stampalia Fdn. Gondolas, photo, Gallimard.
381 San Francesco del Deserto, © Naya, photo sd © O Böhm.
382 Monks on the Island of San Lazzaro degli Armnei, photo J Darblay. Egyptian Mummy, Museum of San Lazzaro degli Armeni © Böhm. Island of San Lazzaro degli Armeni in Isolario Veneto, Coronelli 1969 © Bibl Nat. Mooring posts in the Lagoon, photo, Gallimard.
382-383 San Lazzaro degli Armeni, photo.
383 Isola del Lazzaretto Nuovo in Isolario, Tironi-Sandi, 1779, Private collection. Byron's bedroom, San Lazzaro degli Armeni, photo G Arici. San Clemont, photo, G Rossi.
384 Isola della Grazia delle Capucine, engraving © photo Toso. View of the Lagoon and Islands, F Guardi, Coll. Bentineck, Paris © Scala. Lazzaretto Vecchio, photo G Rossi.
386 Airport, photo, Bertarello.
387 Santa Lucia Station, boat, photo, Gallimard. Piazzale Roma, photo, K Rothfjell. Orient Express, poster © La vie du Rail SNCF/Paris.
388 Vaporetto landing stage, photo, Bertarello.
389 Vaporetto landing stage, Vaporetto, photo, Gallimard. Isola San Giorgio, photo, © Auger.
390 Gondolas, St Mark's Basin, photo, © Auger. Traghetto and motoscafo, photo, Gallimard.
391 Street signs and numbers, photo, Gallimard.
392 Café Quadri, souvenirs, photo, Gallimard.
393 Newspaper kiosk, boat-market, photos Gallimard. Devil, photo, Bertarello. Market stall, photo, Gallimard.
394 Letterbox, cash distributor, photos

Gallimard.
395 Public callbox, photo, Gallimard.
398 Grand Canal, Rialto, Piazzetta, Salute, photos, Gallimard. Piazza San Marco, Café Florian, Accademia Bridge, photo, K Rothfjell.
399 Rialto, sign of Trattoria all Colomba, emblem of La Fenice, Hotel Gabrelli, Il Redentore, photos, Gallimard. Hotel Danieli, photo A Celan/Ciga Hotel. Gates of the Arsenal, photo K Rothfjell.
400-401 Photo Gallimard. Photo K Rothfjell.
402 Child in Piazza San Marco, photo, Gallimard.
404 Legatoria Piazzesi, photo, Gallimard. Lace, photo, idem.
405 Venetia Studium, photo K Rothfjell. Maskmakers Mask, marbled paper, photo, Gallimard.
406 St Christopher, Titian, Doge's Palace © Correr Museum.
407 Musicians, Piazza San Marco, photo, Gallimard. Portal of St Mark's Basilica, photo K Rothfjell. Entrance to La Fenice and sign, photo Gallimard.
408 Senso, L Visconti, 1954, Coll P Zanotto.
409 Vino da Pinto, photo, idem. Venetian Inn, poster, coll della Toffola.
416 Hotel Bellini, photo, Gallimard.
417 Hotel Gabrielli, photo, Gallimard.
418 Hotel Danieli, photo Gallimard.
422 Hotel Gritti Palace, photo Gallimard.
423 Hotel Europa e Regina, photo, idem.
425 Hotel Monaco, photo, Gallimard.
426 Harry's Bar, photo, Gallimard.
427 Rialto Bridge, photo, Gallimard.
428 Cantina Do Spade, photo, Gallimard.
429 Peggy Guggenheim Foundation, photo, idem.
431 The Zattere, photo, Gallimard.
432 View of the Giudecca, photo, idem.

433 Isola San Giorgio, photo, Gallimard.
434 Fondaco dei Turchi, photo Gallimard.
437 Mostra 1935, poster, Archivio Storico delle Arti Contemporanee della Biennale.
440 Glassworker, photo Gallimard.
441 Lacemakers, photo, Gallimard.

Itinerary Maps
Vincent Bruno,
Philippe Lhez: 298-299,
Frédéric Liéval: 156-157.

Color works
Malou Camolli (itinerary maps)
Conchetta Forgia 187-217, 220-221
Jean-Marie Guilloux 104
Sylvaine Pérols 244-247, 368-369 and itinerary maps.

Illustrators:
Philippe Biard: 26-27.
Anne Bodin: 16-17, 20-21, 22-23, 24-25, 26-27,
Christian Broutin: cover, 66.
Jean-Philippe Chabot: 162.
Jean Chevallier: 4th plate, 15, 18-19, 20-21, 24-25, 28,
François Débordes: 18-19, 24-25.
Claire Folloni: 15, 18-19, 28.
Gilbert Houbre: cover, 16-17, 24 25.
Domitille Héron: 100 104.
Olivier Hubert: 315.
Jean-Michel Kacedan ; 20-21, 28.
Maurice Pommier: 385, 390, 392, 393, 394, 398, 404, 405, 407, 416, 417, 422, 423, 424, 425, 426, 428, 429, 438, 439, 442, 443.
Bruno Lenormand: cover, 78-79, 82 to 95, 194.
Ugo Pizzarello: 68-73, 80-81, 96-97.
François Place: 22-23, 104.
Thomas Woltz: 144, 148, 150, 171, 261 272, 283, 289, 290, 346.

Where the city goes unmentioned, VENICE is meant, except in the case of © Auger, Bibl Nat, J Darblay, Gallimard,

Giraudon, RMN PARIS; Electa, G Rossi (MILAN); and Scala (FLORENCE) CVN is an abbreviation of CONSORZIO VENEZIA NUOVA.

The publishers wish to extend their thanks to the following individuals, whose help in compiling this book has been invaluable:
Padre Raffaele Andonian (Palazzo Zenobio, Armenian College),
S Graziano Arici,
S Jacopo Barovier,
S Bertarello,
S Oswaldo Böhm,
Dott. Giorgio Busoto (Curator of the Querini-Stampalia Foundation),
S Paolo Canestrelli,
S Cassio (Correr Museum),
Sra Antonietta dell Toffola,
S Roberto Fontanari (Accademia),
Sa. Margusta Lazzari (Querini-Stampalia Foundation),
Dott.essa Lunardon (Church of Santa Maria dei Dereletti e Ospedaletto),
S Antonio Menegnolo (Loggia of the Houses of St Mark/Procuratoria of St Mark),
Elisabetta Navarbi (La Fenice Theater),
Prof Glandomenico Romanelli (Curator of the Correr Museum),
Patriarchal Chancellor Mario Ronzini (Church of San Giovanni in Bragora),
Sa Rossi (Assistant director of the Biblioteca Marciana),
Dott Francesco Semenzato,
S Francesco Turio Böhm,
Sa Vianello (Querini-Stampalia Foundation),
Sa Nanni Wurmibrand,
Dott Marino Zorzi (Curator of the Biblioteca Marciana).

In some cases we have been unable to contact the heirs to certain copyrighted documents, or their publishers; an account remains open for

◆ A ◆

ACQUA ALTA: High water.
ALTANA: A sort of wooden platform or terrace, built on a roof, like a bird's nest.
ARSENALOTTI: The workers in the old Arsenal dockyards.

◆ B ◆

BACARO: Wine bar.
BAICOLI: Small Venetian cakes.
BALLOTTINO: Child selected to draw the ballots during the election of the Doge.
BARENE: Salt flats in the Venetian Lagoon.
BAUTA: Garment worn during Carnival, consisting of a black silk hood with a lace cloak.
BISSONA: A boat with eight oarsmen, which features in the Venice Historical Regatta.
BRAGOZZO: Chioggia. Typical fishing boat.
BRICOLA: Cluster of pilings in the Lagoon, positioned to mark navigable channels. The term also applies to mooring-posts.
BUSSOLAI: Small Venitian cakes.

◆ C ◆

CA': Abbreviation for casa, house.
CALLE: Alley, street or space between houses in Venice. A small calle is called a calletta.
CAMERLENGHI: The treasurers of the former Venetian Republic.
CAMPO: "Field"; this term applies to all Venice's open spaces, with only St Mark's Square being allowed the title of piazza. The campi used to be covered in grass and planted with trees. A campiello is a small square.
CANALE: Canal.
CANALAZZO: The Grand Canal.
CAORLINA: A boat rowed by six oarsmen.
CASINO: Gaming house.
CICHETTI: Snacks and hors d'oeuvres, usually consumed in bacari.
CONTRADA: Parish.
CORNO: The Doge's hat.
CORSO: Originally a race between competing gondoliers.
CORTE: A courtyard shared by several houses, as opposed to the

cortile, which is the private courtyard of a palace.
CORTELÀ: Decorated sides of a galley.
CROSERA: A junction of several calli.

◆ D ◆

DESDOTONA: A boat with eighteen oarsmen, which features in the Venice Historical Regatta.
DOGE: Head of the Venetian Republic, elected by the Doge.

◆ E ◆

ERBERIA: Fruit and vegetable market at the Rialto.

◆ F ◆

FELZE: Small box-like cabins, which used to be placed on gondolas during the winter.
FERRO: Gondola figurehead.
FONDACO: Warehouse-residence, where merchants both lived and stored their goods.
FONDAMENTA: Quay alongside a canal.
FONTEGO: See fondaco.
FORCOLA: Rowlock of gondola.
FRITTELLE: Fritters.

◆ G ◆

GONDOLIN: Racing gondola.

◆ L ◆

LIAGO: Broad covered balcony.
LISTA: A part of a street which was formerly attached to a foreign embassy, hence outside Venetian territory.

◆ M ◆

MARIEGOLE: "Mother rules" of a guild or brotherhood.
MASCARETA: Light racing skiff, usually reserved for women competitors.
MOTOSCAFO: Launch; a smaller version of the vaporetto.
MURAZZO: Sea wall between the Lagoon and the Adriatic.

◆ O ◆

OMBRA: A glass of wine, as served in the bacari.
OSELLA: A commemorative medallion.
OSPEDALE: Hospice for

abandoned children, usually offering a musical education.

◆ P ◆

PARROCCHIA: During the Republic, Venice was subdivided into about seventy parishes: their numbers were reduced after Napoleon's appropriation of the city.
PESCHERIA: The Rialto fish market.
PIANO NOBILE: First floor of a palace.
PIAZZA: St Mark's Square (only).
PIAZZETTA: Small square adjoining St Mark's.
PISCINA: An arm of the Lagoon which was originally used by Venetian children as a bathing place (nowadays the piscinas are surrounded by buildings, or have been filled in).
PONTILE: Landing stage for vaporetti and motoscafi.
PORTEGO: Main salon, covering the entire width of the piano nobile of a palace.
PUPARIN: Long Lagoon boat.

◆ R ◆

RAMO: A very short calle, often a dead end.
RIDOTTO: Gaming house, place of entertainment in Venice.
RIO: Canal. There are only three "canals", properly speaking, in Venice – the Cannaregio canal, the Grand Canal and the Giudecca Canal.
RIO TERRÀ: A filled-in rio, now a street.
RIVA: Bank.
RUGA: From the French "rue", a street; in Venice, a straight calle full of boutiques.
RUGHETTA: Short ruga.

◆ S ◆

SACCA: A large piscina. More recently, a part of the Lagoon which has been filled in.
SALIZZADA: Paved main thoroughfare; as a rule, the ordinary calli were not paved.
SANDALO DA S'CIOPO: A small, light boat with a flat bottom.
SANPIEROTA: Very stable Lagoon vessel.
S'CIOPON: See Sandalo da s'ciopo.
SCUOLA: Professional corporation or religious

brotherhood.
SESTIERE: One of the six sections of Venice, dating from about 1170.
SOTTOPORTEGO: Portion of a street passing through a building.
SQUERO: Private boatyard, where traditional gondolas are built.
STAZIO: Landing stage for gondolas.

◆ T ◆

TABARRO: Voluminous cape worn during Carnival.
TOLE: Lumber yards.
TOPO: Sailing vessel, used for fishing in the Lagoon.
TRAGHETTO: Publicly maintained gondola with two oarsmen: also, point at which the Grand Canal can be crossed.

◆ V ◆

VAPORETTO: Venetian public transport along the Grand Canal.
VIA: Street.
VOGALONGA: Nineteen-mile boat race.

◆ Z ◆

ZATTERE: Quay in the Dorsoduro sestiere where barges of produce were unloaded.
ZUCCA: Pumpkin.

INDEX

◆ Thematic Index

◆ Scuole ◆

464